COM AND CORBA® SIDE BY SIDE

Architectures, Strategies, and Implementations

Jason Pritchard, Ph.D.

Addison-Wesley

An imprint of Addison Wesley Longman, Inc.

Reading, Massachusetts • Harlow, England
Menlo Park, California • Berkeley, California
Don Mills, Ontario • Sydney • Bonn
Amsterdam • Tokyo • Mexico City

Many of the designations used by manufacturers and sellers to distinguish their products are claimed as trademarks. Where those designations appear in this book and Addison-Wesley was aware of a trademark claim, the designations have been printed in initial capital letters or in all capitals.

The author and publisher have taken care in the preparation of this book, but make no expressed or implied warranty of any kind and assume no responsibility for errors or omissions. No liability is assumed for incidental or consequential damages in connection with or arising out of the use of the information or programs contained herein.

The publisher offers discounts on this book when ordered in quantity for special sales.

For more information, please contact:

Corporate, Government, and Special Sales
Addison Wesley Longman, Inc.
One Jacob Way
Reading, Massachusetts 01867
(781) 944-3700

Library of Congress Cataloging-in-Publication Data

Pritchard, Jason
    COM and CORBA® side by side: architectures, strategies, and implementations /
Jason Pritchard.
      p.   cm.
    Includes bibliographical references.
    ISBN 0-201-37945-7
    1. COM (Computer architecture)   2. CORBA (Computer architecture)
    I. Title.
    QA76.9.A73P755   1999
    005.2'76—dc21   99-23779
                                                  CIP

Screenshots of Microsoft Visual Basic®, Microsoft Visual J++™, Microsoft Management Console, and Microsoft Windows NT® are reprinted by permission from Microsoft Corporation.

Screenshots of ObjectBridge™ COM/CORBA Enterprise Client are reprinted by permission from Visual Edge® Software, Ltd.

ISBN 0-201-37945-7
Text printed on recycled and acid-free paper

1 2 3 4 5 6 7 8 9 10—MA—0302010099
First printing, June 1999

To Mary,
Brenna, and William

Contents

Part II
COM and CORBA on the Server 103

Part IV
Bridging COM and CORBA 317

Chapter 11
Custom Bridging Approaches 319

Chapter 12
Commercial Bridging Approach 333

Preface

Topics Covered in the Preface

- What Is This Book About?
- Who Should Read This Book?
- What Specific Areas Are Covered in This Book?
- What Are the Prerequisites for This Book?
- Where Are the On-line Resources?

COM and CORBA are all too often viewed as strictly competing technologies. In many areas, the competitive nature of these two technologies cannot be denied; however, each technology has its own strengths that differentiate it from the other. The most significant difference is the support for various operating system platforms. COM is oriented toward the Windows platform, while CORBA is inherently multiplatform. The operating system platform is an important consideration when determining where each technology should be deployed, but many other variables that factor into a decision regarding the use of COM and/or CORBA.

Determining where to use COM, CORBA, or both is a decision that is often based on emotional rather than on logical reasoning. Due to vendor marketing and the fervor of various technology proponents, emotion often ends up being one of the biggest factors in the selection of a distributed object architecture. I have seen several cases where the correct choice for using COM or CORBA was quite obvious, but where a different choice was made for emotional rather than for logical reasons. An objective strategy for choosing where to use COM and CORBA is badly needed.

The influence of emotion on the decision-making process is not too surprising in any part of the software industry. Software developers tend to be artisans and not engineers. Artisans rely on their instincts and rules of thumb when making critical decisions. Engineers rely on well-defined processes and formulae. While all of us should strive to evolve software development into an engineering discipline, we just aren't there yet. The processes and formulae usually do not exist for making definitive decisions with regard to software.

Perhaps the greatest difficulty with understanding software technologies, especially technologies like COM and CORBA, is the ever-expanding functionality provided by such technologies. None of us can hope to understand every nuance of COM or CORBA. We must therefore become specialized and focus on very specific areas that meet our current needs. As we become more specialized, we lose sight of the big picture. This has a negative effect on our ability to make rational decisions. To escape specialization, we must rely on other people to make us aware of the key factors that need to be considered when deciding where complex technologies like COM and CORBA should be used.

What Is This Book About?

This book provides a comprehensive comparison of COM and CORBA. It brings together the critical elements that must be considered when deciding where COM and CORBA should be used. This book also discusses various approaches for using COM and CORBA together in situations where the use of both is desired.

Throughout this book, COM and CORBA are compared in a side-by-side manner so that the similarities and differences between COM and CORBA are accentuated. The best way to understand what is meant by the phrase *side-by-side* is to examine the book's table of contents and note that the focus constantly shifts between discussions of COM, CORBA, or both. Within individual sections, comparisons are made between COM and CORBA whenever possible.

While writing this book, I have made every effort to avoid any bias toward either COM or CORBA. This book is definitely not about promoting one technology over the other. I have been fortunate enough to work with COM and CORBA on a multitude of projects, and I very much enjoy using both of them. In this book, I have done my best to objectively present useful information that will be helpful when choosing COM and/or CORBA.

Who Should Read This Book?

Software products based on COM and CORBA will undoubtedly provide the distributed object infrastructures for many future software systems. This book is designed for technical managers and strategists who need to determine where COM and CORBA should be used in their particular organizations. This book will also benefit developers who want to have an impact on such decisions.

This book also allows developers who have a working knowledge of either COM or CORBA to leverage their existing knowledge to better understand both technologies. The side-by-side nature of this book allows developers who are familiar with one approach to easily identify parallels with the other approach. The identification of such parallels provides a powerful mechanism for learning. As a result, a software developer who understands COM can use this book to better understand CORBA; a software developer who understands CORBA can use this book to better understand COM.

What Specific Areas Are Covered in This Book?

This book is divided into four parts that can be read independently of one another. If you are unfamiliar with either COM or CORBA, you should look at Part I first since it provides information on COM and CORBA fundamentals. After completing Part I, the rest of the parts can be read in any order.

- **Part I, Embracing COM and CORBA.** This part of the book provides a brief history leading up to distributed objects and discusses why COM and CORBA currently hold dominant positions in the marketplace. Part I concludes by performing an extensive side-by-side comparison of COM/CORBA technical fundamentals.

- **Part II, COM and CORBA on the Server.** This part of the book discusses the use of COM and CORBA on the server side. It begins by describing an objective strategy for assessing the appropriateness of COM and CORBA for a specific server-side domain. Part II then examines platform issues (including legacy system support), essential services (transactions, security, etc.), and intangibles that must often be considered when choosing between COM and CORBA.

- **Part III, COM and CORBA on the Client.** This part of the book examines client approaches for using COM and CORBA. Because Windows controls the desktop, Part III begins by looking at COM desktop client approaches. It then examines COM/CORBA Internet client approaches and also discusses design issues related to remoting and security. Part III concludes by providing an example that demonstrates a migration path from the desktop to the Internet.

- **Part IV, Bridging COM and CORBA.** This part of the book examines approaches for using COM and CORBA together. It begins by examining custom approaches for bridging COM and CORBA. Part IV then examines commercial bridging approaches based on the OMG's COM/CORBA interworking architecture. Part IV concludes with a discussion of enterprise application servers based on COM, CORBA, and Enterprise JavaBeans.

What Are the Prerequisites for This Book?

The COM examples presented in this book use C++, Java, and Visual Basic. The CORBA examples use C++ and Java. While some chapters in the book are not code-oriented, you will probably have trouble comprehending this book if you are not proficient in C++ or Java.

If you are planning to use COM or CORBA, you have probably already obtained references that focus directly on COM, CORBA, or COM/CORBA bridging. This book provides a comparison of COM and CORBA and also discusses COM/CORBA bridging. It does not, however, attempt to provide a complete reference for any of these areas. Depending on your needs, you may require books that focus exclusively on COM, CORBA, or COM/CORBA bridging to supplement the material contained in this book. For a list of such books that I have found useful, see the references (Appendix A) at the end of the book.

Where Are the On-line Resources?

The best on-line source for information on COM, including the COM specification, can be found at

```
http://www.microsoft.com/com
```

A wealth of information related to CORBA can be found at

```
http://www.omg.org
```

Information related to this book, including code examples, can be found at

`http://www.pobox.com/~pritchard/com_corba.html`

If you would like to get a short description of all the example code available for this book before going to the Web site, see the examples available for download (Appendix B) at the end of the book.

If you still haven't found what you're looking for and think that I can help, send e-mail to

`pritchard@pobox.com`

Acknowledgments

The task of writing a book affects an incredible number of people. The patience and the support shown to me by family members, friends, coworkers, editors, and reviewers have been a source of strength throughout this endeavor. A special thanks goes to Al Cilcius, Michi Henning, Lak Ming Lam, Jishnu Mukerji, Fernando Martinez-Campos, Roger Sessions, and Andreas Vogel for providing candid and insightful reviews.

While it is not possible to thank everyone who made contact with this book, I do want to thank PSW Technologies for providing a safe haven during the many months of effort that went into this book. PSW has provided me with the opportunity to use both COM and CORBA on a wide variety of projects.

I would also like to thank Mary O'Brien and Elizabeth Spainhour for initiating this project and, most importantly, for keeping it on track at Addison-Wesley. This effort would not have flourished without their support. In addition, thanks to Genevieve Rajewski, Jean Peck, and John Fuller for their tremendous assistance during production of this book.

Finally, I could not have succeeded without the patience, support, and love of my family. I know that the sum of my efforts on this book cannot compare to my wife's incredible success at doing the job of two parents—thanks Mary. And thanks to my wonderful children, Brenna and William, who will soon believe that I really don't have to work on the book tonight!

Jason Pritchard
March 1999

Part I

Embracing COM and CORBA

Introduction

Our top priority in Part I is to establish a mindset for embracing the Component Object Model (COM) and Common Object Request Broker Architecture (CORBA) when building distributed systems. If you are already in that mindset, the first section of this book will give you the firepower to win over others with whom you interact. Your success at using COM and CORBA will ultimately depend on your ability to garner support from other key people within your organization. This is especially true in the case of large distributed systems that span disparate groups across an enterprise.

To embrace means *to accept willingly*. The idea of willingly accepting both COM and CORBA is a difficult concept for some to grasp. The plain truth is that it is not an either/or proposition. Each technology possesses significant advantages over the other. Understanding the pros and cons of each technology as well as how to combine both technologies will allow you to solve a wide range of problems. This will make you more successful at dealing with the challenges involved in creating complex distributed systems.

Part I establishes the *embrace* mindset by describing the history leading up to distributed objects, the current positions of COM and CORBA in the marketplace, and the technical fundamentals of these powerful technologies.

- Chapter 1 provides a brief history of the software approaches that led up to the widespread use of distributed objects. It includes a discussion of 2-tier, 3-tier, and *N*-tier approaches. Chapter 1 concludes by describing why the distributed object approach is currently viewed as the best way to build distributed systems.

- Chapter 2 first focuses on a wide range of specific technologies for implementing distributed objects. It then focuses specifically on COM and CORBA and how their different evolutionary paths resulted in each having specific advantages. Chapter 2 concludes by explaining why COM and CORBA both hold dominant positions in the marketplace.

- Chapter 3 first discusses the technical fundamentals of distributed object architectures. It then presents an example that accentuates the similarities and differences between COM and CORBA.

Part I provides an introduction to COM and CORBA as well as a side-by-side comparison of these important technologies. This comparison provides a starting point for choosing between one or the other; however, the comparison also reveals similarities that indicate why COM and CORBA can be used together when the best attributes of both technologies are desired.

Chapter 1

The Arrival of
Distributed Objects

Topics Covered in This Chapter

- Client/Server Beginnings
- 2-Tier, 3-Tier, and *N*-Tier Architectures
- Communicating Between Tiers
- The Power of Distributed Objects
- From Objects to Components
- Managing Distributed Systems
- The State of Distributed Objects

The history of computing has been marked by dramatic changes in the way people interact with computers. You have to admit that it is a giant stretch to go from punching cards to putting on a headset and entering virtual reality to interact with a program. Given these changes in human–computer interaction, it is no wonder that the way in which computer systems are organized has also undergone drastic change.

Early computer systems can best be described as monolithic systems in which all processing occurred on the same machine. Users interacted with the monolithic systems through dumb terminals. For a variety of reasons, which we'll be discussing in this chapter, it became desirable to move away from such monolithic systems and divide the work between several different computers—this change signaled the birth of client/server systems. Of course, there happen to be a large number of strategies for dividing the work among multiple computers. In this chapter, we'll analyze some of these strategies.

Client/Server Beginnings

All major software systems rely on a persistent storage mechanism for maintaining state between program invocations. In such software systems, it is possible to clearly separate processing into two distinct areas:

1. Processing that supports the storage and retrieval of persistent data as well as concurrent access to persistent storage.

2. All other processing required within the software system.

This clear delineation presented a great opportunity for separating the processing between multiple computers.

Splitting the work among multiple machines was not the only motivation for driving client/server technology. Business data is the most important asset that most companies possess. Maintaining a database on a server separate from the client allows for greater security, reliability, and performance with regard to data storage while simultaneously reducing the high cost associated with monolithic systems.

The relational database vendors recognized the opportunity and were instrumental in promoting the first major movement toward client/server distributed systems. These client/server systems were characterized by compute-intensive clients that maintained their persistent data within relational databases located on separate machines. The clients typically used Structured Query Language (SQL) as well as a database network driver to communicate with the database server.

It wasn't long before the strategy began to break down. SQL's biggest strength is that it is a nonprocedural mechanism for accessing data (nonprocedural means that you describe *what* you want rather than *how* to get it). SQL does not allow the user to specify processing semantics within a query. This meant that large amounts of data often needed to be transferred to the client to be processed even if the result after processing was very small. Network congestion was inevitable.

The relational vendors needed a way to move some of the processing back to the database server. As a result, all of the major vendors offered some form of stored procedures. A *stored procedure* is code that executes on the server side within the database management system. The stored procedure can be used to access data within the database and process it before sending the result to the client. Since the result of such processing is likely to be much smaller than the data being processed, the traffic between the client and the server is substantially reduced. Stored procedures can also be shared between multiple clients. The downside of such an approach is that stored procedures are inherently nonportable because they are vendor-specific. Whereas SQL can offer a somewhat portable means for accessing data, the use of stored procedures usually necessitates a large commitment to a specific vendor.

2-Tier, 3-Tier, and N-Tier Architectures

The client/server architecture described in the previous section was a distinctly 2-tier architecture. As illustrated in Figure 1-1, management of the database occurred on one tier and all other processing occurred on the other tier. This imposed a burden on the clients in that each client was required to possess significant processing power. The *stored procedure* approach that was used to better distribute work between client and server was a convenient mechanism to relieve the client in many cases, but it was certainly not appropriate for all situations. An example where it was definitely not appropriate was the case in which a business could not depend on vendor-specific features like stored procedures. A different strategy for distributing the work among multiple computers was required.

To further distribute the work, a new separation of work had to be found. The greatest opportunity for further separation was found in the client, which performed all processing not directly related to database management. It was possible to separate the client-side processing into application presentation and business logic processing. This further separation of processing resulted in

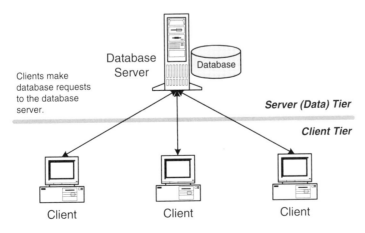

Figure 1-1. A typical 2-tier architecture.

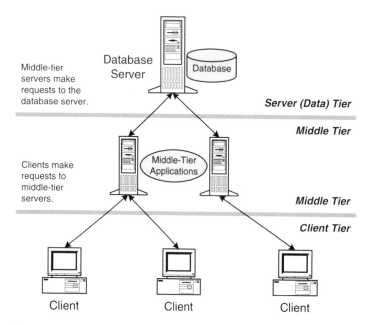

Middle-tier servers make requests to the database server.

Clients make requests to middle-tier servers.

Figure 1-2. *A typical 3-tier architecture.*

three tiers: a client tier for visual presentation, a middle tier for processing based on business logic, and a data tier for persistent data management. An example of a 3-tier architecture is illustrated in Figure 1-2.

Removing the business logic from the client and placing it in the middle tier offers a number of advantages above and beyond better distribution of processing.

- Placing business logic in the middle tier enhances performance by allowing the middle-tier business logic processing to occur in close proximity to the data-tier business data regardless of where clients are located.

- Adding new middle-tier servers to meet the demands of newly added clients can greatly increase the scalability of a 3-tier system.

- Removing the business logic from the client and placing it in the middle tier creates a layer between client-tier applications and data-tier databases, thus allowing client-tier applications to be written that are independent of the data-tier database.

- Placing the business logic in the middle tier centralizes the location of business logic in one place. In the 2-tier approach, business logic was spread across all clients (unless stored procedures were used). This is unacceptable since business rules tend to be dynamic and need to be enforced for the business to survive. Spreading the business logic across the client-tier clients can make enforcement very difficult.

The client and data tiers are very well defined in a pure 3-tier architecture. In contrast, the middle tier is not so well defined and is a catchall for all processing not related to application presentation and persistent data storage. It seems logical to assume that the middle tier might be divided into a number of services. If you consider each major service to be a separate tier, the 3-tier architecture that we've described quickly becomes an *N*-tier architecture. In fact, one could argue that 3-tier architectures are very rare since there is usually more than one service in the middle tier. A prominent example of an *N*-tier architecture is a Web-based application. A Web-based application might consist of the following tiers:

- Tier 1, a client-tier presentation implemented by a Web browser.

- Tier 2, a middle-tier distribution mechanism implemented by a Web server.

- Tier 3, a middle-tier service implemented by a set of server-side scripts.

- Tier 4, a data-tier storage mechanism implemented by a relational database.

An *N*-tier architecture for the Web-based application just described is illustrated in Figure 1-3.

All of this sounds simple enough—the different tiers in an *N*-tier system simply represent a division of work across multiple computers. The next question that you should be asking is, How does one coordinate the multiple tiers and manage communication between them? The Web-based example was a very simple case in which protocols for communication between the tiers are well defined. More complex systems require a much more complex infrastructure to manage the overall system.

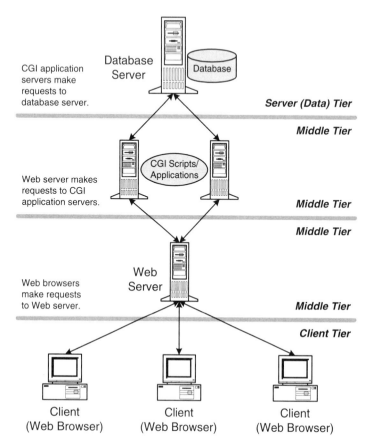

Figure 1-3. *An N-tier Web-based application architecture.*

Communicating Between Tiers

Because client/server applications span multiple computers, they rely on a networking infrastructure such as TCP/IP or IPX to connect the nodes participating in the application. The transition to multi-tier systems would not have been possible if all communication between tiers had to be implemented at such a low level. The evolution of middleware was driven by the need to facilitate usable mechanisms for communication between the participating computers.

In 2-tier systems, the task of abstracting the network protocols was fairly simple. The relational database vendors provided specialized libraries and drivers to access the database that abstracted the various network protocols. Client applications could be written without regard for the actual location of the database. The client-tier applications were able to link in the appropriate library (either statically or dynamically) that allowed communication with the data tier. Abstracting the networking code was not overly difficult since the relational model provided a very structured and generic means for accessing the database. Over time, an embedded SQL standard was created such that data access could be implemented in a portable way. This was followed by several portable dynamic-access approaches such as the Open Database Connectivity (ODBC) standard.

N-tier systems require a much more sophisticated infrastructure for communication across the network. Communication between the client applications and middle-tier services cannot be done in a generic and structured way as had been done in 2-tier systems; instead, clients need a model of communication that blends in with the development platform being used to implement the client applications. As this need was realized, standards began to emerge that provided the middleware foundation needed by such clients.

To meet the needs of various client implementations (i.e., programming languages), middleware evolved much as programming languages have over the last 10 years. The first middleware technology to gain wide acceptance was the *remote procedure call* (RPC). Using remote procedure calls, client applications could make C-language function calls that executed on a remote computer. Open Network Computing RPC (ONC RPC) and the Open Group's Distributed Computing Environment (DCE) are the dominant standards for remote procedure call architectures.

As object-oriented programming languages such as C++ became more prevalent, distributed middleware evolved toward object-oriented semantics. The Object Management Group (OMG), a group consisting of a wide range of computer software and hardware vendors, put forth a specification for the Common Object Request Broker Architecture (CORBA) that outlined an architecture for distributing objects across language, process, and machine boundaries. Many vendors have implemented the CORBA specification and currently market CORBA middleware.

The OMG was not alone in attempting to create an architecture for distributed objects. Microsoft evolved the Component Object Model (COM), an architecture that allows objects to cross language and process boundaries but not machine boundaries. In 1996, Microsoft released DCOM, a distributed version of COM implemented on top of the DCE RPC architecture. With DCOM,

Microsoft controls a technology on par with CORBA in terms of distributed object functionality.

The Power of Distributed Objects

Distributed objects represent an advancement over remote procedure calls just as object-oriented programming languages represented an advancement over procedural programming languages. The very essence of the object-oriented paradigm is that objects maintain state and communicate via messages—an ideal fit in the distributed computing world. Object instances appear to be an excellent unit of distribution (i.e., it doesn't make sense to split an object instance across two different middle-tier servers). Determining distribution can be more difficult with the procedural RPC approach.

Both COM and CORBA achieve language independence by defining object interfaces in a language-independent manner. This means that COM and CORBA objects can be implemented in one language and used by another without significant effort. COM and CORBA interfaces map very nicely into the Java and C++ programming languages. Most COM objects can also be used transparently within Visual Basic. With regard to CORBA, the CORBA 2.2 specification contains official mappings to C, C++, Java, COBOL, Smalltalk, and Ada.

The most important aspect of distributed objects is that they can be used transparently (i.e., without regard for location or implementation) at a fine level of granularity. A distributed object should not simply be a giant grouping of services. Instead, the distributed object can be thought of as any other program object. For example, a C++ programmer can use a COM object representing a customer instance in much the same way as a conventional C++ object. The programmer would not need to worry about the location of the actual running object instance. This blending of distributed objects within the context of the client application program is very powerful.

From Objects to Components

Objects are out. Components are in. The popularity that used to surround object technology now seems to have shifted to the area of component technology. Components represent what objects should have been striving for from the beginning. Object-oriented development tools have assisted developers in creating ever more complex enterprise systems; however, object technology has fallen far short of expectations. This can hardly be blamed on the software developers who worked diligently to use object technology. Instead, it is mostly due to slightly misplaced priorities. Early efforts with object technology focused primarily on two concepts: encapsulation and implementation reuse through inheritance. This is not surprising since both of these concepts initially appear to have great value. It also just so happens that encapsulation and implementation inheritance are also the easiest concepts to appreciate for someone moving from the procedure-oriented paradigm to the object-oriented paradigm.

The encapsulation mechanism offered by object-oriented programming languages provides a strict method for hiding one object's implementation details from another object. Object interfaces represent a contract. As long as the contract is maintained, the implementation can change without creating side effects throughout the rest of the system. Systems built with a procedural language like C are difficult to maintain because there is very little language support for encapsulation. It is therefore difficult to avoid side effects when making even the smallest of changes. Encapsulation is often viewed as a way to ease the maintenance problem evidenced in procedural-based systems. Easing the maintenance problem is certainly a worthwhile endeavor.

Implementation reuse through inheritance has also been given the highest priority in many large system development efforts. This seems like an obvious winner: More implementation reuse should result in less development time, improved time to market, and reduced costs. Large-scale implementation reuse was nearly an unachievable goal with procedural languages. The sad truth is that it has proven almost as difficult with object-based technologies (except in the rare cases that get all the publicity).

The term *component* connotes a very different set of priorities than does the term *object*. Whereas object orientation often resulted in an extreme focus on encapsulation and implementation reuse, component orientation tends to focus on component pluggability. This is so important that it is worth repeating: Component orientation focuses on creating pluggable parts. Creating pluggable parts (i.e., components) has little to do with encapsulation in the object-oriented sense and absolutely nothing to do with implementation reuse.

Components carry encapsulation to an extreme level. They do so by exposing only a public interface. The actual implementation of a component is completely hidden such that

- *The implementation language of the component is unknown.* A Java client is unaware that a component being used is implemented in C++.

In fact, the component might very well not even be implemented as an object!

- *The physical location of the component is unknown.* A Visual Basic client is unaware that a component being used is running within the same process (using a DLL), is running in a different process on the same machine, or is located on a different machine.

By using extreme encapsulation, components each live in their own tiny (or possibly large) universe. The benefit to the outside world is that a properly designed component can be plugged into a diverse set of clients. Clients do not need to worry about the implementation (actual source code) of a component. Clients of a component need to worry only about the interfaces (i.e., the contract) supported by a component. In an ideal setting, different components that support the same interfaces can be used interchangeably. Pluggability of interchangeable components is the goal of component-based systems. In contrast, implementation reuse has a fairly low priority with regard to components.

The goal of implementation reuse (i.e., code reuse) through inheritance is flawed. When we add up all of the effort that goes into a software system (such as requirements gathering, design, planning, implementation, deployment, maintenance, etc.), we find that actual implementation ends up being a very small portion of the overall effort. Implementation inheritance should be a side effect of good design rather than an end goal. Implementation reuse has absolutely nothing to do with component architectures. As stated earlier, components need not even be implemented as objects. Components are more successful from a reuse standpoint because they are pluggable. When you plug a component into your software system, you plug in all of the effort, including requirements gathering, design, implementation, and so forth, that went into making the component a well-defined pluggable unit.

Component models usually include a number of other defining characteristics. Here are a few of the more important traits:

- *Components are managed within a container.* Components obey the rules of their container and have a standard way of sending events to their container.

- *Components derive properties from their container.* For example, a component might use the container's background color as its own background color.

- *Components allow for dynamic discovery and invocation of supported interfaces.* Clients can determine at runtime what functionality is supported by a component and then invoke that functionality.

There are two important things to keep in mind when we discuss components. First, components should not be viewed as necessarily small entities. Many consider components to be small visual artifacts such as controls that can be placed on something like a Visual Basic palette. An example of a fairly large and complex component is the HTML viewer used in Microsoft's Internet Explorer. This HTML control is used in a number of places, including the help system in Microsoft's Visual Studio development environment. Second, components and their containers are not necessarily visual. Components may be completely nonvisual and implement business logic. The container that manages such nonvisual components can control nonvisual characteristics such as activation, security, transactions, and persistence.

Understanding the general benefits of components as opposed to objects is important for the following reason. COM and CORBA are significantly different in their support for component orientation. We need to clearly understand the advantages of components and the support offered by COM and CORBA so that we can determine where COM and CORBA fit into our software solutions.

Managing Distributed Systems

Up to this point, we've spent a considerable amount of time discussing how communication can be achieved between communicating entities in a multi-tiered distributed system. We have not yet discussed how to manage the overall system. To manage a complex distributed system, several different types of high-level services are needed. Just as it would not have been possible to evolve to client/server without abstracting the underlying networking protocols, it will not be possible to evolve to complex *N*-tier systems unless key high-level services are provided with distributed object platforms.

It is quite possible that you will not need all of the described services for your current system. But, as you attack larger problems (as is inevitable in the software industry), the following types of services will be necessary:

- *Naming.* A naming service provides a mechanism for locating distributed objects within the system.

- *Monitoring.* A monitoring service monitors the health of the system and issues alerts when attention by an operator is required.

- *Licensing.* A licensing service ensures that users of the distributed objects have purchased the appropriate usage license.

- *Persistence.* A persistence service provides a uniform mechanism that allows distributed objects to save, update, and restore their state using a persistent data store.

- *Security.* A security service ensures that communication with a distributed object is secure and that the user of the distributed object has obtained the appropriate privileges.

- *Transactions.* A transaction service ensures that a transaction is completed or aborted in its entirety whenever work is performed. A transaction typically defines an atomic unit of work in an enterprise system. A distributed transaction is a single unit of work that spans multiple computers.

- *Messaging.* A messaging service supports an asynchronous programming model as opposed to the typical request-reply model. There are many types of applications that require messaging. An example is an application in which the client and server are required to run at different times.

- *Distributed garbage collection.* A distributed garbage collector automatically deallocates distributed objects when they are no longer being used by clients.

- *Resource management.* A resource manager manages distributed objects in such a way as to maximize scalability, which refers to the ability to support a large number of clients interacting with a large number of distributed objects in a short period of time.

The services just described provide a lot of insight into the many aspects that need to be considered when distributed systems are being developed. Many of these services have fully matured in the RPC domain but not in the COM and CORBA domains; however, all of the major vendors have refocused their efforts on establishing services as described here for their distributed object technologies. The availability and scope of services offered by COM and CORBA vendors will have a significant impact on your decision to use COM and CORBA in your distributed system.

The State of Distributed Objects

Have distributed objects arrived? A more interesting question might be the following: Are we in the middle of a paradigm shift in the software development industry? Consider the following points:

- *Language choice is no longer a primary consideration.* Both COM and CORBA provide a language-independent mechanism for describing distributed object interfaces. Distributed objects can be implemented in one language and used by client applications implemented in a different language. For example, a COM distributed object might be written in Java and then used by a client application written in Visual Basic.

- *Process and machine boundaries are more easily crossed.* It used to be an extremely difficult task to write cooperative applications that communicated across processes or even machines. Interprocess communication relied on a wide range of techniques, including shared memory, named pipes, and so on. Communicating across machine boundaries required in-depth understanding of each machine's architecture to resolve platform idiosyncrasies. COM and CORBA abstract interprocess and multiplatform issues so that interprocess communication is as simple as calling a method on an object.

- *Internet and push technologies offer new delivery mechanisms.* The days of getting new floppies and CDs containing software programs are rapidly coming to an end. Web-based applications can be run using a Web browser without having to install any software on the client system. Push technologies allow client applications and system configuration to be updated without the need for user intervention.

These factors indicate that the development and the deployment of software systems are undergoing a drastic change. Distributed *N*-tier applications will dominate in the enterprise systems arena. It just so happens that distributed object technology provides the most powerful mechanism currently available to create distributed applications.

In the next chapter, we will assess some of the distributed object architectures that have appeared over the last few years. We will then describe why COM and CORBA dominate the distributed object domain. COM and CORBA are being deployed at a feverish rate in a variety of situations. The ever-expanding usage of COM and CORBA in the marketplace is hard evidence that distributed objects have truly arrived.

Chapter 2

The Dominance of COM and CORBA

Topics Covered in This Chapter

- The Distributed Object Landscape

- COM: The Dominant Component Architecture

- CORBA: The Dominant Remoting Architecture

- Evolutionary Trends

- A Test of Wills

- Who Is the Winner?

Distributed objects have the potential to solve a wide range of challenges faced by designers of large software systems. Some of these challenges include component packaging, cross-language interoperability, interprocess communication, and intermachine communication. The distributed object architectures that have been introduced over the last decade exhibit different strengths and weaknesses based on their ability to meet these challenges. In this chapter, we'll first take a quick tour of the primary distributed object architectures that have been created. We'll then discuss the importance of the various architectures in the marketplace.

For this discussion, we will draw a line in the sand and separate distributed object architectures into two categories: component architectures and remoting architectures. We define *component architectures* as architectures that focus primarily on component packaging and cross-language interoperability. We define *remoting architectures* as architectures that focus primarily on support for remote method invocation on distributed objects. The separation that we are making is somewhat arbitrary, as each distributed object technology tends to cross our boundary in some way or another. Creating the separation allows us to categorize the different architectures so that we can more easily identify the strengths of one technology over another technology.

The Distributed Object Landscape

Microsoft's COM/DCOM

In the early 1990s, Microsoft made a strong commitment to Object Linking and Embedding (OLE). Microsoft quickly recognized that to effectively evolve OLE, it needed a standard mechanism for packaging components. Cross-language interoperability was also crucial so that those components could be implemented in a variety of languages and then combined in an arbitrary fashion. Microsoft created the Component Object Model (COM) to provide the infrastructure that was needed to realize its vision for OLE. As time passed, COM became the foundation for a wide range of technologies that included but were not exclusive to OLE. One of the most important new technologies that relied on COM was the OLE Control Extension (OCX).

In 1996, Microsoft announced that ActiveX would be the new name for those technologies based primarily on COM. Microsoft has since changed this position and associates the term *ActiveX* with the visual controls market (formerly known as *OCXs*). By the end of 1996, Microsoft introduced DCOM, a set of RPC-based extensions to COM that allow COM objects to be distributed. COM has been very slow to appear on non-Windows platforms. Because of limited platform support, COM is still identified as being more of a component architecture than a remoting architecture; however, COM has much to offer as a remoting architecture, especially when working on Windows-based platforms. COM is undoubtedly the most mature and prolific component architecture in use today. This is largely due to the dominance of Microsoft's Windows-based operating systems on the desktop.

IBM's SOM/DSOM

Microsoft's COM was not the only component architecture that was made available to developers. IBM introduced the System Object Model (SOM) in the early 1990s. Like Microsoft's COM, SOM is a component architecture that provides cross-language interoperability as well as a standard mechanism for packaging components. Networking extensions were later added to SOM, resulting in the introduction of Distributed SOM (DSOM).

SOM never gained wide acceptance as a component architecture outside of the IBM community for a couple of reasons. First, IBM failed to succeed in making OS/2 a dominant desktop operating system. Had OS/2 gained wider acceptance, SOM might have become the component architecture of choice, at least for OS/2-based systems. Second, IBM's SOM could not compete with Microsoft's COM/OLE on Microsoft's Windows-based platforms. IBM's DSOM also failed to gain wide acceptance as a remoting architecture despite the fact that IBM evolved it toward the OMG's CORBA standard. In recent years, IBM has shifted focus away from SOM/DSOM toward a new set of CORBA-based development tools.

CORBA

The Object Management Group (OMG) is a consortium of vendors who banded together with the intent of creating a standard specification for a remoting architecture. The specification created by the OMG is the Object Management Architecture (OMA), of which CORBA is a fundamental part. The purpose of CORBA as proposed by the OMG is very different from that of COM and SOM. CORBA was intended from the beginning to solve the problem of inter-machine communication and is therefore a remoting architecture. The CORBA specification outlines an infrastructure for communication between processes on the same or different machines. Method invocations on CORBA objects are transparent such that the caller is not aware of where the callee is located.

Component packaging was not the primary objective during early iterations of the CORBA specification; however, CORBA does provide for cross-language, cross-platform, and even cross-vendor interoperability. Because the CORBA specification has been implemented by a fairly wide range of vendors on most hardware platforms (i.e., mainframe, UNIX, and Windows-based platforms), CORBA is the dominant remoting architecture in use today.

In addition to CORBA's excellent support for remoting, the OMG is actively working on a standard CORBA component model. The CORBA component model is one of the most significant artifacts being added to the CORBA 3.0 specification. In addition to providing a rich server-side component framework, the specification for the CORBA component model will also provide a mapping to Enterprise JavaBeans (Sun's Java-based server-side component model), thus leveraging the current Enterprise JavaBeans install base. The mapping will allow an Enterprise JavaBean to be used within a CORBA component container that provides activation, transactions, security, events, and persistence.

Java RMI

The pervasive influence of Java has resulted in several Java-based distributed object architectures. The most ubiquitous is Java Remote Method Invocation (RMI), a remoting architecture that shipped in 1997 with version 1.1 of the Java Development Kit (JDK). Java RMI is a Java-only solution that provides an elegant mechanism for allowing remote method invocations on Java objects.

The use of Java RMI continues to increase because it provides the remoting infrastructure for Enterprise JavaBeans and future systems like Sun Microsystem's JavaSpaces and Jini. The most significant disadvantage of Java RMI is that it can be used only with the Java programming language. This disadvantage can be alleviated by using both Java RMI and CORBA. Efforts are under way to provide wire-level interoperability between CORBA and Java RMI, thereby allowing the efficient use of CORBA servers from RMI clients and vice versa. (For more information, see Enterprise JavaBeans Approach on page 366.)

Because of emerging technologies such as Enterprise JavaBeans, JavaSpaces, and Jini, Java RMI will be used in many large software systems. It currently appears, however, that Java RMI will not dominate as a general-purpose remoting architecture because of its reliance on a single programming language.

ObjectSpace's Voyager

ObjectSpace has entered the distributed object marketplace with a very interesting Java-based product called *Voyager*. Voyager is a remoting architecture that is implemented completely in Java. Although it is a Java-based product, Voyager offers a number of unique advantages. First, the process to remote-enable a Java class is unobtrusive. The Voyager compiler allows almost any Java class to be compiled into a remote-enabled class. Second, Voyager supports code mobility. The Voyager system allows Voyager-compiled Java classes to be shipped to remote locations as necessary. This feature allows for the design of a very dynamic distributed system.

ObjectSpace also plans support for dynamic bidirectional bridging to both CORBA and COM. Voyager will be able to treat CORBA and COM objects as Voyager objects. Voyager will generate CORBA IDL and COM IDL so that CORBA- and COM-based systems can interact with Voyager objects. Despite the advantages offered by Voyager and its planned support for both COM and

CORBA, it cannot dominate as a general-purpose remoting architecture because it can be used only directly from Java.

Summary

It should be clear at this point who the dominant players in the distributed object marketplace are. Microsoft's COM is the dominant component architecture, and the OMG's CORBA is the dominant remoting architecture. Although several other products, such as Java RMI, have established a share of the market, they show no signs of supplanting the positions held by COM and CORBA.

COM: The Dominant Component Architecture

COM is the dominant component architecture in use today. This is not too surprising since COM is the component architecture for today's most dominant desktop operating system—Microsoft Windows. Keep in mind that COM is focused on solving development problems in a desktop environment. The primary focus in desktop software development is to create front-end applications with which users interact. An optimized development environment for creating such applications requires prebuilt high-level components. It therefore makes sense that COM is primarily a component architecture rather than a remoting architecture.

COM supports a language-neutral interface definition language (IDL) that is used to describe the interface of a COM component. Using IDL, the designer of a COM component can describe the interfaces, methods, and properties that are supported by the component. Client applications rely on the IDL definition of the COM component rather than on implementation-specific details such as programming language and implementation platform.

COM supports the following three types of servers for implementing components:

1. *In-process server.* An in-process server is implemented as a dynamic linked library (DLL) that executes within the same process space as the application. The performance overhead of invoking an in-process server is small because an in-process server is located in the same process as the client. An in-process server is commonly referred to as an *ActiveX control.*

2. *Local server.* A local server executes in a separate process space on the same computer. Communication between an application and a local server is accomplished by the COM runtime system using a high-speed interprocess communication protocol. The performance overhead of using a local server is typically an order of magnitude greater than that of using an in-process server.

3. *Remote server.* A remote server executes on a remote computer. DCOM extends COM by providing an RPC-based infrastructure that is used to manage communication between the application and the remote server. The performance overhead of using a remote server is typically an order of magnitude greater than that of using a local server.

An application that uses a COM component is not required to know what type of server it is using. After a COM object instance handle has been obtained by a client, client interaction with the COM object instance is the same regardless of server location. This allows for great flexibility when determining how components should be implemented. Figure 2-1 illustrates a client application that interacts with an in-process, a local, and a remote COM server.

COM is a very mature component architecture that has many strengths. Thousands of third-party ActiveX controls (i.e., in-process COM components) are available that can be used to quickly create sophisticated end-user applications in a wide range of client environments. Microsoft and other vendors have built many tools that accelerate development of ActiveX controls and ActiveX-based applications. These tools include development environments such as Visual Basic and Visual C++. Microsoft is also providing advanced services

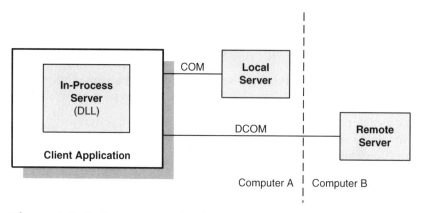

Figure 2-1. *An in-process, a local, and a remote COM server.*

such as Microsoft Transaction Service (MTS) and Microsoft Message Queuing Service (MSMQ) to support development of enterprise multi-tier systems. These tools and services in tandem with a mature component model like COM allow complex multi-tier systems to be built in a fraction of the time previously required.

Several significant weaknesses prevent COM from being an ideal single solution. First and foremost are the platform limitations. COM support is extremely limited on UNIX and mainframe platforms. Microsoft has not announced plans to make advanced services such as MTS and MSMQ available on non-Windows platforms. Another problem is that COM usage within Java requires usage of the Microsoft Java Virtual Machine. The Microsoft JVM that supports COM is not supported on non-Windows platforms. A final problem is the risk involved in depending solely on one vendor (e.g., Microsoft on Windows platforms or Software AG on UNIX platforms) for COM support. Many companies are unwilling to invest so heavily in one vendor's solutions.

CORBA: The Dominant Remoting Architecture

CORBA is the dominant remoting architecture in use today. The CORBA specification defines the foundation of the OMG's Object Management Architecture (OMA). Version 2.2 of the CORBA specification includes the following critical elements:

- *CORBA IDL.*[*] An implementation-independent interface definition language used to describe the interfaces of CORBA objects.

- *Dynamic invocation.* A specification for client-side and server-side APIs supporting dynamic discovery and invocation of CORBA object interfaces.

- *Portable object adaptor.* A specification for creating portable CORBA server implementations.

- *Interoperability.* A specification for interoperability between ORBs implemented by different vendors on different platforms. This specification includes IIOP, the CORBA 2.2 standard protocol used on top of TCP/IP. ORBs that comply with the CORBA 2.2 interoperability standard can communicate using IIOP regardless of the ORB vendor or platform.

---

*The CORBA specification refers to CORBA-based IDL as *OMG IDL*. To avoid confusion, we will refer to CORBA-based IDL as *CORBA IDL* and to COM-based IDL as *COM IDL* throughout the remainder of the book.

- *COM/CORBA bridging.* A formal specification that defines how COM and CORBA can be mapped to allow interoperability between the two architectures. With such a bridge, COM objects appear as CORBA objects to a CORBA client developer, and CORBA objects appear as COM objects to a COM client developer.

- *Multiple programming language mappings.* Standard mappings of CORBA IDL to the C, C++, Java, Smalltalk, COBOL, and Ada programming languages.

CORBA is currently the dominant remoting architecture because it provides robust cross-language, cross-platform, and cross-vendor support for creating servers on a wide range of operating system platforms. The CORBA specification was created and accepted by a large consortium of vendors within the Object Management Group.

CORBA is a very mature remoting architecture that has many strengths. First and foremost, CORBA was intended from the beginning to create a standard for remote method invocation. The CORBA specification has undergone two major revisions and countless implementations. C/C++ language implementations of version 1.1 of the CORBA specification appeared in the early 1990s and culminated in the release of Iona Technologies' Orbix for C++ in June of 1993. Version 2.0 of the CORBA specification was approved in July of 1995 and is now supported by many vendors, including Iona, Inprise, BEA, and IBM. The OMG has also made considerable headway in defining specifications for essential high-level services, including naming, events, security, and transactions. Most of the major vendors have begun marketing implementations of these services along with their base CORBA products.

The use of CORBA allows for incredible versatility when implementing distributed systems. This versatility is a result of

- *Broad language support.* CORBA products support official mappings to C, C++, Java, Smalltalk, COBOL, and Ada.

- *Diverse platform support.* CORBA products exist on mainframe platforms, all major UNIX platforms, Windows NT, Windows 95/98, OS/2, and Vax/VMS platforms. Several Java-based ORBs can be used on any platform that supports the Java Virtual Machine.

- *Multivendor support.* CORBA products are sold and supported by many vendors, including Iona Technologies, Inprise, BEA Systems, Expersoft, and IBM. CORBA ORBs that support the IIOP interoperability standard can be intermixed within the enterprise.

- *Freely available CORBA products.* Freely available CORBA products include Java IDL in Sun's JDK 1.2, OmniORB 2 from the Olivetti and Oracle Research Laboratories, JacORB for Java, and many others.[*]

One of CORBA's greatest strengths is that it is an open standard arrived at by the consensus of a large number of vendors. This also happens to be one of its greatest weaknesses because specifications often take a long period of time (typically greater than 12 months) to gain approval. The vendors then need sufficient time (typically greater than 6 months) to implement products that support the approved specifications. The specifications also require approval by a large number of parties. This tends to restrict innovation in order to create a specification that is capable of being approved.

CORBA currently lacks a component model and advanced tool support. Although the CORBA 3.0 specification will contain a CORBA component model, it will take time for such a model to appear in various commercial implementations. It is also reasonable to assume that additional time will be needed for such commercial implementations to mature and stabilize in the marketplace.

Based on the strengths and weaknesses as identified here, CORBA appears to be a solid choice for creating middle-tier and back-tier servers. This makes sense because middle-tier and back-tier server development relies heavily on a solid remoting architecture and does not necessarily rely on a component architecture. In contrast, CORBA is often not appropriate for creating client-tier applications because it lacks so many of the important component-related advantages offered by COM.

One client-tier advantage that CORBA does currently possess over its COM counterpart is the use of CORBA in Java applets. Several ORB vendors, such as Inprise and Iona, offer a Java-based ORB that can be downloaded at run-time along with a Java applet. After a browser such as Internet Explorer downloads the Java ORB, the ORB functions as a first-class CORBA ORB within the browser's Java Virtual Machine. The Java applet can then use the downloaded ORB to communicate with server-side CORBA objects. As browsers add support for JDK 1.2, clients will be able to take advantage of Java IDL, the CORBA ORB that ships as part of JDK 1.2.

---

*For more information on freely available CORBA products, see http://www.omg.org/corba/freestuff.html.

Evolutionary Trends

In preceding sections, we have identified some strengths and weaknesses of COM and CORBA that make each of them dominant in the marketplace. You may have also noticed that comparing COM and CORBA is like comparing apples and oranges. The only appropriate comparison is between DCOM and CORBA since COM encompasses a variety of technologies that have no parallel in the CORBA universe. When we examine the differences between COM and CORBA, we see that two trends are quite obvious: COM evolved in a bottom-up fashion, and CORBA evolved in a top-down fashion.

Although distributing COM objects was probably a consideration when designing the COM architecture, COM was originally intended to meet the needs of OLE. COM later evolved as a component architecture rather than as a remoting architecture. Extensions to support distribution in COM did not appear until 1996 under Windows NT 4.0. Support for DCOM in Windows 95 was added in the early part of 1997, followed by limited UNIX and mainframe support late in 1997. This is in contrast to CORBA, which has been available on many platforms since the early 1990s. COM clearly evolved in a bottom-up fashion. Each step in the evolution of COM resulted in increased functionality that was used for ongoing product development at Microsoft.

The evolution of CORBA was completely different from that of COM. The OMG was established in 1989 and consisted of a small number of vendors interested in creating a new standard for building distributed applications. The first step involved the creation of the Object Management Architecture that described a low-level object bus as well as high-level services and facilities. The low-level object bus was described in the CORBA specification. This specification identified a language-neutral interface definition language and a C mapping. Vendors then began implementing CORBA products based on the specification. Over the last decade, the specifications have been updated, and new specifications have been created, resulting in the delivery of better CORBA-based products. CORBA clearly evolved in a top-down fashion. Early phases in the specification of CORBA were openly debated and ratified. The specifications were then revised and refined, as were the implementations dependent on those specifications.

A Test of Wills

The software industry is fraught with conflict. Conflict is a natural result of competition and is to be expected in any industry that harbors competition.

One would expect that the best product wins out in the face of healthy competition. This may be the case when natural selection occurs in the wild, but it is rarely the case in human endeavors. Instead, emotion, personality, and politics often dominate the decisions made by vendors and end users. The conflict between COM and CORBA has been brewing for quite some time and has been fueled by both vendors and end users.

Vendor Perspective

The powerful force behind COM is Microsoft. Microsoft controls the world's most prolific operating system (i.e., Windows) and most of the important products that run on that operating system. To maintain its lead in premium software products such as its Office suite, Microsoft is constantly forced to enhance its own development needs. The rest of the development community benefits from the substantial development efforts made by Microsoft on its own behalf.

Microsoft has also demonstrated incredible focus and vision. Microsoft focuses only on software and is not influenced by a need to sell hardware. Although the marketing engine of Microsoft has at times confused outside developers, Microsoft's quest to conquer the enterprise has been pervasive. Microsoft has made a strong commitment to build the arsenal of tools (e.g., Visual C++, Visual Basic, etc.) and services (e.g., MTS, MSMQ, etc.) necessary to make its vision a reality.

The competition has fallen by the wayside in lieu of Microsoft's rise to the top of the software industry. However, there is one area in which Microsoft has struggled—the courtroom. Microsoft has been embroiled in several major lawsuits over the last few years, including an antitrust lawsuit filed against Microsoft by the United States Department of Justice as well as a Java-related lawsuit filed against Microsoft by Sun Microsystems. Another problem with Microsoft is its protectionist attitude when it comes to embracing outside technologies. Microsoft will continue to succeed in this attitude only as long as it dominates the desktop-computing world.

The vendors in the CORBA domain lack the focus and vision shown by Microsoft. Two of the biggest vendors in the CORBA domain are IBM and Sun. Although IBM and Sun have reduced their involvement in the retail sale of CORBA products, they still have a strong influence on the direction of CORBA. These two vendors share many of the same strengths and weaknesses in their quest to promote CORBA (or sabotage COM, depending on your viewpoint). Both IBM and Sun command considerable financial resources. IBM controls the mainframe, while Sun controls Java as well as Solaris, the dominant UNIX platform. Despite these advantages, both companies generate most of their revenues from hardware rather than from software, thus hindering their overall focus on software. This is exhibited in their lack of commitment to CORBA. IBM has a vested interest in non-CORBA technologies such as DCE and CICS for the mainframe. Sun has a vested interest in Java RMI and Java-related technologies such as Enterprise JavaBeans. These distractions fragment IBM's and Sun's attempts to steer the software community.

The primary CORBA vendors, such as Iona, Inprise, BEA, and Expersoft are certainly committed to CORBA, but they lack the resources to successfully compete with Microsoft in making CORBA a dominant technology. Microsoft can afford to forego profits while establishing COM. Vendors like Iona do not have that luxury. Despite these conditions, CORBA still fills a variety of important needs not addressed by COM (e.g., non-Windows support) and is therefore extremely important in the middleware marketplace.

User Perspective

Have you ever been in a meeting that directly discussed choosing between competing technologies such as CORBA and COM? If not, I can tell you that it is not a pretty sight. You're probably wondering whether conflicts over technology preference can be avoided. The answer is, probably not. The existence of sharp divisions in technology preference is nothing new in the software industry. In fact, it seems to be the rule rather than the exception. Here are some obvious (and maybe not so obvious) reasons why user conflicts often occur:

- *Creative endeavor.* Software development continues to be a creative endeavor. Software designers rely on their creative instincts when it comes to selecting specific technology to solve a problem. Relying on instinct is inherently nonobjective.

- *Multiple options.* Most problems can usually be solved using a range of options. To select a specific option, the decisionmaker is forced to convince himself/herself that one specific option is the best in order to defend the decision.

- *Past experience.* Everyone has a past in which somebody else made the decision to use a specific technology. Support for the previously used technology is often based on the outcome of the past experience (good or bad) without regard to how well or how poorly alternatives may have solved the same problem.

- *Current environment.* The current environment in which people work greatly influences their perspective. It is difficult to dislike a technology and continue to work with that technology on a day-to-day basis. When forced to use a specific technology, it is much easier to stay sane if you can avidly support that technology.

- *Backing the winner.* There is often a dominant player in a specific technology area. Some people will always favor the dominant player despite the advantages offered by nondominant players in the market (despite the overall viability of the nondominant players).

- *Backing the underdog.* Just as some people tend to favor the winner, others tend to always favor the underdog.

- *Marketing/propaganda.* Last but not least, the marketing departments (marketing machines) are always looking for an edge when it comes to selling their products. This often has the unfortunate side effect of undermining an entire set of competing technologies.

What is the strongest reason for conflict when debating issues surrounding COM and CORBA? It is too easy to blame vendor marketing and propaganda when, in fact, the other reasons just described contribute equally to the problem. It is important for each of us to identify the forces that sway our decisions so that we can avoid emotion and can objectively take advantage of each technology where it is most appropriate.

Who Is the Winner?

In this chapter, we've made a survey of the various distributed object architectures that have appeared over the last decade. Based on observation, we've identified COM and CORBA as the dominant architectures in the distributed object domain. COM is the dominant component architecture, and CORBA is the dominant remoting architecture. We then looked at the nontechnical issues that have driven COM and CORBA into their current positions in the marketplace. Although it is critically important to be aware of nontechnical driving forces such as politics and emotion, it is best not to let those nontechnical forces drive your decisions.

Who is the winner and who is the loser? As of today, there is no clear winner or loser. As we have stated before, COM and CORBA each possess strengths that the other technology lacks. Clarity with regard to the advantages of each technology will allow you to choose which technology is most appropriate for each situation. In the next chapter, we will examine the technical fundamentals of COM and CORBA. We'll begin by identifying the fundamental traits of distributed object systems. We'll then demonstrate how COM and CORBA provide the infrastructure that is needed to implement and deploy distributed object systems.

Chapter 3

Distributed Object Fundamentals

Topics Covered in This Chapter

- An Overview of the Fundamentals

- A Distributed Object Example

- Demonstrating the Fundamentals

A remoting architecture provides the foundation for a distributed object system. When we consider the remoting architectures available today, it is clear that COM and CORBA dominate the distributed object marketplace. In this chapter, we'll first examine the fundamental traits of distributed object systems. We'll then take a side-by-side look at the mechanisms provided by COM and CORBA that provide the foundation for building distributed object systems.

As we examine COM and CORBA more closely, the differences between these architectures will be apparent; however, the differences are largely syntactic. The general mechanisms and functionality that are provided by COM and CORBA are quite similar. This is to be expected since COM and CORBA both serve the same purpose—to meet the fundamental needs of distributed object systems.

A comparison of COM and CORBA fundamentals will help you to choose the technology that is most appropriate for a specific situation. It is also important to remember that the fundamental mechanisms provided by COM and CORBA are quite similar. This similarity indicates the existence of common ground on which both COM and CORBA can coexist.

An Overview of the Fundamentals

Up to this point, we have kept the discussion of distributed objects within the philosophical realm. The time has come to take a look at the actual software mechanisms used by COM and CORBA. Rather than attempting to perform a comprehensive analysis of each architecture, we will instead identify the fundamental traits of distributed object systems. We will then perform a side-by-side comparison of how COM and CORBA meet these fundamental needs.

The fundamental traits of a distributed object system are given next. For each trait, we provide a brief description of how the trait is handled by COM and CORBA. We expound on these descriptions throughout the remainder of the chapter. The fundamental traits of a distributed object system include

- *Interfaces.* Interfaces are used to define contracts that describe the capabilities of the distributed objects in the system. Interfaces are used in both COM and CORBA to define such contracts.

- *Data types.* A distributed object system must support data types that allow data to be transmitted to and from the distributed objects. Both COM and CORBA provide for a rich set of types as well as support for enumerated types, constants, and structures.

- *Marshaling and unmarshaling.* A distributed object system must ensure that data integrity is maintained when data is transmitted to and from distributed objects. A marshaling process packages data into a standard format so that it can be transmitted. An unmarshaling process unpacks transmitted data.

- *Proxies, stubs, and skeletons.* A distributed object system abstracts access to distributed objects so that the objects can be treated uniformly by client applications regardless of the distributed objects' actual implementation or location. COM and CORBA provide seamless access to distributed objects by proxifying client access to remote objects. *Proxies, stubs,* and *skeletons* are the terms used in COM and CORBA for the mechanisms that allow seamless access to remote objects.

- *Object handles.* Object handles are used to reference distributed object instances within the context of a client's programming language or script. Object handles are referred to as *interface pointers* in COM and as *object references* in CORBA.

- *Object creation.* A distributed object system must provide a mechanism for creating a new instance of a distributed object. A *factory* is a special type of distributed object used to create other distributed objects. COM defines a standard factory interface[*] for all COM objects, while CORBA factory interfaces are user-defined.

- *Object invocation.* A distributed system must provide a mechanism for invoking operations on a distributed object. Both COM and CORBA provide mechanisms that allow for static and dynamic invocation of distributed objects. (We will demonstrate static invocation in Invoking Object Methods on page 87.)

- *Object destruction.* A distributed object system must provide a mechanism for removing a distributed object instance from the system once it is no longer in use. COM supports distributed reference counting and garbage collection. CORBA provides no system support (i.e., distributed objects remain alive forever unless explicitly evicted or timed out).

A Distributed Object Example

Before we can demonstrate COM- and CORBA-based software, we need to define (i.e., contrive) an example that will accentuate the features in which we are interested. The requirements for our example are as follows:

1. The example must demonstrate both a COM distributed object and a CORBA distributed object.

2. The example must demonstrate clients being run locally and remotely in proximity to the distributed object.

3. The example must demonstrate at least two different clients using two different implementation languages communicating with each distributed object.

4. The example must demonstrate interface inheritance using both COM and CORBA.

5. The example must demonstrate multiple interfaces in both the COM and CORBA objects.

---

[*]COM actually defines two factory interfaces, `IClassFactory` and `IClassFactory2`. `IClassFactory` is considered the standard factory interface and is used implicitly by many COM methods.

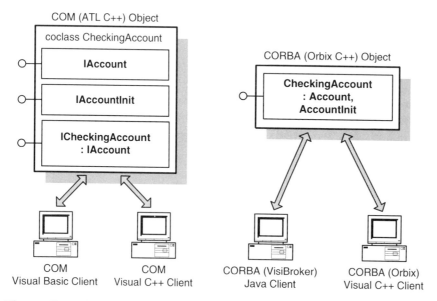

Figure 3-1. *The checking account example.*

6. The example must demonstrate object creation, invocation, and destruction.

A distributed object implementing a simple checking account will meet our needs. Figure 3-1 provides a conceptual view of our example.

Each of our COM and CORBA checking account objects will implement the three interfaces shown in Table 3-1.

Table 3-1. *Checking Account Object Interfaces*

Interface	Properties	Methods
Account	name balance	deposit(amount) withdraw(amount)
AccountInit		init(name)
CheckingAccount		withdrawUsingCheck (checkNumber, amount)

COM Object and Clients

Our first task is to implement a COM object and two COM client applications. Since it does not matter which platform we use to implement the COM object, we will use Microsoft Visual C++ and the Active Template Library (ATL) as a matter of convenience. The COM object will support three interfaces: IAccount, IAccountInit, and ICheckingAccount. (It is typical for a COM object to expose distinct multiple interfaces. We will discuss how to manage multiple interfaces for a COM object in more detail in COM Interface Pointers in C++ on page 65.) To demonstrate interface inheritance in our example, the ICheckingAccount interface will inherit from the IAccount interface.

We have a wide variety of choices when it comes to creating COM clients for our COM checking account object. For this example, we will implement our COM clients using Visual Basic and Visual C++. As opposed to our COM server implementation choice (i.e., Visual C++ ATL), our client platform choices are not arbitrary. The Visual Basic environment provides excellent support for COM object integration. The Visual C++ environment will allow us to see how COM works at the C/C++ API level. The Visual Basic client application is shown in Figure 3-2. The Visual C++ client application (not shown) is functionally identical to the Visual Basic application.

The COM client application is divided into two sections: initialization and account management. The initialization section is used to specify the name of the person for whom the account will be created and the server name of the host on which the COM checking account object is implemented. The COM client will attempt to run against a local server if no server name is specified. The account management section allows the user to perform withdrawals and deposits. The balance is maintained as well as a log of all withdrawals and deposits since the object was created.

CORBA Object and Clients

We also need to create a CORBA object and two CORBA clients. We will implement our CORBA object using Iona's Orbix (a CORBA 2.0 compliant product) and Visual C++. The CORBA object will support one interface called CheckingAccount that inherits from the Account and AccountInit interfaces. Unlike COM, CORBA cannot support multiple interfaces except through the use of multiple inheritance. COM, on the other hand, does not support multiple inheritance in the interface hierarchy but does allow multiple distinct

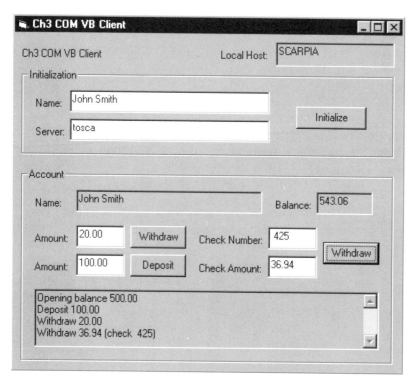

Figure 3-2. *The COM Visual Basic client application.*

interfaces to be supported by a single COM object. We will clarify what we mean by *multiple inheritance* versus *multiple distinct interfaces* when we explore interfaces and object handles later in the chapter.

To demonstrate CORBA clients that are implemented in both C++ and Java, we need to use CORBA products that support both C++ and Java. We will use Orbix/C++ since we already have the ORB installed and working. Our other client application will be implemented using Inprise's VisiBroker Java ORB (a CORBA 2.0 compliant product). This gives us the added bonus of demonstrating interoperability between two distinct vendors' CORBA 2.0 compliant ORB products. The Java client application is shown in Figure 3-3. The Visual C++ client application (not shown) is functionally identical to the Java application.

The CORBA client application is identical to the COM client application with one major exception. Rather than specifying a server name to the client at runtime, the user is instead required to input a string known as a *stringified interoperable object reference* (IOR) identifying the CORBA factory that should

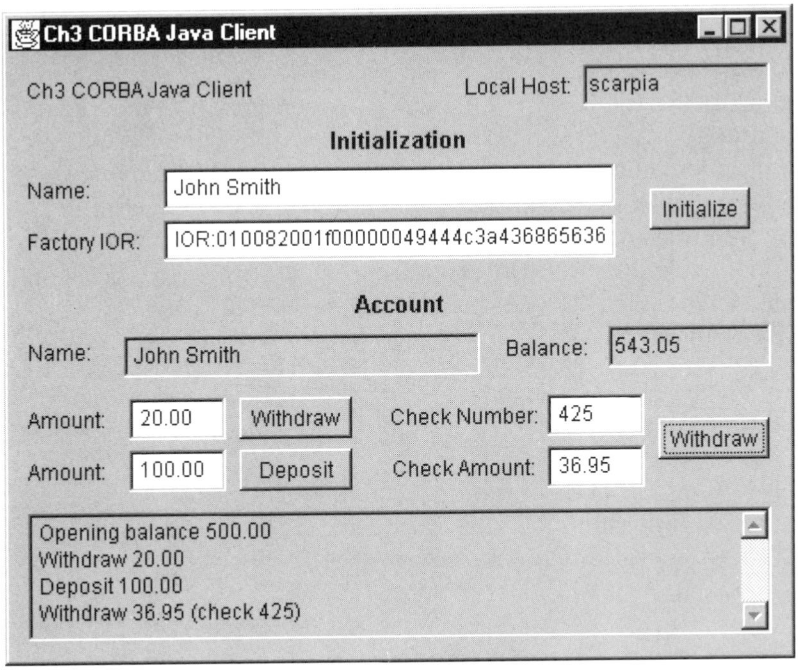

Figure 3-3. *The CORBA Java client application.*

be used to create the CORBA checking account object. IORs are defined in the CORBA 2.0 standard and are used to uniquely identify CORBA object instances. Listing 3-1 shows the IOR that was entered in Figure 3-3.

Manually entering a stringified IOR is not practical (the IOR in Listing 3-1 is 268 characters) but serves our purpose well. Remember that our Java client uses the VisiBroker ORB to communicate with our server object, which is implemented using Orbix. The stringified IOR provides an extremely convenient way to interoperate between the two different ORB products. (We will

Listing 3-1. *CORBA Checking Account Factory IOR*

```
IOR:010082001f00000049444c3a436865636b696e674163636f756e74466163
746f72793a312e3000000010000000000000005000000010100000600000746f
7363610083043c0000003a5c746f7363613a436865636b696e674163636f756e
74466163746f72793a303a3a49523a436865636b696e674163636f756e744661
63746f727900
```

describe how a stringified IOR is generated and used in CORBA Factories on page 82.)

While the use of a stringified IOR is in some ways impractical, it demonstrates the most fundamental approach for achieving interoperability between different CORBA products. For more complex applications, a CORBA-based solution would typically rely on a CORBA naming service. The CORBA naming service allows meaningful names (as opposed to IORs) to be associated with CORBA objects. All of the major CORBA vendors provide implementations of the naming service. Applications that use a naming service do not normally need to manipulate stringified IORs.

Reviewing the Requirements

Before we move on to the task of examining actual code, let's review the requirements for our example to make sure that it meets our needs. The requirements and their resolutions are summarized in Table 3-2.

Demonstrating the Fundamentals

We began this chapter by defining the fundamental traits of distributed object systems. We then defined an example intended to allow us to explore the fundamental mechanisms provided by both COM and CORBA. In this section, we will describe the actual programming code used to implement the example. The following topics will be explored:

- In Selecting Data Types on page 40, we will briefly discuss the data types available in COM and CORBA. We will then describe the data types used in the checking account example.

- In Defining the Interfaces on page 41, we will provide a detailed description of how the interfaces for our COM and CORBA objects are defined using COM IDL and CORBA IDL.

- In Proxies, Stubs, and Skeletons on page 50, we will describe what these terms mean in the context of the COM and CORBA architectures. We will then demonstrate how proxies, stubs, and skeletons are used in the checking account example.

- In Implementing the Servers on page 56, we will discuss how the COM and CORBA checking account servers are implemented.

Table 3-2. *Summary of Requirements for Checking Account Example*

Requirement	Resolution
The example must demonstrate both a COM distributed object and a CORBA distributed object.	Our example implements a checking account object using both COM and CORBA.
The example must demonstrate clients being run locally and remotely in proximity to the distributed object.	Our COM client applications allow the server machine to be specified. Our CORBA client applications use an IOR that can point to a CORBA object on either a local or remote machine.
The example must demonstrate at least two different clients using two different implementation languages communicating with each distributed object.	Our COM clients include a Visual Basic application and a Visual C++ application. Our CORBA clients include a Java application and a Visual C++ application.
The example must demonstrate interface inheritance using both COM and CORBA.	In our COM object, the ICheckingAccount interface inherits from the IAccount interface. In our CORBA object, the CheckingAccount interface multiply-inherits from the Account and AccountInit interfaces.
The example must demonstrate multiple interfaces in both the COM and CORBA objects.	Both the COM and CORBA objects support three interfaces: Account, AccountInit, and CheckingAccount.
The example must demonstrate object creation, invocation, and destruction.	Our client applications demonstrate object creation, invocation, and destruction.

- In Implementing the Clients on page 57, we will describe the basic design of our COM and CORBA client applications. We will then show how the interface definitions for our COM and CORBA objects are used when implementing the client applications.

- In Object Handles on page 64, we will discuss issues related to COM interface pointers and CORBA object references and demonstrate their use in our client applications.

- In Creating Objects on page 75, we will show how the COM and CORBA checking account objects are created from our client applications.

- In Invoking Object Methods on page 87, we will describe how COM and CORBA object methods are invoked.

- In Destroying Objects on page 95, we will describe how COM and CORBA objects are destroyed when they are no longer referenced.

Selecting Data Types

Both COM and CORBA allow for a rich set of data types. This includes support for constants, enumerated types, structures, and arrays in addition to common base types like `long` and `short`. COM also identifies a special subset of data types known as *automation types* that must be used when defining automation-compatible interfaces. (A list of automation types is given later in Table 8-2 on page 232.) The greatest limitation of automation types is the lack of support for user-defined types such as structs. (We will discuss these limitations in COM Client Approaches on page 218.) COM interfaces that are not automation-compatible often do not work with non-C++ COM client environments including Visual Basic. To ensure that our example can utilize a Visual Basic client application, our COM interface must abide by automation restrictions. This is an area where CORBA is clearly superior to COM. In contrast to COM, which must sometimes abide by automation restrictions when defining COM interfaces, any CORBA type can be used in any CORBA interface.

Our checking account example has very few requirements with regard to data types. The interfaces utilize the `string` data type (for the account name), `double` data type (for the balance and amounts), and `long` data type (for the check number). All of these types can be represented as automation types.

Note that because of the automation restrictions just described, our COM interfaces utilize the `BSTR` type when dealing with strings. `BSTR` is the automation type typically used to represent strings. A short explanation of `BSTR` is provided next since `BSTR`s will frequently be used throughout the COM-based examples presented in this chapter.

A `BSTR` (also known as a *Basic string*) is a pointer to a length-prefixed wide-character array. Because a `BSTR` is prefixed with a 4-byte length attribute, a C/C++ `BSTR` pointer does not point at the beginning of the data structure but instead points to the first wide character in the array. This requires special handling when working with a COM interface in C++ since we cannot use the normal memory allocation system calls (i.e., `new` and `delete`). In a C++ application, a `BSTR` instance must be allocated using the `SysAllocString()` method as shown here:

```
static BSTR AllocateBstr(const wchar_t* wstr)
{
    BSTR bstr = ::SysAllocString(wstr);
    return bstr;
}
```

A BSTR instance must be deallocated using the SysFreeString() method as shown here:

```
static void FreeBstr(BSTR bstr)
{
    ::SysFreeString(bstr);
}
```

To assist developers in using BSTRs, Microsoft has defined the _bstr_t helper class in the comdef.h header file. The _bstr_t helper class allows for simplified allocation and deallocation of BSTRs as well as conversions between BSTRs and common C-language string types such as char*. The comdef.h header file is shipped with the Visual C++ development environment.

We have now reached the stage where we have the key ingredients needed to describe our distributed object interfaces. These ingredients include the interfaces (e.g., Account, AccountInit, and CheckingAccount) as well as the properties, methods, and corresponding data types for each interface. The next step is to formally define our interfaces.

Defining the Interfaces

Both COM and CORBA utilize an interface definition language (IDL) to describe their respective interfaces. These IDL descriptions provide the starting point for implementing server objects and client applications. In this section, we will examine how COM IDL and CORBA IDL are used in our checking account example.

COM IDL and Type Libraries

The COM IDL file used to implement the COM checking account object is shown in Listing 3-2. A first look at COM IDL can be somewhat daunting. Remembering the various keywords and syntax is quite challenging unless you happen to work with COM IDL on a daily basis. These problems are alleviated by excellent development tool support. All of the IDL code for our example (except for the oleautomation attribute in the interface definitions) was generated by Visual C++ from within an Active Template Library (ATL) project. The creation of properties, methods, interfaces, and so forth was completely dialog-driven. A problem of higher complexity than our example would require a better understanding of COM IDL. However, superior tool support (as is the case with Visual C++ and ATL) helps to lessen the learning curve.

Listing 3-2. *COM IDL for Checking Account*

```
//
// Ch3ComCppServer.idl (COM IDL)
//

import "oaidl.idl";
import "ocidl.idl";


    [
        object,
        uuid(B5F3E2FE-B376-11D1-BB1E-00207812E629),
        oleautomation,
        helpstring("IAccount Interface"),
        pointer_default(unique)
    ]
    interface IAccount : IUnknown
    {
        [propget, helpstring("property Balance")]
            HRESULT Balance([out, retval] double *pVal);

        [propget, helpstring("property Name")]
            HRESULT Name([out, retval] BSTR *pVal);

        [helpstring("method Deposit")]
            HRESULT Deposit([in] double amount);

        [helpstring("method Withdraw")]
            HRESULT Withdraw([in] double amount);
    };


    [
        object,
        uuid(B5F3E2FF-B376-11D1-BB1E-00207812E629),
        oleautomation,
        helpstring("IAccountInit Interface"),
        pointer_default(unique)
    ]
    interface IAccountInit : IUnknown
    {
        const int E_INVALID_NAME = 0x80040200;

        [helpstring("method Init")]
            HRESULT Init([in] BSTR name);
    };
```

*Listing **3-2.** COM IDL for Checking Account (continued)*

```
    [
        object,
        uuid(B5F3E2FD-B376-11D1-BB1E-00207812E629),
        oleautomation,
        helpstring("ICheckingAccount Interface"),
        pointer_default(unique)
    ]
    interface ICheckingAccount : IAccount
    {
        [helpstring("method WithdrawUsingCheck")]
            HRESULT WithdrawUsingCheck([in] long checkNumber,
                                       [in] double amount);
    };

[
    uuid(B5F3E2F0-B376-11D1-BB1E-00207812E629),
    version(1.0),
    helpstring("Ch3ComCppServer 1.0 Type Library")
]
library CH3COMCPPSERVERLib
{
    importlib("stdole32.tlb");
    importlib("stdole2.tlb");

    [
        uuid(B5F3E300-B376-11D1-BB1E-00207812E629),
        helpstring("Ch3CheckingAccount Class")
    ]
    coclass Ch3CheckingAccount
    {
        interface IAccount;
        interface IAccountInit;
        [default] interface ICheckingAccount;
    };
};
```

In developing client applications, a COM IDL description is often not needed at all. For example, creating a Visual Basic client application to communicate with our checking account object requires no interaction with the IDL description of our COM object. Instead, the VB client application relies on a type library. Visual C++ also supports extensions to the C++ language, thus allowing for direct import of type libraries when working with COM interface pointers. So, what is a type library?

A *type library* is a compiled binary file that contains a standardized description of a COM object. Type libraries can be created from an IDL file using the Microsoft IDL (MIDL) compiler. For our example, running the command

```
c:\book\ch3\midl> midl Ch3ComCppServer.idl
```

results in the creation of several files, including a type library named Ch3ComCppServer.tlb. After the type library has been created, its location needs to be registered in the Windows system registry.* It can then be used by client applications to programmatically obtain information describing the various attributes (e.g., interfaces, methods, properties, etc.) of the COM object that it describes. Our Visual C++ ATL project adds the type library as a resource to our COM object server and automatically registers the server (including the type library) for us.

Given the evolution of COM-related tools, it appears that users may eventually be spared from dealing with COM IDL at all. This is not yet the case, and IDL still plays an important role in developing COM objects. We therefore need to look inside an IDL file to see how it's organized. The IDL file shown in Listing 3-2 can be divided into two parts. The first part contains a list of interfaces (i.e., IAccount, IAccountInit, and ICheckingAccount) to be supported by our COM object. The second part defines a type library containing a single coclass (component object class) called Ch3CheckingAccount that will implement a COM object supporting the three checking account interfaces.

Each COM IDL interface definition is divided into a header (delimited by square brackets) and a body. The IAccount interface is presented here:

```
[
    object,
    uuid(B5F3E2FE-B376-11D1-BB1E-00207812E629),
    oleautomation,
    helpstring("IAccount Interface"),
    pointer_default(unique)
]

interface IAccount : IUnknown
{
    [propget, helpstring("property Balance")]
        HRESULT Balance([out, retval] double *pVal);
```

---

*Non-Windows implementations of DCOM provide a runtime version of the Windows system registry as well as a port of the system registry API.

```
    [propget, helpstring("property Name")]
        HRESULT Name([out, retval] BSTR *pVal);

    [helpstring("method Deposit")]
        HRESULT Deposit([in] double amount);

    [helpstring("method Withdraw")]
        HRESULT Withdraw([in] double amount);
};
```

The header attributes for the IAccount interface have the following meanings:

- object—Signifies that the interface is a COM interface (as opposed to a DCE interface).

- uuid—Specifies a unique 16-byte identifier for the interface. This universal unique identifier is generated by a utility and is computed based on a machine's network address and time stamp (a combination that practically guarantees uniqueness). The uuid is used within the COM runtime system as well as the Windows system registry to uniquely identify the interface.

- oleautomation—Specifies that all data types used are automation types. This attribute guarantees that the interface can be used in Visual Basic. It also allows the automation marshaler to be used with the interface. (We will discuss the automation marshaler further in COM Type Library Marshaling on page 53.)

- helpstring—Specifies a descriptive string to be placed in the type library.

- pointer_default—Used to optimize proxy and stub code that is generated by the MIDL compiler.

The interface definition shows that IAccount inherits from the ubiquitous IUnknown interface. All COM interfaces must inherit (either directly or indirectly) from IUnknown. The IUnknown interface defines basic functionality for COM object interface management and reference counting. (We will describe the IUnknown interface and its methods in COM Interface Pointers in C++ on page 65.) The IAccount interface supports two read-only properties: Balance and Name. Note that there is no way to set the balance or name since we did not define any methods on the interface to do so. The interface also supports two methods: Deposit() and Withdraw(). Because of inheritance, IAccount also supports the methods defined in IUnknown.

The second interface defined in our IDL file is `IAccountInit`. This interface also inherits from `IUnknown`:

```
interface IAccountInit : IUnknown
{
    const int E_INVALID_NAME = 0x80040200;
    [helpstring("method Init")]
        HRESULT Init([in] BSTR name);
};
```

The `IAccountInit` interface supports one method, `Init()`, that is used to initialize an account based on an account name. We have also defined a constant that we will use as an `HRESULT` return value when an invalid name is passed as an argument. This will allow us to perform special error handling when such an error occurs. One other thing to note is that the `Init()` method is not supported by any of the other interfaces. It can be called only by using the `IAccountInit` interface.

The last interface in our IDL file is `ICheckingAccount`. This interface inherits from the `IAccount` interface defined earlier. Note that `ICheckingAccount` still inherits from the `IUnknown` interface via the `IAccount` interface:

```
interface ICheckingAccount : IAccount
{
    [helpstring("method WithdrawUsingCheck")]
        HRESULT WithdrawUsingCheck([in] long checkNumber,
                                   [in] double amount);
};
```

The `ICheckingAccount` interface supports one new method, `WithdrawUsing-Check()`. Because it inherits from `IAccount`, `ICheckingAccount` also supports the `Balance` and `Name` properties, the `Deposit()` and `Withdraw()` methods, and the methods supported in `IUnknown`.

The final section of our COM IDL file is the type library section:

```
[
    uuid(B5F3E2F0-B376-11D1-BB1E-00207812E629),
    version(1.0),
    helpstring("Ch3ComCppServer 1.0 Type Library")
]

library CH3COMCPPSERVERLib
{
```

```
[
    uuid(B5F3E300-B376-11D1-BB1E-00207812E629),
    helpstring("Ch3CheckingAccount Class")
]

coclass Ch3CheckingAccount
{
    interface IAccount;
    interface IAccountInit;
    [default] interface ICheckingAccount;
};
};
```

This section defines two new elements: the Ch3ComCppServer type library and the Ch3CheckingAccount component object class (coclass). Both the type library and the coclass require a uuid since both will be registered in the system registry. The uuids are used by the COM runtime system to uniquely identify the type library and coclass. The Ch3CheckingAccount component object class implements the three interfaces used in our checking account example.

CORBA IDL

CORBA IDL lies at the heart of every CORBA-based system. The CORBA specification is necessarily vendor-neutral. This means that CORBA products cannot as readily depend on vendor-specific tools or specific operating system features like the Windows system registry. In contrast, Microsoft can and does take advantage of the fact that it controls the operating system, the major development tools, and the major programming interfaces. This leads to an interesting debate. Many would argue that building distributed systems inherently relies on tight coupling with the operating system. In terms of fundamentals, CORBA proves them wrong; however, the argument for tight coupling may very well prove to be true when advanced services such as those supporting security and transactions are integrated.

What is the glue that allows CORBA to work across a disparate array of operating systems, vendors, and programming languages? The answer is, CORBA IDL. CORBA IDL has evolved over many years into an elegant implementation-independent language for describing distributed object interfaces; it has also been mapped to many languages, including C, C++, Java, Smalltalk, COBOL and Ada. The CORBA IDL file used to implement our CORBA checking account object is shown in Listing 3-3.

Listing 3-3. *CORBA IDL for Checking Account*

```
// Ch3.idl (CORBA IDL)

module Ch3
{
    exception InvalidNameException
    {
        string reason;
    };

    interface Account
    {
        // Attributes ...
        readonly attribute string name;
        readonly attribute double balance;

        // Methods ...
        void deposit(in double amount);
        void withdraw(in double amount);

        // Destroy this object ...
        void destroy();
    };

    interface AccountInit
    {
        void init(in string name) raises(InvalidNameException);
    };

    interface CheckingAccount : Account, AccountInit
    {
        void withdrawUsingCheck(in long checkNumber,
                                in double amount);
    };

    interface CheckingAccountFactory
    {
        CheckingAccount create();
    };
};
```

Our CORBA IDL code is much simpler than the COM IDL code presented earlier in Listing 3-2. CORBA IDL focuses strictly on interface definition, whereas COM IDL is used to address many noninterface-related issues (e.g., type libraries, etc.). Some of these noninterface elements are absolutely necessary in COM. For example, IDL attributes related to optimization are critical when creating an ActiveX control (i.e., an in-process COM object). Since CORBA focuses mainly on distributed objects and not on in-process objects, such optimizations are irrelevant. The bottom line is that neither IDL (neither COM nor CORBA) is necessarily better but that they serve different purposes. That said, let's take a look at the CORBA IDL file for the checking account.

The first element in our IDL file is a `module` named `Ch3`. A CORBA IDL module is used to scope IDL identifiers when mapping IDL to other languages. For example, when mapping `Ch3.idl` to C++, all generated symbols will be scoped to the C++ namespace named `Ch3`. When mapping `Ch3.idl` to Java, all generated symbols will be placed in a Java package named `Ch3`.

The next element in our IDL file is a definition for `InvalidNameException`. This exception will be raised when an invalid name is passed to the `init()` method of our CORBA object (as defined in the `AccountInit` interface). A CORBA IDL exception can contain members of any IDL data type, including simple types, structs, unions, enums, and references to other CORBA objects. Our exception contains one member called `reason`. This allows our CORBA object to pass a reason (in the form of a character string) back to the client if the exception is raised.

The first interface defined in our IDL file is `Account`. The `Account` interface supports two read-only attributes: `name` and `balance`. The interface also supports two methods: `deposit()` and `withdraw()`. In contrast to our COM interface, the CORBA `Account` interface also specifies a `destroy()` method. This method will be called by clients to explicitly destroy the CORBA `Account` instance when it is no longer needed. Note that we didn't need the `destroy()` method in our COM object because COM automatically takes care of destroying our COM checking account instances when they are no longer referenced by any clients. (We will discuss this in greater detail in Destroying COM Objects on page 96.)

The second interface defined in our IDL file is `AccountInit`. The `AccountInit` interface supports one method, `init()`, that is used to initialize an account based on an account name. This method raises `InvalidNameException` when an invalid name is passed as an argument.

The next interface defined in our IDL file is `CheckingAccount`. The `CheckingAccount` interface multiply-inherits from the `Account` and `AccountInit` interfaces. `CheckingAccount` defines one new method, `withdrawUsingCheck()`. Because it also inherits from `Account` and `AccountInit`, `CheckingAccount` supports the `name` and `balance` attributes as well as the `deposit()`, `withdraw()`, `init()`, and `destroy()` methods. Note that our COM `ICheckingAccount` interface does *not* support the `Init()` method. CORBA relies on multiple inheritance, whereas COM relies on the notion of multiple distinct interfaces; therefore, the CORBA `CheckingAccount` interface must multiply-inherit from both `Account` and `AccountInit`.

The last interface defined is `CheckingAccountFactory`. This type of interface is unique to CORBA since COM uses a standard interface for its factory. (We will discuss COM class factories in COM Factories on page 75.) In CORBA, the factory interface for creating another type of CORBA object is user-defined. For our `CheckingAccountFactory`, we define a `create()` method that can be used by clients to create a `CheckingAccount` instance.

Interface orientation (as opposed to implementation orientation) is a prime factor helping to cultivate the success of COM and CORBA. We've taken a look at how interfaces are defined in both architectures. Next, we'll take a look at how the interface definitions are used to implement our example.

Proxies, Stubs, and Skeletons

The COM and CORBA architectures allow developers to treat distributed objects in much the same manner as native objects. For example, invoking a method on a COM or CORBA object in C++ is no different than invoking a method on a native C++ object. (We will discuss object invocation in greater detail in Invoking Object Methods on page 87.) The developer may need to address certain timing and error-handling issues, but the syntax for the method invocation is identical in both the native and the remote case.

There is nothing magical about remote method invocation. As shown in Figure 3-4, both COM and CORBA rely on client-side and server-side mechanisms to manage issues related to remoting. These mechanisms are referred to as *proxies* and *stubs* in COM. In CORBA, the mechanisms are referred to as *stubs* and *skeletons*. When describing both COM and CORBA, we will refer to the client-side mechanism as a *client stub* and the server-side mechanism as a *server stub*.

A remote method invocation is implemented as follows:

1. A client invokes a remote method. The remote method is actually invoked in the client stub.

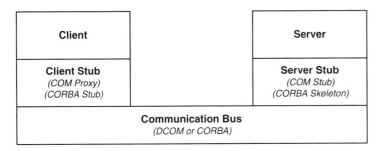

Figure 3-4. *Proxies, stubs, and skeletons in COM and CORBA.*

2. The client stub creates a message containing information needed for the remote invocation. (The message creation process is referred to as *marshaling*.)

3. The client stub sends the message to the server stub using the communication bus.

4. The server stub receives the message and unpacks it. (The unpacking process is referred to as *unmarshaling*.)

5. The server stub calls the appropriate server method based on the information provided in the received message.

6. The server stub creates a message based on the outputs of the call to the server method (i.e., the return value and out parameters).

7. The server stub sends the result message to the client stub using the communication bus.

8. The client stub receives the result message, unpacks the message, and returns the result to the client.

It should be obvious from the steps just outlined that the client stub, server stub, and communication bus do a lot of work. Where do the stubs and communication bus come from? The communication bus is our generic name for the COM or CORBA runtime system. In contrast, the client and server stubs must be created to support the custom interfaces that are used in the system. Hand-coding client and server stubs for every interface would be a tedious and an error-prone task. COM and CORBA solve this problem by providing tools to generate client and server stubs from IDL descriptions.

COM Proxies and Stubs

COM terminology refers to client stubs as *proxies* and to server stubs simply as *stubs*. In COM, the proxy and stub are packaged in a single DLL. The DLL is associated with the appropriate interfaces in the Windows system registry. The COM runtime system then uses the registry to locate proxy–stub DLLs associated with an interface when marshaling of the interface is required.

In the checking account example, we generate the proxy–stub code by running the MIDL compiler on the checking account IDL description as shown here:

```
C:\book\ch3\midl>midl Ch3ComCppServer.idl
Microsoft (R) MIDL Compiler Version 3.01.75
Copyright (c) Microsoft Corp 1991-1997. All rights reserved.
Processing .\Ch3ComCppServer.idl
...
```

The files that are generated by the `midl` command include the following:

```
Ch3ComCppServer.h
Ch3ComCppServer_i.c
Ch3ComCppServer_p.c
dlldata.c
```

These files are all that is needed to generate the proxy–stub DLL for our COM checking account object. To build the proxy–stub DLL, we run the makefile that was generated by the Visual C++ ATL project when we created the IDL file. Once the DLL is built, we register the proxy–stub DLL in the Windows system registry. To do so, we simply use the `regsvr32` utility as shown here:

```
c:\book\ch3\midl> regsvr32 Ch3ComCppServerPS.dll
```

After registering the proxy–stub DLL, the `IAccount`, `IAccountInit`, and `ICheckingAccount` interfaces are all associated with `Ch3ComCppServerPS.dll` in the registry. Figure 3-5 illustrates the structure of the COM client, server, and proxy–stub DLL in the checking account example. Note that the proxy-stub DLL must be installed on every client machine so that the client application can properly marshal data.

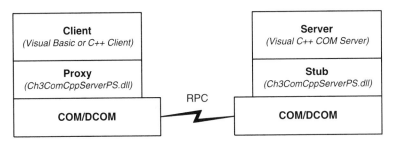

Figure 3-5. *Using a COM proxy–stub DLL.*

COM Type Library Marshaling

The checking account example does not actually require the creation and registration of a proxy–stub DLL. Instead, it can rely on a technique known as *type library marshaling.*

Recall that we exclusively used automation-compatible data types when we defined the COM interfaces for `IAccount`, `IAccountInit`, and `ICheckingAccount` in the checking account example. We did this for several reasons. First, the example does not demand complex data types; our needs are easily met by the subset of automation-compatible types. Second, we want to ensure that the interfaces work in environments that require automation-compatible types (e.g., Visual Basic, etc.). In the IDL description of our COM checking account object, we designated our interfaces as automation-compatible by using the `oleautomation` attribute in the header of each interface.

In the IDL description, we also defined a type library to be generated that describes the COM checking account interfaces. The type library is generated by the MIDL compiler. The type library needs to be registered in the Windows system registry on all client machines so that it can be used by the Visual Basic client application. To register the type library, we use a utility named `regtlb`[*] as shown here:

```
C:\book\ch3\midl> regtlb Ch3ComCppServer.tlb
```

An added benefit of using automation-compatible types and registering a type library is that we can use the automation marshaler instead of a proxy–stub DLL. The automation marshaler (implemented in `oleaut32.dll`) uses the type

---

[*]The `regtlb` utility was written by Mike Nelson and is freely available at
http://www.iapetus.com/dcom/dcomtool.htm.

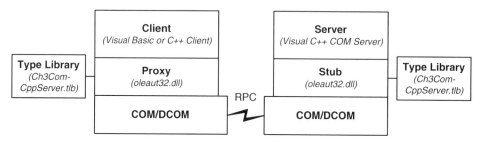

Figure 3-6. *Using the automation marshaler.*

library to marshal data between the client and server—no proxy–stub DLL is required. This is very convenient since the type library is already registered on all client machines anyway. Registering a type library associates all automation-compatible interfaces with the automation marshaler in the system registry. Figure 3-6 illustrates the structure of the COM client, server, type library, and automation marshaler in the checking account example.

CORBA Stubs and Skeletons

CORBA terminology refers to client stubs as *stubs* and to server stubs as *skeletons*. Packaging of the stubs and skeletons is user-defined. For our example, we simply link the appropriate object files corresponding to the stub and skeleton into our C++ client and server. In Java, we create a package that contains all stub files needed by the Java client.

To generate the Orbix stub and skeleton, we invoke the Orbix IDL compiler as shown here:

```
c:\Orbix\bin\idl.exe -B Ch3.idl
```

The following files are generated by the IDL compiler:

```
Ch3.hh     // declarations
Ch3C.cpp   // Orbix client stub
Ch3S.cpp   // Orbix server skeleton
```

Figure 3-7 illustrates the structure of the CORBA client, stub, skeleton, and server in the checking account example. The stub (`Ch3C.obj`) allows the client to connect to the ORB on the client side. The skeleton (`Ch3S.obj`) allows the server to connect to the ORB on the server side. Although we are using the

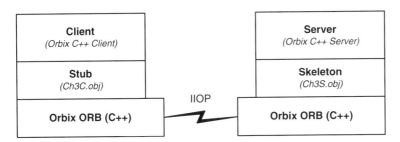

Figure 3-7. *Using an Orbix stub and skeleton.*

same ORB (Orbix) on both the client and server machines, the client and server ORBs communicate using IIOP, which is the CORBA 2.0 standard communication protocol for TCP/IP.

The Java client in our example requires a VisiBroker client stub as well. To generate the VisiBroker stub, we invoke the VisiBroker IDL compiler as shown here:

```
c:\vbroker\bin\idl2java ..\..\servers\idl\Ch3.idl
```

The `idl2java` compiler generates a Java package named `Ch3` corresponding to the `Ch3` IDL module. The `Ch3` package contains the stub classes needed by the VisiBroker Java client. Figure 3-8 illustrates the structure of the VisiBroker client, VisiBroker stub, Orbix skeleton, and Orbix server in the checking account example. The stub (the `Ch3` Java package) allows the client to connect to the VisiBroker ORB on the client side. The skeleton (`Ch3S.obj`) allows the server to connect to the Orbix ORB on the server side. The VisiBroker and Orbix ORBs communicate using IIOP.

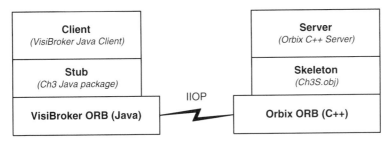

Figure 3-8. *Using a VisiBroker stub and Orbix skeleton.*

Implementing the Servers

The COM and CORBA IDL descriptions provide the basis for our COM and CORBA servers. For our checking account example, implementing the COM server is simply a matter of defining the IDL within a Visual C++ ATL project and then filling in the methods that are automatically created by Visual C++ and the ATL wizard. The ATL framework takes care of the details needed to make our server function in the COM environment (e.g., setting up the class factory, etc.). Since there are a multitude of ways to create COM objects and since a description of how to use ATL is best left to a different source, we will not pursue an in-depth discussion of our COM server's implementation.

Implementing our CORBA server requires a different approach. Rather than generating our IDL and server simultaneously (as is the case with ATL), we need to do the following:

1. We create our IDL description using a generic editor. The IDL description is vendor- and implementation-neutral.

2. We compile our IDL description using the IDL compiler that is provided with the Orbix product. This generates the files `Ch3.hh`, `Ch3C.cpp`, and `Ch3S.cpp`. Note that the names given to these generated files are Orbix-specific.

3. We implement the server using the files generated in step 2 and an Orbix-specific implementation approach.

There is little to be gained by describing our CORBA server implementation since it is vendor-specific. This is in contrast to our CORBA clients, which use IDL-generated code that is highly standardized in both C++ and Java. The most important point to note when using both COM and CORBA is that distributed object clients do not care how the distributed object servers are implemented. Instead, clients rely strictly on IDL definitions (and type libraries when using COM).

At the time of this writing, the implementation of CORBA servers was vendor-specific for all of the major CORBA products, including those offered by Iona, Inprise, and BEA. CORBA vendors have not yet attained compliance with the CORBA 2.2 specification, which includes a specification for a portable object adaptor (POA). As CORBA vendors evolve their products to support the CORBA 2.2 specification and the POA, it will be possible to create portable CORBA server implementations. The POA is an extremely important addition to the CORBA 2.2 specification.

Implementing the Clients

We need to examine some basic design issues before we can examine the distributed object interactions of our clients. Recall that we are required to implement four client applications using three different programming languages. To avoid being distracted by any code not related to distributed objects (e.g., GUI-related code), we have chosen to create four wrapper classes (one for each example) called `MyCheckingAccount`. All COM or CORBA interactions required by the client occur within the confines of the `MyCheckingAccount` class as shown in Figure 3-9.

Each client application uses its wrapper in the following way:

1. The client application starts up and creates an instance of the `MyCheckingAccount` class. This instance is not enabled until it has been initialized. The same `MyCheckingAccount` instance is used for the life of the client application. For example, in the COM VB client application, the `MyCheckingAccount` object is created in the `Form_Load()` subprocedure and is destroyed only when the application is terminated.

2. Whenever the user initializes a new account (by clicking on the *Initialize* button), the client application calls `Init()` on the `MyCheckingAccount` instance.

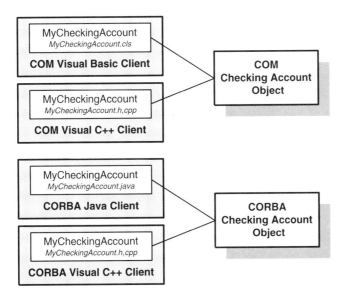

Figure 3-9. *MyCheckingAccount wrappers.*

Table 3-3. *MyCheckingAccount Source Code*

Appendix	Section	Page
Appendix C	COM/C++ MyCheckingAccount Class	391
Appendix C	COM/Visual Basic MyCheckingAccount Class	397
Appendix C	CORBA/C++ MyCheckingAccount Class	400
Appendix C	CORBA/Java MyCheckingAccount Class	405

3. During `Init()`, the `MyCheckingAccount` instance releases any previously held reference and sets its reference to a newly created distributed object. It then enters the enabled state.

4. All wrapped methods (e.g., `Deposit()`, `Withdraw()`, etc.) call the appropriate methods on the distributed object when the `MyCheckingAccount` instance is enabled.

The `MyCheckingAccount` class will be referenced frequently throughout the rest of this section, and it is important to understand how it is used in the context of our client applications. Complete source code listings for each of the `MyCheckingAccount` wrapper classes are provided in the Appendix C sections indicated in Table 3-3.

Now that the design issues are out of the way, we are ready to take a look at how each `MyCheckingAccount` class is implemented. As we shall see, these classes depend heavily on the IDL descriptions and type library defined earlier; however, they are blissfully unaware of any other server implementation details. Before we begin discussing creation and management of COM and CORBA objects, we'll first describe how the IDL and type library are used in each of the client applications.

Using IDL in the COM C++ Client

To communicate with the COM checking account object, the `MyCheckingAccount` wrapper class needs to be able to declare and use interface pointers for `IAccount`, `IAccountInit`, and `ICheckingAccount`. Since the wrapper class also needs to create the COM object and initialize the interface pointers, it must know the `uuids` corresponding to the interfaces and the component class. Where do the `uuids` and declarations like `IAccount` come from? We have two choices: generate the required definitions from the IDL file or use the previously generated type library. For our example, we will generate the definitions from the IDL since using the type library relies on Visual C++ compiler-specific directives such as import and __uuidof(). (The import and __uuidof Visual C++ extensions are described later in The Visual C++ COM Client on page 247.) We generate the definitions by using the midl command:

```
C:\book\ch3\midl> midl Ch3ComCppServer.idl
```

This results in the creation of several files, including two files that we require: Ch3ComCppServer.h and Ch3ComCppServer_i.c. The first generated file that we will use is Ch3ComCppServer.h. This file contains the class definitions for our interfaces. To see what the generated classes look like, the generated IAccountInit interface class definition is presented here:

```
// interface definition contained in Ch3ComCppServer.h
interface DECLSPEC_UUID("B5F3E2FF-B376-11D1-BB1E-00207812E629")
IAccountInit : public IUnknown
{
public:
    virtual /* [helpstring] */
    HRESULT STDMETHODCALLTYPE Init(/* [in] */ BSTR name) = 0;
};
```

Note that IAccountInit is defined as an interface rather than as a class. An interface is defined in the COM header files as

```
// excerpt from "Objbase.h"
#define interface struct
```

Why is interface defined as a struct and not as a class? Because COM interfaces consist strictly of public methods. The only difference between a C++ struct and a C++ class is that a struct's members are declared public by default, whereas a class's members are defaulted to private. A struct is therefore more appropriate than a class. The public access specifier is not really needed in the preceding definition. Including Ch3ComCppServer.h in our wrapper class allows us to declare our interface pointers and call methods on those interfaces:

```
// excerpt from MyCheckingAccount.h
#include "Ch3ComCppServer.h"

class MyCheckingAccount
{
    ...
```

```
private:
    IAccount*        m_pIAccount;
    IAccountInit*    m_pIAccountInit;
    ICheckingAccount* m_pICheckingAccount;
};
```

The `m_pIAccount`, `m_pIAccountInit`, and `m_pICheckingAccount` interface pointers are initialized as described later in COM Object Creation in C++ on page 77.

To create our COM checking account object and initialize the interface pointers, we still need the `uuids`. The other MIDL-generated file, `Ch3ComCppServer_i.c`, provides the `uuids`. This file contains the interface ids (`IIDs`) of our interfaces as well as the class id (`CLSID`) of our checking account:

```
// uuids defined in Ch3ComCppServer_i.c
const IID IID_IAccount = {0xB5F3E2FE,0xB376,0x11D1,
                    {0xBB,0x1E,0x00,0x20,0x78,0x12,0xE6,0x29}};

const IID IID_IAccountInit = {0xB5F3E2FF,0xB376,0x11D1,
                    {0xBB,0x1E,0x00,0x20,0x78,0x12,0xE6,0x29}};

const IID IID_ICheckingAccount = {0xB5F3E2FD,0xB376,0x11D1,
                    {0xBB,0x1E,0x00,0x20,0x78,0x12,0xE6,0x29}};

const CLSID CLSID_Ch3CheckingAccount = {0xB5F3E300,0xB376,0x11D1,
                    {0xBB,0x1E,0x00,0x20,0x78,0x12,0xE6,0x29}};
```

Since the `uuids` are used in the implementation of our wrapper class, we simply include `Ch3ComCppServer_i.c` in the `MyCheckingAccount.cpp` file. No other external files are needed to implement the `MyCheckingAccount` wrapper class.

Using a Type Library in the COM Visual Basic Client

Using the COM checking account object in our C++ client is fairly easy. Visual Basic makes using COM objects even easier. For our example, Visual Basic relies on the type library that we registered in the Windows system registry when we created our ATL COM server. To use the type library, we enable it in the *References* dialog from within our client application's project. This is accomplished by selecting *References...* from the Visual Basic *Project* menu and enabling the `Ch3ComCppServer` type library (see Figure 3-10). To confirm that the COM object is accessible, we can bring up the Visual Basic *Object*

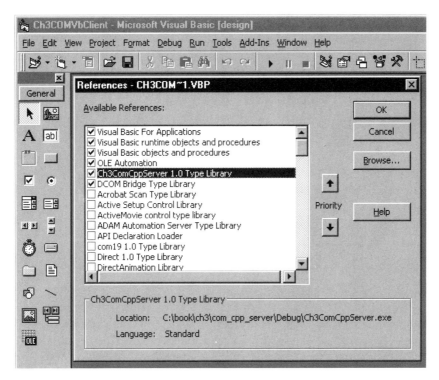

Figure 3-10. *The Visual Basic References dialog.*

Browser by selecting *Object Browser* in the Visual Basic *View* menu (see Figure 3-11).

When we examine the interfaces in the *Object Browser* (Figure 3-11), we notice that the `ICheckingAccount` interface does not appear. The reason is that `ICheckingAccount` is specified as the default interface for the `coclass` `Ch3CheckingAccount`, and Visual Basic assigns the default interface to the `coclass` name:

```
// component object class definition from Ch3ComCppServer.idl
   coclass Ch3CheckingAccount
   {
       interface IAccount;
       interface IAccountInit;
       [default] interface ICheckingAccount;
   };
```

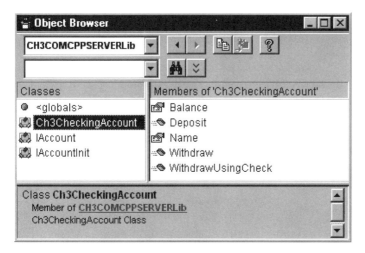

Figure 3-11. *The Visual Basic Object Browser dialog.*

This does not stop us from using the `ICheckingAccount` interface name inside the `MyCheckingAccount` wrapper class. The declarations for the interface pointers are shown next. Once we have enabled the reference to our checking account type library, we treat the checking account object as we would any other Visual Basic object:

```
'excerpt from MyCheckingAccount.cls
Private mIAccount As IAccount
Private mIAccountInit As IAccountInit
Private mICheckingAccount As ICheckingAccount
```

The `mIAccount`, `mIAccountInit`, and `mICheckingAccount` interface pointers are initialized as described later in COM Object Creation in Visual Basic on page 80.

Using IDL in the Orbix CORBA C++ Client

As stated earlier, IDL lies at the heart of any CORBA-based system. Our CORBA C++ client is no exception. The `MyCheckingAccount` wrapper class relies on files that are generated using an IDL compiler. The first step in creating the Orbix client is to run the Orbix IDL compiler on the `Ch3.idl` file:

```
c:\Orbix\bin\idl.exe Ch3.idl
```

The IDL compiler generates several files, including a header file named `Ch3.hh` that we include in our wrapper class header file. This file defines all symbols (i.e., class definitions, constants, etc.) necessary to work with the CORBA checking account object. Our wrapper class uses the IDL-generated definitions when it declares a checking account member variable:

```
// MyCheckingAccount.h
#include "Ch3.hh"

class MyCheckingAccount
{
    ...

private:
    Ch3::CheckingAccount_var m_account;
};
```

The `m_account` object reference is initialized as described later in CORBA Object Creation in C++ and Java on page 85.

The IDL compiler also generates a file named `Ch3C.cpp`. This file contains the client stub that allows the client application to plug into the Orbix ORB. (We discussed CORBA stubs in CORBA Stubs and Skeletons on page 54.) Note that although the stub implementation is vendor-specific, the header file provides a standardized mapping from IDL. In other words, the source code used to implement the `MyCheckingAccount` wrapper class would be the same regardless of the vendor being used. Of course, there are always vendor-specific extensions, but these can be avoided (or at least isolated) if portability is desired. To build the application, we need to link in the compiled CORBA stub, `Ch3C.obj`, as well as the Orbix libraries `initsrv.lib` and `itm.lib`:

```
LINK  /MAP  Ch3C.obj  MyCheckingAccount.obj  main.obj
   /OUT:Ch3CorbaCppClient.exe  wsock32.lib  advapi32.lib
   user32.lib  initsrv.lib  itm.lib
```

Using IDL in the VisiBroker CORBA Java Client

Our VisiBroker Java client uses the same IDL file that our Orbix C++ client did. Remember that CORBA IDL is not vendor-specific. The `MyCheckingAccount` wrapper class in our CORBA Java client imports a number of classes generated by the IDL compiler. The VisiBroker compiler is invoked as shown here:

```
c:\vbroker\bin\idl2java ..\..\servers\idl\Ch3.idl
```

In Java, CORBA IDL modules map directly to Java packages. The `import` statements in `MyCheckingAccount.java` reflect the `Ch3` package name corresponding to the `Ch3` CORBA IDL module:

```
// MyCheckingAccount.java
import Ch3.CheckingAccount;
import Ch3.CheckingAccountFactory;

class MyCheckingAccount
{
    CheckingAccount m_account;
    ...
}
```

The `m_account` object reference is initialized as described later in CORBA Object Creation in C++ and Java on page 85.

Client Implementation Summary

To this point, we have described how each of our client applications has utilized IDL (or a type library in the case of the VB client) to integrate with our distributed checking account object. We have also designed each of our clients to use a wrapper class called `MyCheckingAccount` to isolate COM/CORBA calls so that we can ignore issues not directly related to distributed object interactions. (Complete source code for the wrapper classes can be found in the Appendix C section MyCheckingAccount Classes (from Ch. 3) on page 391.) We are now ready to lower the microscope and take a closer look at the details of how COM and CORBA are used to create and manage distributed objects.

Object Handles

Before we can talk about creating distributed objects, we need to have a firm understanding of how object handles are managed. Object handles are used to reference object instances in a programming language context. An object handle in C++ is an object pointer or an object reference. In Visual Basic, it is a variable referring to a VB object (as opposed to a variable defined as a VB intrinsic data type). To simplify access to distributed objects, object handles referring to COM and CORBA objects need to behave much like their native counterparts. When we use COM and CORBA in languages like Visual Basic, C++, and Java, the syntax for calling an instance method is the same regardless of whether the object instance is native, local, or remote.

COM refers to object handles as *interface pointers* while CORBA refers to them as *object references*. In this section, we will first examine the use of COM interface pointers in our Visual C++ and Visual Basic COM client applications. We will then focus on the use of CORBA object references in our Visual C++ and Java CORBA client applications.

COM Interface Pointers in C++

The term *interface pointer* can sometimes cause confusion. After all, what does it mean to point to an interface? Rest assured that an interface pointer does actually reference a specific COM object instance. One of the most interesting aspects of COM is that a COM object instance supports multiple interfaces. In calling methods on a COM object, it is usually necessary to use multiple interface pointers that point to different interfaces for the same object instance. This is certainly the case in our example; we use multiple interface pointers in both our C++ and Visual Basic COM clients. Recall that our COM checking account object supports three interfaces, as shown in Figure 3-12.

The only way to call the Init() method on the COM object instance is to use the IAccountInit interface. For the same reasons, an IAccountInit inter-

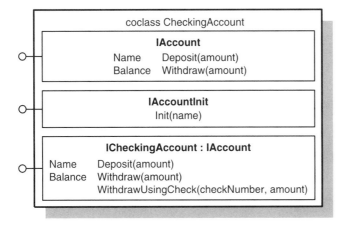

Figure 3-12. *The COM checking account object.*

face pointer cannot call methods like `Deposit()` and `Withdraw()`. To fully access the COM object, we need multiple interface pointers. To illustrate this, consider the wrapper class used in our C++ COM client. In `MyCheckingAccount`, we declare a member variable for each of the interfaces:

```
class MyCheckingAccount
{    ...

private:
    IAccount*        m_pIAccount;
    IAccountInit*    m_pIAccountInit;
    ICheckingAccount* m_pICheckingAccount;
};
```

Assume for the moment that all three interface pointers are currently set to NULL and that we have an `IUnknown` pointer that points to a checking account instance. How do we set our interface pointers to point to the same checking account instance? The answer can be found in the `IUnknown` interface. Recall that all COM interfaces must derive (either directly or indirectly) from `IUnknown`. The `IUnknown` interface is defined as

```
interface IUnknown
{
    HRESULT QueryInterface([in] REFIID riid,
                           [out] void **ppvObject);
    ULONG AddRef();
    ULONG Release();
}
```

The `QueryInterface()` method defined in `IUnknown` (and therefore supported by all COM interface pointers) allows one interface pointer to be queried for another. Using the `IUnknown` pointer, we can initialize our interface pointers in the following manner. In the example here, assume that `pIUnknown` currently references a valid `Ch3CheckingAccount` COM object instance:

```
BOOL MyCheckingAccount::SetInterfaces(IUnknown* pIUnknown)
{
    HRESULT hr;
    void*   pInterface = NULL;

    // Query the IUnknown interface to get the ICheckingAccount
    // interface.
    hr = pIUnknown->QueryInterface(IID_ICheckingAccount,
                                   &pInterface);
```

```
        if ( !SUCCEEDED(hr) ) handle error ...
        m_pICheckingAccount = (ICheckingAccount*)pInterface;

        // Query the ICheckingAccount interface to get the IAccount
        // interface.
        hr = m_pICheckingAccount->QueryInterface(IID_IAccount,
                                                 &pInterface);
        if ( !SUCCEEDED(hr) ) handle error ...
        m_pIAccount = (IAccount*)pInterface;

        // Query the IAccount interface to get the IAccountInit
        // interface.
        hr = m_pIAccount->QueryInterface(IID_IAccountInit,
                                         &pInterface);
        if ( !SUCCEEDED(hr) ) handle error ...
        m_pIAccountInit = (IAccountInit*)pInterface;
        return TRUE;
}
```

In this example, we call `QueryInterface()` from several different interface pointers. This doesn't matter. COM semantics guarantee that, for all interface pointers referencing the same COM object instance, calling `QueryInterface()` with a specific interface id (`IID`) always returns the same result. In the example, we would have obtained the same result if we had used the `IUnknown` pointer in all of the `QueryInterface()` calls. One other point is critical: If the call to `SetInterfaces()` succeeds, `m_pIAccount`, `m_pIAccountInit`, and `m_pICheckingAccount` all point to the same COM object instance (i.e., the checking account instance pointed to by the `IUnknown` pointer).

Before we leave the realm of C++ interface pointers, we need to address the issue of reference counting. A COM object instance uses reference counting to determine when it should be destroyed. Just as COM object clients cannot create a COM object using the `new` operator, they should never destroy a COM object using `delete`. In addition to `QueryInterface()`, the `IUnknown` interface also defines two methods for reference counting: `AddRef()` and `Release()`.

`AddRef()` is used to increment the reference count of a COM object. `AddRef()` is called implicitly when a COM object is created and also when a `QueryInterface()` call succeeds. This is why `AddRef()` was not called in the previous example. `AddRef()` should be called explicitly whenever a copy of the interface pointer is made. For example, if a user defines a method that returns an interface pointer, `AddRef()` should be called on the interface pointer before it is returned.

`Release()` is used to decrement the reference count and should be called whenever an interface pointer is no longer in use. In the `MyCheckingAccount` wrapper class, the interface pointers need to be released before a new COM object can be associated with the wrapper or when the wrapper is deleted. The `Reset()` method shown here releases all interface pointers managed by the `MyCheckingAccount` wrapper instance:

```
void MyCheckingAccount::Reset()
{
    m_isEnabled = FALSE;

    if (m_pIAccount)
    {
        m_pIAccount->Release();
        m_pIAccount = NULL;
    }

    if (m_pIAccountInit)
    {
        m_pIAccountInit->Release();
        m_pIAccountInit = NULL;
    }

    if (m_pICheckingAccount)
    {
        m_pICheckingAccount->Release();
        m_pICheckingAccount = NULL;
    }
}
```

Reference counting, in general, is problematic when the programmer is made responsible for adding and releasing references. If a programmer forgets to call `Release()`, the COM object will never get destroyed. If the user calls `Release()` prematurely, the COM object will be invalid when the next caller tries to use it. How can this problem be avoided? The solution is to use smart pointers.

Smart pointers automatically increment and decrement reference counts. For example, assigning an interface pointer to a smart pointer automatically calls `AddRef()`. A smart pointer's destructor automatically calls `Release()`. Proper use of smart pointers can eliminate many reference-counting errors. The ATL class library as well as the Visual C++ compiler both provide substantial smart pointer support. C++ developers should almost always use smart pointers and avoid direct calls to `AddRef()` and `Release()`.

COM Interface Pointers in Visual Basic

We showed how a Visual Basic project references a type library in Using a Type Library in the COM Visual Basic Client on page 60. Once the reference to the type library has been enabled, Visual Basic makes working with a COM object very simple. The `MyCheckingAccount` wrapper class declares the following interface pointers:

```
'MyCheckingAccount.cls
Private mIAccount As IAccount
Private mIAccountInit As IAccountInit
Private mICheckingAccount As ICheckingAccount
```

In the following example, assume that we have a method for creating a new checking account instance. This creation method returns an `IUnknown` interface pointer that points to the newly created COM object instance. To initialize our checking account interface pointers, we simply assign the `IUnknown` pointer to each of the checking account interface pointers:

```
'MyCheckingAccount.cls
Public Function Init(name As String, _
                     server As String) As Boolean
On Error GoTo ErrorHandler
    Dim account As IUnknown

    'Create an instance of the checking account.
    Set account = CreateSomeCheckingAccount 'pseudo code

    'Initialize the interface pointers.
    Set mIAccount = account
    Set mIAccountInit = account
    Set mICheckingAccount = mIAccount
    ...
End Function
```

After seeing how such assignments occur in the C++ environment (see COM Interface Pointers in C++ on page 65), it should be clear that Visual Basic is calling `QueryInterface()` behind the scenes. Note that we also do not need to worry about the `uuids` (i.e., interface ids) associated with the interface pointers. Visual Basic uses information retrieved from the type library when it calls `QueryInterface()`. Finally, if the call to `Init()` succeeds, all interface pointers point to the same newly created COM object instance.

The other issue regarding the handling of interface pointers is reference counting. As is the case with most memory management in Visual Basic, reference counting is handled automatically. For example, performing an assignment using `Set` does not require an explicit `Release()` before the assignment is made. Visual Basic will call `Release()` automatically if the variable currently references an object. `Set` also adds a reference to the newly assigned object. If an interface pointer needs to be released (because it remains in scope but will no longer be used), the user can assign the interface pointer to `Nothing`, a special keyword used to disassociate Visual Basic variables from their objects. The `Reset()` method shown here releases all interface pointers:

```
'MyCheckingAccount.cls
Public Sub Reset()
    Set mIAccount = Nothing
    Set mIAccountInit = Nothing
    Set mICheckingAccount = Nothing
End Sub
```

CORBA Object References in C++

When we use CORBA with C++, reference counting directly affects how object references are declared. An object reference type that is appended with _ptr never implicitly affects the reference count of the object that it references. An object reference type that is appended with _var implicitly decrements the reference count of any object it currently references when it is destroyed or assigned to a new object. The `MyCheckingAccount` wrapper class uses both _var and _ptr types:

```
// MyCheckingAccount.h
#include "Ch3.hh"

class MyCheckingAccount
{
    ...

private:
    Ch3::CheckingAccount_var m_account;
    Ch3::CheckingAccountFactory_ptr LocateFactory(const char* ior);
};
```

We declare m_account as a _var type so that it will automatically be released when the `MyCheckingAccount` instance is destroyed. If we had declared it as a _ptr type, we would have needed to explicitly release it in the destructor. The

CORBA C++ mapping provides the `CORBA::release(ptr)` function to explicitly decrement the reference count of a CORBA object referenced by `ptr`. The `LocateFactory()` method returns a `_ptr` type so that the object being referenced is not inadvertently released when the call completes. To release the returned pointer, the caller can explicitly call `release()` or assign the pointer to a `_var` type as is done in the `Init()` method of the `MyCheckingAccount` wrapper class:

```
BOOL MyCheckingAccount::Init(const char* name,
                            const char* factoryIOR)
{
    Ch3::CheckingAccountFactory_var factory;
    factory = LocateFactory(factoryIOR);
    ...
}
```

Assigning the factory in this manner ensures that the factory reference count will be decremented when the call to `Init()` is completed. Now that we have covered `release()`, we need to discuss how reference counts are incremented. The CORBA C++ mapping specifies a static `_duplicate()` method to be used for exactly that purpose. We call `_duplicate()` in the `Locate-Factory()` implementation:

```
Ch3::CheckingAccountFactory_ptr
MyCheckingAccount::LocateFactory(const char* ior)
{
    Ch3::CheckingAccountFactory_var factory;
    factory = Get a factory ...
    return Ch3::CheckingAccountFactory::_duplicate(factory);
}
```

If we had returned the factory without calling `_duplicate()`, the factory would have been released as soon as the call completed. It should be noted that this is somewhat tricky. Knowing when to use `_var`, `_ptr`, `release()`, and `_duplicate()` is extremely important and has certainly been the cause of many bugs in CORBA C++-based systems.

The other topic regarding C++ object references that we need to cover is widening and narrowing. CORBA interfaces are organized into a multiple-inheritance hierarchy conceptually rooted at `CORBA::Object`. The hierarchy for our checking account example is shown in Figure 3-13.

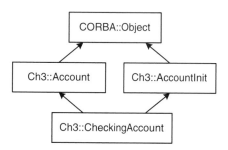

Figure 3-13. *The CORBA/C++ checking account interface hierarchy.*

In mapping CORBA IDL to C++, the CORBA standard does not require that the generated object types (i.e., `Ch3::Account_ptr`, `Ch3::Account_var`, `Ch3::CheckingAccount_ptr`, etc.) be related in any specific manner. To navigate the interface hierarchy in an upward direction, the standard specifies that the generated object reference types support implicit widening (comparable to an implicit upward cast in C++). Downward navigation is accomplished using a static `_narrow()` method that is defined for each interface type. Implicit widening is demonstrated in the following example:

```
// m_account is declared as type Ch3::CheckingAccount_var
Ch3::Account_ptr      pAccount      = m_account;
Ch3::AccountInit_ptr pAccountInit = m_account;
```

In this example, the `Ch3::CheckingAccount_var` reference has been widened to both a `Ch3::Account_ptr` reference and a `Ch3::AccountInit_ptr` reference. Note that the reference count is not incremented when performing implicit widening. The reference count for the checking account object remains the same even though there are two new references to the object referenced by `m_account`. Because implicit widening does not increment the reference count, the CORBA standard disallows implicit widening from one _var reference to another. Allowing implicit widening in such a case would undoubtedly result in having `release()` called too many times. Instead, such conversions require a call to `_duplicate()` as shown here:

```
// m_account is declared as type CheckingAccount_var
Ch3::Account_var vAccount =
    Ch3::CheckingAccount::_duplicate(m_account);
```

As stated earlier, downward navigation of the interface hierarchy is accomplished using the `_narrow()` method. The `MyCheckingAccount` wrapper class relies on _narrow() when locating a factory. The reason is that the Locate-Factory() method uses a CORBA-defined method that returns a generic object reference for the factory. The generic reference then needs to be narrowed to a Ch3::CheckingAccountFactory_ptr as shown here:

```
1  Ch3::CheckingAccountFactory_ptr
2  MyCheckingAccount::LocateFactory(const char* ior)
3  {
4      Ch3::CheckingAccountFactory_var factory;

5      try
6      {
7          // Obtain an object reference corresponding to
8          // the IOR.
9          CORBA::Object_var obj;
10         obj = m_orb.string_to_object((char*)ior);
11         if (CORBA::is_nil(obj)) handle error ...

12         // Narrow to a factory object.
13         factory = Ch3::CheckingAccountFactory::_narrow(obj);
14         if (CORBA::is_nil(factory)) handle error ...
15     }

16     catch (CORBA::SystemException& se) { handle error... }
17     return Ch3::CheckingAccountFactory::_duplicate(factory);
18 }
```

The call to _narrow() on line 13 implicitly increments the reference count of the CORBA object being narrowed. In this example, reference counting for the factory object works in the following way. On line 10, the string_to_object() call results in a reference count of 1. On line 13, the reference count increases to 2 because of the call to _narrow(). On line 16, the reference count decreases to 1 because the obj variable goes out of scope and automatically calls release(). On line 17, the reference count increases to 2 because of the call to _duplicate(). On line 18, the reference count decreases to 1 because the factory variable goes out of scope. The CORBA factory object therefore has a reference count of 1 when the Ch3::CheckingAccountFactory_ptr is returned by the function.

Managing CORBA object references in C++ is hard. The complexity due to reference counting is one factor that makes CORBA/C++ a poor choice for the client tier in an *N*-tier system. The good news is that an alternative exists that eliminates most of the object reference problems faced by the CORBA/C++ developer. That alternative is Java.

CORBA Object References in Java

The Java runtime environment provides many advantages over its C++ counterpart. When it comes to CORBA, one of the most important advantages is Java's support for garbage collection. Java-based CORBA products rely on the Java runtime system to manage CORBA object reference counting rather than forcing the user to correctly use explicit constructs like those used in C++ (i.e., _ptr, _var, duplicate(), and release()). Although the duplicate() and release() methods are specified in the standard IDL to Java mapping, the methods are not supported by most Java-based CORBA products. Instead, CORBA object references are managed as normal Java object references. Garbage collection is used to determine when a CORBA object is no longer referenced.

Navigating the CORBA interface hierarchy in Java is accomplished in much the same way as it is in C++. The IDL to Java mapping supports implicit widening (implemented as an interface cast in Java). Downward navigation of the hierarchy is accomplished using a narrow() method that is defined in a helper class for each CORBA interface.[*] The init() method in the MyCheckingAccount wrapper class illustrates the narrowing of a CORBA object reference to a CheckingAccountFactory reference:

```
public void init(String name, String factoryIOR)
{
    try
    {
        // Locate the factory ...
        org.omg.CORBA.Object obj =
            m_orb.string_to_object(factoryIOR);

        // Narrow to a CheckingAccountFactory reference.
        CheckingAccountFactory factory =
            CheckingAccountFactoryHelper.narrow(obj);
        ...
    }

    catch (org.omg.CORBA.SystemException e)
    {
        e.printStackTrace();
    }
}
```

---

[*]Helper classes are fully described in the IDL to Java mapping contained in the CORBA 2.2 specification.

Note that Java does not require any specific handling related to reference counting. This makes Java much easier to use than C++ when we are working with CORBA object references.

Creating Objects

Creating object instances in languages like C++, Java, and Visual Basic is a simple process: One simply needs to use the new operator. In comparison, creating a distributed object instance requires more effort since the object instance is usually created in a different process on a different machine. An abstraction is needed to redirect creation of a distributed object to a remote location.

COM and CORBA both rely on an abstraction called a *factory* to create distributed object instances. A factory is a special type of distributed object whose main purpose is to create other distributed objects. A factory lives within the same server process as the objects that it creates. Creating a distributed object in COM and CORBA is a two-step process. First, the appropriate factory is located. Then, the factory is used to create the object of interest. This section describes how factories are used in both COM and CORBA to create the checking account object used in the checking account example.

COM Factories

COM defines a standard interface for factories called IClassFactory. An abbreviated IDL definition of IClassFactory is presented here:

```
interface IClassFactory : IUnknown
{
    HRESULT CreateInstance(...);
    ...
}
```

A typical COM server implements the IClassFactory interface, thereby allowing COM object instances to be created. The creation process for COM objects that rely on IClassFactory is always the same.

1. Use the COM object CLSID (i.e., uuid of the coclass) to obtain an IClassFactory interface pointer to the correct factory.

2. Call the IClassFactory::CreateInstance() method to create the COM object instance.

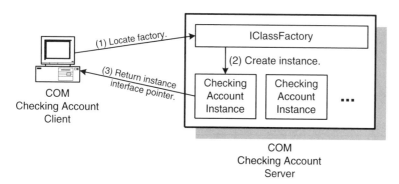

Figure 3-14. *The COM checking account factory.*

After the COM object is created, an interface pointer to the newly created object instance is returned, and the factory interface pointer is discarded. Figure 3-14 illustrates how a factory is used to create a checking account instance in our example.

It would be tedious to repeat the preceding steps every time a COM object instance is created. COM clients typically call one method that combines the steps. As we will demonstrate later in this section, neither our C++ nor our Visual Basic clients directly manipulate the IClassFactory interface pointer associated with the COM checking account. There are still times, however, when the factory needs to be used explicitly.

Explicit use of the factory is required for bulk creation of COM object instances. To make creation of many instances efficient, one needs to first get an interface pointer to the factory and to then create multiple COM object instances using the same factory interface pointer. This eliminates the need to locate a factory for each instance that is created.

A user must also explicitly use a factory when a factory interface other than IClassFactory is needed. COM currently specifies a second standard factory interface, IClassFactory2, that is used to address licensing concerns. The IClassFactory2 interface extends the IClassFactory interface by adding methods that support the use of licensing information when creating a COM object instance. An abbreviated version of the IClassFactory2 interface is presented here:

```
interface IClassFactory2 : IClassFactory
{
```

```
    HRESULT GetLicInfo(...);
    HRESULT RequestLicKey(...);
    HRESULT CreateInstanceLic(...);
    HRESULT RemoteCreateInstanceLic(...);
}
```

COM Object Creation in C++

There are several ways to create a COM checking account object in our C++ client application. One alternative is to use the CoGetClassObject() function to obtain an interface pointer for the checking account factory. The factory can then be used to create one or more checking account instances. A better alternative is to use the CoCreateInstanceEx() function. CoCreateInstanceEx() calls CoGetClassObject() and creates a COM object instance within the context of a single invocation. As shown in Listing 3-4, we call CoCreateInstanceEx() in the Init() method of the MyCheckingAccount wrapper class.

The first section of the Init() method creates the COSERVERINFO structure that will be used to specify the server machine on which the COM checking account server will run. If no server name is specified, a NULL value for the server information will be passed to CoCreateInstanceEx(). Passing a NULL in such a manner alerts CoCreateInstanceEx() to use a server running on the local machine. If no server (local or remote, depending on pServerInfo) is found, CoCreateInstanceEx() will fail. For our example, serverName is set to "tosca." The server name could also have been set to an IP address (192.168.0.1), an IP domain name (tosca.opera.myhouse), or a UNC name (\\tosca).

The next section creates a MULTI_QI array of interface pointers. Recall (from COM Interface Pointers in C++ on page 65) that we need only one interface pointer to obtain all other interface pointers for a specific COM object instance. The QueryInterface() method defined in IUnknown can be used to obtain all other interfaces supported by a COM object. With COM, calling QueryInterface() multiple times can be very inefficient across a slow network connection. CoCreateInstanceEx() allows the user to specify multiple interface pointers to be retrieved when the COM object is created, thus eliminating excessive calls across the network to QueryInterface(). For the checking account example, we create three interface pointers corresponding to the IAccount, IAccountInit, and ICheckingAccount interfaces.

Listing 3-4. *Creating a COM Checking Account Instance in C++*

```cpp
BOOL MyCheckingAccount::Init(const CString& name,
                            const CString& serverName,
                            CString& errmsg)
{
    // Create server info.
    COSERVERINFO  serverInfo;
    COSERVERINFO* pServerInfo;

    if ( serverName.IsEmpty() )
    {
        // Use local server.
        pServerInfo = NULL;
    }
    else
    {
        serverInfo.dwReserved1 = 0;
        serverInfo.dwReserved2 = 0;
        serverInfo.pwszName     = serverName.AllocSysString();
        serverInfo.pAuthInfo    = NULL;
        pServerInfo = &serverInfo;
    }

    // Create MULTI_QI array to get all pertinent interfaces.
    MULTI_QI mqi[] =
    {
        {&IID_IAccount,         NULL, 0},
        {&IID_IAccountInit,     NULL, 0},
        {&IID_ICheckingAccount, NULL, 0},
    };

    // Create a server object instance.
    HRESULT hr;
    hr = CoCreateInstanceEx
            (CLSID_Ch3CheckingAccount, NULL,
             CLSCTX_LOCAL_SERVER | CLSCTX_REMOTE_SERVER,
             pServerInfo, 3, mqi);

    ::SysFreeString(serverInfo.pwszName);
    if ( !SUCCEEDED(hr) ) handle error ...

    // Assign the interface pointers and server name.
    m_pIAccount         = (IAccount*)mqi[0].pItf;
    m_pIAccountInit     = (IAccountInit*)mqi[1].pItf;
    m_pICheckingAccount = (ICheckingAccount*)mqi[2].pItf;
    m_serverName        = serverName;
```

Listing 3-4. *Creating a COM Checking Account Instance in C++ (continued)*

```
    // Initialize the name.
    BSTR bstrName = name.AllocSysString();
    hr = m_pIAccountInit->Init(bstrName);

    if ( !SUCCEEDED(hr) ) handle error ...

    ::SysFreeString(bstrName);

    m_isEnabled = TRUE;
    return TRUE;
}
```

The next section calls `CoCreateInstanceEx()` to create the checking account object. The first argument is the `CLSID` of the checking account `coclass`. (We describe where the `CLSID` and the `IID`s are defined in Using IDL in the COM C++ Client on page 58.) We specify that we will use either a local server (if `pServerInfo` is `NULL`) or a remote server. Finally, we specify the number of interface pointers in our `MULTI_QI` array and pass the `MULTI_QI` array defined in the previous section.

If the call to `CoCreateInstanceEx()` succeeds, the interface pointers are initialized based on the `MULTI_QI` array. The last step is to use the `m_pIAccountInit` interface pointer to initialize the COM object based on the name that was passed to the `Init()` method.

The `CoCreateInstanceEx()` function is convenient in that it allows the user to ignore the factory actually being used to create the instance. `CoCreateInstanceEx()` also increases efficiency in COM by obtaining multiple interface pointers in a single call. As stated earlier, there are still cases when one needs to explicitly use the factory object. Although our checking account example is not one of those cases, we show for completeness, how to create a checking account instance using a factory in the following example:

```
BOOL MyCheckingAccount::InitUsingFactory(
                                    const CString& name,
                                    const CString& serverName,
                                    CString& errmsg)
{
    ...
```

```
// Get the factory ...
IClassFactory* pIClassFactory;
HRESULT hr = CoGetClassObject
        (CLSID_Ch3CheckingAccount,
         CLSCTX_LOCAL_SERVER | CLSCTX_REMOTE_SERVER,
         pServerInfo, IID_IClassFactory,
         (void**)&pIClassFactory);
if ( !SUCCEEDED(hr) ) handle error ...

// Create the instance ...
IUnknown* pIUnknown;
hr = pIClassFactory->CreateInstance(NULL,
                                    IID_IUnknown,
                                    (void**)&pIUnknown);
pIClassFactory->Release();
::SysFreeString(serverInfo.pwszName);
if ( !SUCCEEDED(hr) ) handle error ...

// Set the interfaces using QueryInterface().
...
}
```

To use the factory, we first need to create the COSERVERINFO structure just as we did when using CoCreateInstanceEx() in Listing 3-4. Next, we call CoGetClassObject() to obtain an IClassFactory interface pointer for the checking account server. Finally, we call CreateInstance() on the factory to create a new checking account instance. Note that we release the IClassFactory interface pointer since we no longer need the factory after the checking account instance has been created.

COM Object Creation in Visual Basic

The Visual Basic client application used in the checking account example is implemented using Visual Basic 5.0. The COM extensions needed to specify a remote server are not directly accessible in the VB5 environment.[*] To use a remote COM server from our Visual Basic client, we have two alternatives:

1. Call CoCreateInstanceEx() directly from Visual Basic. Since CoCreateInstanceEx() is part of the Win32 API, it is possible to map the call to Visual Basic; however, the mapping is rather awkward.

---

[*]Note that Visual Basic 6.0 allows a remote server name to be specified when creating a COM object instance. An example that demonstrates this functionality is presented later in The Visual Basic COM Client on page 239.

2. Use a simple in-process COM component (implemented in C++) that calls `CoCreateInstanceEx()` on behalf of the Visual Basic client.

We opt for the second alternative since it illustrates the elegance of using a component-based architecture like COM. It just so happens that a readily available component known as the *DCOM Bridge*[*] meets our needs. We simply install the DCOM Bridge on each of our client machines and then use COM from our Visual Basic client application. Figure 3-10 (given earlier) shows that we also selected *DCOM Bridge Type Library* as a reference when we created our Visual Basic client application. The IDL description of the DCOM Bridge method that we will be using is presented here:

```
interface IDCOMBridge : IDispatch
{
    HRESULT CreateRemoteInstance (
        [in] BSTR szClsid,
        [in] BSTR szServerName,
        [in] BOOL fDispatch,
        [out, retval] IUnknown **punk);
    ...
}
```

The Visual Basic client application creates a COM checking account instance in the `Init()` function of the `MyCheckingAccount` wrapper class as shown next. Two variables are declared in `Init()`. The `account` variable holds the `IUnknown` interface pointer for the checking account instance to be created. The `bridge` variable holds the interface pointer for the DCOM Bridge instance:

```
'MyCheckingAccount.cls

Public Function Init(name As String, _
                     server As String) As Boolean
On Error GoTo ErrorHandler
    Dim account As IUnknown
    Dim bridge As New DCOMBridge

    'Create an instance of the checking account.
    If Len(server) > 0 Then
        'Use the bridge to create a remote instance.
        Set account = bridge.CreateRemoteInstance(CLSIDAccount, _
                                      server, _
                                      False)
```

---

[*]The DCOM Bridge component was written by Mike Nelson and is freely available from `http://www.iapetus.com/dcom/dcomtool.htm`.

```
    Else
        'Create an instance locally.
        Set account = New Ch3CheckingAccount
    End If

    'Initialize the interface pointers.
    Set mIAccount = account
    Set mIAccountInit = account
    Set mICheckingAccount = mIAccount

    'Initialize the account object.
    Call mIAccountInit.Init(name)
    mIsEnabled = True
    Init = True
Exit Function

ErrorHandler:
    Debug.Print "MyCheckingAccount::Init() failed"
    Init = False
End Function
```

The first section creates the checking account instance. If the server parameter contains a name, the `CreateRemoteInstance()` method of the DCOM Bridge component is used to create a checking account instance on the specified server; otherwise, the Visual Basic `New` operator is used to create an instance locally.

If the checking account instance is successfully created, the interface pointers for `IAccount`, `IAccountInit`, and `ICheckingAccount` are initialized. The `IAccountInit` interface pointer is then used to initialize the newly created COM object instance with the customer name specified in the `name` parameter of `Init()`.

CORBA Factories

The CORBA notion of factories is somewhat different from that of COM. CORBA does not specify a standard implementation for factories. Instead, CORBA provides for persistent objects (i.e., objects that can live beyond the lifetime of a single process). A persistent object provides a useful mechanism for creating a factory. The CORBA checking account server used in our example takes such an approach. Recall that the CORBA IDL for our checking account factory is defined as

```
// excerpt from Ch3.idl
module Ch3
{
   ...
   interface CheckingAccountFactory
   {
      CheckingAccount create();
   };
}
```

From the perspective of our CORBA client applications, a single persistent instance of the `CheckingAccountFactory` is always available. To simplify the example, we manually start the CORBA server. The question is, How do the clients locate the `CheckingAccountFactory` instance?

The CORBA clients in our example rely on a stringified interoperable object reference (IOR). A stringified IOR is simply a string of characters that can be used to uniquely identify a CORBA object instance available on the network regardless of vendor or hardware platform. (An example of a stringified IOR was shown earlier in Listing 3-1 on page 37.) For the checking account example, a `CheckingAccountFactory` instance is created when the CORBA checking account server is started. The stringified IOR corresponding to the factory is then written to a file as shown here:

```
// main() routine for the CORBA checking account server

int main()
{
    // Create the factory implementation object.
    Ch3::CheckingAccountFactory_var factory =
        new CheckingAccountFactoryImpl;

    // Get the IOR for the factory.
    char* factoryIOR;
    try
    {
        // This call is Orbix-specific but it does generate
        // a CORBA-compliant IOR.
        factoryIOR = factory->_object_to_string
                            (CORBA::IT_INTEROPERABLE_OR_KIND);
    }
    catch(CORBA::SystemException& sysEx) { handle error ... }
```

```
// Write the IOR to a file.
ofstream strm("ior.txt");
if ( !strm ) handle error ...
strm << factoryIOR; strm.flush(); strm.close();
CORBA::string_free(factoryIOR);

try
{
    // Tell Orbix that we have completed the server's
    // initialization (i.e., enter loop to process events).
    CORBA::Orbix.processEvents(CORBA::Orbix.INFINITE_TIMEOUT);
}
catch (CORBA::SystemException &sysEx ) { handle error ... }

// impl_is_ready() returns only when Orbix times out
// an idle server (or an error occurs).
cout << "server exiting" << endl;
return 0;
}
```

The `main()` function clarifies how the Orbix checking account server works. First, a `Ch3::CheckingAccountFactory` implementation object is created in the server. This implementation object will service all requests made to the factory. Next, the stringified IOR for the `Ch3::CheckingAccountFactory` instance is obtained by calling the `_object_to_string()` method on the factory instance. The stringified IOR is then written to a file (this is done for convenience so that we can cut and paste the IOR into our client applications). An alternative to using the file-based IOR would be to register the factory instance with a CORBA naming service. Clients could then use the naming service to find the `Ch3::CheckingAccountFactory` instance. To keep our example simple, we have chosen to use the file-based IOR approach.

The last step in `main()` is to call the ORB's `processEvents()` method. This method processes events in an infinite loop until either Orbix times out the server or a fatal error occurs in the event loop. Note that several of the calls in the server implementation are vendor-specific. This is not critical.[*] The biggest concern is the ability of the server to interoperate with a variety of clients. The CORBA checking account clients demonstrate that the generated IOR and Orbix server work correctly with both Orbix C++ and VisiBroker Java clients.

---

[*]Note that when CORBA vendors support the CORBA 2.2 specification, most server-side portability problems will be eliminated through the use of a newly introduced portable object adaptor (POA). The Orbix server implementation described in this chapter uses a proprietary implementation of CORBA 2.0's basic object adaptor (BOA).

CORBA Object Creation in C++ and Java

The basic steps required to create a CORBA object in C++ and Java are the same. First, the CORBA object reference for the CheckingAccountFactory instance is located. Next, a checking account instance is created using the create() method provided by the factory. Finally, the checking account instance is initialized with the customer name. Reference-counting issues make locating the factory somewhat complex in C++. The LocateFactory() method for the C++ client is shown here:

```
Ch3::CheckingAccountFactory_ptr
MyCheckingAccount::LocateFactory(const char* ior)
{
    Ch3::CheckingAccountFactory_var factory;

    try
    {
        // Obtain an object reference corresponding to
        // the IOR.
        CORBA::Object_var obj;
        obj = m_orb.string_to_object((char*)ior);
        if (CORBA::is_nil(obj)) handle error ...

        // Narrow to a factory object.
        factory = Ch3::CheckingAccountFactory::_narrow(obj);
        if (CORBA::is_nil(factory)) handle error ...
    }

    catch (CORBA::SystemException& se) { handle error... }
    return Ch3::CheckingAccountFactory::_duplicate(factory);
}
```

As we've already discussed (in CORBA Object References in C++ on page 70), the user has to worry about a myriad of reference-counting issues when using the _ptr and _var reference types as well as the calls to _narrow() and _duplicate() in LocateFactory(). The LocateFactory() method first obtains an object reference corresponding to the stringified IOR that was passed as a parameter. It does this by calling the string_to_object() method on the ORB. The string_to_object() method is specified in the CORBA 2.0 standard C++ mapping. Successful completion of this call returns an object reference to the CORBA object instance uniquely identified by the IOR (in our case, the Ch3::CheckingAccountFactory instance). The CORBA object reference is then narrowed to a Ch3::CheckingAccountFactory object reference and returned to the caller.

The `Init()` method in the `MyCheckingAccount` C++ wrapper class demonstrates how the factory is used to create a checking account instance and how the checking account instance is initialized:

```
BOOL MyCheckingAccount::Init(const char* name,
                            const char* factoryIOR)
{
    BOOL ok = FALSE;

    try
    {
        // Locate checking account factory.
        Ch3::CheckingAccountFactory_var factory;
        factory = LocateFactory(factoryIOR);
        if (CORBA::is_nil(factory)) handle error ...

        // Create a checking account instance.
        m_account = factory->create();

        // Initialize the account for the name.
        m_account->init(name);

        // Finish initialization.
        m_isEnabled = TRUE;
        ok = TRUE;
    }

    catch (Ch3::InvalidNameException& exc)  { handle error... }
    catch (CORBA::SystemException& se) { handle error ... }
    return ok;
}
```

An object reference for the factory is created by calling the `LocateFactory()` method (previously described) with `factoryIOR` passed as a parameter. The checking account instance is then created by calling the `create()` method on the factory. Finally, the `m_account->init()` method is called using the customer name passed in as a parameter to `MyCheckingAccount::Init()`.

Creating a CORBA object in Java is even simpler than it is in C++ because the reference-counting issues do not convolute the solution. Recall that the C++ example previously presented relied on the `LocateFactory()` method, which we described at the beginning of this section. The `LocateFactory()` method was mostly needed to handle reference-counting issues. The `MyCheckingAccount` Java wrapper class shown here does not require a separate method to locate the factory, as was the case with C++:

```java
// MyCheckingAccount.java

    public void init(String name, String factoryIOR)
    {

        try
        {
            // Locate the factory ...
            org.omg.CORBA.Object obj =
                m_orb.string_to_object(factoryIOR);
            CheckingAccountFactory factory =
                CheckingAccountFactoryHelper.narrow(obj);

            // Create an account ...
            m_account = factory.create();

            // Initialize the account ...
            m_account.init(name);

            m_isEnabled = true;
        }
        catch (InvalidNameException e) { handle error... }
        catch (org.omg.CORBA.SystemException e)
                                        { handle error... }
    }
```

The `MyCheckingAccount.init()` method locates the factory by calling the `string_to_object()` method on the ORB (in this case, VisiBroker). As was the case with C++, the `string_to_object()` method is a standardized method that is specified in the standard IDL-to-Java mapping. Successful completion of this call returns an object reference to the CORBA object instance uniquely identified by the `factoryIOR` parameter. The CORBA object reference is then narrowed to a `CheckingAccountFactory` object reference and returned to the caller. Next, the checking account instance is created by calling the `create()` method on the factory. Finally, the `m_account.init()` method is called using the customer name passed in as a parameter to `MyCheckingAccount.init()`.

Invoking Object Methods

In previous sections, we described how COM and CORBA manage object handles and object creation; each architecture has its own set of peculiarities and complexities. However, once an object handle has been obtained for a COM or CORBA object, invoking methods on that object is simple. In fact, a major goal of both COM and CORBA is to make remote method invocation as easy as local method invocation. In other words, the software developer is not required to use a special syntax or special constructs when invoking a method on a remote object.

There is one area where COM and CORBA differ with regard to method invocation. Each architecture has its own strategy for propagating exceptions. The DCOM extensions to COM mandate that every COM interface method return a 32-bit integer known as an HRESULT. The HRESULT contains status information indicating the success or failure of the call. COM also allows users to specify customized HRESULT values (although users should use standard errors whenever possible). In contrast, CORBA supports an exception-based model. CORBA defines standard exception types such as the CORBA SystemException when mapping CORBA IDL to C++ and Java. CORBA also allows users to declare new exception types in CORBA IDL.

The checking account example described in this chapter creates a user-defined HRESULT as well as a user-defined CORBA exception to handle the case when an invalid name is passed to the Init() method of the checking account instance. The COM client applications demonstrate how the user-defined HRESULT is handled in both C++ and Visual Basic. The CORBA client applications demonstrate how the user-defined CORBA exception is caught in C++ and Java.

COM HRESULTs

A COM HRESULT is a simple, efficient, and effective means for conveying status. An HRESULT is a 32-bit integer that is divided into three fields. The most significant bit (bit 31) indicates severity—either success or an error. Bits 16–30 indicate the facility (e.g., RPC, Win32, etc.) with which the HRESULT is associated. Bits 0–15 indicate a specific return code for the facility. Because only one bit is used to indicate success or failure, COM allows for multiple success codes (2^{31} to be exact) as well as multiple failure codes.

DCOM mandates that every COM interface method return an HRESULT. In the event that an error occurs within DCOM during method invocation, the DCOM runtime returns its own error code indicating the problem that occurred. Since DCOM requires that each method return an HRESULT, it is good practice to do so for all COM interfaces. This may seem restrictive, but it is generally not a problem since COM IDL also allows a parameter to a COM interface method to be specified as a return value using the retval keyword. Consider the following COM IDL definition:

```
interface ISomeInterface : IUnknown
{
    HRESULT FetchName([out, retval] BSTR *pVal);
};
```

In Visual Basic, the `FetchName()` method just defined would be treated as a method that returns a name. The Visual Basic error-handling facility would manage the actual return value (i.e., `HRESULT`) and create an exception if the returned `HRESULT` indicates failure.

Creating a user-defined `HRESULT` for general use in a system requires some care. First, the user must decide whether the `HRESULT` indicates success or an error. Next, the user should use the `FACILITY_ITF` constant. `FACILITY_ITF` indicates that the `HRESULT` is specific to the interface that defines the method. Finally, the user should select a return code between `0x0200` and `0xFFFF` since all return codes between `0x0000` and `0x01FF` are already reserved by COM for the `FACILITY_ITF` facility.

In the checking account example, we define an `HRESULT` called `E_INVALID_NAME`, indicating that an invalid name was passed to the `Init()` method. We compute the `HRESULT` using the `MAKE_HRESULT` macro provided in Visual C++. Our newly defined `HRESULT` will indicate an error condition specific to the `IAccountInit` interface. We use `0x0200` as the return code since it is the first available code not already reserved by COM. We then create a constant in the COM IDL for our `IAccountInit` interface as shown here:

```
interface IAccountInit : IUnknown
{
    // 0x80040200 ==
    //    MAKE_HRESULT(SEVERITY_ERROR, FACILITY_ITF, 0x0200);
    const int E_INVALID_NAME = 0x80040200;
    HRESULT Init([in] BSTR name);
};
```

The only remaining task is to return `E_INVALID_NAME` when an invalid name is passed to the `Init()` method in our COM server. The `Init()` method used in our COM server implementation class is shown here:

```
// COM server implementation of Init()
STDMETHODIMP CCh3CheckingAccount::Init(BSTR name)
{
```

```
    if (wcslen(name) == 0)
        return E_INVALID_NAME;

    // Finish initialization ...
    return S_OK;
}
```

The STDMETHODIMP return type is a macro that expands to an HRESULT return
type. To check for an invalid name, we simply check the length of the name
passed to Init() and return E_INVALID_NAME if the length is equal to 0. Otherwise, we finish initialization and return S_OK to indicate that the call was
successful.

COM Error Handling in the C++ Client

The MyCheckingAccount wrapper class used in the COM C++ client application relies on HRESULTs to determine whether a COM object method invocation has succeeded or failed. The use of an HRESULT is illustrated in the
following Init() method:

```
BOOL MyCheckingAccount::Init(const CString& name,
                            const CString& serverName,
                            CString& errmsg)
{
    ...

    BSTR    bstrName = name.AllocSysString();
    HRESULT hr       = m_pIAccountInit->Init(bstrName);

    if ( !SUCCEEDED(hr) )
    {
        if (hr == E_INVALID_NAME)
            errmsg = "Invalid name!";
        else
            errmsg = "Failed to initialize account!";
    }

    ...
}
```

COM provides two macros, SUCCEEDED and FAILED, to test the status of a
COM method invocation. These macros check the severity bit of the HRESULT
to determine success or failure. The preceding example initially sets the status code to the value returned by the call to m_pIAccountInit->Init(). The

status code is then tested using the SUCCEEDED macro. If the status code indicates that the call to m_pIAccountInit->Init() has failed, the status code is compared to E_INVALID_NAME to determine whether the cause for failure was an invalid name.

COM Error Handling in the Visual Basic Client

Visual Basic does not allow for direct manipulation of an HRESULT. Instead, an error handler defined in an On Error statement is invoked if the severity bit of the resulting HRESULT indicates failure. The Init() method of the MyCheckingAccount wrapper class is shown here:

```
'MyCheckingAccount.cls
Public Function Init(name As String, _
                     server As String) As Boolean

    On Error GoTo ErrorHandler
        Call mIAccountInit.Init(name)
        mIsEnabled = True
        Init = True
    Exit Function

    ErrorHandler:
        Debug.Print "Err.Description : " + Err.Description
        Debug.Print "Err.Number      : " + "0x" + Hex(Err.Number)
        Init = False
End Function
```

In this example, an error handler is created to trap any errors that might occur. The mIAccountInit.Init() method is then called. If an error occurs, the error handler is invoked. Visual Basic provides an Err object that can be used to determine what caused the error. If we pass an empty string to the Init() method, we get the following debug output from our error handler:

```
Err.Description : Automation error
Err.Number      : 0x80040200
```

Note that the value returned by Err.Number in the error handler correctly matches the E_INVALID_NAME value defined in our IDL file.

CORBA Exceptions

CORBA provides robust support for exceptions. In addition to standard system exception types defined in the C++ and Java mappings for CORBA IDL, the CORBA standard also allows for user-defined exceptions. The CORBA IDL describing the CORBA checking account object declares a user-defined exception as shown here:

```
// Account.idl

exception InvalidNameException
{
    string reason;
};

...

interface AccountInit
{
    void init(in string name) raises(InvalidNameException);
};
```

An IDL exception can contain members of any IDL data type, including simple types, structs, unions, enums, and references to other CORBA objects. InvalidNameException contains one member called reason. This allows the CORBA server object to pass a reason (in the form of a character string) back to the client if the exception is raised. The InvalidNameException is thrown by the init() method defined in the AccountInit interface. The following init() method is taken from the Orbix checking account server implementation:

```
// Orbix server implementation of init()
void CheckingAccountImpl::init(const char* name,
                               CORBA::Environment& IT_env)
{
    if (name == (char*)0  ||  name[0] == '\0')
        throw Ch3::InvalidNameException("initialization error");
    strcpy(m_name, name);
    ...
}
```

The CORBA runtime system takes care of propagating the thrown exception back to the client that called the init() method. The client can then use the reason attribute of the exception to get a textual reason describing why the exception was thrown. In the preceding example, `reason` would be set to `"initialization error"` if the exception is thrown.

CORBA Exception Handling in the C++ and Java Clients

The handling of CORBA exceptions in C++ and Java is basically the same. CORBA method invocations from C++ and Java should always be made within a try–catch block. Failure to catch an exception thrown by the CORBA runtime will result in abnormal program termination. The `Init()` method in the `MyCheckingAccount` C++ wrapper class illustrates a CORBA method invocation:

```cpp
// MyCheckingAccount.cpp (wrapper class)
BOOL MyCheckingAccount::Init(const char* name,
                             const char* factoryIOR)
{
    try
    {
        ...
        m_account->init(name);
        ...
    }
    catch (Ch3::InvalidNameException& exc)
    {
        cerr << "MyCheckingAccount::Init: "
             << "InvalidNameException! - "
             << exc.reason << endl;
    }
    catch (CORBA::SystemException& se)
    {
        cerr << "MyCheckingAccount::Init: "
             << "CORBA::SystemException!" << endl;
    }
    ...
}
```

The call to `m_account->init()` is made within a try block. Catch blocks are defined for the `Ch3::InvalidNameException` as well as the CORBA `SystemException`. The biggest concern when using C++ is that the C++ compiler does not force the user to catch exceptions. We could have left out the `Ch3::InvalidNameException` catch block, and the program would have still compiled. Forgetting a catch block can lead to abnormal termination of the client application at runtime. It should be noted that this is a weakness of C++ and not of CORBA.

The init() method in the MyCheckingAccount Java wrapper class treats the CORBA method invocation much as the C++ version did. The call to m_account.init() is made within a try block. Catch blocks are defined for the InvalidNameException as well as the CORBA SystemException:

```java
// MyCheckingAccount.java (wrapper class)

    public void init(String name, String factoryIOR)
    {
        try
        {
            ...
            m_account.init(name);
            ...
        }
        catch (InvalidNameException e)
        { e.printStackTrace(); }

        catch (org.omg.CORBA.SystemException e)
        { e.printStackTrace(); }
    }
```

Java enforces usage of all exceptions not derived from the RuntimeException class defined in the java.lang package. The CORBA SystemException class derives from java.lang.RuntimeException; therefore, the compiler will not complain if we do not create a catch block for it. This is not the case with InvalidNameException. If we attempt to leave out the catch block for InvalidNameException, we get the following error from the Java compiler:

```
MyCheckingAccount.java:68: Exception ch3.InvalidNameException
    must be caught, or it must be declared in the throws
    clause of this method.
```

In general, CORBA relies heavily on exceptions, and Java provides much better exception support than C++. This is another area where Java proves to be a better choice than C++ for CORBA-based development.

Destroying Objects

Object lifetimes are managed differently in different programming environments. In C++, an object is destroyed using the `delete` operator. In Java, the garbage collector locates objects no longer in use and destroys them. When we are dealing with distributed objects, managing an object's lifetime is a much more complex task since it requires cooperation between multiple clients and the distributed object server.

COM and CORBA have very different approaches for destroying distributed object instances. Although both COM and CORBA use reference counting to determine when an object is no longer in use within a specific process (client or server), the similarities end there.

COM supports distributed reference counting and garbage collection whereby a server object is destroyed when there are no longer any clients referencing it. As we shall soon see (in Destroying COM Objects on page 96), supporting such a mechanism is not a simple task. Many issues related to efficiency and reliability must be addressed. COM's built-in management of object destruction is an extremely useful and important feature.

CORBA takes the stance that a server object's reference count should not be affected by the uncontrollable actions of an arbitrary client. In CORBA, server-side reference counts are maintained separately and have no direct relationship to client-side reference counts. The reference count maintained in a CORBA server for a specific instance can be manipulated only within the context of the server. This means that the responsibility for releasing all references to a server object requires a customized solution rather than a standardized approach. (We will examine how the checking account example handles this situation as well as other alternatives in Destroying CORBA Objects on page 97.)

The difference in the approaches taken by COM and CORBA has spawned many debates over the superiority of a particular architecture. Some members of the CORBA community have stated that COM's mechanism for managing an object's lifetime is not scalable or reliable in many situations. Members of the COM community are quick to point out that a distributed object architecture requires such a mechanism since custom implementation (as is required in CORBA) is tedious and difficult. Our goal here is to simply achieve awareness of how both COM and CORBA handle object destruction.

Destroying COM Objects

COM normally destroys a COM server object instance when there are no longer any clients referencing it. To destroy a COM checking account instance in our example, we simply need to ensure that all interface pointers for the COM object are released. Recall that the `MyCheckingAccount` wrapper class maintains an interface pointer for each of the checking account's interfaces after it is initialized. We release the interface pointers in the `Reset()` method of the `MyCheckingAccount` wrapper class as shown here:

```
void MyCheckingAccount::Reset()
{
    if (m_pIAccount) m_pIAccount->Release();
    m_pIAccount = NULL;

    if (m_pIAccountInit) m_pIAccountInit->Release();
    m_pIAccountInit = NULL;

    if (m_pICheckingAccount) m_pICheckingAccount->Release();
    m_pICheckingAccount = NULL;
}
```

Calling `Reset()` reduces the reference count to 0 for the COM checking account instance associated with the wrapper instance. Since no clients currently reference the checking account instance after `Reset()` is called, COM ensures that the checking account instance gets deleted on the server.

As shown next, the VB checking account client releases the interface pointers by setting its COM interface pointers to `Nothing`. The `Nothing` value is used in Visual Basic to disassociate an object reference from the actual object. Setting a COM interface pointer to `Nothing` effectively calls `Release()` on that interface pointer:

```
'MyCheckingAccount.cls
Public Sub Reset()
    Set mIAccount = Nothing
    Set mIAccountInit = Nothing
    Set mICheckingAccount = Nothing
End Sub
```

COM uses two mechanisms to determine when a COM object instance needs to be destroyed. The first mechanism is reference counting. From a logical standpoint, a COM object instance maintains one reference count in the server that is directly manipulated by all clients of the instance. In reality, allowing clients to directly manipulate the server-side reference count could result in a tremendous amount of network traffic. For this reason, COM caches calls to `AddRef()` and `Release()` in order to optimize traffic between the clients and the server while maintaining the illusion of a single server-side reference count.

In an error-free environment, reference counting is all that is needed; however, distributed computing environments are never error-free. Consider the case where an application terminates abnormally before it can call `Release()` on its interface pointers. In such a situation, the server object instance would never be destroyed. In a distributed environment, the consequences become more severe when a node or even an entire subnet becomes inoperable.

To handle situations like network outages, COM uses a pinging mechanism to determine when clients can no longer access a server. Clients are expected to ping the server periodically (e.g., every 2 minutes) to let the server know that they are still using the server. If a COM server does not receive a ping within a fixed number of ping periods (e.g., 3 ping periods, or 6 minutes), it assumes that the client can no longer access the server object. If no other clients hold references to the server object instance, the instance is destroyed.

Pinging is potentially expensive when we are dealing with a large number of clients and servers. Imagine thousands of clients pinging thousands of servers. A naive approach to pinging can result in intolerable network traffic. To overcome this problem, COM uses several optimization strategies to minimize traffic. One of the strategies used is known as *delta-pinging*. Delta-pinging combines client ping requests that are destined for the same server machine into a single ping set. Another optimization strategy used by COM combines delta-pings with normal COM packets, thus reducing ping overhead even further. A specific ping packet is created only if the COM client remains idle (i.e., has no communication with the COM server) for more than 2 minutes.

Given the extensive amount of optimization built into COM, pinging imposes minor performance overhead in most COM-based solutions.

Destroying CORBA Objects

The lifetime of a CORBA object instance depends solely on the reference count maintained within its CORBA server implementation. A CORBA object's server-side reference count is initialized when the object is created. In the checking account example, a checking account instance is created by the factory as shown here:

```
1  CheckingAccount_ptr
2  CheckingAccountFactoryImpl::create(CORBA::Environment& IT_env)
3  {
4      CheckingAccount_ptr account = new CheckingAccountImpl();
5      return CheckingAccount::_duplicate(account);
6  }
```

On line 4, the reference count for the newly created checking account instance is set to 1 when the object is created. On line 5, the reference count is increased to 2 because of the call to _duplicate(). Note that CORBA/C++ memory management rules dictate that release() will be called on a _ptr type returned by a server method; hence, the reference count of the newly created checking account reverts to 1 when the create() call is completed. The reference count will remain at 1 until the instance is explicitly released by some other method in the server, thus keeping the checking account instance alive (possibly forever).

Several approaches are commonly used to decrement the server-side reference count. The simplest approach is to create an interface method that releases the object. This is the approach used in the checking account example. The CORBA IDL for the Account interface includes a destroy() method:

```
interface Account
{
    ...
    void destroy();
};
```

The destroy() method simply calls release() on the CORBA server instance, thereby reducing its reference count to 0. Once the reference count reaches 0, the ORB automatically calls delete on the instance. The implementation of destroy() in the Orbix server is presented here:

```
// destroy() method in the server implementation

void CheckingAccountImpl::destroy(CORBA::Environment& IT_env)
{
    CORBA::release(this);
}
```

Given the fact that CORBA clients are unable to directly affect server-side reference counts, one might wonder why client-side reference counts exist at all.

When a client references a CORBA object, it uses a client stub to communicate with that object. Resources associated with the client stub cannot be deallocated until the client-side reference count for the CORBA object goes to 0.

It is important to note that although client stub resources are freed when the client's reference count goes to 0, the actual server object instance is unaffected. To destroy the server object instance (i.e., checking account instance) in the checking account example, the Orbix C++ client must first call destroy() as shown here:

```
void MyCheckingAccount::Reset()
{
    if ( !CORBA::is_nil(m_account) )
    {
        m_account->destroy();
        m_account = Ch3::CheckingAccount::_nil();
    }
}
```

The VisiBroker Java client calls destroy() in the same manner as the Orbix C++ client:

```
// MyCheckingAccount.java
    public void reset()
    {
        if (m_account != null)
        {
            m_account.destroy();
            m_account = null;
        }
    }
```

Simply providing a destroy() method is a naive approach and is subject to several problems. If multiple clients are referencing the same server object instance, calling destroy() will invalidate all of the clients' object references since the server object instance will no longer exist. If the destroy() method is never called due to program error or abnormal program termination, the server object instance will never get destroyed.

To guarantee the eventual destruction of unused CORBA object instances, the CORBA developer is required to implement an eviction scheme within the CORBA server. Eviction schemes are usually based on time-outs. An eviction scheme might work as follows. A CORBA server maintains a list of object references and time stamps for all object instances created in the server. The time stamp is used to indicate the last time the object instance was invoked. A time-out value is set to 10 minutes. A sweep method is run every 2 minutes that evicts objects not used within the last 10 minutes. To keep a server object instance alive, the object provides a method called `keepAlive()` that must be called every 10 minutes by the client if no other methods are invoked.

The eviction scheme places an additional burden on the CORBA developer. The implications in the server are obvious: Data structures and support mechanisms for the eviction scheme must be implemented. The eviction scheme also adds complexity to clients. In the example just described, a client would need to create a thread that periodically called `keepAlive()` to prevent the server from unexpectedly evicting the object.

The important point to note is that eviction schemes are inherently customized solutions. The CORBA standard does not define a specific method for handling object destruction.

Summary

We have covered a lot of ground by demonstrating the fundamental traits of COM and CORBA distributed objects. To maintain perspective, Table 3-4 summarizes the similarities and differences between COM and CORBA that were made evident by the demonstration.

A thorough understanding of the fundamentals along with knowledge pertaining to differences and similarities allows us to do two things. First, we can grasp the architecture-specific strengths resulting from the differences in COM and CORBA. Second, we can identify common ground where both COM and CORBA can be used based on the similarities in their core functionality. The end result is reduced risk since we will better understand when and where to use each architecture.

When we began Part I, our goal was to establish a mindset for embracing COM and CORBA when building distributed systems. In Chapter 1, we provided a brief summary of events leading up to the use of distributed objects. In Chapter 2, we described why COM and CORBA are currently the dominant distributed object architectures. In this chapter, we provided a side-by-side demonstration of COM and CORBA fundamentals. You should now have an understanding of the core capabilities and advantages afforded to users of

Table 3-4. *COM/CORBA Similarities and Differences*

Trait	Similarities	Differences
Interfaces	• COM and CORBA each use their own interface definition language (IDL) to describe interfaces.	• CORBA IDL is simpler and more elegant than COM IDL. • COM has better tool support for creating and managing IDL than CORBA.
Data types	• COM and CORBA support a rich set of data types. • COM and CORBA also support constants, enumerated types, structures, and arrays.	• COM identifies a subset of data types known as *automation types*. Automation-compatible interfaces are supported in more client environments than noncompatible interfaces. COM interfaces that are not automation-compatible are not guaranteed to work in environments other than C++. • Any CORBA interface can be used from any CORBA client.
Marshaling and unmarshaling	• COM and CORBA handle marshaling in client stubs and server stubs. Users do not normally need to worry about marshaling.	• COM allows automation-compatible interfaces to use type library marshaling, thus eliminating the need for customized stubs.
Proxies, stubs, and skeletons	• COM and CORBA rely on client stubs and server stubs to handle remoting issues. • COM and CORBA generate client stubs and server stubs from IDL.	• COM calls client stubs *proxies* and server stubs *stubs*. CORBA calls client stubs *stubs* and server stubs *skeletons*. • COM proxy–stub DLLs are used by all language environments. In CORBA, a separate stub–skeleton must be generated for each ORB/language combination.
Object handles	• COM and CORBA support reference-counted handles on object instances.	• COM calls object handles *interface pointers*. CORBA calls object handles *object references*. • CORBA supports multiple inheritance in the interface hierarchy. COM supports single inheritance only; however, a COM object supports one or more distinct interfaces.

Table 3-4. *COM/CORBA Similarities and Differences (continued)*

Trait	Similarities	Differences
Object creation	• COM and CORBA use factories to create object instances.	• COM has a standard factory interface called IClassFactory. CORBA factories are customized persistent CORBA objects.
Object invocation	• COM and CORBA allow for method invocation similar to native environment method invocation.	• COM's error-handling mechanism is based on HRESULT return values. CORBA supports user-defined exception types in IDL.
Object destruction	• COM and CORBA rely on reference counting to determine when an object can be destroyed.	• COM supports distributed reference counting and garbage collection (i.e., clients affect server reference counts). CORBA reference counts are maintained separately in the client and server (i.e., this makes it difficult to ensure that server objects get destroyed).

COM and CORBA infrastructures. These core capabilities and advantages provide a compelling case for using COM or CORBA to create distributed systems.

In Part II, we will examine the use of COM and CORBA on the server side of the enterprise. Deciding where to use COM and CORBA on the server side depends on an incredible range of factors such as platform, tool support, and high-level services. In the next chapter, we will outline an assessment strategy for determining where COM and CORBA should be used. The assessment strategy is then used to motivate the exploration of server-side issues throughout the remainder of Part II.

Part II

COM and CORBA
on the Server

Introduction

Strategists in charge of maintaining and evolving today's enterprise systems are faced with a formidable task—that of staying competitive while leveraging a new and diverse range of technical innovations. The rules of the game are changing when it comes to evolving server-side systems. It is no longer cost-effective to continue using legacy technology to develop and deploy new server-side applications. Instead, new tools that are built on top of COM and CORBA provide a speedier and more maintainable development path in the long term.

An example of the radical changes occurring in the server-side landscape is the introduction of Windows NT as a viable server platform. On Windows NT, Microsoft offers a host of new COM-based technologies (Microsoft Transaction Server, Microsoft Message Queue Server, etc.) that can speed development and deployment of sophisticated server-side systems. On the CORBA front, vendors are making essential services (object transaction service, security service, etc.) available along with their base ORB offerings.

Our mission in Part II is to aid you in discovering which approach (COM or CORBA) is most appropriate for a specific domain in your server-side system.

- Chapter 4 establishes the criteria and strategy used to assess the application of COM and CORBA in a server-side enterprise domain. The assessment criteria are divided into three primary areas: server platform, essential services, and intangibles.

- Chapter 5 focuses on the platform issues to be considered when selecting COM or CORBA. These platform issues include legacy system support, operating system platform, and availability of development tools.

- Chapter 6 focuses on the essential services needed to properly develop and deploy COM- or CORBA-based applications. Services provide ready-made distributed object plumbing so that developers can focus on business logic rather than on core infrastructure.

- Chapter 7 focuses on the intangibles that must be considered when selecting COM or CORBA, such as vendor perception, vendor lock-in, and availability of development staff.

After completing Part II, you should be able to extend the assessment strategy presented in Chapter 4 to meet the needs of your specific situation. You will then be ready to make rational choices concerning COM and CORBA in your overall enterprise solution.

Chapter 4

Assessing the
Server Side

Topics Covered in This Chapter

- What Constitutes the Server Side?

- Partitioning the Enterprise

- Strategic Directions of COM and CORBA

- The Need for an Assessment Strategy

- Assessment Criteria

- An Assessment Strategy

- COM and CORBA in Your Enterprise Solution

A battle is raging in the middleware arena between COM and CORBA. Both camps are guilty of spreading fear, uncertainty, and doubt about the other camp's technology. This has disastrous consequences when we are dealing with a technology area that is often misunderstood by key enterprise decision-makers. The worst consequence is a commitment to the wrong technology due to irrational reasoning.

In this chapter, we will attempt to move past the fear and uncertainty and present a strategy for making informed rational choices when selecting COM- and CORBA-related technology. This is not an easy task. A naive approach would be to survey the marketplace and rate the various technology choices in a general way. Such an approach would be inaccurate because of the rapid changes taking place in the marketplace as well as the diversity that exists across various enterprise systems.

Instead of assigning pluses and minuses to existing products, we'll first present technology-independent assessment criteria. We'll then describe a basic strategy for applying the criteria and allow it to be tailored to meet specific needs. In Chapters 5, 6, and 7, we will provide some insight into how the assessment criteria defined in this chapter relate to COM and CORBA.

What Constitutes the Server Side?

The definition of the term *server* becomes somewhat fuzzy as distributed systems become more complex. In a classical 2-tier client/server architecture, the role of server is clear. The server is a physical machine or group of machines on which the persistent data store resides.

In a classical 3-tier architecture consisting of a presentation tier, middle tier, and data tier, the delineation remains physical. As is the case with the 2-tier architecture, the data tier is still a server. The middle tier, however, takes on both the client and server roles. The middle tier acts as a client to the data tier while also acting as a server to the presentation tier.

The physical delineation of tiers breaks down in a distributed object system. In such a system, there is no distinct physical tier where middle-tier logic resides. Instead, the middle-tier logic is spread across a diverse range of distributed objects, which may reside in several different physical locations. Some systems even allow the distributed objects to change their location during runtime. This is referred to as *mobile* or *agent-based* computing.

Despite the lack of clear physical boundaries in distributed object systems, there is one physical boundary that remains. The presentation tier generally exists in the form of a lightweight or thin client separate from the rest of the system. A good example of a thin client is an application that runs in a Web browser. A Web client such as a CGI forms-based Web page runs in a Web browser that is separate from the rest of the system. The "rest of the system" is what we refer to as *server side*. In other words, the phrase *server side* is a catchall for everything but the client. Such a division can also be applied to Windows-based applications where the Windows client runs on a machine that is separate from the rest of the server-side system. The division between client side and server side is shown in Figure 4-1.

The physical distinction between client side and server side exists because of the different requirements for each side. Clients typically require less processing power and reliability since external systems do not rely upon them. Server-side systems must provide for high availability, performance, scalability, and security in order to support a diverse set of clients.

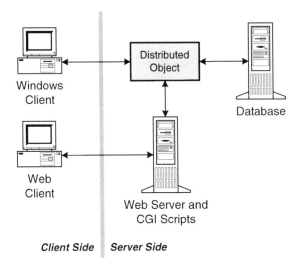

Figure 4-1. *Division between client side and server side.*

Partitioning the Enterprise

The server-side installation of a large enterprise system is usually huge, often ranging from hundreds to thousands of machines (if not more). To properly organize and maintain a large system, it must be partitioned into smaller and more manageable pieces that we hereafter call *domains*. Many factors influence how enterprise systems can be partitioned. Here are some:

- *Business logic.* The software system is partitioned based on the organization of business logic. For example, a company involved in the importing and exporting of foreign goods organizes its software system in a similar fashion. This is the most prevalent partitioning strategy.

- *Business data.* The software system is partitioned based on the organization of the business data. For example, a company stores its data in five distinct databases, and the software system is organized in a similar fashion.

- *Business organization.* The software system is partitioned based on the business organization. For example, the software system is organized by business unit or department.

- *Security.* The software system is partitioned based on security restrictions. For example, a company that manages medical records organizes its software system into one part that manages sensitive medical records and one part that manages less sensitive data such as equipment inventory.

- *Platform.* The software system is partitioned based on hardware and software platforms. For example, a company that uses mainframes and UNIX systems organizes its software system in a similar fashion.

- *Maintenance.* The software system is partitioned for maintenance purposes. For example, a company that manages huge amounts of data partitions the data and software system into smaller and more manageable systems.

All of the factors just mentioned are certainly valid in many situations; however, additional factors need to be considered when adding COM or CORBA to the equation. Middleware such as COM and CORBA is the glue that holds a system together. As such, middleware needs to orchestrate the entities in the software system. Such orchestration requires high levels of cooperation between the middleware components managing the various domains—a level of cooperation that cannot be attained when using multiple middleware products. Partitioning of the server-side system must therefore also consider the following factors:

- *Transactions.* Transaction boundaries should stay within domains managed by the same middleware product. Relying on interoperability between different vendors' object transaction services adds additional risk to the solution.

- *Security.* Security issues should be handled by the same middleware product except in the case where specific best-of-breed products (e.g., message encryption products, certificate providers, firewall solutions, etc.) are required. As was the case with transactions, relying on interoperability between different vendors' products adds additional risk to the solution.

- *Scalability and fault tolerance.* Middleware implementations that provide object pooling, load balancing, fault tolerance, and so forth must be managed by the same middleware product. Because few standards exist in this area, each vendor's middleware implementation of scalability and fault tolerance mechanisms will be different.

Although a certain level of interoperability exists between various CORBA vendors' ORBs (or even COM and CORBA), it is prudent to avoid multiple middleware products in a specific system domain. Interoperability across different middleware vendors' products such as transaction managers, security managers, and so on, will never keep pace with the advantages offered by committing to a single vendor. Always remember that vendors must differentiate themselves in order to stay competitive.

The intermixing of COM and CORBA products boils down to the issue of granularity. If the server-side system is partitioned into reasonable domains, any appropriate COM or CORBA middleware product can be used in any domain. If transactional boundaries, security contexts, or scalability requirements cross multiple domains, the same COM or CORBA middleware product should be used across those domains. This intermixing approach occurs at a necessarily coarse granularity. Intermixing COM and CORBA products at a finer granularity on the server side is probably unwise and will increase integration problems due to the lack of interoperability.

Strategic Directions of COM and CORBA

One of the greatest differences between COM and CORBA is the competitive nature by which each is driven. Microsoft's goal is to elevate Windows NT (and its successors) to the status of dominant server technology. Microsoft's goal is very ambitious considering the youth of Windows NT. The use of Windows NT as a server platform continues to increase, and Microsoft may eventually dominate the competition in much the same way as it has done in the client arena. Microsoft's platform strategy is vertical in that Microsoft controls the technology from the operating system level all the way up to end-user applications. COM is the middleware glue that unifies Microsoft's vertical product offerings.

The strategy behind CORBA is significantly different from that of COM. The Object Management Group (OMG) is an organization whose charter includes the creation of specifications (including CORBA 2.2) that are aimed at creating interoperable and portable distributed object solutions across many platforms. The CORBA vendors implement products based on those specifications. Because most CORBA vendors do not control a single operating system (as does Microsoft), they generally cover multiple platforms, thus resulting in a fairly horizontal platform strategy. In this section, we will take a closer look at the server-side strategies at work behind COM and CORBA. Understanding these very different strategies will help you to better understand the assessment criteria presented later in this chapter.

COM: A Vertical Strategy

Microsoft's strategy for dominating the server side can best be described as a commodity approach. Microsoft provides inexpensive, full-featured software that runs on inexpensive hardware. This is made possible because both the software and hardware are sold in very high volumes. In terms of hardware and software cost, it is relatively inexpensive for corporations to experiment with and deploy Wintel (Windows/Intel)-based server-side systems.

To become a commodity, demand for a specific product needs to be extremely high. Microsoft has established Windows as a commodity product by offering irresistible applications and development tools that run on top of the Windows operating system. This is demonstrated by the popularity of Microsoft's Office suite as well as development tools like Visual Basic. For all intents and purposes, Microsoft has won the battle for client-side domination. It seems logical that they would next pursue the server side.

Microsoft has worked relentlessly to evolve Windows NT into a viable server platform—an amazing feat given that Windows NT was only introduced onto the market in the summer of 1993. UNIX systems evolved for over a decade before they were considered viable. In addition to issues related to maturity, the viability of Windows NT as a commodity server platform also depends greatly on the availability and performance of commodity hardware.

Until recently, commodity hardware was not available for meeting server-side demands. This is one of the reasons that Windows NT was originally ported to the MIPS, DEC Alpha, and PowerPC hardware platforms, none of which ever attained real commodity status. In the past, non-Windows server-side systems required performance attainable only through the use of specialized noncommodity hardware. The combination of powerful commodity hardware like Intel's most recent incarnations as well as an ever-maturing Windows NT Server operating system results in a server-side approach that is hard to resist. This combination provides the core for Microsoft's vertical server-side strategy as demonstrated by the following layers in Microsoft's vertical offering:

- *Hardware.* Intel-based computers dominate the commodity market for desktop computer systems. This provides powerful and inexpensive hardware for hosting Microsoft's software.

- *Server operating system.* Microsoft Windows NT Server is a full-featured and secure operating system. By controlling the operating system, Microsoft also controls essential services such as process activation, the Windows system registry, file system, security mechanisms, and so on.

- *Middleware.* COM is bundled with every copy of Microsoft Windows. COM can be used by any developer writing for the Microsoft Windows platform.

- *Services.* Services bundled with Windows NT Server include Microsoft Transaction Server (MTS), Microsoft Message Queue Server (MSMQ), and Internet Information Service (IIS). The next version of Windows NT (Windows 2000) will also provide a directory service, Active Directory. In addition, Microsoft's COM+ will add several new features to COM, including a publish/subscribe event model, improved security, and load balancing.

- *Client/server development tools.* Microsoft offers sophisticated development tools, such as Visual Basic, Visual C++, and Visual J++, that include integrated support for COM and COM-based services such as MTS.

- *Clients.* The Windows operating system family is the predominant desktop client platform. Microsoft also provides the Internet Explorer Web browser for running Web-based client applications.

The layers just mentioned all map to one vertical platform—Microsoft Windows. Many people have wondered why Microsoft does not embrace industry standards such as CORBA. Given Microsoft's vertical strategy with COM, what does CORBA offer Microsoft in terms of competitive advantage? By controlling COM, Microsoft adds greatly to its control of the Wintel server-side marketplace, a high-volume lucrative arena that continues to look more inviting as Microsoft delivers advanced software integration tools like Microsoft Transaction Server.

CORBA: A Horizontal Strategy

The Object Management Group's charter includes the creation of specifications such as CORBA 2.2 that are aimed at creating interoperable and portable distributed object solutions across many platforms. This charter is a challenging and worthwhile goal that has, in fact, been realized by over 20 commercial vendors on a wide variety of server platforms. Some CORBA vendors support all of the primary UNIX platforms as well as Windows 98, Windows NT, and mainframe platforms like MVS. Support for CORBA on a wide range of platforms allows those platforms to cooperatively participate in a multiplatform distributed solution—a strategy far different from that of Microsoft.

Given that all of the CORBA vendors support the same OMG specifications, you might wonder how the CORBA vendors differentiate themselves in a highly competitive marketplace. There is no need for concern over the vendors' fates. There are many areas for differentiation, including the following:

- *Wide platform coverage.* Several CORBA vendors offer ORB products across a wide range of operating systems and programming languages. This approach most accentuates the horizontal platform strategy embodied by CORBA. These vendors are favored when a CORBA product is selected for a software system built on top of a diverse range of platforms.

- *Strategic platform support.* Several CORBA vendors target strategic programming languages such as Smalltalk, Ada, and COBOL. Other CORBA vendors target strategic operating systems such as VMS and MVS. CORBA support for these strategic environments allows applications developed in these environments to participate in a large CORBA-based distributed system.

- *Vendor-specific features.* Most CORBA vendors offer vendor-specific features in addition to their base specification products. This is similar to the way that relational database vendors differentiate themselves in the database arena. These vendors are favored when such features are required to implement a complex system.

- *Services.* The OMG has defined many services (e.g., transaction service, security service, etc.) that have yet to be implemented on many platforms and programming languages. Vendors that offer such services in addition to their base CORBA offerings are favored when such services are required.

One area where most CORBA vendors are weak is the area of development tools. Since most CORBA vendors are not in the development tools business, this area will probably continue to be a weakness of the CORBA approach. Since CORBA products are not commodity items, it is unlikely that a third-party solution can do much to improve on this situation.

The most important point to remember is that CORBA's greatest strength is its ability to bridge a wide range of operating systems and programming languages when creating a distributed system. In contrast to COM, CORBA has always been supported by multiple vendors on most major platforms. This broad support for a diverse range of environments is indicative of CORBA's horizontal strategy.

The Need for an Assessment Strategy

Based on the observations made so far in this chapter, you might already be starting to form an opinion as to which technology you want to use in your solution. One conclusion might be that if you can deploy on Windows, use COM; otherwise, use CORBA. This may indeed be the correct conclusion, but, then again, it may not. Consider the following facts. Most of the products being sold by CORBA vendors have been proven to work extremely well on Windows platforms. In addition, despite Microsoft's vertical focus on Windows, Microsoft provides a number of solutions that support interaction with legacy systems, databases, and so forth, on non-Windows platforms.

It is very easy to draw the wrong conclusion when selecting COM or CORBA. Even worse, a wrong decision can have a severe negative impact on the life of your system. An assessment strategy is needed because of the many factors that must be considered before committing to a middleware product. It would be convenient at this point in our discussion to simply assess the available technology and evaluate which products are superior. Such an approach is not practical for the following reasons:

- *Technology is changing at a rapid pace.* The results of such an assessment would be obsolete in a very short period of time.

- *System needs are situation-specific.* Software development is still a craft and, as such, relies on many customized features. An assessment could never take into account the individual factors likely to be faced in your particular situation.

For these reasons, we choose instead to present assessment criteria as well as a basic assessment strategy that can be used to evaluate your specific situation. An ideal assessment strategy has the following characteristics:

- *Flexible.* The assessment strategy allows for customization so that it can work in user-specific situations. Several iterations may be needed to ensure that the assessment considers all necessary factors.

- *Objective.* The assessment strategy avoids any bias toward one technology or the other.

- *Systematic.* The assessment strategy consists of a well-defined set of steps to be followed.

- *Deterministic.* An assessment provides a clear and definitive result.

Demonstrating that your assessment is flexible, objective, systematic, and deterministic will aid in enlisting support from all decisionmakers. This is not an easy task, but it is well worth the effort given the importance of choosing the right middleware product for your server-side system. Critical server-side systems have a much longer lifetime than their client-side counterparts. Making the right choices when it comes to COM and CORBA will likely have a long-term impact on your server-side environment.

Assessment Criteria

In many situations, choosing between COM and CORBA requires consideration of many factors. In this section, we will present general criteria that apply to a wide range of situations. It is to be expected that these general criteria will not meet all of your specific needs. You will need to add and remove criteria in order to establish criteria that make sense given your specific situation. The assessment criteria presented in this section are organized into three categories: platform, services, and intangibles. In all cases, the criteria are stated in an implementation-independent manner. As such, they can be used as objective standards of judgment for determining when to use COM or CORBA in your specific situation.

Platform Criteria

The following criteria should be considered when selecting programming language and operating system platforms:

- *Legacy system support.* In most situations, newly developed software needs to interact with various legacy systems. This criterion is used to determine whether adequate legacy system support exists when using COM or CORBA.

- *Operating system support.* New development will be targeted at one or more operating system platforms. This criterion is used to determine whether COM or CORBA is adequately supported on the target operating systems.

- *Programming language support.* New development will occur using one or more programming languages. This criterion is used to determine whether COM or CORBA is adequately supported in the target programming languages.

- *Availability of development tools.* Highly interactive development tools can greatly increase productivity in the area of distributed system programming. This criterion is used to determine whether adequate development tools exist when using COM or CORBA.

Essential Services

Services provide ready-made plumbing so that developers can focus on business logic rather than on core infrastructure. There are many services that may be of interest in your specific situation. For this discussion, we will focus on transactions, security, messaging, and system management. These particular services require support that is built into the middleware engine; it is extremely difficult to build customized infrastructure for these areas. For this reason, we will focus on the following service-related criteria:

- *Distributed transaction support.* Distributed transactions are transactions that occur across multiple distributed resources. Coordinating a transaction across multiple resources requires a two-phase commit protocol that is managed by a distributed transaction manager. This criterion is used to determine whether COM or CORBA can be used with an appropriate distributed transaction manager.

- *Security and privacy.* Security requires user authentication and authorization. Privacy requires encryption of transmitted data. This criterion is used to determine whether adequate levels of authentication, authorization, and encryption are achievable using COM or CORBA.

- *Messaging support.* Messaging allows for an asynchronous programming model as opposed to the typical request-reply model. There are many types of applications that require messaging. An example is an application in which the client and server are required to run at different times. This criterion is used to determine whether messaging semantics can be used with COM or CORBA.

- *Distributed object management.* High-performance server-side systems require infrastructure for complex application management. Before distributed objects, this realm was dominated by transaction-processing monitors such as BEA's TUXEDO, NCR's TOP END, and IBM's CICS. This criterion is used to determine whether an adequate degree of object system management is provided with COM or CORBA.

Intangibles

The criteria presented next usually factor into the decision-making process. The criteria are often not clear and are sometimes irrational. Because the following criteria lack clarity, we refer to them as *intangibles*:

- *Vendor perception.* A customer's perception of a vendor is based on the vendor's reputation and any previous experiences with the vendor. This criterion is used to ensure that the current perception of a COM or CORBA vendor supports a long-term relationship with that vendor.

- *Vendor commitment and viability.* In today's market, vendors often change direction quickly or, in the case of severe financial difficulty, disappear completely. Some vendors have a reputation for excellent customer support, while others do not. This criterion is used to ensure that the vendor (or a viable alternative) will continue to support its customers' COM or CORBA needs over the long term.

- *Vendor lock-in.* Some vendors hold exclusive rights to specific software products. This criterion is used to determine whether locking into a single COM or CORBA vendor's products is tolerable.

- *Availability of product.* The availability of products can range from free evaluations to expensive up-front commitment. This criterion is used to determine whether the availability of selected COM or CORBA products is adequate.

- *Availability of development staff.* The software industry continues to be plagued by a shortage of qualified software developers. This criterion is used to determine whether developers with sufficient COM or CORBA expertise can be obtained for present and future development and maintenance.

- *Product cost.* Cost always factors into acceptance of a particular software product. Given the importance of server-side systems, product cost should not factor in as much as it often does. This criterion is used to determine whether the cost of selected COM or CORBA products is acceptable.

An Assessment Strategy

At some point, you will need to build a convincing case for using either COM or CORBA in your server-side software system. One way to defend a decision is to show that an objective assessment was completed that validates your choices. In this section, we will present a strategy for objectively assessing the appropriateness of COM or CORBA for a specific software domain.

Prerequisites

Before the assessment can begin, several prerequisites need to be completed. The task of completing the prerequisites described next is by no means trivial. There is no universal approach for accomplishing these prerequisites because such an endeavor tends to be situation-specific.

- *Identify an enterprise domain.* We described the need to partition the enterprise into units that we refer to as domains in Partitioning the Enterprise on page 107.

- *Identify legacy systems and their platforms.* Once a domain has been identified, the legacy systems associated with that domain must be identified.

- *Identify platforms for new development.* Choosing a platform for new development is often dependent on the strategic direction of the entire enterprise. The platforms used for new development do not necessarily need to include the platforms that currently support legacy systems. (We will discuss this in more detail in Selecting Platforms for New Development on page 124.)

Recording the Assessment History

The assessment strategy presented in this section is iterative. While iterating, it may become necessary to change the parameters used for evaluation. To properly defend the assessment, a historical record should be maintained that keeps track of the following:

- *Platform changes.* During the assessment, it may be decided that a different target platform is required. Such platform changes and the rationale for making those changes should be recorded.

- *Candidate disqualifications.* The reasons for disqualifying a candidate should be recorded. This aids in supporting the final candidate that is chosen. It also helps to avoid redundant review of the same candidate.

- *Changes in criteria.* The criteria may need to be relaxed to support specific candidates or strengthened to reduce the number of candidates. Such a change can result in the need to review all possible candidates based on the new criteria.

Rating the Criteria

Each criterion should be rated from 1 to 5 as shown in Table 4-1.

Table 4-1. Rating a Criterion

Rating	Name	Description
1	Disqualify	The product cannot support this criterion.
2	Poor	The product poorly supports this criterion.
3	OK	The product supports this criterion.
4	Good	The product has good support for this criterion.
5	Desirable	The product is desirable because of its excellent support for this criterion.

Assessment Steps

The assessment steps are as follows:

1. *Identify the criteria.* To maintain objectiveness in your assessment, you must ensure the objectiveness of any criteria that you add to those that were identified earlier in this chapter (see Assessment Criteria on page 114).

2. *Identify COM/CORBA product candidates.* You should use the criteria identified in step 1 as general guidelines for selecting candidates to be evaluated.

3. *Assess the candidates.* For each candidate, assign a rating between 1 and 5 for each criterion of the candidate being evaluated. If a rating of 1 is made, disqualify the candidate. If all candidates are disqualified, return to step 1 and adjust the assessment criteria.

4. *Weight the criteria.* Weight each criterion based on its importance. Multiply the weight by each rating above 2. Do not multiply the weight by the rating if the rating is less than or equal to 2.

5. *Select the optimal candidate.* The simplest approach is to add up the ratings for each candidate and select the candidate with the highest overall rating.

Selecting the optimal candidate is an area in which you might want to customize your approach. For example, you might want to disqualify a candidate that receives a rating of 2 (Poor) for more than a preset number of criteria (e.g., 3 or more).

As we indicated earlier (in The Need for an Assessment Strategy on page 113), our assessment strategy should be flexible, objective, systematic, and deterministic. The assessment strategy presented here is *flexible* in that it allows the user to adjust the criteria to be used for assessment. The assessment strategy is *objective* since it mandates that all criteria used in an assessment must be objective. The assessment strategy is *systematic* and *deterministic* in that the steps listed herein can be followed systematically to determine the optimal choice.

An Assessment Example

An example of an assessment is shown in Table 4-2. Note that the data presented is artificial and has been fabricated for example purposes only.

In the assessment, the rating for each criterion is calculated by multiplying the weight by the actual rating (which is shown in parentheses) unless the rating is less than or equal to 2. As indicated in Table 4-2, the optimal choice in this example would be the CORBA product from vendor A. If you look closely at the results, you will notice that legacy system support was the greatest determining factor. Note that this should not bias your opinion of COM-related legacy support. As we shall see in the next chapter, there are many COM-related technologies that provide legacy system support.

COM and CORBA in Your Enterprise Solution

In this chapter, we have described a technology-independent assessment strategy for determining when COM or CORBA should be used in a specific server-side domain. This strategy can be used to assess your particular situation. Furthermore, it can be used to show that your decision is objective and that it was reached in a systematic manner. This is critical when garnering support for such a crucial decision.

Table 4-2. *Assessment Example*

Criterion	Weight (1–5)	COM	CORBA (Vendor A)	CORBA (Vendor B)
Platform:				
Legacy system support	5	2 (2)	20 (4)	1 (1)
Operating system support	3	9 (3)	9 (3)	9 (3)
Programming language support	3	9 (3)	12 (4)	9 (3)
Availability of development tools	2	10 (5)	6 (3)	6 (3)
Essential Services:				
Transaction support	5	20 (4)	20 (4)	1 (1)
Security and privacy	2	8 (4)	8 (4)	1 (1)
Messaging support	1	4 (4)	3 (3)	4 (4)
Distributed object management	1	2 (2)	2 (2)	2 (2)
Intangibles:				
Vendor perception	1	4 (4)	3 (3)	2 (2)
Vendor commitment and viability	2	8 (4)	6 (3)	6 (3)
Vendor lock-in	1	2 (2)	3 (3)	3 (3)
Availability of product	1	3 (3)	3 (3)	3 (3)
Availability of development staff	3	12 (4)	2 (2)	6 (2)
Cost	1	4 (4)	3 (3)	3 (3)
Overall Rating		**97**	**100**	**Disqualified**

Now that we have established sound assessment criteria, we possess a coherent roadmap for assessing COM- and CORBA-related technology. In the next chapter, we will explore COM and CORBA support for the platform criteria identified in this chapter. In Chapters 6 and 7, we will explore the assessment criteria related to services as well as the intangibles that we have identified. After completing these chapters, you will possess the foundation that you need to objectively assess COM and CORBA for your enterprise solution.

Chapter 5

The Server Platform

Topics Covered in This Chapter

- Review of the Platform Criteria
- Legacy System Support
- The Development Platform
- Availability of Development Tools

In examining the evolution of server-side systems, one cannot help but notice that the pace of change is fairly slow. Server-side systems must be highly reliable, performant, and scalable. The ability to meet all of these requirements depends greatly on the maturity of the server platform—hence, the slow rate of change that usually occurs in favor of mature computing platforms. Nowhere is this more evident than in the continued use of mainframes in corporations throughout the world; mainframes have been used to manage critical enterprise assets for decades. In recent years, UNIX-based systems have emerged that also meet the stringent requirements of the server side. Over the next few years, Microsoft intends to provide the software infrastructure that is needed to propel Windows NT into the demanding server arena as well.

In this chapter, we will focus our attention on COM- and CORBA-based technology for the server platform. Platform considerations extend well beyond simply choosing the most appropriate hardware, operating system, and programming language. One must also consider the legacy systems currently used in a specific enterprise environment since those systems can have a major impact on future server platform directions. In practically every large system, legacy support is a pivotal issue. We'll first examine general approaches for supporting legacy systems as well as several COM- and CORBA-related technologies for interfacing with legacy systems. We'll then look at the development environments for creating COM and CORBA applications on various server platforms.

Review of the Platform Criteria

In Chapter 4, we identified the following platform criteria to be evaluated in assessing the use of COM and CORBA in a specific server-side domain:

- Legacy system support

- Operating system support

- Programming language support

- Availability of development tools

Legacy system support is a major factor in most large development efforts. In this chapter, we will focus on a range of legacy system issues. We'll first identify specific legacy systems (e.g., CICS, DB2, TUXEDO, etc.) that pervade major enterprise systems. We'll then describe general approaches for interfacing with legacy systems when developing new server-side applications. We will conclude the discussion of legacy system support by describing specific approaches for using COM and CORBA with legacy systems.

Operating system and programming language support in COM and CORBA are dependent on the development and deployment platforms that are offered by product vendors. In this chapter, we will examine development platforms that are currently available for COM and CORBA. We will compare COM and CORBA by identifying the advantages and disadvantages of using COM and CORBA with specific operating systems and programming languages.

The availability of powerful development tools (e.g., Microsoft's Visual C++) can greatly enhance productivity when we are building complex server-side systems. In this chapter, we will discuss development tools that are currently available to aid in COM and CORBA server-side development.

Legacy System Support

When new software systems are being implemented, the importance of legacy support can range from extremely critical to totally insignificant. In large enterprise systems, legacy support is almost always a critical requirement. This is due to the large investment in information technology assets that corporations make over a long period of time. There are several approaches for interfacing with legacy systems when creating new applications. In this section, we will examine these approaches and how they can be applied in creating COM- and CORBA-based systems.

General Approaches for Supporting Legacy Systems

The need to support legacy systems is not specific to COM- and CORBA-related software development efforts. Software developers have always had to grapple with legacy system interactions. Various approaches for supporting legacy systems have been devised as client/server systems have evolved from simple 2-tier systems to more complex 3-tier and *N*-tier systems. Before discussing these approaches, we need to examine some of the more significant legacy systems that currently exist.

Identifying Significant Legacy Systems

While there are an infinite number of proprietary legacy systems to be considered in the world at large, there exists a smaller subset of strategic legacy products that dominate today's major enterprise systems. A small number of legacy platforms support the dominant legacy products because of the reliability, performance, scalability, and maturity exhibited by such platforms. These platforms include

- *IBM's S/390 running OS/390 (MVS).* This is IBM's dominant mainframe product.

- *IBM's AS/400 running OS/400.* This is IBM's midsize product for situations where full mainframe functionality is not required.

- *Compaq/Digital's Vax and Alpha running OpenVMS.* Compaq eventually hopes to integrate the best features of OpenVMS into Windows NT; however, there are currently more than 400,000 users of OpenVMS.

- *High-end servers from Sun, Hewlett-Packard, IBM, and Compaq/Digital running various flavors of UNIX.*

Critical legacy products that run on the preceding platforms include

- *Data storage systems.* Relational database management systems (RDBMSs) are used to store a significant amount of legacy data. There are many proven approaches for accessing relational databases (e.g., ODBC, embedded SQL, etc.). Despite the popularity of RDBMSs, it is widely acknowledged that an even greater amount of critical enterprise data continues to be stored in nonrelational systems such as MVS VSAM files, OS/400 files, and IMS/DB (IMS/DB is IBM's venerable hierarchical DBMS). Accessing such nonrelational data poses many legacy integration risks and challenges.

- *Transaction monitors.* Transaction monitors tend to do far more than coordinate and monitor transactions across multiple data resources. They also enhance the performance, reliability, and scalability of server-side systems. Transaction monitors achieve these enhancements by establishing a framework for creating server-side applications. A transaction monitor can reliably and efficiently manage the resources needed by applications that conform to the transaction monitor's rules. Given this description, transaction monitors might more aptly be called *application managers.* On the mainframe, IBM's CICS and IMS/TM are the predominant transaction monitors (IMS/TM is actually a message-based transaction manager). On UNIX systems, BEA's TUXEDO, BEA's TOP END, and IBM's Encina have all captured parts of the transaction monitor market.

- *Messaging systems.* While most communication that occurs between client/server applications is synchronous (i.e., a request blocks until a reply is received), some applications require asynchronous communication. The predominant messaging product for managing asynchronous communication between applications is IBM's MQSeries product. MQSeries has been ported to all major server platforms.

The group of products that we have identified is by no means exhaustive; however, the legacy products identified here are pervasive on legacy platforms and are supported by a wide range of COM and CORBA vendors. Before describing the approaches for interacting with these legacy systems, we need to select the platforms on which new development will occur.

Selecting Platforms for New Development

In selecting a development platform, it is critical to focus on the needs of the system being developed and not on legacy system constraints. There are many different ways to interact with legacy systems; it is therefore unwise to let legacy interaction strategies drive the platform selection for new development. Instead, you should focus on issues such as

- *Development and deployment support.* Whenever possible, choose platforms that enhance both development and deployment. Note that, in some situations, it is possible to develop on one platform and deploy on another. For example, it may be desirable to develop a Java-based product under Windows and deploy the product on a UNIX-based server. In such a case, a number of Windows-based Java development tools can be used to create a product that would later be deployed on a powerful UNIX-based server.

- *Platform reliability, performance, and scalability.* These qualities need to be present in any robust server-side system. It is possible that a server platform does not currently meet these requirements but that it will meet such requirements when the newly developed system is deployed. This is indicative of an early-adopter approach that is typically used to gain competitive advantage at some point in the future.

- *Platform viability.* As stated earlier, the pace of change with regard to server-side systems is fairly slow. It should be rather easy to determine whether the platform will remain viable for the perceived lifetime of the newly developed system.

- *Migration path to future strategic platforms.* Always keep in mind that the platform chosen today is likely to be a future generation's legacy problem. If it is known that an alternate platform will need to be supported in the future, it may be wise to map out and understand the migration path early on.

The criteria just stated are fairly loose. The main point is that there are many ways to interact with legacy systems. Remember that it is almost always better to let proper platform selection drive the legacy interaction approach rather than the other way around. Now that we have discussed development platform selection, we are ready to take a look at several approaches for interacting with legacy systems from our server-side applications. These approaches focus on making legacy artifacts (e.g., CICS and IMS applications) available in a distributed object environment.

Wrapper Approach

Wrappers are often presented as a strategy for evolving legacy systems. In a wrapper approach, a legacy artifact is wrapped with a general interaction mechanism such as a distributed object implemented in COM or CORBA. Newly developed clients can then invoke the distributed object rather than having to directly manipulate the legacy artifact. The distributed object can be extended, and the legacy artifact can eventually be replaced without affecting the clients as long as the distributed object's interface is not changed. An example of a distributed object wrapper approach is shown in Figure 5-1. In the example, three clients interact with two distributed objects that are used to wrap two MVS/CICS applications. The clients are not aware that the distributed object functionality is implemented using the CICS applications.

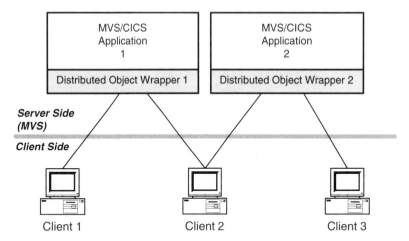

Figure 5-1. *A distributed object wrapper approach.*

Wrappers are often presented as the best approach for evolving legacy systems. If evolving legacy systems signifies new development of business logic on the legacy platform, wrappers are an excellent choice. The wrappers can be extended and can eventually replace legacy artifacts such as CICS COBOL programs with more extensible and maintainable distributed objects. A wrapper approach is therefore appropriate when new development is intended for a legacy platform that also supports the legacy artifact being wrapped.

At this point, you might be tempted to begin wrapping all of your legacy artifacts so that you can use them as distributed objects. Such an approach might work, but it would be inappropriate when the development platform and legacy platform are different. It also requires an employee base that is highly skilled in development on the legacy platform.

Gateway Approach

In many situations, the platform selected for new development is different from the legacy platform. Rather than creating a distributed object wrapper on the legacy platform, it is often more advantageous to create a distributed object gateway on the development platform and use some other strategy to communicate with the legacy artifact. An example of a distributed object gateway approach is shown in Figure 5-2. In the example, three clients interact with two distributed objects that are used as gateways to two MVS/CICS applica-

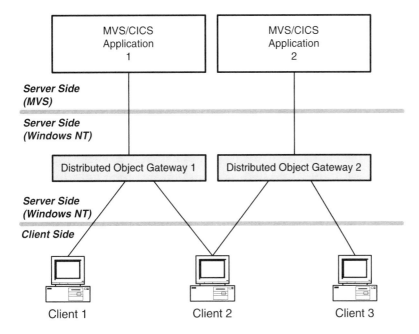

Figure 5-2. A distributed object gateway approach.

tions. The clients are not aware that the distributed object functionality is implemented using the CICS applications.

The advantages of using a gateway approach as opposed to a wrapper approach are significant and include the following:

- *Minimal impact on legacy platform.* No additional software needs to be installed on the legacy platform. The distributed object gateways rely on well-defined legacy protocols or third-party tools to interface with the legacy artifacts.

- *Proper use of development staff expertise.* Development on the legacy platform is minimized. This is highly desirable since the skill set of the development staff will most likely be geared toward the primary development platform rather than toward the legacy platform.

- *Proper leverage of development platform.* The development platform was probably selected because of its suitability for distributed object development. It should therefore be a desirable platform for creating the distributed object gateways.

- *Better distribution of system processing.* The gateway can handle all translation and processing that would otherwise need to occur in the client and legacy platform. This can significantly reduce the workload on the client and legacy systems.

The primary disadvantage of the gateway approach is the presence of an extra network indirection when navigating between the client and the legacy platform. In most cases, processing time on the legacy platform will be several orders of magnitude greater than the network delay caused by the indirection, thereby diminishing the effect of the network delay. In the rare event that the performance impact of the indirection is unacceptable, you may have to revert to a wrapper approach or even change your primary development environment. Another disadvantage is the additional point of failure introduced by the gateway tier. Failure of the gateway obviously prevents gateway clients from reaching legacy platform servers.

In most cases, the advantages of the gateway approach far outweigh the disadvantages just noted. It is therefore generally recommended that the gateway approach be used when the development platform differs from the legacy platform.

Legacy Support When Using COM

The greatest strength of COM is its maturity on the Microsoft Windows platform. Microsoft's vertical focus on Windows has resulted in a mature component-based infrastructure. Because of the vertical focus, Microsoft and several partners have also been able to establish excellent connectivity products from Windows to legacy platforms such as MVS and OS/400. The combination of a mature component infrastructure and excellent connectivity makes COM/Windows an excellent candidate for a distributed object gateway to legacy systems.

In contrast to its strength as a gateway server, COM/Windows is not well suited for a wrapper approach. The greatest weakness of COM has been Microsoft's inability (or lack of desire) to establish COM on non-Windows platforms. COM continues to appear on more non-Windows platforms, but it continues to lack the development tools and advanced services available on the Windows platform. Still, the presence of base COM services on non-Windows platforms does allow for a basic wrapper approach.

COM and the Wrapper Approach

In early 1998, Microsoft announced an initiative to make COM available on all major non-Windows platforms. To meet this goal, Microsoft licensed COM to a variety of vendors, including Software AG, Hewlett-Packard, Compaq/Digital, Silicon Graphics, and Siemens Nixdorf. The availability of COM on all major platforms will eventually allow COM wrappers to be used in almost any environment. Despite the future availability of COM, CORBA continues to be the more proven cross-platform distributed object technology since it is already supported by a multitude of vendors on all major platforms.

Of all the COM licensees, Software AG has been the most aggressive vendor to port COM to multiple platforms. Software AG provides DCOM support on OS/390, Sun Solaris, Digital UNIX, AIX, and Linux. Of particular interest is Software AG's support for MVS legacy systems in its EntireX product suite. The EntireX Developer's Kit for MVS includes a port of DCOM to OS/390 UNIX System Services[*] as well as a legacy application integration product called *EntireX Broker*.

Software AG's EntireX Broker simplifies communication with a variety of legacy artifacts, such as CICS applications, IMS applications, and MQSeries. Also included in the EntireX Developer's Kit is a COM wrapper for the EntireX Broker. Through the COM wrapper, EntireX allows COM clients to access a wide range of MVS legacy artifacts.

COM and the Gateway Approach

Any platform that supports COM can be used as a COM gateway to legacy systems. Of greater interest is COM-related technology that can be used to connect a gateway platform with strategic legacy platforms. Microsoft has focused considerable effort on connectivity from Windows NT to the MVS and AS/400 platforms.

To position Windows NT as a viable enterprise server platform, Microsoft quickly realized that it needed to provide connectivity solutions for bridging Windows NT and strategic legacy platforms. To meet this need, Microsoft created the SNA Server product. SNA Server provides a number of tools that provide legacy platform connectivity. This connectivity allows enterprises to more gradually migrate their critical IT assets from well-established legacy plat-

---

[*]OS/390 UNIX System Services was formerly known as *OpenEdition* and adds UNIX capabilities to the MVS core in OS/390.

forms to Windows NT Server. As Windows NT Server improves in terms of reliability, performance, and scalability, assets can be migrated from expensive legacy systems to inexpensive Windows-based systems.

Recall that we identified three groups of legacy products that pervade most large enterprise systems. These legacy product groups are

- *Data storage systems.* Legacy artifacts include relational DBMSs, IBM's IMS/DB, VSAM flat files, and OS/400 flat files.

- *Transaction monitors.* Legacy products include IBM's CICS and IBM's IMS/TM.

- *Messaging systems.* Legacy products include IBM's MQSeries.

Microsoft has created a number of COM-based technologies that can be used to interact with all of the legacy products just mentioned. In the remainder of this section, we will explore specific COM technologies that are used to access key legacy systems.

Using COM to Access Legacy Data

Accessing legacy data requires connectivity to a wide range of data storage systems. OLE DB is Microsoft's strategic COM data access technology for accessing both relational and nonrelational data sources. To use OLE DB, an OLE DB provider is needed for each specific data source. Microsoft provides a generic OLE DB provider that encapsulates ODBC, thereby allowing OLE DB to be used with existing ODBC data sources.

Because the OLE DB interface is low-level and fairly complex, Microsoft also provides ADO (ActiveX Data Objects), a more usable COM client interface for accessing OLE DB data sources. Although ADO adds a layer on top of OLE DB, its simplicity outweighs the overhead of an extra layer in most situations. The combination of ADO, OLE DB, and ODBC provides a simple way for COM clients to access most major relational databases.

In addition to relational data, a substantial amount of legacy data exists in nonrelational data sources such as VSAM and OS/400 flat files. To access this nonrelational data from Windows NT, Microsoft offers an OLE DB provider for AS/400 and VSAM in its SNA Server product. The combination of ADO and SNA Server provides a simple way for COM clients to access VSAM and OS/400 flat files on the MVS and AS/400 platforms.

COM Integration with CICS and IMS

CICS and IMS are the transaction-processing workhorses of the mainframe environment. A CICS/IMS application is often referred to as a *transaction program* (TP). A CICS/IMS TP provides access to a database (e.g., IMS, DB2, etc.) and sometimes implements business logic as well. Communication with a mainframe TP is accomplished using the LU6.2 protocol (the de facto mainframe standard for distributed transaction processing) and the APPC API (a standard communication API used by CICS/IMS TPs).

Microsoft's COM Transaction Integrator (COMTI) is a tool used to integrate CICS and IMS TPs into a Windows NT Server environment. Microsoft includes COMTI in its SNA Server product. SNA Server also supports the LU6.2 protocol and APPC API previously described. COMTI consists of the following parts:

- *Management Console.*[*] COMTI includes a Management Console snap-in for administration.

- *Component Builder.* The COMTI Component Builder uses COBOL copybooks to generate Microsoft Transaction Server (MTS) components that encapsulate existing CICS and IMS TPs. Because the CICS and IMS TPs are encapsulated in MTS components, they can take part in distributed transactions with other MTS components.[†]

- *Runtime Proxy.* The COMTI Runtime Proxy manages communication at runtime between the COMTI component on the Windows NT Server and the corresponding CICS/IMS TP on the mainframe. SNA Server provides the LU6.2 connection between the Runtime Proxy and the mainframe.

COMTI offers the following significant advantages when used with Windows NT. First, CICS programs can be intermingled with MTS objects in a fully distributed transactional environment. Second, developers can manipulate legacy CICS and IMS applications as COM objects rather than having to use low-level protocols such as LU6.2 and APPC. This allows developers to use advanced COM-based development tools when working with arcane legacy applications.

---

[*]The Microsoft Management Console is a utility used to monitor and administrate a wide range of Windows NT services such as IIS, MTS, MSMQ, COMTI, and so forth.

[†]At the time of this writing, the current version of COMTI does not support IMS transactions. IMS transaction support will be added in a future release.

COM Integration with IBM's MQSeries

IBM's MQSeries is the predominant messaging system on today's legacy platforms. In late 1997, Microsoft introduced its own messaging system, Microsoft Message Queue Server (MSMQ). Given the success of IBM's MQSeries product line, it is not surprising that MSMQ and MQSeries offer much the same functionality. The similarity in products has been exploited to create a commercial bridging product.

Level 8 Systems, a Microsoft partner, has released FalconMQ Bridge, a product that offers seamless, wire-level interoperability between MSMQ and MQSeries. Seamless interoperability is accomplished by mapping the MQSeries API to the MSMQ API. FalconMQ Bridge allows MSMQ applications to seamlessly use MQSeries Queue Managers. In other words, Windows developers can use the MSMQ API and associated COM interfaces when developing systems that require connectivity to MQSeries on legacy platforms.

Summary of COM-Related Legacy Support

In this section, we have discussed a number of COM-related technologies used to achieve connectivity between the Windows NT platform and several legacy platforms. To recap the discussion, these technologies are summarized in Table 5-1.

Table 5-1. COM-Related Legacy Support on Windows NT

Client Interface	Connectivity Approach	Legacy Artifact
ADO	OLE DB, ODBC/DRDA, SNA Server	DB2 on MVS
ADO	OLE DB provider for AS/400 and VSAM, SNA Server	VSAM files on MVS
ADO	OLE DB provider for AS/400 and VSAM, SNA Server	OS/400 flat files on AS/400
COM automation interface	COM Transaction Integrator, SNA Server	CICS TP on MVS
COM automation interface	COM Transaction Integrator, SNA Server	IMS TP on MVS
MSMQ COM interface	FalconMQ Bridge, Level 8 Systems	MQSeries application

The results provided in Table 5-1 demonstrate that the Windows NT platform offers a diverse range of legacy support. It should also be noted that none of the connectivity approaches are intrusive with regard to the legacy platforms. This may be an important factor, depending on the accessibility of legacy platforms in your enterprise solution.

Legacy Support When Using CORBA

The greatest strength of CORBA is its proven track record on a wide range of established server platforms. The OMG envisions a heterogeneous environment consisting of many diverse platforms unified by CORBA middleware. In contrast, Microsoft envisions a COM-oriented Windows-centric environment that provides connectivity to legacy systems. Because CORBA focuses on multiple platforms as opposed to a single platform, CORBA products can be used to wrap a variety of legacy systems.

CORBA and the Wrapper Approach

The CORBA 1.0 specification did not adequately address the issue of interoperability between different ORB products. To remedy this problem, the General Inter-ORB Protocol (GIOP) was introduced in the CORBA 2.0 specification. GIOP is a general protocol in that it can be implemented on any reliable transport. Because of the popularity of the Internet and TCP/IP, a specific version of GIOP over TCP/IP was created. It is the Internet Inter-ORB Protocol (IIOP). To encourage the use of IIOP, the OMG currently mandates that vendors must support IIOP in order to claim compliance with CORBA interoperability as defined in Chapters 10–14 of the CORBA 2.2 specification.

Forcing all compliant vendors to support IIOP has greatly enhanced the value of CORBA in the marketplace. All of the major CORBA products now support IIOP, and it is now possible to cross vendor boundaries in a distributed environment. The interoperability provided by IIOP is the key to CORBA's ability to wrap legacy systems. Legacy artifacts can be wrapped by IIOP-compliant CORBA products. IIOP-compliant clients can then access those legacy artifacts from practically any operating system and programming language.

Several CORBA products have emerged that provide direct support for legacy systems. These products include

- *Iona's Orbix for MVS.* Iona has adapted its popular CORBA product for MVS. Orbix for MVS supports legacy artifacts in several ways. Orbix for MVS allows CORBA server objects to be created using either C++ or COBOL. Orbix for MVS also comes with CICS and IMS adaptors that accelerate the development of Orbix wrappers for CICS and IMS transaction programs.

- *Inprise's VisiBroker ITS.* Inprise provides a CORBA-based transaction service, the Integrated Transaction Service (ITS). Inprise also offers an optional extension to VisiBroker ITS, ITS TransFuse, that allows transactions managed under ITS to coordinate with resources managed under IBM's CICS, IMS/TM, and MQSeries as well as BEA's TUXEDO.

- *BEA Systems' M3.* BEA is the maker of TUXEDO, the predominant UNIX-based transaction monitor. M3 is a CORBA offering that includes support for TUXEDO and MessageQ. In addition, BEA also plans to add a framework to M3 that will provide connectivity to CICS and IMS transaction programs.

- *IBM's Component Broker.* Given IBM's dominance on the mainframe, it makes sense that IBM offers a CORBA product that supports a wide range of mainframe-related legacy products. In Component Broker, IBM plans to offer adaptors to many types of legacy artifacts, including adaptors for CICS, IMS, and MQSeries.

The products just described represent a mere sampling of CORBA products that can be used to wrap legacy artifacts. The important point is that almost any CORBA-enabled client (regardless of vendor) can communicate using IIOP with legacy artifacts that are wrapped using such products.

CORBA and the Gateway Approach

CORBA's wide platform availability also allows it to be used as a gateway to legacy systems. In a gateway approach, a CORBA object is created on some middle-tier platform. The CORBA object then communicates with an application on some legacy platform. Clients interact with the legacy artifact via the gateway CORBA object. This is in contrast to a wrapper approach, where clients interact with CORBA object wrappers that coexist with corresponding legacy artifacts on the same legacy platform.

Although wrapping seems like a logical approach when using CORBA, it may not necessarily be the best approach. Consider a scenario where a company plans to phase out MVS in favor of UNIX over a period of time. There is little reason to expend effort creating CORBA wrapper objects under MVS. Instead, it is better to create CORBA objects on the UNIX platform and use the most efficient strategy possible to communicate between the UNIX-based CORBA objects and the MVS legacy applications.

Creating wrappers on legacy platforms can be an expensive proposition. First, a CORBA ORB must be purchased and installed on the legacy platform. Next, developers of the wrappers must be trained and have access to the legacy platform. Finally, the CORBA object wrappers must be maintained on the legacy platform.

With CORBA, a gateway approach generally allows for greater flexibility and is less expensive than a wrapper approach. In a gateway approach, there is no need to install a CORBA product on the legacy platform. Instead, CORBA is used only to create the gateway objects on the middle-tier platform. Communication between the middle-tier CORBA objects and the legacy applications can be accomplished using legacy connectivity products that are not even CORBA-related. Vendors that sell such legacy connectivity products include NetDynamics, Active Software, I-Kinetics, and Neon Systems. Such products may be substantially less intrusive than a CORBA wrapper approach, thereby requiring far less developer expertise and maintenance costs.

Summary of CORBA-Related Legacy Support

CORBA has proven itself on all major server platforms. Because of its wide platform support, CORBA can effectively be used to wrap legacy systems on a wide range of legacy platforms. In many situations, however, wrappers are not the best approach. For example, the cost of developing and deploying CORBA wrapper objects on a mainframe system such as MVS might be prohibitive. In such situations, CORBA should be used only as a gateway to legacy platforms. Non-CORBA products that are more cost-effective can then be used to achieve connectivity between the CORBA gateway objects and legacy systems. The burden of deciding when to use wrappers and when to use gateways is situation-specific. The good news is that because of CORBA's maturity as a cross-platform solution, many choices are available to suit a variety of needs.

The Development Platform

COM and CORBA are supported to some extent on virtually all major server platforms. Because CORBA is more mature and is supported by more vendors, it tends to offer better language support and enhanced services on a broader range of platforms than does COM. As expected, the one exception to this claim is Microsoft Windows, where COM offers many advantages over its CORBA counterparts. This is especially true with regard to development tools. In this section, we will discuss development issues related to operating systems and programming languages. (We will focus on development tools in Availability of Development Tools on page 140.)

COM Development Platforms

In the COM world, there are two distinct development domains. The first domain consists strictly of Windows-based platforms where COM is supported in a wide variety of ways. The other domain consists of non-Windows platforms where support for COM is extremely limited. Before discussing these limitations, we will first describe COM support under Windows. On the Windows platform, most COM server-side development is accomplished using Microsoft's C++, Java, and Visual Basic compilers.

COM/Windows/C++ Development Platform

COM and C++ have been related since COM's inception. In fact, the binary standard for calling COM object methods is actually based on the virtual function table (vtable) layout that is created when compiling C++ classes. Because of this kinship, all functionality of COM is generally accessible from C++ applications. To ease the use of COM with C++, Microsoft has begun to introduce a number of nonstandard additions to its Visual C++ compiler. One of the most significant additions is the `#import` directive as illustrated here:

```
// Some C++ file ...
#import "c:\tlb\SomeComObject.tlb"
```

Importing a type library in such a manner automatically creates COM object definitions that can be used to manipulate the corresponding COM object. In addition to `#import`, the Visual C++ compiler also supports several nonstandard functions, such as `__declspec()` and `__uuidof()`, that allow interface ids to be more easily stored and accessed within the context of a COM/C++ application. The following code, which is generated by the `#import` directive, uses `__declspec()` and `__uuidof()` to create a smart pointer type definition:

```
// SomeComObject.tlh (a header file generated using #import)
struct __declspec(uuid("ef9fb98c-cfd8-11d1-bb42-00207812e629"))
    ISomeComObject;

_COM_SMARTPTR_TYPEDEF(ISomeComObject, __uuidof(ISomeComObject));
```

In the preceding example, the __declspec() function is used to associate the appropriate uuid with ISomeComObject. The uuid is then retrieved using the __uuidof() function when creating the smart pointer type definition. While features such as #import and __uuidof() simplify COM development, it is important to note that they are nonstandard and will not work when using a C++ compiler other than Visual C++.

COM/Windows/Java Development Platform

To make Java work within the COM framework under Windows, Microsoft provides a COM-aware Java Virtual Machine (JVM). Microsoft also provides a COM-aware Java compiler that is required when using COM in Java applications. This COM-aware Java compiler recognizes COM directives within Java code as shown here:

```
import com.ms.com.IUnknown;

/** @com.interface(iid=EF9FB98C-CFD8-11D1-BB42-00207812E629,
                 thread=AUTO, type=DUAL) */
public interface ISomeComObject extends IUnknown
{ ...
}
```

In the preceding example, the @com.interface() directive ties the ISomeComObject Java interface to the appropriate COM interface identified by iid. To create a COM class that implements the ISomeComObject interface, the @com.register() directive is used as shown here:

```
/** @com.register(clsid=EF9FB98D-CFD8-11D1-BB42-00207812E629,
                 typelib=EF9FB97F-CFD8-11D1-BB42-00207812E629) */
public class SomeComObject implements ISomeComObject
{ ...
}
```

It is important to note that, due to a lawsuit filed against Microsoft by Sun, Microsoft may be forced to change its Java/COM support at some point in the future. The following message is currently displayed by the Visual J++ development tool when attempts are made to use the COM extensions in a Visual J++ project:

> *Note: Use of the Microsoft language extensions for Java results in compiled code that will run only on Windows systems with the Microsoft Virtual Machine for Java installed and may not run on other virtual machines. The Microsoft Virtual Machine for Java is installed with Windows 98 and a freely redistributable version is included with this product. While future versions of Microsoft Java's development tools may be prohibited by court order from incorporating keyword extensions and compiler directives not contained in Sun's Java language specification, any code written and compiled with this version of the product will be unaffected by such a ruling.*

COM/Windows/Visual Basic Development Platform

Visual Basic's support for COM has matured through a large number of product releases. While Visual Basic is generally acknowledged as a client-side development environment, it is also being widely used as a server-side component development environment. It is quite simple to create a Visual Basic COM object; Visual Basic allows class modules to be mapped directly to COM objects. Because it is so easy to create COM objects, Visual Basic is a powerful prototyping tool. In many cases, Visual Basic COM objects meet final deployment requirements as well. In such cases, Visual Basic is a better alternative than C++ in terms of ease of development.

Non-Windows COM Development Platforms

To achieve dominance as a distributed object technology, COM must be adequately supported on non-Windows platforms. Even with Microsoft's support, it will be difficult for COM to displace CORBA, which has had a presence on those platforms for many years. The following factors also diminish COM's ability to dominate non-Windows platforms:

- *COM licensing.* COM must be licensed in order to port it to non-Windows platforms. The COM license that Microsoft has extended to most vendors includes the COM core libraries, Microsoft RPC (to enable DCOM), a subset of the Win32 API, the MIDL compiler, and the Active Template Library (ATL). This license is intended to allow for porting of COM/C++. Other critical technologies, such as Microsoft Transaction Server, are not included in the license.

- *Java support.* The use of COM with Java necessitates the availability of a COM-aware JVM. Such a JVM does not yet exist on any platform other than Microsoft Windows. Large vendors such as Sun are unlikely to support COM in their JVMs. COM must provide both C++ and Java support in order to be viable on non-Windows server platforms.

- *C++ portability.* Microsoft has added several COM extensions to the C++ language supported by the Visual C++ compiler. This trend is likely to continue as Microsoft attempts to make COM more usable from Visual C++. Users who wish to utilize COM/C++ on multiple platforms (including non-Windows platforms) must avoid the use of such extensions. This is problematic since Microsoft does not provide support for avoiding such nonportable extensions in its Visual C++ development environment.

The establishment of COM on non-Windows platforms will ultimately depend on Microsoft's mindset with regard to strategic advantage. If Microsoft determines that its competitive advantage is best served by stifling COM on non-Windows platforms, COM will fail to dominate on any platform other than Windows.

CORBA Development Platforms

By its very design, CORBA supports an incredible number of development platforms. C++ and Java-based CORBA products are offered by multiple vendors on every major server platform. In addition, CORBA products supporting Smalltalk, Ada, and COBOL are also available. This is in contrast to COM, which supports only C++ on most non-Windows platforms.

The marriage of CORBA and Java has significantly added to CORBA's presence on multiple platforms. Unlike COM, which relies on a COM-aware JVM, CORBA/Java products such as Inprise's VisiBroker for Java and Iona's OrbixWeb are written entirely in Java. This approach allows CORBA/Java products to run on any standard JVM on any platform. One other advantage of such an approach is that CORBA/Java objects can easily be developed on one platform and deployed on another.

CORBA's wide platform coverage also gives it an interesting advantage over COM when developing server-side components under Windows NT. Although COM may be easier to use under Windows NT, CORBA offers the ability to more easily migrate server objects from one platform to another. Several major CORBA vendors offer stable CORBA products for Windows NT as well as UNIX platforms. Therefore, if migration from Windows NT to a non-Windows platform (e.g., UNIX) is a possibility, CORBA is a much better choice than COM.

Availability of Development Tools

The disparity between COM and CORBA is greatest in the area of development tools. This is certainly true on Windows platforms where a huge number of tools exist for creating COM objects. In contrast, very few tools exist to aid in creating COM and CORBA server objects on non-Windows platforms. If an enterprise is capable of committing to Microsoft Windows for the long term, the availability of COM-oriented development tools is a strong reason for using COM over CORBA.

COM Development Tools

Microsoft Windows is today's predominant desktop operating system. Because of its popularity, an incredible number of software development tools have been created for Windows. As COM became the primary component architecture for Windows, development platforms evolved to better support COM. As a result, the Windows platform hosts a large number of powerful development tools that can be used to develop COM server-side objects.

In the preceding section, we established C++, Java, and Visual Basic as the primary languages used to create COM server-side objects. Microsoft provides an extremely powerful integrated development environment (IDE) for each of these languages in its Visual Studio product suite. Visual Studio is made up of several products, including Visual C++, Visual Basic, and Visual J++. Microsoft's Visual C++ and Visual Basic products have each matured over more than five major releases. Because of Java's youth, Visual J++ is currently in its second major release. Several other third-party vendors also offer development products that can be used to create COM objects. These development products include environments such as Inprise's Delphi and Sybase's PowerBuilder.

While the Visual Studio products work extremely well when we are developing for the Windows platform, they create problems when we attempt to build COM objects for non-Windows platforms.

- Visual Basic can be used only on the Windows platform.

- Visual J++ creates components that rely on a COM-aware JVM.

- Visual C++ continues to support an ever-increasing number of features that are not supported by non-Windows C++ compilers.

Despite the cross-platform limitations imposed by the Visual Studio products, they are incredibly useful when we are targeting the Windows platform.

CORBA Development Tools

In general, a very small number of CORBA development tools exist for any platform. This is to be expected since CORBA products tend to cover a wide range of programming language and operating system platforms rather than focusing on a single platform. In addition, most of the CORBA vendors do not sell development tools in addition to their CORBA offerings. This is in contrast to Microsoft, a vendor that controls operating systems, development tools, and middleware products.

Despite the general shortage of CORBA development tools, there are exceptions where vendors do offer CORBA-related development support. The acquisition of Visigenic (a major CORBA vendor) by Inprise (a development tools vendor) in 1998 has resulted in direct CORBA support within several outstanding development environments. Inprise provides direct support for the VisiBroker CORBA ORB in enterprise versions of its JBuilder, C++Builder, and Delphi development environments. Another exception is Black & White Software, which offers CORBA-related add-ons for development environments such as Symantec's Visual Cafe for Java and Microsoft's Visual C++.

Summary

In this chapter, we have focused on many issues related to the platform criteria used in our assessment strategy. First, we examined a number of strategies for supporting legacy systems when using COM and CORBA. Next, we described programming language and operating system platforms that support COM and CORBA. Finally, we described development tools that currently exist in the COM/CORBA arena. Keep in mind that the specific products that we discussed in this chapter represent a limited view of all the technology that is currently available in the marketplace.

The focus of this chapter was on platform issues related to basic support for COM and CORBA. In the next chapter, we will examine essential services that are required for implementing large enterprise systems. The essential services that we will look at include distributed transaction support, distributed security, messaging, and system management.

Chapter 6

Essential Services

Topics Covered in This Chapter

- Review of the Service Criteria

- Distributed Transaction Support

- Distributed Security

- Messaging Support

- Distributed Object Management

There is an old and very wise saying: *You have to walk before you can run.* This saying applies to many things, including technical manifestations such as COM and CORBA. The core technology behind COM and CORBA had to properly evolve before high-level services could be created to support advanced system development. Early adopters of COM and CORBA were forced to develop much of the technical infrastructure by hand when creating complex distributed systems. This resulted in a couple of problems. First, there tended to be more failures than successes. Early adopters had very little guidance in the area of distributed objects, and failures in such efforts abounded. Second, developers working on different systems reinvented the same infrastructure components over and over again.

Current distributed object technology vendors recognize the need for high-level services that can be used to provide more robust technical infrastructures. Although such high-level services have some unique characteristics when it comes to distributed objects, the critical services are fundamentally the same for any type of distributed system. COM and CORBA vendors can gain experience from a variety of existing distributed system architectures and services. In this chapter, we will focus on four critical areas: distributed transactions, security, messaging, and distributed object management. In each of these areas, we will explore COM and CORBA services that address advanced system needs.

Review of the Service Criteria

In Chapter 4, we identified the following service-related criteria to be evaluated in assessing the use of COM and CORBA in a specific server-side domain:

- Distributed transaction support

- Security and privacy

- Messaging support

- Distributed object management

Large enterprises rely on transaction management to guarantee the consistency of critical information assets. In nondistributed systems, a transaction is usually managed by a single database management system. In distributed object systems, a transaction can be distributed across multiple distributed objects and data resources. Managing transactions in a distributed object system requires coordination by a distributed transaction coordinator. In this chapter, we will examine how distributed transactions are coordinated in COM and CORBA environments.

Data consistency is critically important within an enterprise, but it means nothing without security. The integrity of unsecured data is always questionable. Managing security within a distributed environment can be a complex task. In this chapter, we will examine how varying levels of security are achieved when using COM and CORBA.

Most programming models use a conversational approach. A request is made, and processing is stopped until a reply is received. For some applications, a request-reply model is inappropriate. An alternative to the request-reply model is messaging. In a messaging approach, applications communicate by sending messages to one another without expecting immediate replies. In this chapter, we will examine messaging approaches that are commonly used in COM and CORBA environments.

The last service-related area that we will discuss is distributed object management. Distributed object management encompasses many areas, such as resource management, load balancing, fault tolerance, and so forth. Very few object management solutions exist today in the distributed object marketplace. In this chapter, we will take a brief look at Microsoft Transaction Server, which is a COM-based management system, as well as BEA Systems' M3, a CORBA-based management system.

Distributed Transaction Support

Transactions define the boundaries between distinct units of work in large enterprise systems. When using COM and CORBA, transactions can be spread across multiple distributed objects and multiple data resources. In this section, we will examine how distributed transactions are coordinated in COM and CORBA environments. We'll first describe a generic scenario for a distributed object transaction. We'll then discuss how the scenario is handled in both a COM solution and a CORBA solution.

A Scenario for a Distributed Object Transaction

A classic example of a transaction is the transfer of money between two bank accounts. Ensuring transactional semantics can be difficult when each bank account is maintained in a separate database. The complexity increases even more when each account is managed by a separate distributed object. Consider the scenario illustrated in Figure 6-1.

In this scenario, the following steps occur:

1. The client makes a request to the *Teller* object to transfer $100 from *Account A* to *Account B*.

2. The *Teller* object makes a request to the *Account_A* object to withdraw $100.

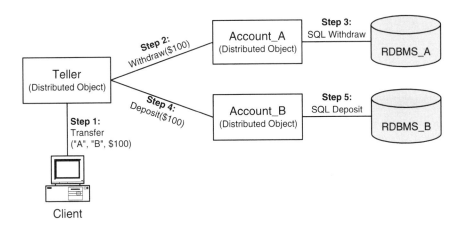

Figure 6-1. *A scenario for a distributed object transaction.*

3. The *Account_A* object updates the account information in *RDBMS_A* so that the balance of *Account A* is reduced by $100.

4. The *Teller* object makes a request to the *Account_B* object to deposit $100.

5. The *Account_B* object updates the account information in *RDBMS_B* so that the balance of *Account B* is increased by $100.

Acceptable outcomes of the scenario are illustrated in Figure 6-2. The transfer either succeeds in its entirety or fails in its entirety. The way to ensure that only these two outcomes occur is to execute the transfer within the confines of a single distributed transaction. If the transfer succeeds and the transaction is successfully committed, the balance of *Account A* in *RDBMS_A* will be $400 and the balance of *Account B* in *RDBMS_B* will be $110. If the transfer fails for any reason (e.g., lack of funds, software failure, hardware failure), the transaction will be rolled back and *RDBMS_A* and *RDBMS_B* will both be returned to a consistent state (i.e., the state before the transfer was initiated).

Who is responsible for managing the distributed transaction? It should be obvious that neither the *Client*, *Teller*, *Account_A*, or *Account_B* objects can manage the transaction. None of those objects is aware that both *RDBMS_A* and *RDBMS_B* are even being used. Instead, the transaction must be managed by a third-party distributed transaction coordinator. To illustrate how such a coordinator is used, an interaction diagram demonstrating a commit for the scenario is shown in Figure 6-3.

The following interactions occur:

1. *Client* asks *Teller* to transfer $100 from *Account A* to *Account B*.

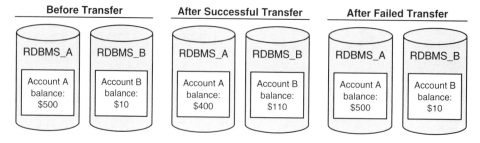

Figure 6-2. Acceptable outcomes of the transfer scenario.

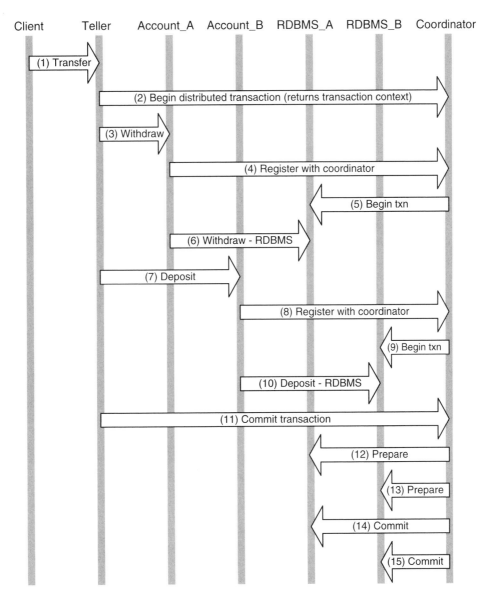

Figure 6-3. *Committing the transfer operation across two databases.*

2. *Teller* asks *Coordinator* to begin a distributed transaction. *Coordinator* replies with a transaction context identifying the distributed transaction. The transaction context is passed to all participants in the distributed transaction.

3. *Teller* asks *Account_A* to withdraw $100.

4. *Account_A* registers with *Coordinator* and lets *Coordinator* know that it will be using *RDBMS_A*.

5. *Coordinator* begins a transaction (txn) in *RDBMS_A* on behalf of *Account_A*.

6. *Account_A* reduces the balance of its account in *RDBMS_A*.

7. *Teller* asks *Account_B* to deposit $100.

8. *Account_B* registers with *Coordinator* and lets *Coordinator* know that it will be using *RDBMS_B*.

9. *Coordinator* begins a transaction in *RDBMS_B* on behalf of *Account_B*.

10. *Account_B* increases the balance of its account in *RDBMS_B*.

11. *Teller* asks *Coordinator* to commit the distributed transaction.

12. *Coordinator* is now ready to perform a two-phase commit. *Coordinator* asks *RDBMS_A* whether it can commit the transaction. *RDBMS_A* tells *Coordinator* that it can commit.

13. *Coordinator* asks *RDBMS_B* whether it can commit the transaction. *RDBMS_B* tells *Coordinator* that it can commit.

14. *Coordinator* tells *RDBMS_A* to commit the transaction.

15. *Coordinator* tells *RDBMS_B* to commit the transaction.

Steps 12–15 represent a two-phase commit protocol. In the first phase of the two-phase commit, each of the RDBMSs is asked whether or not it is willing to commit its portion of the distributed transaction. The second phase involves commit or rollback. If either of the RDBMSs indicates that it cannot commit the transaction, the entire transaction is rolled back; otherwise, both RDBMSs are committed, and the transfer is successfully completed. Of course, many other details are involved when using a specific transaction-processing engine. However, the generic example provided here should convey a general understanding of the coordinator's role in a typical distributed object transaction.

COM, MTS, and the Distributed Transaction Coordinator

Microsoft provides the Microsoft Transaction Server (MTS) and the Distributed Transaction Coordinator (DTC) to orchestrate distributed transactions in the COM environment. The purpose of MTS with regard to distributed object transactions is mainly to initiate and signal completion of transactions. The purpose of the DTC is to manage the actual commit and rollback of specific data resources participating in a distributed transaction. The DTC (and not MTS) is responsible for managing transaction contexts and coordinating two-phase commits. The DTC usually works behind the scenes when COM components live within the MTS framework. MTS allows COM objects to participate in transactions without worrying about how those transactions are started and ended.

The name *Microsoft Transaction Server* is actually a misnomer. As we shall see throughout the rest of this chapter, MTS does far more than initiate and signal completion of transactions. MTS provides a framework for managing the COM runtime system. In addition to its distributed transaction role, MTS can be used in conjunction with COM security, COM resource management, and COM system monitoring.

In the distributed object transaction scenario described on page 145, a *Teller* distributed object is used to transfer money between two *Account* distributed objects. When performing a transfer operation, these three distributed objects must participate in a single distributed transaction in order to maintain consistency across both *RDBMS_A* and *RDBMS_B*. We therefore implement the *Teller* and *Account* COM components as MTS components. This allows us to use distributed transactions when transferring money from one account to another.

First, we create an in-process COM component (DLL) for the *Account* distributed object in an ATL project named `Ch6Account`. In our `Ch6Account` component implementation, we use Microsoft's ADO (ActiveX Data Objects) to access the SQL Server RDBMS. Then, we set up two ODBC data sources, "RDBMS_A" and "RDBMS_B," that map to two SQL Server databases. ADO takes advantage of the ODBC/SQL Server driver that is supported in the MTS environment.

Next, we implement the *Teller* distributed object in an ATL project named `Ch6Teller`. The `Ch6Teller` implementation does not directly access a database but instead uses two `Ch6Account` objects to transfer money from one account to another. Source code listings for the `CTeller` and `CAccount` classes can be found in the Appendix C sections listed here:

- Ch6Teller MTS Component (page 408)

- Ch6Account MTS Component (page 411)

At this point, we have created two in-process COM components (i.e., `Ch6Teller` and `Ch6Account`), but we have not added any support for distributed transactions. We are now ready to host the in-process components under MTS. To do so, we invoke the Microsoft Management Console[*] for MTS and create an MTS package to host the in-process components. We then add the `Ch6Teller` and `Ch6Account` COM components to the package. The Management Console, as it appears after the `Ch6Teller` and `Ch6Account` components have been added, is shown in Figure 6-4.

If you look closely at Figure 6-4, you will notice that both the `Ch6Account` and `Ch6Teller` components indicate that a transaction is *Required* when using those components. This is accomplished by setting the transaction property for the components as shown in Figure 6-5.

By selecting the *Requires a transaction* choice, we have indicated that invocations against this component must be performed within the context of a distributed transaction. If a transaction has not begun when the component is

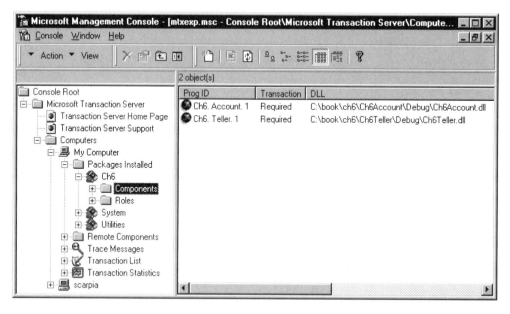

Figure 6-4. *Viewing MTS components in the Microsoft Management Console.*

---

*The Microsoft Management Console is a utility used to monitor and administrate a wide range of Windows NT services, such as MTS, IIS, MSMQ, COMTI, and so forth.

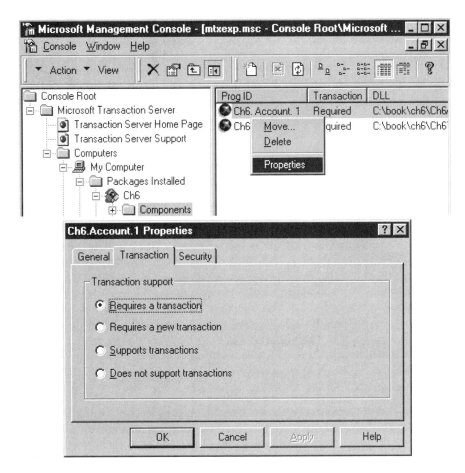

Figure 6-5. *Setting the transaction property for an MTS component.*

invoked, a new transaction will be implicitly started by MTS. If the instance is created in the context of a currently running transaction, the invocation will run in the transaction that is already taking place.

Recall that the Ch6Teller component does not directly access the database and yet we have still identified Ch6Teller as requiring a transaction. The reason is that the Ch6Teller instance initiates the transaction that spans the multiple Ch6Account instances across which the transfer operation is done. The two Ch6Account instances must join the transaction started by the Ch6Teller instance. If the Ch6Teller component did not require a transaction, each `Ch6Account` instance would run in its own transaction, which is not what we require when transferring money from one account to another.

Being able to implicitly start transactions without affecting the client or component code base is very powerful; however, we still have not discussed two important issues. First, how do the `Ch6Account` instances take part in a transaction that is started by a `Ch6Teller` instance? And second, how do the `Ch6Teller` and `Ch6Account` instances indicate that the transaction should be committed or rolled back? The resolution to these issues is that MTS components must be able to interact with the MTS framework.

To solve problems such as these, MTS associates a context object with every component instance under its control. This context object is used for a variety of purposes, including MTS's support for transactions. Instances of MTS components typically obtain handles to their respective contexts and then use the context handles to communicate with the MTS framework. The MTS context object supports the `IContextObject` interface and includes a number of required methods. The most commonly used methods are

- `IContextObject::CreateInstance()`—Used to create another MTS component that needs to participate in the current context. The `Ch6Teller` instance calls this method when creating the `Ch6Account` instances so that the `Ch6Teller` and `Ch6Account` instances participate in the same transaction.

- `IContextObject::SetComplete()`—Used to indicate that the component has successfully completed its portion of the transaction. Note that a call to `SetComplete()` does not do a commit on a data source. Committing and rolling back are the responsibility of the DTC.

- `IContextObject::SetAbort()`—Used to indicate that the component cannot do its work and that the entire distributed transaction must be rolled back. A call to `SetAbort()` is usually made when a database access error occurs.

In Figure 6-3, we identified 15 interactions that take place when a transfer operation occurs in the distributed object transaction scenario. Let's now examine how those 15 interactions occur in the COM/MTS/DTC environment using the `Ch6Teller` and `Ch6Account` MTS components.

1. *Client* asks *Teller* to transfer $100 from *Account A* to *Account B*. From the client's perspective, the `Ch6Teller` instance is just another COM object available for use. The client is unaware that the `Ch6Teller` component is running in the MTS framework.

2. *Teller* asks *Coordinator* to begin a distributed transaction. Because Ch6Teller's transaction property is set to *Required* (as shown in Figure 6-4), MTS will direct the DTC to begin a distributed transaction on behalf of the Ch6Teller instance as soon as the Transfer() method is invoked on the Ch6Teller instance.

3. *Teller* asks *Account_A* to withdraw $100. To interact with an account, the Ch6Teller instance must first create the Ch6Account instances. As shown in Listing 6-1 on line 7, an IObjectContext interface pointer is first obtained by calling GetObjectContext(). The GetObjectContext() method is defined by MTS. On lines 12–28, the object context is used to create two Ch6Account instances. Since each of the Ch6Account components requires a transaction (as shown in Figure 6-4), the newly created

Listing 6-1. *InitializeAccounts( ) Method in Teller MTS Component*

```
1 void CTeller::InitializeAccounts()
2 {
3     HRESULT hr;
4
5     // Get a handle on the MTS context object.
6     CComPtr<IObjectContext> spObjectContext;
7     ::GetObjectContext(&spObjectContext);
8
9     // Create an Account object instance in the transaction
10    // context of this Teller object. This object will be
11    // associated with Account A.
12    IAccount* pIAccount;
13    hr = spObjectContext->CreateInstance(__uuidof(Account),
14                                         __uuidof(IAccount),
15                                         (LPVOID*)&pIAccount);
16    if (FAILED(hr)) return;
17
18    m_pIAccount_A.Attach(pIAccount);   // Account A's object
19
20    // Create another Account object instance in the transaction
21    // context of this Teller object. This object will be
22    // associated with Account B.
23    hr=spObjectContext->CreateInstance(__uuidof(Account),
24                                       __uuidof(IAccount),
25                                       (LPVOID*)&pIAccount);
26    if (FAILED(hr)) return;
27
28    m_pIAccount_B.Attach(pIAccount);   // Account B's object
29 }
```

`Ch6Account` instances participate in the transaction that was started for the `Ch6Teller` instance when `Transfer()` was called. The `Ch6Teller` instance then makes a call to the `Ch6Account` instance corresponding to *Account A* to withdraw $100 as shown on line 15 in Listing 6-2.

4. *Account_A* registers with *Coordinator* and lets *Coordinator* know that it will be using *RDBMS_A*. The `Ch6Account` `Withdraw()` method is shown in Listing 6-3. The first thing that must be determined is the database name. Since the withdrawal will occur on an account named "A," "RDBMS_A" will be used. Next, the `AdjustBalanceInDatabase()` method is called on line 14. This method connects to the ODBC data

Listing 6-2. *Transfer( ) Method in Teller MTS Component*

```
1 STDMETHODIMP CTeller::Transfer(BSTR fromAccount,
2                                BSTR toAccount,
3                                double amount)
4 {
5     // Initialize account objects.
6     InitializeAccounts();
7
8     // Get a handle on the MTS context object.
9     CComPtr<IObjectContext> spObjectContext;
10    ::GetObjectContext(&spObjectContext);
11
12    try
13    {
14        // Transfer the money.
15        m_pIAccount_A->Withdraw(fromAccount, amount);
16        m_pIAccount_B->Deposit(toAccount, amount);
17    }
18    catch (...)
19    {
20        // If either Withdraw() or Deposit() throws an
21        // exception, abort the transaction.
22        spObjectContext->SetAbort();
23        return E_FAIL;
24    }
25
26    // The call to SetComplete() will begin the two-phase
27    // commit of the Transfer() operation.
28    spObjectContext->SetComplete();
29    return S_OK;
30 }
```

Listing 6-3. *Withdraw( ) Method in Account MTS Component*

```
 1 STDMETHODIMP CAccount::Withdraw(BSTR acctName, double amount)
 2 {
 3     // Get a handle on the MTS context object.
 4     CComPtr<IObjectContext> spObjectContext;
 5     ::GetObjectContext(&spObjectContext);
 6
 7     // Determine the database that the account is
 8     // associated with.
 9     const char* db = (_bstr_t("A") == _bstr_t(acctName)) ?
10                     "RDBMS_A" :
11                     "RDBMS_B";
12
13     // Adjust the balance in the database.
14     if ( !AdjustBalanceInDatabase(db, acctName, amount * -1.0) )
15     {
16         // Abort the transaction.
17         spObjectContext->SetAbort();
18         return E_FAIL;
19     }
20
21     // Let MTS know that this part of the transaction
22     // is complete.
23     spObjectContext->SetComplete();
24     return S_OK;
25 }
```

source named "RDBMS_A" using ADO. Since the ODBC driver is supported by MTS as a distributed transaction resource, it is the responsibility of the ODBC Driver Manager to tell the DTC that this Ch6Account instance will be using "RDBMS_A."

5. *Coordinator* begins a transaction in *RDBMS_A* on behalf of *Account_A*. The DTC begins a transaction on the ODBC data source named "RDBMS_A" on behalf of the Ch6Account instance.

6. *Account_A* reduces the balance of its account in *RDBMS_A*. The balance is adjusted for the account named "A" in the ODBC data source named "RDBMS_A." The Withdraw() method then calls SetComplete() on line 23 if the withdrawal was successful; otherwise, it calls SetAbort() on line 17. Note that no commits or rollbacks have occurred on any databases. The call to SetComplete() or SetAbort() simply indicates to the DTC that the Ch6Account instance has completed its portion of the distributed transaction.

7. *Teller* asks *Account_B* to deposit $100. This step is similar to step 3.

8. *Account_B* registers with *Coordinator* and lets *Coordinator* know that it will be using *RDBMS_B*. This step is similar to step 4.

9. *Coordinator* begins a transaction in *RDBMS_B* on behalf of *Account_B*. This step is similar to step 5.

10. *Account_B* increases the balance of its account in *RDBMS_B*. This step is similar to step 6. Note that a different database ("RDBMS_B") is updated as opposed to that in step 6.

11. *Teller* asks *Coordinator* to commit the distributed transaction. In Listing 6-2 on line 28, the `Teller` instance calls `SetComplete()` on its object context to indicate that the distributed transaction is ready to commit.

12. *Coordinator* is now ready to perform a two-phase commit. *Coordinator* asks *RDBMS_A* whether it can commit the transaction. *RDBMS_A* tells *Coordinator* that it can commit. This is handled by the DTC.

13. *Coordinator* asks *RDBMS_B* whether it can commit the transaction. *RDBMS_B* tells *Coordinator* that it can commit. This is handled by the DTC.

14. *Coordinator* tells *RDBMS_A* to commit the transaction. This is handled by the DTC.

15. *Coordinator* tells *RDBMS_B* to commit the transaction. This is handled by the DTC.

Managing distributed transactions is a complex task. MTS makes participating in distributed transactions very simple. The MTS framework automatically begins distributed transactions on behalf of components under its control. The ODBC Driver Manager lets the DTC know when specific ODBC data sources are needed by transactional components. The only responsibility of the component is to call `SetComplete()` or `SetAbort()` on its object context when it has completed its portion of the distributed transaction.

CORBA and the Object Transaction Service

The OMG's Common Object Services Specification includes an Object Transaction Service (OTS) for CORBA. OTS adds robust transactional behavior to objects that live on the CORBA object bus. Because transactions are essential in most distributed systems, almost all of the leading CORBA vendors have added an OTS implementation to their CORBA product suites.

OTS implements a CORBA IDL module called `CosTransactions`[*] that contains OTS-related interface definitions. The interfaces that we will mention in this section are

- `CosTransactions::Control`—Defines methods that can be used to control all elements related to a specific OTS transaction. A `Control` instance is essentially a handle on a specific OTS transaction.

- `CosTransactions::TransactionFactory`—Defines methods to manually create transactions within OTS. The `create()` method provided by this interface returns a `Control` instance.

- `CosTransactions::Current`—Defines methods that simplify the use of OTS for most applications. These methods include `begin()`, `commit()`, and `rollback()`. The OTS runtime system provides a `Current` object instance that is associated with the current thread of control in an OTS application. In contrast to `Control` instances, users are not required to create a `Current` instance.

OTS offers two modes for creating and managing a transaction context within an OTS application:

1. *Direct context management.* An application manipulates the transaction context directly by using a `Control` object instance. With the direct approach, applications usually create a `Control` instance using a `TransactionFactory` instance provided by OTS.

2. *Indirect context management.* An application creates and manages a transaction context indirectly using the `Current` instance provided by OTS. The indirect approach is substantially easier to program than the direct approach.

OTS also offers two approaches for propagating transaction contexts to target CORBA objects:

1. *Explicit context propagation.* With the explicit approach, a `Control` object reference is passed as a parameter when invoking OTS objects.

2. *Implicit context propagation.* The ORB passes the transaction context maintained in the `Current` instance as an implicit argument when invoking OTS-related CORBA objects. OTS provides the `CosTransactions::TransactionalObject` interface that transactional CORBA objects must inherit from in order to receive the

---

[*]The interfaces for `CosTransactions` are defined in CORBA IDL. The prefix, *Cos*, stands for Common Object Services and is used as a prefix for CORBA IDL modules defined in the OMG's Common Object Services Specification.

implicit argument. The implicit approach is easier to program than the explicit approach since the ORB takes care of making sure that the transaction context is propagated where necessary.

Based on the descriptions just presented, the simplest approach for managing transaction contexts in an OTS environment is to use indirect transaction context management and implicit transaction context propagation. The indirect and implicit approaches both rely on the OTS-provided `Current` object instance. The `Current` instance also provides the simplest method for beginning, committing, and rolling back distributed transactions.

The last issue that must be discussed is the registering of resources with OTS. The method for registering recoverable resources such as RDBMSs with OTS is often vendor-specific. For our purposes, we will assume that such registration is done during initialization (i.e., the `main()` function) of transactional OTS server objects. We will not examine vendor-specific approaches for performing such registration.

We are now ready to reexamine our scenario. In the distributed object transaction scenario described on page 145, a *Teller* distributed object is used to transfer money between two *Account* distributed objects. When performing a transfer operation, these three distributed objects must participate in a single distributed transaction in order to maintain consistency across both *RDBMS_A* and *RDBMS_B*. We therefore implement the *Teller* and *Account* CORBA objects using OTS. This allows us to use distributed transactions when transferring money from one account to another.

To simplify implementation of our transactional objects, we use the implicit propagation approach. Our `Account` CORBA interface must therefore inherit from the `CosTransactions::TransactionalObject` interface. The CORBA IDL descriptions for the `Teller` and `Account` CORBA interfaces are shown in Listing 6-4.

In Figure 6-3, we identified 15 interactions that take place when a transfer operation occurs in the distributed object transaction scenario. Let's now examine how those 15 interactions occur in a CORBA/OTS environment using the `Ch6::Teller` and `Ch6::Account` CORBA objects.

1. *Client* asks *Teller* to transfer $100 from *Account A* to *Account B*. From the client's perspective, the `Ch6::Teller` instance is just another CORBA object available for use. The client is unaware that the `Ch6::Teller` object uses OTS.

Listing 6-4. CORBA IDL for Teller and Account Objects

```
#include <OTS.idl>

module Ch6
{
    exception DatabaseExc
    {
        string reason;
    };

    interface Teller
    {
        void transfer(in string fromAccount,
                      in string toAccount,
                      im double amount) raises(DatabaseExc);
    };

    interface Account : CosTransactions::TransactionalObject
    {
        void deposit(in string accountName,
                     in double amount) raises(DatabaseExc);

        void withdraw(in string accountName,
                      in double amount) raises(DatabaseExc);
    };
};
```

2. *Teller* asks *Coordinator* to begin a distributed transaction. In Listing 6-5 on line 12, `current` is used in the `transfer()` method to begin the distributed transaction.

3. *Teller* asks *Account_A* to withdraw $100. In Listing 6-5 on line 15, a `Ch6::Account` instance is created. Because the `Ch6::Account` interface inherits from `CosTransactions::TransactionalObject` (as shown in Listing 6-4), the transaction context associated with `current` will be implicitly passed to `accountA` when the `withdraw()` method is invoked on line 16.

4. *Account_A* registers with *Coordinator* and lets *Coordinator* know that it will be using *RDBMS_A*. As mentioned earlier, techniques for performing such registration are usually vendor-specific. We will assume here that the registration was done during initialization (i.e., the `main()` function) of the `Ch6::Account` server object.

Listing 6-5. Implementation of Teller's transfer( ) Method

```
 1  void TellerImpl::transfer(const char* fromAccount,
 2                            const char* toAccount,
 3                            CORBA::Double amount,
 4                            CORBA::Environment& env)
 5  {
 6    try
 7    {
 8        // Obtain a handle on the Current instance.
 9        CosTransactions::Current_ptr current = getCurrent();
10
11        // Begin the transaction.
12        current->begin();
13
14        // Transfer the money from account A to account B.
15        Ch6::Account_var accountA = createAccount();
16        accountA->withdraw(fromAccount, amount);
17
18        Ch6::Account_var accountB = createAccount();
19        accountB->deposit(toAccount, amount);
20
21        // Commit the transaction.
22        current->commit(1);
23    }
24    catch(DatabaseExc& exc)
25    {
26        // Roll back the transaction if an error occurs.
27        current->rollback();
28        throw exc;
29    }
30    catch(...)
31    {
32        // Roll back the transaction if an error occurs.
33        current->rollback();
34        throw DatabaseExc("transfer failed");
35    }
36  }
```

5. *Coordinator* begins a transaction in *RDBMS_A* on behalf of *Account_A*. In the CORBA implementation, OTS begins a transaction on the RDBMS named "RDBMS_A" on behalf of the `Ch6::Account` instance.

6. *Account_A* reduces the balance of its account in *RDBMS_A*. The `Ch6::Account` instance reduces the balance of an account named

"A" in "RDBMS_A." The important point to note is that although the `Account` instance changes the value in "RDBMS_A," it does not do a commit or rollback on the database. The commit/rollback of transactions is the responsibility of OTS.

7. *Teller* asks *Account_B* to deposit $100. This step is similar to step 3.

8. *Account_B* registers with *Coordinator* and lets *Coordinator* know that it will be using *RDBMS_B*. This step is similar to step 4.

9. *Coordinator* begins a transaction in *RDBMS_B* on behalf of *Account_B*. This step is similar to step 5.

10. *Account_B* increases the balance of its account in *RDBMS_B*. This step is similar to step 6.

11. *Teller* asks *Coordinator* to commit the distributed transaction. In Listing 6-5 on line 22, `current` is used to commit the distributed transaction.

12. *Coordinator* is now ready to perform a two-phase commit. *Coordinator* asks *RDBMS_A* whether it can commit the transaction. *RDBMS_A* tells *Coordinator* that it can commit. This is handled by OTS.

13. *Coordinator* asks *RDBMS_B* whether it can commit the transaction. *RDBMS_B* tells *Coordinator* that it can commit. This is handled by OTS.

14. *Coordinator* tells *RDBMS_A* to commit the transaction. This is handled by OTS.

15. *Coordinator* tells *RDBMS_B* to commit the transaction. This is handled by OTS.

OTS makes participating in distributed transactions very simple. CORBA objects simply need to inherit from `CosTransactions::TransactionalObject` in order to automatically participate in transactions. The `Current` object provided by OTS makes it easy for clients to begin, commit, and roll back distributed transactions.

The fact that clients must initiate and end transactions differentiates OTS from the Microsoft Transaction Server approach that we discussed in the last section. This differentiation does not apply to all CORBA-based systems. For example, BEA's M3 uses a proprietary approach that allows transactions to be automatically started upon method invocation in a similar way to MTS. As other CORBA vendors' products mature, their systems are likely to allow for similar functionality as well.

Distributed Security

Although distributed systems offer great flexibility and power, they also introduce a number of security issues that must be addressed when building large enterprise systems. COM and CORBA provide different approaches for managing security. COM tends to rely on security mechanisms provided by the underlying operating system. CORBA manages security within the confines of a security-enabled ORB or by using IIOP over the Secure Sockets Layer (SSL). Despite these differences, both COM and CORBA must meet the following basic security requirements:

- *User authentication.* One of the first concerns of any security system is the ability to determine the true identity of a user. While there are many ways to make such a determination, the most common form of authentication is the use of login names and passwords.

- *Data integrity.* Once the identity of the user has been determined, the security system must guarantee the integrity of data. The security provider must ensure that no one has tampered with data passed between clients and servers. Integrity is usually guaranteed by performing a checksum on the data being transmitted.

- *Privacy.* In addition to data integrity, it is sometimes important to keep others not only from tampering with data but also from viewing it. In such cases, data must be encrypted.

- *User authorization.* Before a server can perform its assigned task, it must ensure that the client is authorized to make such a request. Authorization tends to be the most difficult aspect of security to administrate. Just as security providers must prevent access by unauthorized users, they must also ensure proper access to authorized users. Getting either aspect of authorization wrong can be costly.

To guarantee security, the mechanisms for maintaining security must pervade all parts of a distributed system. Because of the pervasive nature of security, it is critically important to make security as unobtrusive as possible. In an ideal situation, client and server applications can be developed without regard for security constraints. Meanwhile, the security manager quietly performs its duties in the background. Both COM and CORBA have evolved to provide a security framework that provides for robust and yet unobtrusive security.

Whereas authentication, integrity, and privacy are fairly simple to configure and manage when using COM and CORBA, authorization usually requires a significant amount of administration. In large systems, keeping track of the users that are allowed to access specific services can be a complex task. Microsoft Transaction Server (MTS) plays an important role in managing authorization in the COM environment. The CORBA Security Service specifies an access control model for managing authorization in the CORBA environment. Both the COM and CORBA camps recognize the importance of security in the enterprise systems arena.

DCOM Security

The introduction of DCOM in 1996 resulted in a number of security-related additions to COM. The COM architecture prior to DCOM was already well suited to distribution, as it allowed clients to access both in-process DLLs and local servers transparently. Communication between COM clients and COM local servers is accomplished using a lightweight RPC mechanism. DCOM naturally extends COM to use an enhanced version of RPC (often referred to as *Object RPC*) as its underlying transport. Transparency is maintained so that clients do not usually need to worry whether a server is in-process, local, or remote. Because of its dependence on RPC, DCOM's security services are a natural outgrowth of DCE RPC security services, and the security features added to the COM API reflect the parameters needed to manage the Object RPC transport layer.

DCOM security under Windows NT 4.0 relies heavily on NT's native security mechanism, NTLM. However, because RPC allows for replaceable security packages, DCOM also supports a similar notion. In order to be used with DCOM, replaceable security packages must conform to the Security Support Provider Interface (SSPI), an interface based on the Internet Proposed Standard GSSAPI. In the next version of Windows NT, Windows 2000, Microsoft plans to support multiple security packages by supporting MIT's Kerberos in addition to NTLM.

DCOM provides various levels of support for user authentication, data integrity, and privacy. These levels are the same as those provided in DCE RPC. As the levels increase, each level adds more security and subsumes the levels below it. The authentication levels are defined as

```
#define RPC_C_AUTHN_LEVEL_DEFAULT      0
#define RPC_C_AUTHN_LEVEL_NONE         1
#define RPC_C_AUTHN_LEVEL_CONNECT      2
#define RPC_C_AUTHN_LEVEL_CALL         3
```

```
#define RPC_C_AUTHN_LEVEL_PKT            4
#define RPC_C_AUTHN_LEVEL_PKT_INTEGRITY  5
#define RPC_C_AUTHN_LEVEL_PKT_PRIVACY    6
```

In each of the levels greater than RPC_C_AUTHN_LEVEL_NONE, the user's identity is authenticated by the server. The strategy for authenticating the user is based on the security package. Under the NTLM package, a client is asked to encrypt a server-specified value (known as a *challenge*) using an encoded version of the client's password. The server then encrypts the same value using the same encoded password. If the encrypted values match, the server has successfully authenticated the client. This challenge approach negates the need to transmit the client's password when performing authentication.

RPC_C_AUTHN_LEVEL_PKT_INTEGRITY is used to guarantee that transmitted data has not been modified. This is accomplished by performing a checksum

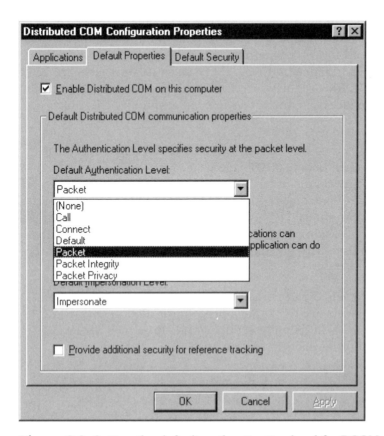

Figure 6-6. *Setting the default authentication level for DCOM.*

on all transmitted data. Note that such a check adds significant overhead since the security package is forced to examine all transmitted data.

The highest authentication level is RPC_C_AUTHN_LEVEL_PKT_PRIVACY. This level ensures that all transmitted data will be encrypted to prevent unauthorized examination. Below this level, data is sent as clear text. Since this level is higher than all others, it subsumes the features of all levels below it such as data integrity and user authentication. The method used to encrypt the data is dependent on the security package.

The authentication level used by COM clients and required by COM servers can be set in several ways. Each process that uses COM must call CoInitializeSecurity() exactly once either explicitly or implicitly. In most cases, the call is made implicitly, and a systemwide default value for the authentication level is used. On Windows NT, users typically configure a default setting for the authentication level in the dcomcnfg.exe utility as shown in Figure 6-6. This value is then stored in the system registry.

In addition to using CoInitializeSecurity() to explicitly set the authentication level on a per-process basis, COM also allows a client to control the authentication level on a per-interface basis. This is accomplished by controlling the proxy used by the client to communicate with the COM server object. To better understand how the client manages interface-level security, consider the following COM interface:

```
interface IComAgent : IDispatch
{
    [id(1), helpstring("method WhoAreYou")]
    HRESULT WhoAreYou([out] BSTR* name);

    [id(2), helpstring("method GetSecretMessage")]
    HRESULT GetSecretMessage([out] BSTR* message);

    ...
};
```

The IComAgent interface defines a method called GetSecretMessage() that requires encryption. Let us assume that none of the other methods defined in the interface requires encryption and that the client would like to avoid the overhead of packet privacy and packet integrity when making any of the other calls. To control the security settings of the client-side proxy, COM provides the IClientSecurity interface, which defines the following methods:

- IClientSecurity::QueryBlanket()—Used to determine the security options currently associated with the proxy.

- `IClientSecurity::SetBlanket()`—Used to set the security options associated with the proxy.

- `IClientSecurity::CopyProxy()`—Used to create a copy of the proxy so that the original proxy remains unchanged when specific security settings are needed for a particular call (as is the case in our example).

For our example, we want to create an interface pointer that will use encryption when invoking the `GetSecretMessage()` method on the COM server object. This is accomplished by setting the security blanket to use encryption for a specific interface pointer as shown here:

```
IComAgent* GetSecretAgent(IComAgent* pAgent)
{
    HRESULT          rc;
    IComAgent*       pSecretAgent = NULL;
    IClientSecurity* pcs          = NULL;

    // Step 1: Get the security interface for the proxy
    //         associated with pAgent.
    rc = pAgent->QueryInterface(IID_IClientSecurity,
                                (void**)&pcs);
    if ( FAILED(rc) ) ; // do error handling

    // Step 2: Make a copy of the proxy so that we only use
    //         encryption when we absolutely need to.
    rc = pcs->CopyProxy(pAgent, (IUnknown**)&pSecretAgent);
    if ( FAILED(rc) ) ; // do error handling

    // Step 3: Set the auth level for the secret agent.
    rc = pcs->SetBlanket(pSecretAgent,
                         RPC_C_AUTHN_WINNT,
                         RPC_C_AUTHZ_NONE, 0,
                         RPC_C_AUTHN_LEVEL_PKT_PRIVACY,
                         RPC_C_IMP_LEVEL_IDENTIFY,
                         0, EOAC_NONE);
    pcs->Release();
    if ( FAILED(rc) ) ; // do error handling

    return pSecretAgent;
}
```

The purpose of `GetSecretAgent()` is to create a second `IComAgent` interface pointer that uses encryption when interacting with the COM object referenced by `pAgent`. We will refer to the interface pointer that uses encryption as the secret agent. Creating the secret agent requires these three steps:

1. Obtain the `IClientSecurity` interface pointer for the proxy object associated with `pAgent`. This is accomplished by simply calling `QueryInterface()` on the original `pAgent` interface pointer.

2. Make a copy of the proxy. This will result in two interface pointers referencing the same server-side object. The original interface pointer, `pAgent`, will be unchanged, while the secret agent interface pointer will use encryption. This allows `pAgent` to be used for all calls not requiring encryption.

3. Set the authentication level to `RPC_C_AUTHN_LEVEL_PKT_PRIVACY` when setting the security blanket for the secret agent interface pointer.

By utilizing `IClientSecurity`, a client can specify that privacy be used in specific situations. For our example, we also want the COM server object to guarantee that clients have chosen packet privacy when retrieving secret messages. COM provides a method for checking the calling context of a COM server object invocation. The following example demonstrates how the server can guarantee packet privacy:

```
STDMETHODIMP CComAgent::GetSecretMessage(BSTR* message)
{
    IServerSecurity *pss = NULL;

    // Step 1: Get the context for the current call.
    HRESULT rc = ::CoGetCallContext(IID_IServerSecurity,
                                    (void**)&pss);
    if ( FAILED(rc) ) ; // handle error

    // Step 2: Determine the auth level from the context.
    DWORD authLevel;
    rc = pss->QueryBlanket(0, 0, 0, &authLevel, 0, 0, 0);
    pss->Release();
    if ( FAILED(rc) ) ; // handle error

    // Step 3: Abort if auth level is insufficient.
    if (authLevel < RPC_C_AUTHN_LEVEL_PKT_PRIVACY)
        return E_FAIL;

    // Step 4: Get the secret message.
    _bstr_t msg("This is the very secret message.");
    *message = msg.copy();
    return S_OK;
}
```

COM provides the `CoGetCallContext()` method to retrieve a server security-related object that supports the `IServerSecurity` interface. This allows the

COM server object to perform a number of tasks. The following method can be used to retrieve the security blanket information associated with the client:

- `IServerSecurity::QueryBlanket()`—Used as the server-side equivalent of the query capability found in `IClientSecurity`. The server implementation in the example calls `QueryBlanket()` to determine the security settings made by the client and fails if packet privacy has not been specified.

Up to this point, we have focused solely on user authentication, data integrity, and privacy. We have not yet discussed user authorization. To determine whether a client is authorized to access a server and server-side resources, the COM developer has two options. The first option is to determine authorization based on the information retrieved when calling

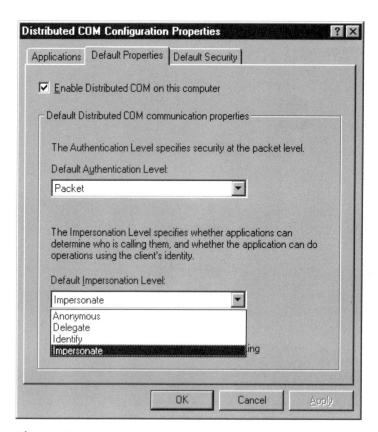

Figure 6-7. Setting the default impersonation level for DCOM.

`IServerSecurity::QueryBlanket()`. The second option is to use impersonation—a COM server object can temporarily impersonate the client to access server-side resources. When using impersonation with COM, the burden of authorization is transferred to the operating system.

This opens up another security issue regarding the trust that must exist between client and server in order to allow a server to impersonate a client. Note that the client has final say as to whether or not a server should have the ability to impersonate the client. The client can control the impersonation level in much the same manner as the authentication level by using the `dcomcnfg.exe` utility as shown in Figure 6-7 to set a systemwide default value or by using `CoInitializeSecurity()` and/or the `IClientSecurity` interface programmatically.

In addition to `QueryBlanket()`, the `IServerSecurity` interface defines the following methods for supporting impersonation in a COM server:

- `IServerSecurity::ImpersonateClient()`—Used to associate the current thread of execution with the client making the call.

- `IServerSecurity::RevertToSelf()`—Used to revert back to the server process owner after the server has completed impersonation.

- `IServerSecurity::IsImpersonating()`—Used to determine whether the server is currently impersonating the client.

To demonstrate impersonation, consider the addition of the following method to our initial `IComAgent` interface:

```
STDMETHODIMP CComAgent::ImpersonateClient(BSTR* clientName)
{
    IServerSecurity *pss = NULL;

    // Step 1: Get the context for the current call.
    HRESULT rc = ::CoGetCallContext(IID_IServerSecurity,
                                    (void**)&pss);
    if ( FAILED(rc) ) ; // handle error

    // Step 2: Use the context to impersonate the client.
    rc = pss->ImpersonateClient();
    if ( FAILED (rc) ) ; // handle error

    // Step 3: Get the client's user name ...
    char nameBuff[128];
    ULONG size = 127;
    if ( !::GetUserName(nameBuff, &size) ) ; // handle error
```

```
    // Step 4: Revert to self.
    pss->RevertToSelf();
    pss->Release();

    // Step 5: Return the result to the user.
    _bstr_t bstr(nameBuff);
    *clientName = bstr.copy();
    return S_OK;
}
```

The use of impersonation with DCOM is limiting in several ways. When using the NTLM Security Manager with DCOM, the ability to impersonate a client is limited to one hop. A server cannot impersonate a client when communicating with DCOM objects on a third machine. Perhaps the biggest problem with impersonation is that it does not provide a scalable solution. Impersonation relies on very fine granularity—each user has specific access permissions. Authorization mechanisms scale better when they rely on groupings of individuals as opposed to unique individual permissions. To meet this need, a role-based security mechanism for COM is provided by the Microsoft Transaction Server framework.

MTS Security

MTS greatly simplifies security management under COM by providing a declarative security framework as well as a simplified programmatic model. Declarative security allows administrators to configure user authorization without changing applications programmatically. Programmatic security provides security-aware COM objects with a coding mechanism for enforcing user authorization. As we saw in the last section, COM's native security mechanism is strictly programmatic and often relies on impersonation. While impersonation can be implemented in a generic manner, it moves user authorization control from COM to the underlying operating system. In many cases, it is often desirable to maintain control of user authorization at the COM level.

MTS provides a role-based model for managing user authorization. MTS relies on the underlying COM mechanisms described in the last section to provide user authentication, data integrity, and privacy. In the MTS framework, a role represents a particular type of user rather than distinct users' identities. These roles are then used to determine when access to a specific MTS COM component is allowed. The MTS administrator can assign distinct users to each role, thereby allowing access to the COM objects. To better understand how roles are used with MTS, consider the following interface:

```
interface IMtsSecureAccount : IDispatch
{
    HRESULT Deposit    ([in] double amount);
    HRESULT Withdraw   ([in] double amount);
    HRESULT GetBalance([out, retval] double* );
};
```

The `IMtsSecureAccount` interface defines methods for depositing money into, withdrawing money from, and getting the balance of an account. We therefore implement an MTS object that implements the `IMtsSecureAccount` interface and create an MTS package called `Ch6` to manage that object.

To secure such an account, it is decided that there are two types of users: spenders and savers. Spenders have permission to withdraw money from the account, while savers have access only to deposit money into the account. Figure 6-8 illustrates how the MTS Explorer appears after adding the roles and users for `Spenders` and `Savers`.

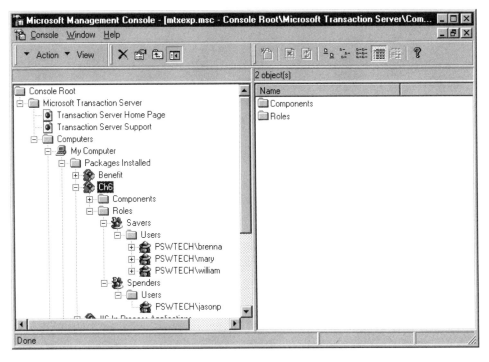

Figure 6-8. *Associating MTS roles with the Ch6 package.*

For the `MtsSecureAccount` example, we have limited the `Savers` role to the users named `brenna`, `mary`, and `william`. The only spender is the user named `jasonp`. The next step is to declare what roles can access the `MtsSecureAccount` object. MTS supports role membership at both the component and interface levels. Since our component supports only one interface, we modify the role membership at the component level rather than at the interface level. Figure 6-9 illustrates how the MTS Explorer appears after adding the `Spenders` and `Savers` roles to the role membership for the `Ch6.MtsSecureAccount` component.

The most important point to note is that the `MtsSecureAccount` component is not aware of specific users. Instead, it is concerned only with the two roles, `Savers` and `Spenders`, that are part of its role membership. New users can be given permission to access the `MtsSecureAccount` component simply by adding their user ids to the appropriate role for the `Ch6` package.

There are two roles associated with the `MtsSecureAccount` component. The next question is, How does the component limit withdrawals to only `Spenders`

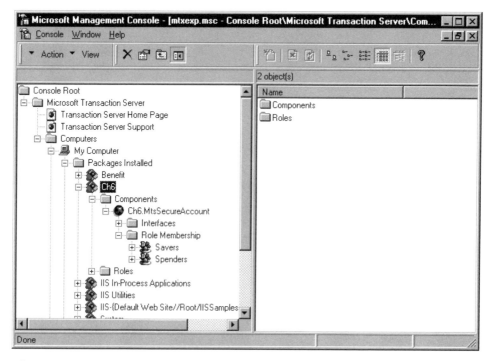

Figure 6-9. *MTS role membership for the Ch6.MtsSecureAccount component.*

and deposits to only `Savers`? This is where the need for a programmatic security model is still required. In COM, MTS, and the Distributed Transaction Coordinator on page 148, we described how a context object is associated with each MTS component. In addition to transaction-related functionality, the context object also provides the following methods for interacting with the MTS security mechanism:

- `IObjectContext::IsSecurityEnabled()`—Used to determine whether security is currently enabled for the MTS component.

- `IObjectContext::IsCallerInRole()`—Used to determine whether the caller is in a specific role when the call is made.

For simplicity, we have implemented the `MtsSecureAccount` component in Visual Basic. The `Withdraw()` method as shown next uses programmatic security to determine whether the client has permission to withdraw money. If the caller is not a `Spender`, the `Withdraw()` method fails. It is important to note once again that MTS places the emphasis on roles rather than on distinct users. The `Withdraw()` method shown here examines the role rather than specific user ids:

```
Public Sub Withdraw(ByVal amount As Double)
    'Step 1: Get MTS context object associated with this component.
    Dim ctx As ObjectContext
    Set ctx = GetObjectContext()

    'Step 2: Programmatically determine whether user has permission
    '        to withdraw.
    Dim isSecure As Boolean
    isSecure = ctx.IsSecurityEnabled And _
            ctx.IsCallerInRole("Spenders")

    'Step 3: Make the withdrawal.
    If isSecure Then
        'Withdraw money from the account.
    Else
        'Handle security violation.
    End If
End Sub
```

As we noted earlier in the chapter, the name *Microsoft Transaction Server* is actually a misnomer. MTS does far more than manage distributed transactions. The security model afforded by MTS is another reason for using MTS to host COM objects when secure access is required.

CORBA and the Secure Sockets Layer

The primary communication protocol used by CORBA ORBs in the marketplace today is the Internet Inter-ORB Protocol (IIOP). IIOP does not include inherent support for a security mechanism. To compensate for this lack of security, several vendors have created add-on security packages for their CORBA ORBs that rely on the Secure Sockets Layer (SSL).

SSL was originally created by Netscape Communications and has emerged as a de facto standard for secure communication across the Internet. SSL uses RSA* public key cryptography to realize secure connections. From the CORBA perspective, SSL is unobtrusive in that it has very little influence on a CORBA client or server application. The reason is that SSL exists as a separate secure layer between IIOP and TCP/IP, as shown in Figure 6-10. CORBA clients and servers usually need to interact only with SSL-related functionality when initializing an SSL-enabled ORB.

The primary security benefits enjoyed by SSL-enabled CORBA clients and servers are

- *Authentication.* With SSL, a client can authenticate the validity of the server, and the server can optionally authenticate the validity of the client. This is accomplished by executing an SSL handshake protocol that uses public and private keys. Note that the authentication mechanism applies to applications rather than to individual users.

- *Data integrity.* SSL ensures against data tampering by including a message authentication code (MAC) with each transmitted message.

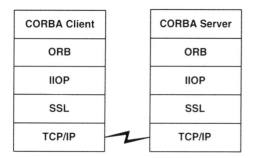

Figure 6-10. *The SSL layer in an SSL-enabled CORBA solution.*

---

*The acronym *RSA* stands for Rivest, Shamir, and Adleman, the names of the three people after whom this cryptography is named.

This code is a computed checksum that is used to validate the transmitted data.

- *Privacy.* Once an SSL session has been initiated, another key, known as a *secret*, is securely exchanged using the public and private keys. This secret is then used to encrypt and decrypt all data passed across the SSL connection. Since all data being transmitted is encrypted, privacy is assured.

Despite the advantages just listed, CORBA/SSL still does not meet the distributed security requirement for user authorization. SSL does, however, provide an effective and lightweight solution for ensuring authentication, data integrity, and privacy—traits that are essential when using CORBA clients and servers on the Internet. For environments where authorization is required as well as authentication, data integrity, and privacy, CORBA vendors provide implementations of the CORBA Security Service.

The CORBA Security Service

The CORBA Security Service is an impressive and comprehensive specification that outlines in great detail how security should be managed in a CORBA environment. The comprehensive nature of the specification is evidenced by its size (almost 300 pages) and the fact that it required over two years of effort before it was first approved in 1996. After its approval, it took almost two more years for the first implementations to appear in the marketplace.

The great length of time needed to bring CORBA security to the marketplace can be blamed on two problems. First, distributed security is a difficult and complex problem that requires considerable effort to effectively solve. Second, extensive security as provided by the CORBA specification is usually required only in the largest of systems, very few of which have relied on CORBA until recently. The demand for a heavyweight security solution will continue to increase as CORBA becomes a more dominant technology in large enterprise systems.

The CORBA Security Service addresses a broad range of security-related issues. In addition to the basic security requirements such as authentication, integrity, privacy, and authorization, CORBA Security also addresses a number of other important issues, most important of which are the following:

- *Delegation.* In distributed object systems, chaining of calls often occurs across multiple objects. For example, *Object_A* calls *Object_B*, which, in turn, calls *Object_C*. Delegation deals with how the original caller's security credentials are managed during the calling process. CORBA Security defines a number of delegation schemes to be supported by a compliant implementation.

- *Auditing.* To monitor security, notable events such as authentication failures, privilege changes, and so forth, must be audited. CORBA Security defines policies and interfaces for auditing activity within a security-enabled ORB.

- *Nonrepudiation.* In client/server systems, there are times when clients and servers must be held accountable for their actions. CORBA Security addresses nonrepudiation as defined in the ISO 7498-2 specification.

- *Interoperability.* One of the hallmarks of CORBA is its constant focus on interoperability. CORBA Security defines the Secure Inter-ORB Protocol (SECIOP), a protocol designed to allow for interoperability across distinct security-enabled ORBs. CORBA Security also addresses how security information should be managed within an interoperable object reference (IOR).

- *Replaceability.* Wherever possible, CORBA Security allows for replaceability of key security services such as authentication services, auditing services, and so forth. This is a natural side effect of the OMG's efforts to specify protocol rather than specific implementation details.

While these issues have significant merit, they do not distract from CORBA Security's focus on basic requirements.

User authentication is the first order of business when working in a CORBA-secured environment. CORBA Security provides several objects that manage security for the client. These objects include

- `PrincipalAuthenticator`—Encapsulates the ORB's underlying authentication mechanism. The client identifies himself/herself to the `PrincipalAuthenticator` and is then granted a set of credentials to be used when performing secure operations.

- `Credentials`—Represents all security-related attributes that are associated with an authenticated user. These attributes include the information related to the roles, groups, clearances, and privileges of the user. Of special note is the fact that roles under CORBA Security can be made universal across the distributed system. This is in contrast to roles under Microsoft Transaction Server, which must be defined on a per-package basis.

- Current—Associated by the ORB with the authenticated user's Credentials object. Users do not directly manipulate their credentials. (Current was first introduced in CORBA and the Object Transaction Service on page 156.) CORBA Security extends the concept of Current to also encompass security as well as transactional information. Whenever a client calls a secure method, the ORB implicitly passes a reference for the client's Credentials object to the server so that authorization can occur.

Communication between clients and servers must also be secure in that data integrity and privacy must be provided when needed. CORBA Security does not provide specific interfaces for interacting with data integrity and privacy mechanisms. Instead, CORBA Security identifies the QOP (quality of protection) that is provided by the underlying security mechanism. This characteristic is defined by an enum in CORBA IDL as

```
// Quality of protection
enum QOP
{
    SecQOPNoProtection,
    SecQOPIntegrity,         // uses checksum to guarantee integrity
    SecQOPConfidentiality,   // uses encryption to guarantee privacy
    SecQOPIntegrityAndConfidentiality
};
```

CORBA Security also provides the following method for overriding the QOP for a specific object reference:

```
// The following method is defined in the CORBA IDL for
// the SecurityLevel2::Object interface definition.
void override_default_QOP(in Security::QOP qop);
```

User authorization is generally handled by the security-enabled ORB when using CORBA Security. Recall that an authenticated user is associated with a Credentials object and that a reference to the Credentials object is passed to the server whenever the client calls a secure method. To determine whether or not access is allowed, these credentials are compared with the rights required to access a particular object method. If the credentials are insufficient to meet the rights required, the call is rejected. CORBA Security defines the following interfaces for managing user authorization:

- RequiredRights—Defines methods for accessing information related to required rights in the underlying ORB's security information repository. Rights are set at the interface-method level. A `RequiredRights` object is available as an attribute of `Current` in every execution context. The CORBA IDL description is as follows:

```
interface RequiredRights
{
    void get_required_rights(
        in Object obj,
        in CORBA::Identifier operation_name,
        in CORBA::RepositoryId interface_name,
        out Security::RightsList rights,
        out Security::RightsCombinator rights_combinator);

    void set_required_rights(
        in string operation_name,
        in CORBA::RepositoryId interface_name,
        in Security::RightsList rights,
        in Security::RightsCombinator rights_combinator);
};
```

- `AccessDecision`—Contains one method that is used to determine whether the credentials of the user meet the rights required of the interface method. The CORBA IDL description is as follows:

```
interface AccessDecision
{
    boolean access_allowed (
        in SecurityLevel2::CredentialsList cred_list,
        in Object target,
        in CORBA::Identifier operation_name,
        in CORBA::Identifier target_interface_name);
};
```

CORBA Security automatically calls the `access_allowed()` method every time a secure method is invoked by a user. In addition, applications can define their own access policies. The specification recommends that such access mechanisms also implement the `AccessDecision` interface.

The access control model provided by CORBA Security offers very fine granularity when controlling authorizations. Access to each interface method can be controlled at any level of use such as group, role, or distinct user. Control at too fine a granularity can become unwieldy in a sizable system. To allow for reasonable administration of system security, access should be done at the role level for groups of objects whenever possible.

The short overview presented herein cannot do justice to the completeness of the CORBA Security Service. Robust implementations of CORBA Security will be a major factor in allowing large enterprise entities to move away from legacy systems toward CORBA-based infrastructures. The combination of distributed transaction support, security, messaging, and object management creates an exciting avenue for future enterprise system development.

Messaging Support

In large enterprise systems, situations often arise where components need to communicate asynchronously. For example, consider a distributed system that supports on-line trading. In such a system, an on-line trader needs to rapidly place multiple orders to be executed in the stock market. The trader has no control over when a specific order will be fulfilled or by whom. Depending on the bid (or ask) price made by the trader, the order may never be completed. In addition, a trader may decide to place orders when the market is closed in the expectation of having those orders fulfilled soon after the market opens. Based on the very nature of on-line trading, it is impossible for a trader to interactively communicate with the market. Instead, the trader must issue multiple orders at a time and wait (perhaps indefinitely) for replies from the market.

There are many situations similar to the on-line trading scenario. These situations are characterized by a high degree of autonomy exhibited by the entities at work in such systems. Furthermore, the autonomous entities tend to perform their operations at different times. The request-reply model traditionally offered by COM and CORBA is inappropriate for building such asynchronous systems. For example, a trader would be greatly handicapped if a reply was required for each order placed before the next order could be issued. Instead, such systems are typically built using specialized messaging software.

Two of the most popular messaging software systems currently available are Microsoft's MSMQ and IBM's MQSeries. Both of these systems rely on the abstraction of queues to relay messages between components. Figure 6-11 illustrates the use of message queuing to implement the on-line trading scenario.

In Figure 6-11, the trader communicates asynchronously with the stock market by placing orders on the order queue and receiving fulfillment notifications on the notification queue. A message-queuing approach allows the trader

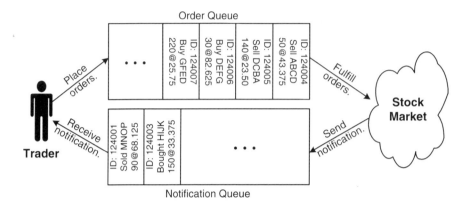

Figure 6-11. *Using message queuing in an on-line trading scenario.*

and stock market to operate autonomously. The trader can always place orders, even when the stock market is unavailable. The stock market can fulfill orders without regard for the actual availability of the trader.

Implementing an asynchronous system with the request-reply semantics of traditional COM and CORBA would require an extra component to handle the indirection accomplished by the message queues in Figure 6-11. Because the need for such an indirection is common in large systems, several companies offer specialized messaging software. Messaging software products provide a rich set of features, including the following:

- *Guaranteed delivery.* Messages are stored in queues until they can be delivered.

- *Recoverable messages.* Recoverable messages can survive failures such as a system reboot.

- *Automatic expiration.* Messages can be timed out if they are not retrieved from the queue in a timely manner.

- *Temporal ordering.* Messages can be ordered based on a first-in-first-out (FIFO) policy.

- *Priority ordering.* Messages can be ordered based on priority rather than on time.

- *Security.* Access to queues can be restricted to authorized users only. In addition, messages in transit can be encrypted.

The autonomy afforded by a messaging approach greatly decreases coupling across components in large enterprise systems. Until recently, messaging software products have been split off from mainstream COM and CORBA. This has been due to two factors. First, messaging products such as IBM's MQSeries are well established in the marketplace and have been used since long before COM or CORBA became popular. Second, messaging is appropriate for the asynchronous problem space, whereas COM and CORBA are more appropriate for synchronous request-reply problems.

Given the robust features offered by messaging products, it appears that messaging might be the final solution for implementing asynchronous solutions. This is not the case. Messaging software tends to oversimplify when creating solutions. The interface for communicating with message queues is very strict. Also, the messaging approach lacks the rich set of data types and expressive interface concepts that are offered in COM and CORBA. Messaging support can therefore greatly enhance COM and CORBA. Because messaging support and COM/CORBA are complementary, both Microsoft and the OMG are working aggressively to merge messaging semantics into the COM and CORBA architectures.

COM and Microsoft Message Queue Server

To support messaging in the COM environment, a robust message-queuing product is required. Microsoft has met this requirement with its MSMQ product. MSMQ provides functionality that is comparable to IBM's venerable MQSeries product. In addition to a C-language API, Microsoft also provides a COM interface for MSMQ. Note that this does not constitute a merger of COM and MSMQ. The COM wrapper simply allows any COM-enabled client to access MSMQ.

The power of message queuing as well as the use of the COM interface to MSMQ are best demonstrated in an example. The rest of this section describes an MSMQ-based solution for the on-line trading problem illustrated in Figure 6-11.

The on-line trading solution will require two MSMQ queues named

- `stock_market_orders`—Used to manage market orders placed by a trader. Orders placed by a trader must expire if they have not been removed from the queue within 10 minutes. In addition, "sell" orders must always take precedence over "buy" orders in order to maximize cash flow for the trader.

- `trader_notifications`—Used to manage notification messages indicating that a specific order has been fulfilled. It is imperative that MSMQ guarantee delivery of notifications to the trader so that the trader can keep track of executed orders. For this reason, messages placed in the `trader_notifications` queue will never expire and will be recoverable with regard to system failure.

The solution will also require the creation of a *Trader* application and a *Stock Market* application. (Complete source code for these applications can be found in Appendix C on page 415.) Since a COM interface to MSMQ will be used and since Visual Basic provides the simplest tool for creating COM client applications, both applications will be implemented using Visual Basic. To use the MSMQ COM interface, we first need to reference the MSMQ type library in both the *Trader* and *Stock Market* Visual Basic projects as shown in Figure 6-12.

The *Trader* application has two main purposes. First, the trader must be able to place both buy and sell orders. Second, the trader must be notified when a

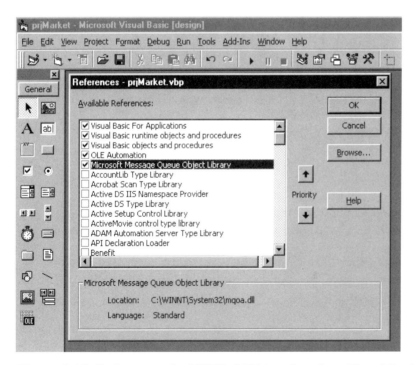

Figure 6-12. *Referencing the MSMQ COM interface from Visual Basic.*

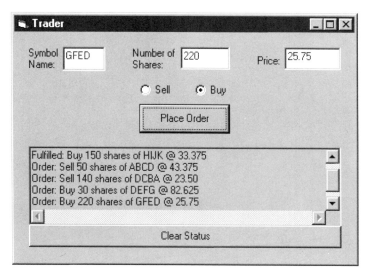

Figure 6-13. *The Trader MSMQ application.*

previously placed order has been fulfilled by the market. The *Trader* application is shown in Figure 6-13.

The trader can set a symbol name, number of shares, price per share, and indicate whether the order is a buy or a sell. The trader can also view a status window showing placed orders as well as fulfilled orders. When the *Trader* application starts, it needs to open the order and notification queues. If the queues do not exist, the application creates the queues. The Visual Basic method shown here indicates how an MSMQ queue is opened (and possibly created) in Visual Basic:

```
Private Sub OpenQ(ByVal qHost As String, _
              ByVal qLabel As String, _
              ByVal qGuid As String, _
              ByVal qMode As Long, _
              ByRef q As MSMQQueue)


    Dim query As New MSMQQuery
    Dim qinfos As MSMQQueueInfos
    Dim qinfo As MSMQQueueInfo
```

```
    'Locate the queue.
    Set qinfos = query.LookupQueue(Label:=qLabel, _
                                   ServiceTypeGuid:=qGuid)
    Set qinfo = qinfos.Next

    'Create the queue if the query did not find one.
    If qinfo Is Nothing Then
        Set qinfo = New MSMQQueueInfo
        qinfo.PathName = qHost + "\" + qLabel
        qinfo.Label = qLabel
        qinfo.ServiceTypeGuid = qGuid
        qinfo.Create
    End If

    'Open the queue (qMode can be set to peek, send, or receive)
    Set q = qinfo.Open(qMode, 0)
End Sub
```

Once the order and notification queues have been opened, the *Trader* application must handle MSMQ events related to the notification queue. We will discuss MSMQ event handling in a moment when we look at the *Stock Market* application. Of more interest in the *Trader* application is the *Place Order* functionality. Recall that we placed several constraints on stock market orders (e.g., orders must expire after 10 minutes). The method used to place orders is as follows:

```
Private Sub cmdPlaceOrder_Click()
    Dim msg As New MSMQMessage
    Dim order As String

    'Determine priority of the message.
    If optSell.Value = True Then
        msg.Priority = 7    'Sell orders have highest priority
    Else
        msg.Priority = 3    'Buy orders have lower priority
    End If

    'We want orders to time out if they haven't been fetched
    'from the queue within 10 minutes (600 seconds).
    msg.MaxTimeToReceive = 600

    'Track the order placement in the status area.
    order = GetOrderString
    txtStatus.Text = txtStatus.Text + "Order: " + _
                     order + vbCrLf
```

```
    'Set the message body and label and send the message.
    msg.Body = GetOrderString
    msg.Label = "Order"
    msg.Send gOrderQ
End Sub
```

After creating the message instance, we set the priority of each sell order message to 7 and each buy order message to 3. This ensures that sell orders will be placed ahead of buy orders in the order queue. Next, we set the time-out of order messages to be 10 minutes. Finally, we generate a message body, set the message label, and send the order message to the order queue. Note that the *Stock Market* application does not need to be running since we are not communicating directly with it. Instead, order messages are sent to the order queue. The *Stock Market* application is then able to receive messages from the order queue as desired.

The *Stock Market* application has two main purposes. First, the market needs to be alerted when orders are placed by the trader. Second, the market fulfills orders and sends notifications back to the trader. Assume that the trader has placed 4 outstanding orders. When the *Stock Market* application starts, it will be notified of the 4 orders waiting in the order queue as shown in Figure 6-14.

The *Stock Market* application first needs to open the order queue and notification queue just as the *Trader* application did. After the queues are open, the market needs to listen for trader orders. The MSMQ COM interface provides an

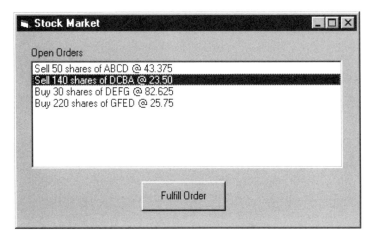

Figure 6-14. *The Stock Market MSMQ application.*

event mechanism allowing clients to be notified when messages have been queued. An `MSMQEvent` object is initialized and declared as follows:

```
Dim WithEvents gOrderQEvents As MSMQEvent
Dim gOrderQ As MSMQQueue

Private Sub Form_Load()
    'Open the order queue to receive orders
    ...

    'Receive event notification when new messages are added
    'to the order queue.
    Set gOrderQEvents = New MSMQEvent
    gOrderQ.EnableNotification gOrderQEvents
End Sub
```

After the event object is initialized, the following method gets fired whenever a message appears in the order queue:

```
Private Sub gOrderQEvents_Arrived(ByVal q As Object, _
                                  ByVal cursor As Long)
    Dim msgIn As MSMQMessage
    Dim strTextIn As String

    'Get an MSMQQueue interface pointer for the orderQ
    Dim orderQ As MSMQQueue
    Set orderQ = q

    'Get the message out of the queue
    '(time out after 100 milliseconds)
    Set msgIn = orderQ.Receive(ReceiveTimeout:=100)
    If Not msgIn Is Nothing Then
        strTextIn = msgIn.Body        'Read the message body
        lstOrders.AddItem (strTextIn) 'Add the order to the list
    End If

    'Reenable event firing
    orderQ.EnableNotification gOrderQEvents
End Sub
```

The *Stock Market* application simply provides a mechanism for a user to select an order from a list and fulfill the order. The *Trader* and *Stock Market* applications are extremely robust in that each operates independently of the other. This allows for improved performance, scalability, and reliability at the cost of increased generalization as is necessary when using message queuing.

The establishment of MSMQ in Microsoft's suite of server products is extremely important. MSMQ is an essential building block for creating large enterprise systems in the Windows NT Server environment. In addition to the basic need for message queuing software, the establishment of MSMQ also allows Microsoft to use MSMQ as an underlying transport mechanism for an asynchronous form of COM. Microsoft plans to add support for its Queued Components product using MSMQ in COM+.

CORBA and Messaging Support

The CORBA programming model is inherently synchronous (as is COM). To address asynchronous issues, the OMG provides the CORBA Event Service and the CORBA Notification Service.[*] While these services offer a callback architecture for event-oriented distributed object programming, they do not provide a general approach for supporting the asynchronous invocation of CORBA methods. Instead, the Event Service and Notification Service rely on the use of intermediate CORBA objects known as *event channels*. CORBA applications that utilize the Event Service or Notification Service must necessarily interact with event channels.

To support asynchronous method invocation as well as the quality-of-service features typically associated with messaging systems, several vendors have combined CORBA ORBs with commercial messaging products. One of the most interesting products in the CORBA messaging arena is TIBCO's TIB/ObjectBus CORBA ORB. TIBCO's primary messaging software product, TIB/Rendezvous, is a highly versatile messaging system that is offered on all major server platforms. The TIB/ObjectBus CORBA ORB can use TIB/Rendezvous instead of IIOP as an underlying transport mechanism.

In addition to TIBCO's efforts, Iona has created two different products that combine a commercial messaging product with Orbix. The first is Orbix+MQSeries, a product that integrates Orbix and IBM's MQSeries. The other is Orbix+PIPES, a product that integrates Orbix with PeerLogic's PIPES. Both of these products use a special adaptor that allows the Orbix runtime to use the messaging system rather than IIOP as an underlying transport.

Products such as TIB/ObjectBus, Orbix+MQSeries, and Orbix+PIPES demonstrate the need for messaging support in CORBA. To meet this need, the OMG

---

[*]The CORBA Notification Service is actually a successor to the CORBA Event Service. The CORBA Notification Service preserves backward compatibility with the CORBA Event Service while adding important new features such as event filtering and quality of service.

has approved a CORBA Messaging specification. The CORBA Messaging specification is a joint submission presented by 11 companies, including BEA Systems, IBM, Inprise, Iona, PeerLogic, and TIBCO.[*] This messaging specification represents a major addition to the next version of CORBA (CORBA 3.0) and addresses three fundamental areas:

1. *Quality-of-service management.* The specification outlines how quality of service (e.g., automatic expiration, temporal ordering, priority ordering, etc.) is managed within the CORBA Messaging environment. The specification also describes how quality-of-service settings are propagated throughout the runtime system.

2. *Message routing.* Because CORBA was initially intended as a request-reply synchronous model, its underlying communication protocol (as specified in the General Inter-ORB Protocol, GIOP) does not adequately support message routing. The CORBA Messaging specification addresses changes that need to be made to GIOP in order to adequately support CORBA Messaging.

3. *Programming model.* The specification outlines callback and polling models for CORBA Messaging. The specification also presents programming examples using CORBA IDL and a C++ mapping.

As just stated, the programming model presented in the CORBA Messaging specification discusses two distinct models: callbacks and polling. To understand how these models would work, consider once again the on-line trading scenario illustrated in Figure 6-11. The following CORBA IDL would represent a synchronous approach for placing orders in a trading system:

```
interface StockMarket
{
    void placeOrder(in string order, out string result);
};
```

For simplicity, we use a string to represent both the order and the result. The method, `placeOrder()`, is synchronous in that it will block until the `order` is handled and a `result` is returned. Let us first examine the callback model described in the CORBA Messaging specification. Use of the callback model would result in the following IDL declarations:[†]

---

[*]The CORBA Messaging specification can be obtained from the OMG at `http://www.omg.org`.

[†]Note that the IDL descriptions of the callback- and polling-related declarations contained in this section are strictly notional in order to describe how the callback and polling interfaces would be used from client applications. For brevity, we have not included exception support code that would also appear in the notional IDL.

```
interface AMI_StockMarketHandler;

interface StockMarket
{
    // Original declaration.
    void placeOrder(in string order, out string result);

    // Async callback declaration.
    void sendc_placeOrder(in AMI_StockMarketHandler ami_handler,
                          in string order);
};

interface AMI_StockMarketHandler : Messaging::ReplyHandler
{
    void placeOrder(in string result);
}
```

When using the callback model, the user would not directly invoke the
placeOrder() method. Instead, the user would first create an instance of a
CORBA object supporting the AMI_StockMarketHandler interface that implemented the placeOrder(result) method. This callback object is referred to
as the *reply handler*. The user would then invoke the sendc_placeOrder()
method and pass the reply handler reference. The call to sendc_placeOrder()
would return immediately. The result of the invocation would be passed to the
placeOrder() method of the reply handler that was passed as a parameter.

The other asynchronous model is polling. Use of the polling model would
result in the following IDL declarations:

```
value AMI_StockMarketPoller;

interface StockMarket
{
    // Original declaration.
    void placeOrder(in string order, out string result);

    // Async polling declaration.
    AMI_StockMarketPoller sendp_placeOrder(in string order);
};

value AMI_StockMarketPoller : Messaging::Poller
{
    void placeOrder(in unsigned long timeout,
                    out string result);
};
```

When using the polling model, the user would not directly invoke the `placeOrder()` method. Instead, the user would invoke the `sendp_placeOrder()` method. The call to `sendp_placeOrder()` would immediately return an `AMI_StockMarketPoller` object. The implementation of the poller object is provided by the messaging-aware ORB. The user could then periodically query the poller object to determine the result.

Note that the poller object is declared as a `value` rather than as an `interface`. The `value` keyword signifies that the poller object returned from the `sendp_placeOrder()` call is a stateful local object (and will therefore be performant since calls to the poller object will be in-process). The `value` keyword is a newly introduced feature in CORBA that indicates the passing of objects by value.[*]

The OMG has approved the CORBA Messaging specification and will include it as a significant part of CORBA 3.0. The CORBA Messaging specification is supported by all of the major vendors in the CORBA and messaging domains. Based on early efforts by companies such as TIBCO and Iona to integrate CORBA with messaging software, it appears likely that CORBA messaging will become mainstream in the short term.

Distributed Object Management

High-performance server-side systems require an infrastructure for complex application management. Before distributed objects, this realm was dominated by transaction-processing monitors such as IBM's CICS and BEA Systems' TUXEDO. Transaction-processing monitors (TP monitors) do far more than manage transactions. They establish the infrastructure necessary to create robust, scalable, and performant systems. TP monitors are actually distributed application managers that enforce well-defined rules for developing scalable distributed applications. The enforcement of these rules results in a disciplined approach for creating applications that can exist within the TP monitor framework and therefore provide the demanding needs of critical server-side systems.

TP monitors provide the benefits that are typically needed by critical server-side systems. These benefits include

- *Efficient start-up and shutdown of services.* TP monitors can be configured to anticipate system load and prestart services to handle that

---

[*]For more information, see the Objects by Value specification at `http://www.omg.org`.

load. TP monitors are also able to shut down services and minimize resource usage when services are not needed.

- *Resource pooling.* Server-side systems often rely on scarce resources. The most prevalent example of a scarce resource is a database connection. In servicing a large number of clients, it is not possible to provide one unique database connection per client. TP monitors are able to pool scarce resources such as database connections and share those resources across multiple clients.

- *Load balancing.* A server-side system may need to service a large number of requests at any given time. TP monitors allow for deployment of redundant servers and provide load-balancing functionality that can spread the workload across those redundant servers.

- *Fault tolerance.* Mission-critical systems rely on redundancy to guard against failure. TP monitors allow for deployment of redundant servers and provide fail-over mechanisms that can automatically switch over to a redundant server when a specific server fails.

Only recently have COM and CORBA products been realized that provide the benefits offered by traditional TP monitors. Examples of these products are Microsoft's MTS, which is a COM object management system, and BEA Systems' M3, a CORBA object management system. These distributed object management products are redefining how distributed object systems are designed and implemented using COM and CORBA. They are also making the distributed object community acutely aware of several requirements for making distributed objects scalable. The most significant of these requirements is the requirement for stateless objects.

The Need for Stateless Objects

The greatest misconception about distributed objects is that they are simply a distributed extension to traditional object-oriented programming. Many object-oriented developers attempt to create distributed objects that look and behave exactly like normal object-oriented programming objects. Such a goal is not attainable because distributed systems have very different requirements in comparison to nondistributed systems. One such requirement in a distributed system is the requirement to minimize network traffic. Another requirement is the ability to handle load balancing and automatic fail-over when the network becomes congested or fails completely.

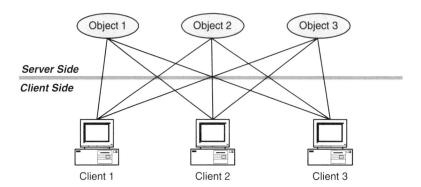

Figure 6-15. *A scenario where three stateful objects are used by three clients.*

In nondistributed object-based systems, object instances are tied to both state and methods. An object instance is created, and its state is changed over its lifetime by calling methods on the object. We refer to such objects as *stateful objects*. Consider a scenario where three stateful distributed objects are being used concurrently by three client applications. This scenario is depicted in Figure 6-15.

The scenario shown in Figure 6-15 illustrates that even a small system requires a large number of connections. Dedicated connections are an expensive resource in both COM and CORBA. Consider the case where 100 clients concurrently use 100 distributed objects. In such a situation, 10,000 dedicated connections would need to be tracked and maintained within the COM or CORBA runtime system. Dedicated connections also make it extremely difficult to perform load balancing and provide fault tolerance with regard to the server objects.

In many situations, dedicated connections as described here are not even necessary. It is unlikely that all connections would be active at the same time. This is where TP monitor functionality is best applied. Distributed object management systems such as Microsoft's MTS and BEA's M3 are intended to solve these problems. To minimize connection cost and provide load balancing and fault tolerance, these management systems require that the majority of distributed objects supported by their frameworks be stateless.

The term *stateless* tends to cause a great deal of anxiety among object-oriented developers. In distributed object management systems such as Microsoft's MTS and BEA's M3, objects are stateless only in that they are constantly being activated and deactivated. Objects are activated on demand and are deactivated when they are no longer needed.

Distributed object management systems have different approaches for determining when objects should be deactivated. Deactivation usually occurs when an object method has completed or when a transaction involving the method has completed. Deactivating objects reduces system load. When a deactivated object is again needed by a client, the object management system automatically activates another object to service the client's request. Note that after an object has been activated, it is once again stateful.

Clients that utilize distributed objects supported by an object management system do not possess direct handles on server objects. As shown in Figure 6-16, clients actually hold a handle that is managed by the object management system. This level of indirection allows the object management system to perform its magic. Clients are completely unaware if a handle references a distributed object that is currently activated or not. From the client's perspective, the handle on a deactivated object continues to be valid. The object management system takes care of automatically activating the object if it is used by the client.

Based on the scenario illustrated in Figure 6-16, it appears that the number of dedicated connections is still excessive. This is precisely the goal when using an object management system. Clients can be developed as if they possess dedicated connections. In reality, clients just possess handles to the object management system—handles that are very inexpensive to maintain.

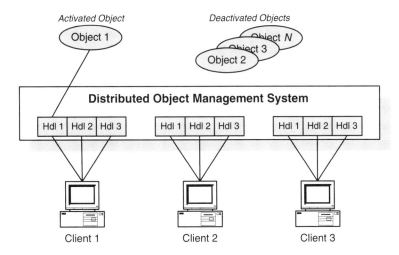

Figure 6-16. *Using an object management system to manage server activation.*

The indirection provided by an object management system also allows load balancing and automatic fail-over to occur. In the case where objects are activated and deactivated on a per-method basis, each method call to a distributed object can occur within a different server process. The object management system can therefore perform load balancing on a per-method basis and can also direct an object invocation toward a healthy server process when failure occurs.

A distributed object system must support stateless objects in order to be robust, scalable, and performant. Stateless objects allow a distributed object system to better manage its resources by automatically activating and deactivating actual object instances as required. This allows the overall system to support a much larger number of clients and servers.

COM Object Management Under Microsoft's MTS

Microsoft Transaction Server (MTS) is the cornerstone of Microsoft's COM object management system for the Windows platform. As we have seen in previous sections, MTS participates in a number of COM management activities, including transactions and security. MTS also allows server objects to be automatically deactivated and reactivated in order to reduce system load and increase scalability.

At the heart of MTS is the MTS Executive. The MTS Executive manages each COM object that is under MTS control. We will refer to MTS-controlled COM objects as *MTS objects*. To manage MTS objects, the MTS Executive associates a context wrapper with each MTS object. This context wrapper allows the MTS Executive to intercept all calls destined for the MTS object. The interception capability provided by such an indirection allows the MTS Executive to deactivate an object and then reactivate it the next time that it is needed. As illustrated in Figure 6-17, the client of an MTS object holds a reference to the MTS Executive's context wrapper rather than to the actual MTS object.

Holding references to MTS context wrappers is inexpensive in the MTS runtime environment. The deactivation of unneeded MTS objects greatly reduces system load and increases overall scalability because of the small overhead used by the context wrappers. In fact, it is generally recommended that MTS clients obtain references to MTS objects early and hold on to those references for a long period of time because the cost of reconnecting is greater than the overhead of maintaining a reference to the context wrapper.

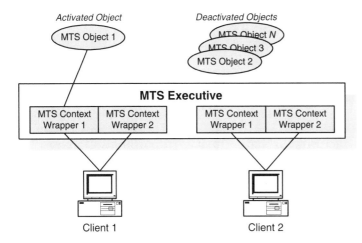

Figure 6-17. *The MTS Executive and MTS context wrappers.*

The ultimate key to scalability is the ability of an object management system to proactively deactivate unused objects. MTS provides both implicit and explicit mechanisms to force deactivation of MTS objects. The implicit deactivation mechanism is based on the transactional setting of an MTS object. In Figure 6-5 (given earlier), we illustrated how an MTS object's transaction property can be set to require a transaction. If an MTS object requires a transaction, the MTS object will be deactivated when the transaction that it participates in completes (whether it commits or rolls back). This means that clients of an MTS object cannot rely on the instance state of an MTS object to live across multiple transactions. In fact, the MTS object instance that gets activated upon the next client request will probably be a different MTS object instance altogether.

While transaction boundaries provide a logical approach for deactivating objects, it is also important to have the ability to deactivate nontransactional MTS objects. In COM, MTS, and the Distributed Transaction Coordinator on page 148, we described the context object with which all MTS objects are associated. An MTS object obtains a reference to its associated object context by calling `GetObjectContext()` as shown here:

```
STDMETHODIMP CAccount::Deposit(BSTR accountName, double amount)
{
    IObjectContext* pObjectContext;
    ::GetObjectContext(&pObjectContext);
    ...
```

```
    // Let MTS know that this part of the transaction is
    // complete. SetComplete() causes deactivation of the
    // MTS object even if it does not require a transaction.
    pObjectContext->SetComplete();
    pObjectContext->Release();

    return S_OK;
}
```

The `IObjectContext` interface supports a number of important methods, including the methods `SetComplete()` and `SetAbort()`. In addition to signaling that a distributed transaction should complete or abort, `SetComplete()` and `SetAbort()` can also be called by nontransactional MTS objects to explicitly signal that the MTS object should be deactivated. In the case where the object is transactional, a call to `SetComplete()` or `SetAbort()` can speed up the deactivation process, thereby reducing system load as quickly as possible.

An MTS object needs to be notified when it is being activated or deactivated. To meet this requirement, MTS provides the `IObjectControl` interface. If an MTS object supports the `IObjectControl` interface, MTS will call `IObjectControl::Activate()` immediately after activation of the MTS object. The MTS Executive will also call `IObjectControl::Deactivate()` immediately before deactivation. Here is an example of an MTS object implemented with Visual C++ that supports the `IObjectControl` interface:

```
#include <mtx.h>

class ATL_NO_VTABLE CAccount :
    public CComObjectRootEx<CComSingleThreadModel>,
    public CComCoClass<CAccount, &CLSID_Account>,
    public IObjectControl,
    public IDispatchImpl<IAccount, &IID_IAccount,
                        &LIBID_CH6ACCOUNTLib>
{
public:
    ...
```

Because MTS objects can be pooled,[*] it is important to perform initialization during `Activate()` and perform finalization during `Deactivate()`. When implementing an MTS object with C++, the constructor and destructor should not be used for instance-level initialization and finalization since the MTS object instance might be placed in a pool and later reactivated when the next

---

[*]Support for pooling of MTS objects is not yet supported and will be added in COM+.

client request for an MTS object of that type arrives. The implementation of `Activate()` and `Deactivate()` is shown next. In this example, a smart pointer to the object context is obtained in `Activate()` and released in `Deactivate()`. Note that an explicit `Release()` needs to be called on the smart pointer so that the object context reference gets released when the MTS object is deactivated. This ensures that the object context is released even if the MTS object instance is placed in the pool after deactivation:

```
HRESULT CAccount::Activate()
{
    HRESULT hr = ::GetObjectContext(&m_spObjectContext);
    if (SUCCEEDED(hr))
        return S_OK;
    return hr;
}

void CAccount::Deactivate()
{
    m_spObjectContext.Release();
}
```

One major weakness of the `IObjectControl::Activate()` method is that it cannot be used to fully restore an MTS object instance to a previous state because it does not take any arguments. As we shall see in the next section, BEA's M3 addresses this problem by passing an object id[*] as a string to methods that perform activation and deactivation.

In the current release of MTS, users are forced to pass in activation state (i.e., the object identity) as a parameter to each method as demonstrated here:

```
interface IAccount : IDispatch
{
    [id(1), helpstring("method GetBalance")]
    HRESULT GetBalance([in] BSTR accountName,
                        [out,retval] double* balance);

    [id(2), helpstring("method Deposit")]
    HRESULT Deposit([in] BSTR accountName,
                     [in] double amount);
```

---

[*]The object id that is used by BEA's M3 is actually the Object Id as defined for the POA in the CORBA 2.2 specification. Management of the Object Id is handled implicitly by the POA.

```
        [id(3), helpstring("method Withdraw")]
        HRESULT Withdraw([[in] BSTR accountName,
                         [in] double amount);
};
```

Note that each method in the `IAccount` interface takes an explicit `account-Name` parameter so that the account object can be restored when the method is invoked. This is a significant weakness when compared to BEA M3's implicit management of a unique object id.

The current version of MTS has addressed many critical requirements of large enterprise systems, including distributed transactions, security, and scalability; however, it does not yet support load balancing and fault tolerance. Microsoft will address these issues in COM+. The most important point is that Microsoft's MTS has laid the proper foundation for supporting load balancing and fault tolerance in the future by providing key features such as interception, automatic object activation, and proactive object deactivation.

CORBA Object Management Under BEA Systems' M3

The advent of CORBA object management systems such as BEA's M3 elevates CORBA from an innovative architectural approach to an industrial-strength enterprise infrastructure. Although CORBA products have been available for many years on most major platforms, very few large-scale efforts have been able to attribute their success solely to CORBA. To build large-scale systems with early CORBA products, system planners were forced to provide non-CORBA infrastructure to ensure reliability, performance, and scalability. The early CORBA products provided a general-purpose object bus with very little support for CORBA object management.

BEA's M3 is a complete CORBA object management system as opposed to a CORBA ORB with add-on CORBA services. The fact that BEA is one of the first vendors to offer a complete CORBA object management solution is hardly surprising. BEA currently controls the leading transaction monitors for UNIX (TUXEDO and TOP END) as well as one of the oldest and most mature CORBA ORBs (ObjectBroker). It is only natural that BEA's architects would desire to merge the best features of TUXEDO with ObjectBroker.

Scalability is one of the biggest strengths of TUXEDO, but it is also one of the greatest weaknesses in traditional CORBA products. Achieving scalability with traditional CORBA products typically relied on proprietary mechanisms to effectively manage CORBA-related resources. Creating scalable CORBA applications therefore required a great deal of expertise with specific CORBA products. In other words, developers could not rely on the CORBA standard to guide them in their attempts to create highly scalable CORBA-based systems.

The introduction of the POA in the CORBA 2.2 specification provides a portable infrastructure for creating highly scalable CORBA-based systems. Among other features, the POA defines policies for object activation, object deactivation, and threading. As vendors add support for the POA to their commercial CORBA ORBs, it will be easier and more standardized to create scalable CORBA applications. However, even with support for the POA, the creation of highly scalable CORBA applications still requires a considerable amount of effort. BEA's M3 provides a proprietary TP framework on top of the POA that makes development of scalable CORBA applications much simpler than using the POA directly.

To achieve scalability as well as fault tolerance and load balancing, M3 provides a level of indirection between clients and server objects. This level of indirection allows M3 to intercept all calls to an M3 server object and manage that object within the M3 framework. As illustrated in Figure 6-18, the client of an M3 server object holds a reference to an M3 IIOP client handler rather than to the actual M3 server object.

The M3 client handler approach offers many advantages while imposing minimal overhead. The most fundamental advantage is that client handlers allow M3 to intelligently manage server objects under its control by allowing for

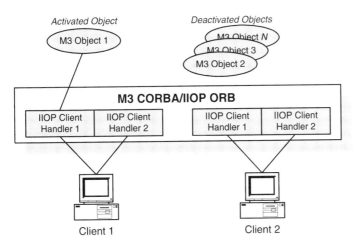

Figure 6-18. *M3 and IIOP client handlers.*

interception. Overhead is minimized since connections between clients and handlers are far less expensive to maintain than dedicated CORBA connections from clients to CORBA server objects. Client handlers make object deactivation possible since the handler can intercept the next call to a deactivated object and reactivate it on demand. Behind the scenes, M3 uses its implementation of the POA to handle activation and deactivation of M3 server objects.

M3 client handlers also play a fundamental role in load balancing and fault tolerance. The M3 framework allows multiple server processes on multiple machines to service client requests. When failures occur, client handlers can reroute requests to healthy servers. M3 can also prestart server processes to handle anticipated load and can gracefully shut down server processes when they are no longer needed. Whenever a client handler needs to activate an object, M3 uses two heuristics to determine which server process can best meet the client's needs:

1. *Transaction clustering.* Client requests that participate in a transaction are routed to servers that are already participating in the transaction whenever possible.

2. *Load optimization.* Client requests for which no transaction exists are routed to the least busy server.

Scalability, load balancing, and fault tolerance all depend on M3's ability to proactively deactivate server objects. To ensure deactivation of server objects, M3 allows activation policies, which are actually *deactivation* policies, to be associated with CORBA IDL interfaces at runtime. The three activation policies that M3 provides are

1. `atMethodEnd`—Means the server object is deactivated at the end of every method call.

2. `atTransactionEnd`—Means the server object is deactivated when the transaction in which it participates ends.

3. `atProcessEnd`—Means the server object is deactivated when the server process is terminated. (This is the approach used in traditional CORBA products.)

The control of deactivation is not explicitly programmed into the M3 CORBA object implementation as is the case with MTS when using `SetComplete()` and `SetAbort()` for such purposes. M3 activation policy information is stored in an environment file that is used by the M3 framework at runtime. All interfaces for the objects managed by the M3 framework must be associated with one of the three activation policies just described. In most cases, M3 server objects should use the `atMethodEnd` or `atTransactionEnd` policy to promote scalability, load balancing, and fault tolerance; however, there are situations where the cost of deactivating an object is prohibitive. In such cases, it may be better to use the `atProcessEnd` policy.

M3 server objects need to be notified whenever activation and deactivation occur so that state associated with an object instance can be appropriately saved and restored. When using C++, all M3 CORBA server implementations derive from the `Tobj::ServantBase` class. This class provides two virtual functions that can be overridden by a CORBA server implementation to handle activation and deactivation:

- `Tobj::ServantBase::activate_object()`—Called whenever an M3 object is activated. Here is an example:

```
void Account::activate_object(char* objectID)
{
    // Restore the account object associated with objectID.
}
```

- `Tobj::ServantBase::deactivate_object()`—Called when an M3 object is deactivated. Here is an example:

```
void Account::deactivate_object(char* objectID,
                                DeactivateReason reason)
{
    // Save the account object and associate it with
    // objectID in case it needs to be reactivated later.
}
```

Both the `activate_object()` and `deactivate_object()` methods take an object id as a parameter. The object id (as described by the POA) can be used to uniquely identify the object instance in the M3 environment. This allows the state of an M3 object to be restored and saved strictly within the confines of these method calls. The rest of the methods in the object implementation can be implemented as if the object is completely stateful since those methods will not be called until after activation has occurred. In addition, the `deactivate_object()` method also takes a `DeactivateReason` parameter. This parameter is generally used to determine whether the object is being deactivated for one of the following reasons:

- `DR_TRANS_COMMITTING`—Means the transaction was committed.

- `DR_TRANS_ABORT`—Means the transaction was aborted.

From the client's perspective, the object id associated with an M3 server object is transparent; the object id is completely encapsulated inside the object references held by clients. Clients using any IIOP-compliant ORB (e.g., Orbix, VisiBroker, Java IDL, etc.) can access M3 server objects. Clients remain totally unaware of the activities being performed by the M3 framework on the server side.

BEA's experience in the enterprise middleware arena is clearly evident in their M3 product offering. BEA has addressed scalability, load balancing, and fault tolerance while also supporting distributed transactions, security, and messaging. The initial release of M3 supports C++ on Windows NT, Sun SPARC Solaris, IBM AIX, Digital UNIX, and HP/UX. Because of the magnitude of the M3 offering, it will probably remain somewhat limited in terms of supported programming languages for the near term. Such time, however, will be well worth the wait given the robust features provided in the first release of M3.

Summary

The availability of high-level services makes the implementation of large, robust, and scalable COM- and CORBA-based systems a superior alternative to traditional approaches. While some early adopters of COM and CORBA were able to work around the lack of services in early efforts, the failure rate was high. The availability of high-level services reduces risk and development time by providing prefabricated distributed object plumbing that is required in most large systems.

The most critical service discussed in this chapter is the transaction service. Transactions define the boundaries between distinct units of work in all large enterprise systems. Without the support of a distributed object transaction service, it is practically impossible for COM- and CORBA-based systems to guarantee consistency across the enterprise.

In some situations, security and messaging support are also vital. COM addresses security in both COM and MTS. CORBA vendors offer various levels of support for the Secure Sockets Layer (SSL) and the OMG-specified CORBA Security Service. With regard to messaging support, neither COM nor CORBA directly supports message-oriented middleware (MOM) today, but both Microsoft and the OMG have outlined plans for supporting MOM in the future. Microsoft will support Queued Components using MSMQ in COM+, and the OMG will include the CORBA Messaging specification in CORBA 3.0.

The most exciting advance in the area of COM- and CORBA-based system development is the introduction of distributed object management systems such as Microsoft's MTS for COM and BEA Systems' M3 for CORBA. These object management systems are a natural next step in the evolution toward distributed objects from traditional TP monitors. Using a distributed object management system requires a disciplined approach for creating distributed objects that can exist within a well-defined distributed object framework. Discipline is critical in order to create distributed object systems that are robust, scalable, and performant.

We have now completed a discussion of the fundamental technical issues surrounding the use of COM and CORBA on the server side of the enterprise. In the next chapter, we will focus on nontechnical intangibles that must also be considered when committing an enterprise to COM and/or CORBA. Such intangibles can be the determining factors in shifting an enterprise toward distributed object technology.

Chapter 7

Server-Side Intangibles

Topics Covered in This Chapter

- Vendor Perception
- Vendor Commitment and Viability
- Vendor Lock-in
- Availability of Product
- Availability of Development Staff
- Product Cost

In Chapter 4, we described an assessment strategy to determine when and where COM and CORBA should be used on the server side. In Chapters 5 and 6, we covered a wide range of specific technical issues that factor into such a determination. While technical issues must always be considered when making technical decisions, the nontechnical issues are just as important. Strategists planning for the long term must consider many issues other than the hottest and newest technology in the technical pipeline. We refer to these mostly nontechnical issues as *intangibles* because of the vague and unpredictable manner in which they become prominent.

Committing a large organization to COM and/or CORBA requires consensus among many groups of individuals who often possess very different viewpoints. Developers tend to focus on development issues such as vendor commitment and support. Marketing and sales personnel concentrate on issues such as customer perception and strategic vendor relationships. Human resources personnel focus on staffing issues and staff retention. Each of these groups affects the decision-making process when selecting sophisticated technologies like COM and CORBA to build large systems. It is important to address nontechnical as well as technical concerns. Achieving consensus across a group of both technical and nontechnical individuals is a difficult challenge that must usually occur in order to adopt COM and/or CORBA.

Vendor Perception

The perception of a vendor in the software world is the result of many different factors. The most obvious of these factors is marketing. To generate profits, all commercial vendors must actively market their products and services in some manner. As vendors and their wares become established, the perception of a particular vendor is also influenced by media exposure in technical journals and on-line technical forums. Finally, the most popular software products create a momentum that results in large (and often vocal) user groups.

In the distributed objects arena, Microsoft has exhibited a tremendous ability to promote its distributed object architecture. Despite a substantial early lead by CORBA in the distributed object marketplace, COM has quickly overtaken CORBA on the Windows platform. While CORBA has been available on the Windows platform much longer than DCOM, Microsoft has quickly established DCOM as the dominant distributed object framework for Windows. Although there are a multitude of reasons for DCOM's dominance, much of its success can be attributed to successful marketing efforts rather than to technical superiority over CORBA.

The incredible effectiveness of Microsoft's marketing is demonstrated in the transition over the last few years from OLE to ActiveX to COM. In early 1996, Microsoft began its rigorous marketing of ActiveX and downplayed the term *OLE* in its core technologies. Due to intense marketing, it appeared at first that ActiveX encompassed all technologies related to the Internet, OLE, and COM. Microsoft has since reigned in the marketing hype, and it now appears that COM, ActiveX, and OLE each represent unique domains (although ActiveX and OLE are both built on top of COM).

The CORBA vendors cannot compete with Microsoft in terms of mass marketing. Most of the major CORBA vendors do not possess the financial resources or customer install base to make Microsoft-like marketing worthwhile. Recall (from COM: A Vertical Strategy on page 110) that Microsoft products tend to behave like commodities because of the huge number of copies sold. In contrast, CORBA vendors attack a more specialized marketplace that is influenced more by user experience than by intense marketing.

User experience often leads to sharply divided camps when assessing COM and CORBA vendors. This division is quite understandable. COM offers significant advantages with regard to development tools, programming language integration, and services on the Windows platform. It is difficult for Windows/COM developers to give up the sophisticated development tools and integrated development environments afforded on the Windows platform. Developers that have enjoyed working under Windows have a natural tendency to perceive Microsoft in a positive manner.

Despite its advantages, the Windows NT platform is still immature and is not an acceptable server platform for many mission-critical situations. In contrast to COM, CORBA vendors offer products that are built to run well in mission-critical situations. Specific CORBA vendors have established excellent reputations in the enterprise server marketplace. For example, IBM is acknowledged for its dominance in the mainframe and midrange systems arena. BEA's TUX-EDO is the predominant UNIX-based transaction monitor. Iona has offered its Orbix product on an incredible range of platforms since 1993. The OMG has also documented a large number of cases where CORBA has been used successfully.[*] On all major platforms, CORBA vendors have earned a great deal of respect, and their products are often perceived as being more appropriate than COM for mission-critical situations.

Vendor Commitment and Viability

Microsoft is unquestionably committed to COM on the Windows platform. After all, COM provides the core infrastructure for all of Microsoft's major products. In contrast, Microsoft has lacked commitment on non-Windows platforms. It appears that Microsoft has struggled to determine whether its strategic advantage is served by supporting non-Windows platforms. It is clear that COM/C++/ATL will soon be supported on all major platforms. The question remains whether or not other key technologies such as MTS, MSMQ, and a COM-capable Java environment will ever be fully supported on anything besides Windows. Without these key technologies, COM will not be able to compete with CORBA head-to-head on non-Windows platforms.

Commitment among CORBA vendors must be examined on a per-vendor basis. The CORBA world has recently undergone a significant amount of flux. IBM has phased out SOM and replaced it with the ComponentBroker suite of products. At the end of 1997, Sun Microsystems dropped support for NEO, its CORBA offering. In the beginning of 1998, Inprise (formerly Borland) purchased Visigenic. While most of these changes have resulted in improved CORBA offerings, they still represent the fast pace of change occurring in the CORBA marketplace. The pace of change leads one to question the long-term viability of CORBA products in general. Despite recent changes in the market-

---

*For more information on specific CORBA success stories, see http://www.omg.org.

place, almost all of the major CORBA vendors continue to earn profits and are financially viable for the foreseeable future.

Vendor Lock-in

Microsoft's ownership of the COM specification automatically creates a lock-in situation when using COM. To best leverage COM, one cannot avoid using at least some of the COM-based development tools offered by Microsoft. The addition of MTS and MSMQ to the COM arsenal increases user dependence on Microsoft. This can be a dangerous situation for a customer. In such a situation, a dominant vendor is less likely to be responsive to a single customer's needs since the customer does not have access to an alternate vendor.

Despite Microsoft's dominance, there are a number of non-Microsoft tools that can be used to create COM components. For example, Inprise's Delphi is a popular development environment that can also be used to create COM components. Note that the use of non-Microsoft development tools does not decrease reliance on the COM runtime system, which is still controlled by Microsoft on Windows.

Because all CORBA-compliant products support a common specification, it would appear that CORBA offers a portable solution, thereby preventing vendor lock-in. This is not the case. The OMG has always tried to avoid specifying detailed product implementation when creating specifications such as CORBA. As a result, many of the CORBA vendors offer vendor-specific constructs that can make porting of CORBA-based code difficult from one product to the next.

The best example of nonportable CORBA constructs can be found in each vendor's support for a basic object adaptor (BOA). The BOA is used to implement CORBA server objects. The OMG left the implementation details for the BOA open in the CORBA 2.0 specification. As a result, each CORBA vendor offers a different approach for supporting the BOA. To alleviate this problem, the OMG has specified a new adaptor—a portable object adaptor (POA)—in the CORBA 2.2 specification. Widespread use of the POA will solve many of the portability problems previously faced when using the BOA.

CORBA vendors will always search for innovative ways to differentiate their products. This situation is analogous to the manner in which relational database vendors differentiate themselves in the database marketplace. Differentiation is a natural outcome of competition. Despite the differentiation that must occur among vendors, CORBA still offers the best approach for creating distributed object solutions that can be ported to another vendor's product if required. This is not the case with COM since COM is supported only by a very small number of vendors on each server platform.

Availability of Product

Product availability can be a very important issue when adopting emerging technologies such as COM and CORBA. Enterprise strategists must perform a significant amount of experimentation before committing the company's future to new technological trends. While major vendors usually allow for free evaluation of their products, some vendors make it easier than others.

Microsoft makes it effortless to evaluate almost all of their major server-side products. Individuals can obtain trials of Windows NT Server as well as most of the major server products such as MTS and MSMQ. With the low cost of Wintel-based hardware, individuals can experiment with and learn complex server technology in the workplace or at home. These individuals can then carry that experience into the workplace and accelerate the acceptance of COM-based technology in the enterprise. Before the advent of commodity hardware and software, users were forced to gain almost all of their technical expertise in the workplace. The high availability of COM-based products provides COM with tremendous momentum.

The CORBA vendors do not enjoy the incredible install base that Microsoft does; however, many CORBA products are also very easy to obtain. Several robust CORBA products exist in the public domain. In addition, many CORBA vendors, such as Iona, Inprise, and Expersoft, offer downloadable evaluations of their CORBA products. Sun offers Java IDL, a lightweight CORBA/Java ORB, as part of the Java Development Kit (JDK). With the inclusion of a CORBA ORB in the Java JDK, the OMG's vision of *CORBA everywhere* has been realized.

Availability of Development Staff

Perhaps the greatest challenge facing the enterprise is the availability of qualified and dedicated development staff. Architecting complex distributed systems requires technical depth, long-term commitment, and the ability to master emerging technology at a rapid pace. The availability of COM- and CORBA-based technology has helped to increase the number of developers familiar with distributed object technology. Familiarity does not, however, equate to design and architectural prowess.

COM and CORBA offer tremendous infrastructures for building complex server-side systems. In response to the availability of this infrastructure, enterprise strategists are now attempting to solve problems that are a magnitude more difficult than those attempted just a few years ago. The greatest problem with building large systems is a lack of qualified individuals who know how to properly leverage COM and CORBA infrastructures. This lack of qualified individuals can be attributed to several factors, including the following:

- *Loyalty.* The relationship between employees and their employers has deteriorated over the last 5 to 7 years. As a result, employees (and employers) do not make long-term commitments to one another.

- *Breadth of technology.* Because the software technology base continues to expand, software developers are forced to become more specialized and therefore lose sight of the big picture. A lack of breadth results in missed opportunities to best leverage currently available technology.

- *Focus on tools rather than on design.* The early 1990s were characterized by considerable focus on design. The last few years have been dominated by rapid application development (RAD) techniques. As a result, developers have become more focused on how to best utilize RAD tools rather than on how to provide fundamental design.

The shift from design orientation to rapid application development is indicative of the positions of COM and CORBA in the marketplace. While CORBA was painstakingly designed by committee over many years, COM and a set of development tools were developed rather quickly to meet the needs of an aggressive software vendor—Microsoft.

Out of necessity, businesses are working on new strategies to attract and retain software development staff. Employers are beginning to focus on innovative benefits that will help to retain employees. Training is becoming more important to both employees and employers in order to compensate for the ever-expanding technology base. A renewed focus on design has emerged in an attempt to eliminate some of the wasted efforts that have occurred using the RAD approach. The bottom line is that employee retention and commitment are vitally important to enterprises that rely on sophisticated technology like COM and CORBA.

Product Cost

A great many factors contribute to the overall cost of developing software. Most software life cycle descriptions identify phases for requirements analysis, design, implementation, deployment, and maintenance. All phases of software development tend to be expensive. Strangely enough, implementation is often the least expensive of the major phases. And yet, the costs of software products (e.g., COM- and CORBA-related products) are overemphasized despite their negligible impact on overall development cost.

Over the long term, it appears that both COM and CORBA will be virtually free on all major server platforms. COM and CORBA provide generic object buses that connect distributed system components. To generate revenue, COM and CORBA vendors will create high-level specialized services that can be sold at a premium.

The most important point is that with the small portion of overall cost expended during actual software implementation, the cost of COM and CORBA products should not be given much importance. In fact, it should be the least significant consideration when selecting server-side technology. Rather than arguing over the cost benefits of COM versus CORBA, one should always make sure to stress other factors such as platform, vendor lock-in, and staff availability.

Server-Side Summary

When we began Part II, our goal was to discover where COM and CORBA should be used on the server side of the enterprise. In Chapter 4, we discussed the need for partitioning a large enterprise into manageable coherent domains. We then identified assessment criteria and presented an assessment strategy for objectively assessing the suitability of COM or CORBA for a specific enterprise domain.

The assessment criteria that we identified in Chapter 4 provided a basis for exploring many of the factors that must be considered when selecting COM or CORBA. These factors run the technical gamut from fundamental issues such as development platform to high-level services supporting transactions, security, messaging, and scalability. We explored a plethora of technical issues surrounding COM and CORBA in Chapters 5 and 6. In addition, many nontechnical concerns must also be considered and resolved in the selection process. These nontechnical intangibles have been discussed in this chapter.

Choosing between COM and CORBA can be incredibly difficult given the large number of issues that factor into such a decision. Neither COM nor CORBA is appropriate for all situations. Each distributed object environment offers a unique set of advantages for any specific enterprise domain. Rather than locking an organization into a one-size-fits-all solution, it is wiser to objectively select the best technology on a domain-by-domain basis. The challenge then remains as to how COM and CORBA can coexist in a mixed setting.

Before we attack the interoperability issues related to mixing COM and CORBA in server environments, we first need to understand the client side of the equation. In Part III, we will examine approaches for creating COM- and CORBA-based client applications. Microsoft Windows has dominated the client desktop for many years; however, the power of the Internet has produced dramatic changes in the client application arena. We will discuss how COM and CORBA can be used to build robust client applications within both the Windows and Internet models.

Part III

COM and CORBA on the Client

Introduction

Large enterprise systems are expensive to deploy and even more expensive to maintain. Much of the expense is often due to the large number of client installations that must be maintained. Supporting a large install base of clients requires careful planning and painstaking attention throughout the life of the system. The need for such attention results in high maintenance costs over the long term.

The reduction of client deployment and maintenance costs has always been a high priority for enterprise system planners and system administrators. Such costs are directly proportional to the innate complexity of client applications. To reduce client costs, various methods have been used to reduce the complexity of client applications. Client/server systems reduce client complexity by moving data management complexity to the server tier. Distributed object approaches using COM and CORBA also allow business logic to be transferred to the server tier, thus reducing client complexity even further.

Part III focuses on COM and CORBA client approaches as well as several key design issues that must be considered when constructing COM- and CORBA-based systems.

- Chapter 8 focuses on the use of COM and CORBA in desktop client applications. The desktop realm is dominated by Microsoft Windows and COM. Various COM client approaches as well as the primary COM client development environments are discussed.

- Chapter 9 focuses on the use of COM and CORBA in Internet client applications. The COM and CORBA camps have addressed the Internet client problem space in different ways. The use of COM with Microsoft's Active Server Pages (ASP) as well as the use of CORBA with Java are demonstrated.

- Chapter 10 examines design issues that must be considered when creating COM- and CORBA-based clients. A conflict often occurs when attempts are made to meet remoting requirements and client interface needs. Techniques for addressing this conflict are discussed. Chapter 10 also presents a scenario in which COM and CORBA are used together. The issues that arise in such a scenario are discussed.

After completing Part III, you should have a firm grasp of the primary client approaches that can be used in conjunction with COM and CORBA. The COM and CORBA approaches allow complexity to be moved from the client tier to the server tier. The end result is a thinner client that is less costly to deploy and maintain.

Chapter 8

The Desktop Client

Topics Covered in This Chapter

- Impact of Distributed Objects
- Dominance of COM on the Desktop
- COM Client Approaches
- Installing Remote COM Clients
- COM Development Environments

In recent years, the typical desktop client has evolved into a thinner client as client/server systems have evolved toward distributed objects. The first generation of client/server systems left most of the business logic and complexity in the client tier. Client applications were therefore complex and needed to run on robust hardware platforms. The advent of distributed object architectures such as COM and CORBA encourages movement of business logic from the client tier to the server tier. This reduces complexity in the client and allows client applications to run on less expensive desktop computers.

The Microsoft Windows family of operating systems currently dominates the desktop client arena. This can be attributed to several factors. First, a huge number of applications and productivity tools run on the Windows platform. Second, Microsoft has evolved a powerful component architecture in COM that allows for rapid assembly of Windows applications. Finally, a large number of powerful integrated development environments exist that simplify the creation of Windows-based applications.

Of all the Windows-based development tools, Microsoft's Visual Studio family of products has the largest market share. The Visual Studio suite includes Visual C++, Visual Basic, and Visual J++. These tools provide excellent support for utilizing COM within desktop client applications. This is not surprising since the operating system, component architecture, and primary development tools are all controlled by a single vendor—Microsoft.

Impact of Distributed Objects

The first generation of client/server architectures placed most of the business logic and application complexity on the client tier; the server tier was strictly used for data management. Even today, coordination among multiple clients in a typical client/server system is accomplished by sharing a common data repository such as a relational database. The server tier is used for little else. As a result, a large amount of processing still occurs on desktop client machines, thus requiring substantial hardware resources on the client side. Due to hefty processing requirements and high levels of complexity, such client applications are typically referred to as *rich* clients.

A strict client/server approach suffers from several deficiencies. As mentioned, a large amount of processing power is often required on each client machine. In addition, rich client applications are difficult to maintain and extend. Since the business logic of the system is implemented in each client application, each client machine potentially needs to be updated whenever business logic changes. Such updates can become unwieldy as a large software system evolves.

To resolve the problems posed by rich client approaches, software designers have used a number of strategies for slimming down client applications. In most cases, the best approach is to separate business logic from visual presentation and move business logic processing from the client tier to the server tier. The end result is a thin client (as opposed to a rich client) since most of the processing and complexity actually occurs on the server side. The thin client application running on the client machine is simply a visual interface for interacting with server-side applications. In the thin client approach, updates to business logic need to be made only on the server side. In many cases, the client hardware requirements are reduced as well.

Implementing business logic on the server tier necessitates a communication mechanism that allows client applications to tap the business logic on the server side. Early approaches relied on low-level networking mechanisms such as TCP/IP. Later approaches included the use of general-purpose messaging middleware (e.g., IBM's MQSeries) and remote procedure calls (RPCs). Today, distributed objects provide the best approach for distributing application logic.

Distributed object architectures such as COM and CORBA offer an object-based approach for distributing business logic across multiple tiers. In most cases, client applications can treat a distributed object as if it is running locally, regardless of the distributed object's actual location. This allows distribution of business logic to occur without imposing significant overhead in terms of overall system complexity. In addition, COM and CORBA are supported on a wide range of platforms. As tool support and platform support continue to improve, the use of COM and CORBA will encourage the creation of thin clients, thereby reducing the cost of deploying and maintaining desktop client applications across the enterprise.

Dominance of COM on the Desktop

The Microsoft Windows family of operating systems currently dominates the desktop client arena. In the early 1990s, other operating systems, such as UNIX, also vied for market share in the enterprise desktop realm. UNIX was often required because UNIX desktop systems offered more powerful hardware and greater stability than their Windows counterparts. The continued strengthening of Intel-based hardware as well as the release of the more stable Windows NT and Windows 95/98 operating systems allowed Windows to become the dominant desktop platform. Today's end users demand that enterprise client applications work on Windows so that they can also use the huge number of other tools (word processing, spreadsheet, etc.) that run on the Windows platforms. The dominance of COM on the desktop hinges on the continued success of Microsoft Windows as the primary desktop operating system.

The high degree of support for COM in Windows-based development tools ensures COM's continued dominance on the desktop. Microsoft continues to aggressively improve support for COM in its Visual Studio suite of development tools. Since DCOM is simply COM with a longer wire (at least from the client's perspective), the Visual Studio development tools make it very simple to use DCOM distributed objects from client applications. Despite the best efforts of vendors such as Inprise, support for CORBA in desktop client development environments is not nearly as extensive as support for COM.

In terms of desktop client environments, CORBA is most appropriate for creating client applications that must run on multiple platforms including both Windows and non-Windows platforms. Although CORBA is not well supported in development tools, it is very easy to use with Java. Java and CORBA make up a powerful combination when creating cross-platform client applications. Java/CORBA is also a powerful combination when creating Java applets that can run in a Web browser (see Using CORBA in a Java Applet on page 267).

While there are many CORBA ORBs that can be used with Visual C++ and Visual J++, there is no support for CORBA when using Visual Basic and VBScript. Instead, CORBA vendors tend to offer bridging solutions that provide COM interfaces to CORBA servers. We will discuss commercial COM/CORBA bridging products in Chapter 12. Because of COM's dominance in desktop client applications, the rest of this chapter will focus on COM client approaches and COM client development environments.

COM Client Approaches

COM provides several approaches for achieving communication between COM client applications and COM server objects. The diversity in approaches is a result of performance and development considerations as well as the diverse range of client environments that COM supports. At its core, COM relies on interfaces to provide client entry points into COM objects. The COM client approaches vary based on the types of interfaces that COM objects support. The different COM client approaches are

- *Custom interface approach.* With this approach, a COM object supports a customized interface defined by the COM object creator.

- *Automation interface approach.* With this approach, a COM object supports a standard COM interface named `IDispatch`.

- *Dual interface approach.* With this approach, a COM object supports both a customized interface and the `IDispatch` interface.

The key differentiator between the COM client approaches is the support provided in each approach for `IDispatch`. `IDispatch` is a standard COM interface that allows for dynamic invocation of a COM object. *Dynamic invocation* in this case refers to the ability of a client application to discover and invoke COM object methods at runtime rather than at compile time. Dynamic invocation is critical when using COM in interpreted environments such as VBScript or Visual Basic for Applications. (The use of `IDispatch` and dynamic invocation will be discussed more thoroughly in Automation Interfaces on page 227.)

One of the most substantial differences between COM and CORBA is the mechanism by which dynamic invocation is supported. COM provides a standard COM interface, `IDispatch`, for allowing dynamic invocation. This means that COM developers must explicitly design their COM objects to support `IDispatch` in order to provide dynamic invocation. In contrast, CORBA specifies the Dynamic Invocation Interface (DII). CORBA developers do not need to explicitly allow for dynamic invocation. Instead, support for the DII is the responsibility of the CORBA ORB. CORBA ORBs that implement the DII support dynamic invocation for all user-defined CORBA interfaces.

The use of IDispatch as opposed to the use of a custom interface has several performance and development implications. In terms of performance, the use of IDispatch adds overhead to the COM method call since the method must be dynamically dispatched. In contrast, the overhead produced by calling a method on a custom interface is approximately the same as the cost of making a virtual function call in C++. Perhaps more important are the software development implications. Since custom interface method calls must be managed at compile time, the compiler can perform static type checking to ensure that the call is being made correctly. Such checking is not possible when using IDispatch, therefore making the risk of an incorrect method call more likely. Despite the overhead involved with using IDispatch, the impact is noticeable only when invoking a COM object that is running within the client application's process (i.e., the COM object is an in-process DLL). The overhead of using IDispatch is insignificant when a COM object is called across process or machine boundaries because of the overhead due to other factors such as marshaling.

Client environment support is the most important reason for having multiple COM client approaches. Client applications created with development tools such as Visual C++ and Visual Basic can invoke custom interfaces and can assist the user with compile-time support to help ensure correctness. Client applications that rely on VBScript (e.g., Active Server Pages) require automation interfaces because VBScript is an interpretive environment. Systems that intend to provide both types of client applications (e.g., Visual Basic and VBScript) should provide dual interfaces in order to best support both types of client development environments (compiled and interpreted) with a single set of COM objects.

Custom Interfaces

The fundamental technique for creating external entry points into COM server objects is through the creation of COM interfaces. One of the principal rules of COM is that once an interface has been assigned a uuid and has been published for general use, it should never be changed. Instead, COM server objects should support new additional interfaces as well as the original interfaces when new functionality needs to be supported. In fact, most COM objects do support multiple interfaces.

Over the years, a large number of standard COM interfaces have been published. These standard interfaces include a range of important protocols such as IMarshal, IClassFactory, and IStream. The IDispatch interface implemented by OLE Automation components is also a standard interface (we will discuss IDispatch in the next section). Standard interfaces cannot realistically meet the needs of all situations. To use COM in custom applications, developers often need to create COM objects that support custom interfaces.

COM IDL is generally used to describe COM interfaces (we first discussed COM IDL in COM IDL and Type Libraries on page 41). As expected, COM IDL supports basic types such as int, long, float, and double. In addition to the basic types, COM IDL also supports the marshaling of complex and user-defined data types, including the following:

- *Arrays*. COM IDL allows arrays of data to be passed between clients and servers. Depending on the task at hand, COM allows for arrays to be specified in several ways. For example, if the array length is known at compile time, COM IDL allows for the declaration of a fixed-length array (e.g., long vals[10]).

- *NULL-terminated strings*. A string is often represented as an array of characters terminated by a NULL character. COM IDL allows for the definition of such strings in a special manner.*

- *Structs*. COM IDL allows for the definition of user-defined structs. COM IDL allows structs to be nested as well.

- *Unions*. COM IDL allows for the definition of user-defined unions.

Support for complex data types varies greatly across development environments. Since the MIDL compiler generates C++ proxy code, Visual C++ clients can access any interface that can be defined in COM IDL. The same cannot be said for Visual Basic and Visual J++. To better understand the limitations of Visual Basic and Visual J++, consider the COM IDL description shown in Listing 8-1. The key elements in this IDL description are

- struct Ch8Struct (line 4 of Listing 8-1)—A user-defined struct containing a single attribute.

- struct Ch8NestedStruct (line 9 of Listing 8-1)—A user-defined struct containing a single attribute that is also a struct.

---

*Note that NULL-terminated strings are not supported in COM environments such as Visual Basic. Because of the greater support for the BSTR automation type, it is generally recommended that COM IDL strings be declared as BSTRs rather than as NULL-terminated strings. (BSTRs were described in greater detail on page 40.)

Listing 8-1. *COM IDL with struct, nested struct, and array*

```
 1 import "oaidl.idl";
 2 import "ocidl.idl";
 3
 4     typedef struct Ch8Struct
 5     {
 6         long longVal;
 7     } Ch8Struct_t;
 8
 9     typedef struct Ch8NestedStruct
10     {
11         Ch8Struct_t structVal;
12     } Ch8NestedStruct_t;
13
14     [
15         uuid(17BCA30E-44F1-11D2-B2C2-00207812E629),
16         pointer_default(unique)
17     ]
18     interface ICh8Custom1 : IUnknown
19     {
20         HRESULT GetStruct([out] Ch8Struct_t* data);
21
22         HRESULT GetNestedStruct([out] Ch8NestedStruct_t* data);
23
24         HRESULT GetArray([in]  long max,
25                          [out] long* actual,
26                          [out, size_is(max), length_is(*actual)]
27                                long* vals);
28     };
29 [
30     uuid(17BCA300-44F1-11D2-B2C2-00207812E629),
31     version(1.0)
32 ]
33 library CUSTOM1Lib
34 {
35     importlib("stdole32.tlb");
36     importlib("stdole2.tlb");
37
38     [
39         uuid(17BCA30F-44F1-11D2-B2C2-00207812E629),
40     ]
41     coclass Ch8Custom1
42     {
43         [default] interface ICh8Custom1;
44     };
45 };
```

- interface ICh8Custom1 (line 18 of Listing 8-1)—An interface with methods that manipulate a struct, a nested struct, and an array.

- coclass Ch8Custom1 (line 41 of Listing 8-1)—A COM class that implements the ICh8Custom1 interface.

To demonstrate the limitations of various client environments when using custom interfaces, the Ch8Custom1 coclass defined in Listing 8-1 is implemented using Visual C++ and ATL. Next, client applications are written in Visual C++, Visual Basic, and Visual J++ that exercise the ICh8Custom1 interface. These client applications demonstrate several current limitations of Visual Basic and Visual J++ and are the focus of the remainder of this section.

For this discussion, assume that the Visual C++ client has obtained a valid ICh8Custom1 interface pointer. The TestStruct() function shown next demonstrates how the Visual C++ client retrieves a Ch8Struct instance from the server:

```
static void TestStruct(ICh8Custom1* iPtr)
{
    HRESULT    hr;
    Ch8Struct myStruct;
    hr = iPtr->GetStruct(&myStruct);
    if (FAILED(hr)); // handle error
    cout << "struct: longVal = " << myStruct.longVal << endl;
}
```

The TestNestedStruct() function shown next demonstrates how the Visual C++ client retrieves a Ch8NestedStruct instance from the server:

```
static void TestNestedStruct(ICh8Custom1* iPtr)
{
    HRESULT          hr;
    Ch8NestedStruct myNestedStruct;
    hr = iPtr->GetNestedStruct(&myNestedStruct);
    if (FAILED(hr)); // handle error
    cout << "nestedStruct.structVal.longVal = ";
    cout << myNestedStruct.structVal.longVal << endl;
}
```

The TestArray() function shown next demonstrates how the Visual C++ client retrieves an array of longs from the server:

```
static void TestArray(ICh8Custom1* iPtr)
{
    HRESULT hr;
    long    vals[3];
    long    len = 0;

    hr = iPtr->GetArray(3, &len, vals);
    if (FAILED(hr)); // handle error

    cout << "Array: ";
    for (long i=0; i < len; i++)
    {
        if (i > 0) cout << ", ";
        cout << vals[i];
    }
}
```

As expected, the Visual C++ client application has full access to the struct, nested struct, and array as defined in the COM IDL in Listing 8-1. Next, we examine the Visual Basic client and its usage of the custom interface.

Visual Basic facilitates access to various COM objects by specifying references to COM object type libraries in the *References* dialog. (We will discuss this technique in The Visual Basic COM Client on page 239.) For this discussion, assume that a valid ICh8Custom1 interface pointer has already been obtained. The TestStruct() function shown next demonstrates how the Visual Basic client retrieves a Ch8Struct instance from the server:

```
Private Function TestStruct(obj As ICh8Custom1) As String
    Dim data As Ch8Struct
    Call obj.GetStruct(data)
    TestStruct = "struct.longVal = " & data.longVal
End Function
```

The TestNestedStruct() function shown next demonstrates how the Visual Basic client retrieves a Ch8NestedStruct instance from the server:

```
Private Function TestNestedStruct(obj As ICh8Custom1) As String
    Dim data As Ch8NestedStruct
    Call obj.GetNestedStruct(data)

    TestNestedStruct = "nestedStruct.structVal.longVal = " & _
                        data.structVal.longVal
End Function
```

The `TestArray()` function shown next demonstrates how the Visual Basic client retrieves an array of `longs` from the server:

```
Private Function TestArray(obj As ICh8Custom1) As String
    Dim actualLength As Long
    Dim vals As Long
    Call obj.GetArray(1, actualLength, vals)
    TestArray = "Array : " & vals
End Function
```

Notice that the `TestArray()` function does not work since it is not possible to define an array of `longs` as required by the `ICh8Custom1::GetArray()` method. The Visual Basic client can retrieve only the first `long` value in the array. The *Object Browser* view shown in Figure 8-1 clearly shows how Visual Basic maps the `ICh8Custom1::GetArray()` method to the Visual Basic language. The Visual Basic environment interprets the `long* vals` declaration on line 27 in Listing 8-1 as a pointer to a single `long` rather than to an array of `longs`.

It is not surprising that Visual Basic does not support the array defined in the example. Instead, Visual Basic relies on `SAFEARRAYS`. A `SAFEARRAY` is an automation-compatible data type for managing arrays. If a custom interface using an array needs to be used from a Visual Basic client, the array must be

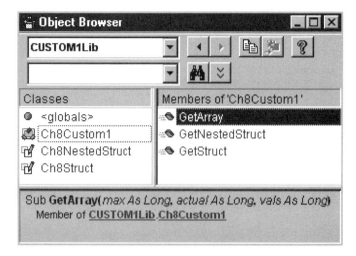

Figure 8-1. *The Visual Basic mapping of the GetArray( ) method.*

declared as a SAFEARRAY. The last custom interface client that we need to examine is the Visual J++ client.

Visual J++ facilitates access to various COM objects by generating Java class wrappers based on COM object type libraries. (We will discuss this technique in The Visual J++ COM Client on page 242.) For this discussion, assume that a valid ICh8Custom1 interface pointer has already been obtained. The TestStruct() function shown next demonstrates how the Visual J++ client retrieves a Ch8Struct instance from the server:

```
private static void TestStruct(ICh8Custom1 obj)
{
    Ch8Struct myStruct = new Ch8Struct();

    obj.GetStruct(myStruct);
    System.out.println("struct.longVal = " +
                        myStruct.longVal);
}
```

In Visual J++, it is not possible to access the nested struct in the Ch8NestedStruct instance. As mentioned, Visual J++ generates a Java class wrapper for the Ch8NestedStruct. The generated wrapper is shown here:

```
public final class Ch8NestedStruct
{
// UNMAPPABLE: structVal: Cannot be used as a structure field.
//   /** @com.structmap(UNMAPPABLE structVal) */
//   public UNMAPPABLE structVal;
}
```

The generated wrapper is unable to map the COM IDL definition of Ch8NestedStruct to Java, thereby making Ch8NestedStruct unusable from the Visual J++ client.

The TestArray() function shown next demonstrates how the Visual J++ client retrieves an array of longs from the server:

```
private static void TestArray(ICh8Custom1 obj)
{
    int[] len  = new int[1];
    int[] vals = new int[3];

    obj.GetArray(3, len, vals);
```

```
System.out.print("Array: ");

for (int i=0; i < len[0]; i++)
{
    if (i > 0) System.out.print(", ");

    System.out.print("" + vals[i]);
}
}
```

The custom interface defined in Listing 8-1 worked correctly from the Visual
C++ client but was problematic in several ways when used in the Visual Basic
and Visual J++ clients. Table 8-1 summarizes some of the issues that arose
when using the custom interface in the example.

The data provided in Table 8-1 is by no means comprehensive. It is quite prob-
able that several of the problems noted within this section will be fixed as
Microsoft improves the mapping between COM IDL and its primary non-C++
COM development environments, Visual Basic and Visual J++. The main point
is that any COM custom interface must be carefully tested to ensure that it
works properly in COM client environments other than Visual C++. In contrast, CORBA interfaces map to all supported languages equally without
restriction. To ensure that COM interfaces will work across the greatest possible range of environments, COM dual interfaces should be used. (We will discuss the use of COM dual interfaces in greater detail on page 229.)

Table 8-1. *Custom Interface Summary*

	Visual C++ Clients	**Visual Basic Clients**	**Visual J++ Clients**
Arrays	OK	Not supported. SAFEARRAY must be used.	OK
NULL-Terminated Strings	OK	Not tested; however, BSTR must be used.	Not tested.
Structs	OK	OK; however, struct members must be VB compatible.	Partially supported. Nested structs do not work.
Unions	OK	Not tested.	Not tested.

Automation Interfaces

Custom interfaces provide the ultimate in power and flexibility when creating COM servers. This power, however, comes at a fairly steep price in that custom interfaces are unusable in some client development environments. Although Microsoft continues to increase support for custom interfaces in its mainstream development tools (as is exemplified by the evolution of Visual Basic), some specialized environments demand a different approach. In particular, interpreted environments such as VBScript and JScript require a mechanism for dynamically invoking COM objects. (We will discuss VBScript further in Using COM with Active Server Pages on page 261.)

Microsoft's strategy for supporting dynamic invocation is through the use of the `IDispatch` interface. COM objects that support the `IDispatch` interface are often referred to as *automation objects* (or *automation servers*); hence, interfaces to automation objects are often referred to as *automation interfaces*. Although an automation object is not required to support any interface besides `IDispatch`, it is still important to specify the interface supported by the automation object. The interface definition can then be saved in a type library and used by development environments. In COM IDL, an automation interface is specified by declaring a `dispinterface` as illustrated in Listing 8-2.

In Listing 8-2, a type library is declared that defines the `Ch8Dispinterface_Dispatch` dispinterface and the `Ch8Dispinterface` coclass. Note that a dispinterface is not a normal COM interface as we defined in the last section. In reality, the `Ch8Dispinterface` coclass actually only supports the `IDispatch` COM interface (as well as `IUnknown`). However, it is still necessary to publicly expose the underlying methods that the automation object supports. The definition of a dispinterface within a type library serves this purpose well. From a developer's perspective, the dispinterface simply indicates which calls can be made via `IDispatch` to the COM server object. In the context of the Visual Studio development tools, a dispinterface definition supplies valuable information that can be used to provide more structured access to an automation object and eliminate the need to use `IDispatch` directly.

Accessing an automation object directly through the `IDispatch` interface is tedious and error-prone. To provide a generic dynamic interface, the `IDispatch` interface must use very low-level semantics. The actual COM IDL definition of `IDispatch` is shown in Listing 8-3.

The `IDispatch` interface consists primarily of four methods. The first three methods can be used at runtime to dynamically discover which methods are

Listing 8-2. *Ch8Dispinterface Example*

```
[
  uuid(DB225AA2-4792-11D2-B2C3-00207812E629),
  version(1.0),
  helpstring("Ch8 Dispinterface Example Type Library")
]
library Ch8DispinterfaceTypeLib
{
    importlib("STDOLE2.TLB");
    dispinterface Ch8Dispinterface_Dispatch;


    [
      uuid(70A14883-4795-11D2-B2C3-00207812E629)
    ]
    dispinterface Ch8Dispinterface_Dispatch
    {
        properties:
        methods:
            [id(1)] BSTR TestString([in] BSTR Parameter0);
            [id(2)] long TestLong([in] long Parameter0);
    };


    [
      uuid(DB225AA3-4792-11D2-B2C3-00207812E629)
    ]
    coclass Ch8Dispinterface {
        [default] dispinterface Ch8Dispinterface_Dispatch;
    };
};
```

supported by the automation object. The fourth method, `Invoke()`, is used to dynamically invoke a specific method of the automation object.

Most client development environments allow developers to use a more elegant approach for invoking automation object methods than directly calling the `IDispatch` methods. For example, Visual Basic, Visual C++, and Visual J++ can automatically generate helper classes based on a dispinterface defined in a type library. These helper classes then provide the developer with a high-level mechanism for invoking automation objects that only support `IDispatch`. (We will examine how automation objects are supported in the Visual Studio development tools in COM Development Environments on page 238.)

Listing 8-3. *IDispatch COM IDL Definition*

```
[
    object,
    uuid(00020400-0000-0000-C000-000000000046),
    pointer_default(unique)
]
interface IDispatch : IUnknown
{
    HRESULT GetTypeInfoCount(
            [out] UINT * pctinfo
        );
    HRESULT GetTypeInfo(
            [in] UINT iTInfo,
            [in] LCID lcid,
            [out] ITypeInfo ** ppTInfo
        );
    HRESULT GetIDsOfNames(
            [in] REFIID riid,
            [in, size_is(cNames)] LPOLESTR * rgszNames,
            [in] UINT cNames,
            [in] LCID lcid,
            [out, size_is(cNames)] DISPID * rgDispId
        );
    HRESULT Invoke(
            [in] DISPID dispIdMember,
            [in] REFIID riid,
            [in] LCID lcid,
            [in] WORD wFlags,
            [in, out] DISPPARAMS * pDispParams,
            [out] VARIANT * pVarResult,
            [out] EXCEPINFO * pExcepInfo,
            [out] UINT * puArgErr
        );

    .
    . Rest of IDispatch definition ...
    .
}
```

Dual Interfaces

Custom interfaces offer power and flexibility, while automation interfaces offer a *least common denominator* approach. Recall that, in addition to COM's remoting capabilities, COM also allows components to be used in-process. An in-process COM component runs as a DLL within the same operating system process as the client application. The ability to use in-process components is very important from an efficiency standpoint when remoting is not required. The most prominent example of the need for in-process component support is a visual ActiveX control.

When invoking a COM object within the same process as the caller, it is important to reduce the overhead of the call as much as possible. Invoking a COM object through IDispatch is at least 10 times more costly than invoking a conventional COM interface method directly. Rather than having to choose between a custom interface or an automation interface simply for performance reasons, COM supports a third approach known as *dual interfaces*. A dual interface simultaneously supports a conventional COM interface as well as an automation interface. COM client environments that are capable of accessing custom interfaces directly can use a dual interface and still enjoy the benefit of optimal performance. Interpreted environments can still use automation when invoking a dual interface method as well. A dual interface is represented in COM IDL as shown in Listing 8-4.

The dual interface described in Listing 8-4 has several attributes that differentiate it from a custom interface. On line 4, the interface is identified as being of type dual. On line 7, the interface is declared as inheriting from IDispatch. On lines 9 and 12, dispatch ids are associated with each of the dual interface methods.

A dual interface is ideal from a client perspective, but it requires additional complexity when actually creating a dual interface COM server. For obvious

Listing 8-4. *COM IDL for a Dual Interface*

```
1    [
2        object,
3        uuid(E5BB118D-4945-11D2-B2C3-00207812E629),
4        dual,
5        pointer_default(unique)
6    ]
7    interface IVcDual : IDispatch
8    {
9        [id(1)] HRESULT TestLong([in] long val,
10                                 [out,retval] long* result);
11
12       [id(2)] HRESULT TestString([in] BSTR str,
13                                  [out,retval] BSTR* result);
14   };
```

reasons, it is highly desirable that the burden imposed by the additional complexity fall on the development environment rather than on the developer. Visual C++, Visual Basic, and Visual J++ all excel in their ability to implement dual interface components.

- *Visual C++ dual interface creation.* The Visual C++ development environment includes the Active Template Library (ATL), a class library that greatly simplifies creation of dual interface COM components. ATL provides a wizard that allows the user to specify support for a dual interface when implementing a COM object. ATL implements the automation interface automatically. The developer simply implements the methods one time and is not required to deal directly with `IDispatch`.

- *Visual Basic dual interface creation.* The Visual Basic development environment provides several project types for creating COM objects. The COM object developer simply implements a VB class, and that class forms the interface and implementation of the dual interface COM object.

- *Visual J++ dual interface creation.* In Visual J++, Microsoft does not provide direct support for creating the COM IDL dual interface definition. Instead, the developer must use another tool (e.g., VC++/ATL) to generate a dual interface IDL description and type library. The type library can then be used by Visual J++ to define the COM object to be implemented. As with Visual C++ and Visual Basic, the developer is not forced to deal directly with `IDispatch`.

Dual interfaces have one major restriction that prevents their use in all situations: Dual interfaces can use only automation data types. This restriction on data types makes sense since a dual interface simultaneously supports `IDispatch` as well as a conventional COM interface. The automation types that are most frequently used are described in Table 8-2.

To better understand how each of the automation types described in Table 8-2 should be defined in an actual COM dual interface, we define the `ITestAutomationTypes` dual interface in Listing 8-5. One special point to note about Listing 8-5 is that all `[out]` parameters are specified using a pointer to the automation type.

A number of issues must be considered when using the automation types. The `VARIANT_BOOL` type should always be used instead of `BOOL`. Note that although the MIDL compiler does allow `BOOL` to be specified for Boolean types when defining COM dual interfaces, it is more desirable to use `VARIANT_BOOL` for a

Table 8-2. *Most Frequently Used COM Automation Types*

COM IDL Type	Description
short	16-bit signed integer
long	32-bit signed integer
float	32-bit floating-point number
double	64-bit floating-point number
BSTR	length-prefixed wide-character array
VARIANT_BOOL	short integer used to indicate true or false
DATE	64-bit floating-point number representing the fractional number of days since December 30, 1899 (e.g., 12/31/1899 6:00:00 AM == 1.25)
IUnknown*	generic interface pointer
IDispatch*	automation interface pointer
VARIANT	discriminated union of all automation types
SAFEARRAY	data type that manages variable-sized multidimensional arrays

couple of reasons. First, Visual Basic always defines Boolean fields as
VARIANT_BOOL when creating COM objects using Visual Basic. For reasons of
consistency, it is better to use VARIANT_BOOL consistently regardless of the
development environment used. Second and more importantly, the MIDL compiler maps BOOL to a long when creating a type library, whereas it leaves
VARIANT_BOOL as is. Visual Basic and Visual J++ environments therefore identify a BOOL as a long instead of their native Boolean type when accessing a
type library interface definition. In contrast, Visual Basic and Visual J++ both
map VARIANT_BOOL to their native Boolean types.

As shown in Listing 8-5, automation supports both the IDispatch and
IUnknown interface pointers. Both types of interface pointers are required in
order to support all client environments. For environments such as Visual C++,
Visual Basic, and Visual J++ that can use the IUnknown::QueryInterface()
method to access any interface from any other interface, IUnknown is all that
is needed. However, in interpreted environments that can manipulate only
IDispatch interfaces (e.g., VBScript), the use of IDispatch is mandatory.

The VARIANT type can contain any of the automation types (including a nested
variant) and is therefore extremely useful when the actual parameter type is

Listing 8-5. *COM Dual Interface That Uses Most Automation Types*

```
[
    object,
    uuid(397DF8BD-4A9D-11D2-B2C4-00207812E629),
    dual,
    pointer_default(unique)
]
interface ITestAutomationTypes : IDispatch
{
    [id(1)]  HRESULT TestShort([in] short val,
                               [out,retval] short* result);

    [id(2)]  HRESULT TestLong([in] long val,
                              [out,retval] long* result);

    [id(3)]  HRESULT TestFloat([in] float val,
                               [out,retval] float* result);

    [id(4)]  HRESULT TestDouble([in] double val,
                                [out,retval] double* result);

    [id(5)]  HRESULT TestBstr([in] BSTR val,
                              [out,retval] BSTR* result);

    [id(6)]  HRESULT TestVariantBool(
                              [in] VARIANT_BOOL b,
                              [out,retval] VARIANT_BOOL* result);

    [id(7)]  HRESULT TestDate([in] DATE val,
                              [out,retval] DATE* result);

    [id(8)]  HRESULT TestIUnknown([in] IUnknown* unk,
                                  [out,retval] IUnknown** ip);

    [id(9)]  HRESULT TestIDispatch([in] IDispatch* dsp,
                                   [out,retval] IDispatch** ip);

    [id(10)] HRESULT TestVariant([in] VARIANT val,
                                 [out,retval] VARIANT* result);
};
```

unknown at design time. In addition, the VARIANT type is required when supporting client environments such as VBScript and Visual Basic for Applications. In those environments, the VARIANT type must be used when defining [out] parameters that are not return values. For example, the following method would be unusable from VBScript:

```
[id(1)]   HRESULT TestShort([in] short val,
                             [out] short* outval,
                             [out,retval] VARIANT_BOOL* status);
```

In the `TestShort()` method just shown, `outval` cannot be specified since VBScript cannot define a variable of type `short` to be passed by reference when making the call. Instead, the `TestShort()` method should be defined as follows:

```
[id(1)]   HRESULT TestShort([in] short val,
                             [out] VARIANT* shortOutval,
                             [out,retval] VARIANT_BOOL* status);
```

The second `TestShort()` method works from any COM client environment. The rule of using a `VARIANT` as an `[out]` parameter does not apply when arguments are specified as return values since no parameter needs to be passed by reference, as was the case with `outval` in the original example.

One automation type that we did not demonstrate in Listing 8-5 is the `SAFEARRAY` type. Describing how to use `SAFEARRAY`s is a complex task and falls outside the scope of this book. However, it is worth noting that, in general, it is probably wiser to simply declare an array argument as a `VARIANT` and wrap the actual `SAFEARRAY` within the `VARIANT` when invoking COM methods that use arrays. This simplifies the interface and allows for greater flexibility.

The greatest weakness of requiring automation types is that it is not possible to create user-defined types such as `struct`s and `union`s. The need for such user-defined types is closely related to several other design issues that must be considered when creating distributed object systems. (We will examine this issue further in Remoting Requirements and Design Issues on page 278.)

Before leaving the topic of dual interfaces, we will demonstrate the calling of a dual interface object using both its conventional interface as well as its automation interface. Exercising both aspects of a dual interface is simple to do using Visual Basic. Consider the following dual interface:

```
interface IVcDual : IDispatch
{
    [id(1)] HRESULT TestString([in] BSTR str);
};
```

The `IVcDual` interface is a dual interface that supports a single method. The first test is to directly call the `TestString()` method supported by the `IVcDual` interface. This is accomplished from Visual Basic as shown here:

```
Private Sub IVcDualTest()
    Dim obj As IVcDual
    Set obj = CreateObject("Ch8.VcDual", txtServerName.Text)
    txtStatus.Text = obj.TestString()
End Sub
```

In the `IVcDualTest()` method just shown, an `obj` is declared of type `IVcDual`. Next, a COM instance that implements the `IVcDual` interface is created. The `TestString()` method is then called on the `IVcDual` instance.

The `IDispatchTest()` method shown next attempts to call the `TestString()` method using `IDispatch` rather than the `IVcDual` interface:

```
Private Sub IDispatchTest()
    Dim obj As Object
    Set obj = CreateObject("Ch8.VcDual", txtServerName.Text)
    txtStatus.Text = obj.TestString()
End Sub
```

Note that the `IDispatchTest()` method is identical to the `IVcDualTest()` method except for one detail. In the `IDispatchTest()` method, the `obj` is declared as an `Object` rather than as an `IVcDual`. In Visual Basic, calls made against such `Object`s are invoked using `IDispatch`. The `TestString()` method in `IDispatchTest()` is therefore invoked against the `IDispatch` interface rather than against the `IVcDual` interface.

Of the three COM client approaches discussed, it should be obvious that a dual interface should be used most of the time. Pure dispinterfaces should not usually be used since dual interfaces provide both `IDispatch` and conventional interface entry points. Custom interfaces should be used only sparingly due to compatibility problems with non-C++ COM client environments.

Installing Remote COM Clients

The diversity in COM client approaches naturally leads to a diversity in the steps necessary to make remote COM clients operate correctly. In this section, we will describe the steps necessary to configure a client machine to work with remote COM servers. It is assumed that clients must be able to specify the server name at runtime (as opposed to hard-coding the server name in the client machine's system registry).

The first step is to install the `ProgID` (e.g., `Ch8.VcDual`) on the client computer. Recall that in C/C++, the `CoCreateInstanceEx()` function must be used to dynamically create a remote instance of a server object. `CoCreateInstanceEx()` relies on the `CLSID` of the COM object that is to be instantiated in order to locate the COM object's implementation. The `CLSID` is used as a key to find implementation information in the Windows system registry. A typical `CLSID` is a `uuid` and is defined in COM IDL as shown in the following example:

```
[
    uuid(E5BB118E-4945-11D2-B2C3-00207812E629)
]
coclass VcDual
{
    [default] interface IVcDual;
};
```

The `CLSID` is not a human-readable string and is not used by most COM client programs (Visual C++ is one exception). Instead, environments such as Visual Basic and VBScript use a `ProgID` when creating COM object instances. The `ProgID` is simply a mapping to the actual `CLSID` in the Windows system registry. The registry entries that would need to be set for the "`Ch8.VcDual`" `ProgID` are as follows:

```
REGEDIT4

[HKEY_CLASSES_ROOT\Ch8.VcDual]
"" = "Ch8 VcDual Class"

[HKEY_CLASSES_ROOT\Ch8.VcDual\CLSID]
"" = "{E5BB118E-4945-11D2-B2C3-00207812E629}"
```

The `ProgID` would be used in a Visual Basic client application as shown here:

```
Private Sub IVcDualTest()
    Dim obj As IVcDual
    Set obj = CreateObject("Ch8.VcDual", txtServerName.Text)
End Sub
```

The only other requirement is that client applications must be able to obtain a client proxy implementation that can marshal any requests made to a remote

COM server. This can be accomplished in several ways, depending on the COM client approaches used on the client machine. The various marshaling approaches are summarized in Table 8-3.

The final step needed to support remoting is to ensure that the type library or proxy–stub DLL gets installed on the client machine. Note that this is required only if client applications will be using interfaces other than `IDispatch` (as is indicated in Table 8-3). Regardless of the minimum requirements, it is probably best to always install both the `ProgID` and type library. A type library offers potential users of the interface a wealth of information that might otherwise be difficult to discover.

Table 8-3. *Marshaling Approaches for Various COM Clients*

Client Approach	Typical Clients	Marshaling Approach
Custom interface	Visual C++	A proxy–stub DLL must be registered on the client machine (see COM Proxies and Stubs on page 52).
Custom interface marked as [oleautomation]	Visual Basic Visual J++ Visual C++	Interfaces marked as [oleautomation] can take advantage of type library marshaling (see COM Type Library Marshaling on page 53). A type library that defines the interface must be registered on the client machine. A proxy–stub DLL can be used instead if desired.
Dual interface	Visual Basic Visual J++ Visual C++ VBScript (Active Server Pages)	Interfaces marked as [dual] can take advantage of type library marshaling (see COM Type Library Marshaling on page 53). A type library that defines the interface must be registered on the client machine. A proxy–stub DLL can be used instead if desired. Nothing is required if clients will be using only IDispatch since the marshaler for IDispatch is already installed.
Automation interface dispinterface (IDispatch)	Visual Basic VBScript Visual Basic for Applications	Nothing is required since the marshaler for IDispatch is already installed.

COM Development Environments

COM development environments rely on a standard mechanism for determining the availability and capabilities of COM server objects. The type library is the standard mechanism for conveying COM server object information. Most COM environments rely on type libraries to determine the interfaces that a particular COM object supports.

Visual Basic, Visual J++, and Visual C++ all provide mechanisms that rely on type libraries to simplify COM object usage when creating COM client applications. In this section, we will create examples to demonstrate how Visual Basic, Visual J++, and Visual C++ applications manipulate COM objects that support both automation interfaces (i.e., dispinterfaces) and dual interfaces. It is assumed in all of the examples that the type libraries being used have been properly registered.

The `Ch8Disp` dispinterface that is presented next will serve as the dispinterface for all relevant client application examples. It is assumed that the `Ch8Disp` dispinterface is implemented by a COM object whose registered ProgID is "Ch8.Dispinterface." Here is the dispinterface:

```
dispinterface Ch8Disp
{
    methods:
        [id(1)] BSTR TestString([in] BSTR Parameter0);
};
```

The `IVcDual` dual interface that is presented next will serve as the dual interface for all relevant client application examples. It is assumed that the `IVcDual` interface is implemented by a COM object whose registered ProgID is "Ch8.VcDual." Here is the dual interface:

```
interface IVcDual : IDispatch
{
    [id(1)] HRESULT TestString([in] BSTR str,
                              [out,retval] BSTR* result);
};
```

The IDL definitions for the dispinterface and dual interface just described will not be directly exposed during development of the example applications. Instead, the development environments will derive helper classes based on the appropriate type libraries. This relieves client application developers from the burden of having to generate mappings from IDL to the native language being used. As Microsoft continues to expand the scope of COM, it will most certainly expand the capabilities of type libraries and their usage in COM-oriented development tools.

The Visual Basic COM Client

When compared to Visual J++ and Visual C++, Visual Basic is unique in its support for automation. Whenever a COM object is declared as an `Object` in Visual Basic, the COM object is invoked using automation (i.e., `IDispatch`). It should be noted that Visual Basic supported automation long before it supported the calling of custom COM interfaces directly. Here is an example of how automation is used from a Visual Basic client:

```
Private Sub IDispatchTest()
    Dim obj As Object
    Set obj = CreateObject("Ch8.VcDual", txtServerName.Text)
    txtStatus.Text = obj.TestString("Test")
End Sub
```

In the `IDispatchTest()` subroutine, `obj` is declared as a Visual Basic `Object`. Any invocation made against `obj` will be made using the `IDispatch` interface. If the COM object does not support `IDispatch`, Visual Basic raises an error.

The ability to use `IDispatch` has both advantages and disadvantages. If the client application uses only `IDispatch`, it is not necessary to install a proxy–stub DLL or type library on the client machine (see Table 8-3). In addition, Visual Basic provides an excellent rapid prototyping environment for testing a COM component's automation capabilities. This is very useful when testing a component for later use with environments such as VBScript.

The disadvantages of using automation in a Visual Basic client outweigh the advantages when using COM objects that support dual interfaces. The use of `IDispatch` is inefficient compared to calling the dual interface directly. Another disadvantage is that the IntelliSense feature is not available when automation is used. IntelliSense is a feature of the Visual Basic editor that relies on type library information and assists the user by performing name completion and providing parameter information. An example of IntelliSense is demonstrated in Figure 8-2. Note that as the `TestString()` method is typed into the Visual Basic editor, IntelliSense pops up a small window indicating

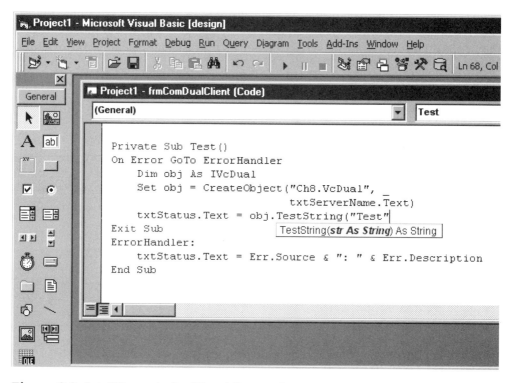

Figure 8-2. _IntelliSense in the Visual Basic editor._

the call and argument type. IntelliSense is very helpful when writing Visual Basic programs.

Perhaps the biggest disadvantage of using IDispatch as opposed to the actual dual interface is the lack of compile-time checking. When automation is used, errors cannot be detected until the method is invoked at runtime. In contrast, the Visual Basic compiler can perform static type checking and detect errors at compile time when dual interfaces are used.

To use a COM interface directly (as opposed to using IDispatch), Visual Basic first requires that a reference be made to the type library in which the interface is defined. The type library to be referenced must be registered in the Windows system registry. For our example, we wish to reference the Ch8 VcDual type library that defines the IVcDual dual interface. In Visual Basic, we simply select _Project_ on the menu bar and then select _References..._ to bring up the _References_ dialog. The _References_ dialog used to select the Ch8 VcDual type library is shown in Figure 8-3.

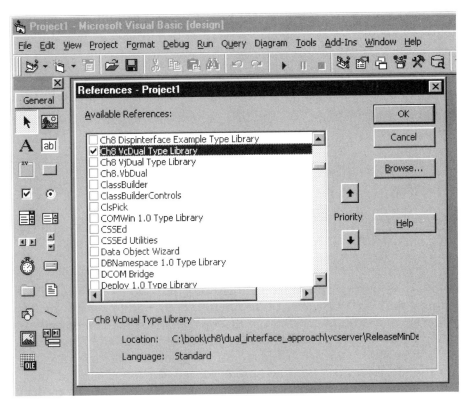

Figure 8-3. *Referencing the Ch8 VcDual type library in Visual Basic.*

Once the reference to the type library has been made, all interfaces defined in the type library become first-class types in the Visual Basic environment. Because the Visual Basic environment has a reference to the `Ch8 VcDual` type library, all invocations against the interface can be type-checked at compile time. The `IVcDual` interface would be used as shown here:

```
Private Sub Test()
    Dim obj As IVcDual
    Set obj = CreateObject("Ch8.VcDual", txtServerName.Text)
    txtStatus.Text = obj.TestString("Test")
End Sub
```

Up to this point, we have not commented on how a Visual Basic application creates a reference to a remote COM object. Recall (from COM Object Creation in Visual Basic on page 80) that we described several alternatives for creating such a reference when using version 5.0 of Visual Basic, including the use of a COM bridging component that wraps `CoCreateInstanceEx()`. In Visual Basic 6.0, Microsoft has extended the `CreateObject()` method to take a remote server name as an optional parameter. In our example, we hold the server name in a Visual Basic `TextBox` named `txtServerName`. The server name can be specified as the local network name (e.g., "tosca"), as a UNC name (e.g., \\tosca), as an IP address (e.g., 192.168.0.1), or as an IP domain name (e.g., tosca.opera.myhouse).

The call to `CreateObject()` in the example uses a `ProgID` and server name to instantiate a remote COM object. The `ProgID` is needed to look up (in the client machine's registry) the `CLSID` of the COM object to be instantiated. While the support for a remote server name in `CreateObject()` is a valuable new feature, a COM component that wraps `CoCreateInstanceEx()` might still be required if data such as security information needs to be passed to the server when creating the server object.

Visual Basic is undoubtedly the simplest environment in which to create client applications that use COM. What it lacks in flexibility and power, it makes up for in ease of use. Although we did not discuss support for COM objects that provide pure dispinterfaces and custom interfaces, the method for using such objects is the same as when using a dual interface object. As long as a type library that describes the interfaces is registered, the interfaces can be used from Visual Basic (assuming the interfaces use types that can be understood in Visual Basic). Because Visual Basic lacks power when it comes to certain programming tasks (such as multithreading), developers sometimes need to use other development tools. Next, we will examine how the Visual J++ development environment supports COM-based client application development.

The Visual J++ COM Client

Visual J++ uses a very different strategy for supporting COM objects than does Visual Basic. Recall from the previous section that the Visual Basic programmer does not directly manipulate the underlying mechanism that supports calling COM objects. In contrast, Visual J++ uses the `JActiveX.exe` tool to generate COM/Java wrapper classes from type libraries. The Visual J++ programmer uses these generated classes to invoke their corresponding COM objects.

After a type library has been installed, it is very simple to use that type library within the Visual J++ development environment. Visual J++ provides a dialog-based interface for using `JActiveX.exe`. For our example, we first need to create COM wrappers for the `Ch8Disp` dispinterface and the `IVcDual` dual interface. In Visual J++, we simply select *Project* on the menu bar and then select *Add COM Wrapper...* to bring up the *COM Wrappers* dialog. The *COM Wrappers* dialog used to select the `Ch8 Dispinterface` and `Ch8 VcDual` type libraries is shown in Figure 8-4.

The COM wrappers that get generated by Visual J++ contain COM-specific comments. These comments can be interpreted only by the COM-aware Java compiler that ships with Visual J++. The COM-specific comments are actually extensions to Sun's Java language description. Microsoft and Sun are currently involved in a legal dispute over Microsoft's right to use such extensions. (For more information, see COM/Windows/Java Development Platform on page 137.)

For COM to work with Java, a COM-aware Java Virtual Machine (JVM) must also be available. Microsoft ships such a JVM with every version of its Internet

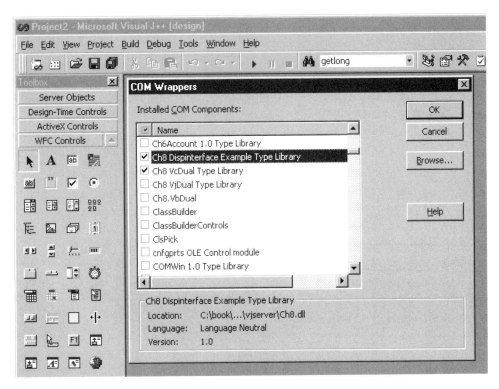

Figure 8-4. *Creating COM wrappers in Visual J++.*

Explorer Web browser, thus making the Microsoft JVM universally available on the Windows platform. Before we examine a generated COM wrapper, consider once again the COM IDL used to define the `Ch8Disp` dispinterface:

```
dispinterface Ch8Disp
{
    methods:
        [id(1)] BSTR TestString([in] BSTR Parameter0);
};
```

The following Java code is generated by Visual J++ for the `Ch8Disp` dispinterface:

```
/** @com.interface(iid=70A14883-4795-11D2-B2C3-00207812E629,
                   thread=AUTO, type=DISPATCH) */
public interface Ch8Disp extends IUnknown
{
    /** @com.method(dispid=101, type=METHOD,
                    name="TestString", returntype=VOID)
        @com.parameters([in,type=STRING] Parameter0,
                        [type=STRING] return) */
    public String TestString(String Parameter0);
}
```

Note that in the `Ch8Disp` Java class, both the `Ch8Disp` class and the `TestString()` method are prefaced by COM-specific comments. The `Ch8Disp` class is identified as a COM interface of type `DISPATCH`. A generated interface id (`iid`) also appears in the comment. The `TestString()` method is associated with a dispatch id (`dispid`), and its parameters are identified. These comments allow invocations against the `Ch8Disp` class to be mapped to the actual `IDispatch` implementation of the corresponding COM object.

The following example demonstrates how the `Ch8Disp` wrapper class is used in a client application:

```
private static void Test(String serverName)
{
    Ch8Disp obj = (Ch8Disp)CreateObject("Ch8.Ch8Dispinterface",
                                         serverName);

    System.out.println(obj.TestString("vjtest"));
}
```

Visual J++ handles a dual interface in the same manner as a dispinterface. Let us now consider the COM IDL associated with the `IVcDual` dual interface:

```
interface IVcDual : IDispatch
{
    [id(1)] HRESULT TestString([in] BSTR str,
                               [out,retval] BSTR* result);
};
```

The following Java code is generated by Visual J++ for the `IVcDual` interface:

```
/** @com.interface(iid=E5BB118D-4945-11D2-B2C3-00207812E629,
                   thread=AUTO, type=DUAL) */
public interface IVcDual extends IUnknown
{
  /** @com.method(vtoffset=4, dispid=1, type=METHOD,
                  name="TestString", addFlagsVtable=4)
     @com.parameters([in,type=STRING] str, [type=STRING] return) */
  public String TestString(String str);
}
```

As was the case with the `Ch8Disp` Java class, both the `IVcDual` class and the `TestString()` method are prefaced by COM-specific comments. However, the content of the comments is significantly different when we compare a disp-interface COM wrapper to a dual interface COM wrapper. The `IVcDual` class is identified as a COM interface of type `DUAL` (as opposed to `DISPATCH` in the previous case). The `TestString()` method is still associated with a dispatch id, but it also contains a `vtoffset` field. The `vtoffset` field identifies the `TestString()` method's position in the `IVcDual` interface. This information is used by the Java Virtual Machine when calling the `IVcDual` interface directly.

The following example demonstrates how the `IVcDual` wrapper class is used in a client application:

```
private static void TestVcDual(String serverName)
{
    IVcDual obj = (IVcDual)CreateObject("Ch8.VcDual",
                                        serverName);
    System.out.println(obj.TestString("vcdualtest"));
}
```

In both the dispinterface and dual interface examples, a call was made to `CreateObject()` to create the appropriate COM object. Unlike Visual Basic and Visual C++, Visual J++ does not provide a convenient approach for creating a remote COM object instance. We therefore rely on a readily available component called the *DCOM Bridge* (introduced on page 81). To use the DCOM Bridge component, we first need to create a COM wrapper for it using the *COM Wrappers* dialog in Visual J++. We then use the `DCOMBridge` wrapper classes to implement the `CreateObject()` method as follows:

```
private static Object CreateObject(String progid,
                                   String serverName)
{
    IDCOMBridge bridge = new DCOMBridge();
    return bridge.CreateRemoteInstance(progid, serverName, 0);
}
```

The Java runtime system relies on garbage collection to clean up system resources when they are no longer in use. Note that, in the preceding Java examples, we have created object references but have never released them. Since the Java Virtual Machine runs the garbage collector at arbitrary times, it might sometimes be necessary to explicitly force the release of unused COM object references.

One approach to cleaning up resources more quickly is to explicitly invoke Java's garbage collector. This is accomplished as follows:

```
System.gc();    // Run the Java garbage collector.
```

While there is a good chance that running the garbage collector will release the appropriate COM objects, it is not guaranteed. For efficiency reasons, garbage collection schemes do not usually try to reclaim 100% of unused resources. For this reason, you may be required to explicitly release COM object references.

Microsoft provides the `com.ms.com.ComLib` class to assist developers with Java/COM integration. The `ComLib` class implements a `release()` method that can be used to release all references to a specified COM object. The following example demonstrates how `ComLib.release()` is used:

```
private static void TestVcDual(String serverName)
{
    IVcDual obj = (IVcDual)CreateObject("Ch8.VcDual",
                                        serverName);
```

```
        System.out.println(obj.TestString("vcdualtest"));
        com.ms.com.ComLib.release(obj);
}
```

With the advent of MTS, it is rarely necessary to explicitly release COM object references. If MTS is used and if the MTS objects are deactivated upon completion of each method call, references to the MTS objects are relatively inexpensive to maintain. In this case, it is almost always wiser to simply let the garbage collector worry about cleaning up such references.

A multitude of features make the use of COM in Visual J++ almost as simple as Visual Basic. Like Visual Basic, Microsoft's latest version of Visual J++ (version 6.0) supports IntelliSense. As the user enters code into the Visual J++ editor, name completion and parameter information are interactively displayed. In addition, Visual J++ can also interactively check source code for syntax errors (in much the same way that Microsoft Word interactively checks for spelling and grammatical errors). Despite the fact that Visual J++ is a more robust programming language, Visual Basic continues to be a more mature and reliable product. This is due to Visual Basic's widespread use as well as the incremental improvements in reliability and efficiency that have been made to Visual Basic over a long period of time.

The Visual C++ COM Client

C++ is unquestionably the most powerful and efficient language to use when working with COM. It is also, however, one of the most difficult languages in which to use COM (especially when compared to Visual Basic and Visual J++). These difficulties stem from problematic issues such as memory and pointer management—issues that must constantly be considered when working with C++ in general. To compensate for these difficulties, Microsoft has taken an approach that is totally different from that of Visual Basic and Visual J++.

Recall that Visual Basic and Visual J++ provide GUI-based tools to generate helper and wrapper classes. Rather than providing such GUI-based support for creating helper classes, Microsoft has instead chosen to extend its version of the C++ programming language. While these extensions present portability problems on non-Windows platforms, they are extremely useful when creating Windows-based desktop clients. In this section, we will briefly examine a few of the extensions and features that simplify COM client development under Visual C++.

Consider once again the COM IDL definition that describes the `IVcDual` interface and `VcDual` COM class:

```
[ object, uuid(E5BB118D-4945-11D2-B2C3-00207812E629), dual ]
interface IVcDual : IDispatch
{
    [id(1)] HRESULT TestString([in] BSTR str,
                               [out,retval] BSTR* result);
};
[ uuid(E5BB1180-4945-11D2-B2C3-00207812E629) ]
library Ch8VCSERVERLib
{
    ...
    [ uuid(E5BB118E-4945-11D2-B2C3-00207812E629) ]
    coclass VcDual
    {
        [default] interface IVcDual;
    };
};
```

In Using IDL in the COM C++ Client on page 58, we demonstrated how such an IDL definition could be used from a C++ client application. Using IDL in such a manner has several drawbacks when developing COM client applications. The client developer must run the MIDL compiler on all IDL files and then manage the generated code. More important is the fact that many environments (such as Visual Basic and Visual J++) do not even generate COM IDL. Instead, they create type libraries when creating COM interfaces and classes. While it is certainly possible to reverse-engineer COM IDL from a type library,[*] it is much simpler to use a type library directly from C++. Microsoft has added an `import` statement to its Visual C++ language that can be used to directly import a type library into a Visual C++ program. The following example demonstrates the `import` of the `Ch8VcDual` type library:

```
#include <comdef.h>
#include <iostream.h>
#import "../vcserver/Ch8VcDual.tlb" no_namespace
```

Importing a type library results in the automatic generation and inclusion of two files, `<typelib>.tlh` and `<typelib>.tli`. The `import` statement allows for the specification of several attributes, including one for namespace. In this

---

[*]The `OLEView.exe` utility that ships with Visual Studio 6.0 is able to present an IDL description for a specified type library.

case, we have chosen not to place all generated definitions in a C++ namespace. The following files would be generated when importing the `Ch8VcDual` type library:

- `Ch8VcDual.tlh`—Contains several typedefs and definitions, including a C++ interface definition for the `IVcDual` interface. In addition to the raw interface methods that are defined in the type library, the `import` statement also generates a wrapper method for each interface method. These wrapper methods provide for a number of important features, including exception support and simpler calling semantics.

- `Ch8VcDual.tli`—Contains implementations for the wrapper methods that are defined in the `Ch8VcDual.tlh` file.

When importing a type library, the `uuid`s associated with the interfaces and coclasses must be generated. Rather than creating constants (as is done with the MIDL compiler), the `import` directive takes advantage of the `__declspec` directive and associates types with their respective `uuid`s. The following definitions demonstrate how the `IVcDual` interface and `VcDual` coclass are associated with their respective `uuid`s:

```
// The following is an excerpt from Ch8VcDual.tlh
struct
    __declspec(uuid("e5bb118d-4945-11d2-b2c3-00207812e629")) IVcDual;

struct
    __declspec(uuid("e5bb118e-4945-11d2-b2c3-00207812e629")) VcDual;
```

Once the `__declspec` has occurred, the `uuid` can be retrieved at any time by using the `__uuidof` directive as shown next. This mechanism provides a very intuitive and readable approach for working with `uuid`s in C++ client applications:

```
IID    interfaceID = __uuidof(IVcDual);
CLSID classID     = __uuidof(VcDual);
```

A C++ interface corresponding to the type library interface must also be generated. The following definition is created for the `IVcDual` interface:

```
// The following is an excerpt from Ch8VcDual.tlh
struct __declspec(uuid("e5bb118d-4945-11d2-b2c3-00207812e629"))
IVcDual : IDispatch
{
```

```
   // Raw methods provided by interface
   virtual HRESULT __stdcall raw_TestString(BSTR str,
                                              BSTR* result)=0;

   // Wrapper methods
   _bstr_t TestString(_bstr_t str);
};
```

The C++ interface definition that gets created when doing an `import` is substantially different from the one that gets generated by running MIDL. All of the method names are prepended with `raw_`. In addition, wrapper methods that wrap the raw calls are also created. The calling semantics of the wrapper method are simplified in certain cases. Notice that because `result` was specified as a `retval` in the type library, the wrapper method actually returns a `BSTR`, whereas the raw method treats `result` as another parameter and returns an `HRESULT`. The implementation of the `TestString()` wrapper method is as follows:

```
// The following is an excerpt from Ch8VcDual.tlh
inline _bstr_t IVcDual::TestString ( _bstr_t str ) {
    BSTR _result;
    HRESULT _hr = raw_TestString(str, &_result);
    if (FAILED(_hr)) _com_issue_errorex(_hr, this, __uuidof(this));
    return _bstr_t(_result, false);
}
```

Import-generated wrapper methods implement an exception-handling approach instead of using the traditional `HRESULT` return values. As is shown in the preceding `TestString()` implementation, the wrapper method calls `_com_issue_errorex()` if the call to `raw_TestSTring()` fails. The end result is that an exception of type `_com_error` is thrown. The following example demonstrates how exceptions should be handled when calling import-generated wrapper methods:

```
static void TestVcDual(const char* serverName)
{

    IVcDual* pIVcDual = (IVcDual*)0;

    try
    {
        pIVcDual = (IVcDual*)CreateObject(__uuidof(VcDual),
                                          __uuidof(IVcDual),
                                          serverName);
```

```
        cout << pIVcDual->TestString("testException") << endl;
    }

    catch (_com_error e)
    {
        _bstr_t desc = !e.Description() ? "" : e.Description();
        cerr << "TestVcDual: " << desc << endl;
    }

    if (pIVcDual) pIVcDual->Release();
}
```

The `_com_error` class supports a number of methods that can be used to access a variety of error information when exceptions occur.

Note that, in the `TestVcDual()` method, we are still required to call `Release()` on the interface pointer when the method is completed. Instead of manually releasing the interface pointer, it is better to use a smart pointer that will automatically call `Release()` when it goes out of scope. A smart pointer type is automatically created when a type library is imported. The `IVcDualPtr` smart pointer type definition is shown here:

```
// The following is an excerpt from Ch8VcDual.tlh
_COM_SMARTPTR_TYPEDEF(IVcDual, __uuidof(IVcDual));
```

The `_COM_SMARTPTR_TYPEDEF` macro just shown creates the `IVcDualPtr` smart pointer type. The following example demonstrates how the `IVcDualPtr` is used:

```
static void TestVcDual2(const char* serverName) throw(_com_error)
{
    IVcDual* ip = (IVcDual*)CreateObject(__uuidof(VcDual),
                                         __uuidof(IVcDual),
                                         serverName);
    IVcDualPtr sp(ip, false);
    cout << sp->TestString("vcdualtest") << endl;
}
```

In `TestVcDual2()`, a `VcDual` COM object is created. Next, the `IVcDualPtr` smart pointer is declared. This smart pointer takes ownership of the `IVcDual*` interface pointer. Note that there is no explicit call to `Release()` in the `TestVcDual2()` method. The smart pointer, `sp`, automatically calls `Release()` as soon as it goes out of scope, even if `TestString()` throws an exception.

Up to this point, the examples that demonstrate `import` have all focused on the use of a dual interface. The `import` directive can also be used with type libraries that define automation interfaces. From the client perspective, an automation interface is used like any other interface. The `import` directive generates wrapper methods that invoke `IDispatch` correctly. The following wrapper method demonstrates how an automation interface is actually invoked when importing an automation interface:

```cpp
inline _bstr_t Ch8Disp::TestString(_bstr_t Parm0)
{
    BSTR _result;

    _com_dispatch_method(this, 0x65, DISPATCH_METHOD, VT_BSTR,
                          (void*)&_result, L"\x0008", (BSTR)Parm0);
    return _bstr_t(_result, false);
}
```

In several of the examples, we have used the `CreateObject()` function to create a remote instance of a COM object. An example of this usage is shown here:

```cpp
IVcDual* ip = (IVcDual*)CreateObject(__uuidof(VcDual),
                                     __uuidof(IVcDual),
                                     serverName);
```

The `CreateObject()` function simply calls `CoCreateInstanceEx()`:

```cpp
static void* CreateObject(REFCLSID clsid,
                          REFIID ifcid,
                          const char* srvName) throw(_com_error)
{
    // Create server info.
    COSERVERINFO  serverInfo;

    serverInfo.dwReserved1 = 0;
    serverInfo.dwReserved2 = 0;
    _bstr_t bstr(srvName);
    serverInfo.pwszName  = (wchar_t*)bstr;
    serverInfo.pAuthInfo = NULL;

    // Create MULTI_QI array to hold the desired interface.
    MULTI_QI mqi[] = { {&ifcid, NULL, 0} };

    // Create a server object instance.
    HRESULT hr = ::CoCreateInstanceEx(clsid, NULL, CLSCTX_ALL,
                                      &serverInfo, 1, mqi);
```

```
    if (FAILED(hr)) throw _com_error(hr);

    return mqi[0].pItf;
}
```

Using COM with Visual C++ is much more complicated than using COM with Visual Basic and Visual J++. This is mostly due to the added power and flexibility afforded to the user when deploying in C++. Despite the extensions that Microsoft has added to Visual C++ (e.g., `import`, `__declspec`, smart pointers, etc.), Visual Basic continues to excel as a superior development environment for creating end-user COM-based applications. There are always exceptions to any generalization, but the low-level nature of C++ tends to make it more appropriate for the server than for the client.

Summary

Distributed objects have had a profound impact on the desktop client landscape. The level of complexity required to bridge process and even machine boundaries has been greatly reduced. This reduction in complexity allows client application logic to be distributed across the enterprise. The ultimate benefits are lower maintenance costs, reduced client hardware requirements, and quicker deployment.

The desktop client arena is dominated by the Microsoft Windows family of operating systems. Because COM is tightly coupled with Windows, it also enjoys a dominant position on Windows platforms. To meet the needs of a diverse set of clients, several approaches have evolved for using COM in client applications. In this chapter, we discussed the custom interface approach, automation interface approach, and dual interface approach. We explored the strengths and weaknesses of each approach.

COM's momentum on the desktop is fueled by the powerful development environments that currently support it. Of all the COM-capable development environments, Microsoft's Visual Studio continues to lead in market share. Visual Studio allows developers to create and use COM objects in Visual Basic, Visual J++, and Visual C++. Each of the environments (VB, VJ++, and VC++) has specific advantages and disadvantages when compared to the others.

In recent years, the Web application paradigm has begun to attract an increasing number of applications away from the traditional desktop. In the next chapter, we will examine the positions of both COM and CORBA in the Web application domain. Unlike the desktop domain, the verdict is still out as to which technology will dominate in Web-based applications.

Chapter 9

The Internet Client

Topics Covered in This Chapter

- Distributed Object Internet Strategies
- Using COM with Active Server Pages
- Using CORBA in a Java Applet
- The Push Technology Alternative

The Internet is undeniably the most significant force to impact the software industry in the last decade. Given Microsoft's dominance on the traditional desktop, only the most significant of forces could sway Microsoft's substantial user base to consider anything besides a traditional Windows desktop solution. The Internet has provided enough benefits to alter the demands of end users and drive the need for Web-based application development. While most users continue to use Windows to host their browsers, users actually rely on the almost painless accessibility afforded by the Web browser rather than the conveniences of Windows itself. The end result is that the Web browser becomes the client target platform rather than a particular operating system. This is a radical departure from traditional client approaches.

The use of COM and CORBA in creating Web-based applications has taken a few different directions as Web application development has become mainstream. With regard to remoting capability, COM has mostly been confined to the server side. COM is rarely used to communicate with a remote server from a client's browser. In contrast, CORBA has been used in CORBA/Java applets. In Java applets, CORBA can be used directly from the client's Web browser.

Highly sophisticated browser-based applications can cause a range of problems, including extremely high download times and cross-browser incompatibilities. In some cases, push technology offers an alternative to browser-based deployment. In this chapter, we will explore the use of COM and CORBA in Internet client applications.

Distributed Object Internet Strategies

In browser-based applications, distributed objects can be used in several different ways. In some cases, all access to the distributed objects is restricted to the server side. In other cases, distributed objects are used directly from the browser-based client application. These two approaches are illustrated in Figure 9-1.

The first scenario shown in Figure 9-1 illustrates a browser-based client application that does not interact with any distributed objects. In such a scenario, all of the interactions between client and server occur through the Web server via HTTP. The distributed objects are used only by the Web server when it processes HTTP requests and generates HTTP responses.

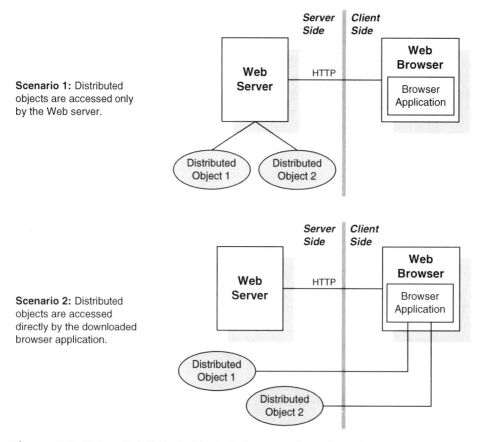

Scenario 1: Distributed objects are accessed only by the Web server.

Scenario 2: Distributed objects are accessed directly by the downloaded browser application.

Figure 9-1. *Using distributed objects in browser-based applications.*

The second scenario shown in Figure 9-1 illustrates a browser-based client application that interacts directly with distributed objects. In such a scenario, the Web server first downloads an executable client application (e.g., Java applet, VBScript, etc.) to the browser. The running client application then directly uses the distributed objects.

Each strategy has advantages and disadvantages. Limiting distributed object access to the Web server increases security since the Web server is the only server entry point from the client. Also, the client application is less complex since it is not required to access the distributed objects. The lower complexity makes such an approach easier to implement and more maintainable. The main disadvantage is that of power and performance. The client application in such an approach must constantly access the Web server (using HTTP) when it needs to access any server-side systems. This imposes a severe amount of overhead on the Web server.

The ability to access distributed objects directly from the client's browser application is extremely powerful. Providing such access, however, has several drawbacks. To support such an approach, the browser application requires a complete distributed object infrastructure on the client side. This requires a great deal of control over the client's environment and can be difficult to deploy and maintain.

Both COM and CORBA support either approach. Their unique characteristics, however, tend to favor one approach over the other.

COM Internet Strategies

A multitude of products exist in the marketplace for building Web applications. Despite the competition, one product dominates on the Microsoft Windows NT Server platform. Microsoft supports Active Server Pages (ASP) as part of Internet Information Server (IIS) for Windows NT Server. Because IIS ships with every copy of NT Server, it naturally has a huge install base. The ASP framework provides a powerful architecture for creating COM-based Web applications. Figure 9-2 illustrates how an application that uses Active Server Pages is typically implemented.

When using an ASP application, clients (using a Web browser) request URLs with an `.asp` extension rather than with an `.htm` or `.html` extension. If IIS identifies the ASP page as being part of a predefined ASP application, it processes the ASP page before sending a response to the client. This processing allows

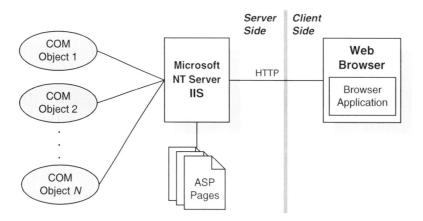

Figure 9-2. *A typical Active Server Pages application.*

implementors of the ASP application to add scripts to the ASP pages that execute on the server side. ASP pages typically consist of a mix of HTML, server-side script, and client-side script. The scripting languages used for server-side processing (VBScript and JScript) support interaction with COM objects. All such interactions usually occur only on the server side, and the client browser is unaware that COM is being used. (To better understand how ASP pages are used with COM, see Using COM with Active Server Pages on page 261.)

Another alternative is to use DCOM directly from a browser-based client application. It is certainly possible to use DCOM from VBScript or JScript running within a client's browser. Such an approach, however, is problematic for the following reasons:

- *Browser support for scripts.* The client's browser must support the VBScript and/or JScript extensions to support COM.

- *Operating system support for DCOM.* The operating system on which the browser is running must support DCOM.

- *Client configuration.* The client machine must be configured to support usage of the DCOM object. For example, the ProgID must be associated with the appropriate CLSID. Such configuration depends greatly on the types of COM objects being used by the client (see Installing Remote COM Clients on page 235).

- *Security.* Security must be configured correctly on both the client and server machines to allow access to the COM server object from the client machine. Allowing such access while also ensuring proper server-side protection is perhaps the greatest challenge.

Microsoft's Active Server Pages provides a portable and maintainable solution. If care is taken to ensure that generated pages contain only pure HTML and basic JavaScript, the pages generated by the IIS Active Server Pages engine work on virtually any browser. In contrast, attempting to use DCOM directly from the client browser is problematic at the very least.

CORBA Internet Strategies

In the client domain, CORBA has inextricably tied its future as a client-based ORB to Java. This statement should in no way lower CORBA's importance as a server-based ORB when languages other than Java, such as C++, are used. On the client, however, support for CORBA in languages such as Visual Basic, VBScript, and JScript is nonexistent unless a vendor-provided COM/CORBA bridging product is used. While CORBA support is available for C++, C++ tends to be a poor environment for creating client applications. This leaves Java as the only widely supported language for client application development with CORBA. Given this situation, the success of CORBA in Internet client application development depends greatly on the success of Java in Internet client environments.

JavaServer Pages (JSP)[*] is a Java-based technology that is similar to Microsoft's Active Server Pages. JSP allows Java to be intermixed with HTML just as ASP allows for the use of VBScript and JScript. JSP offers several advantages over ASP. The most important advantage is that the JSP approach is more portable since it runs on any platform that supports a JSP-enabled Web server and Java. In contrast, the use of ASP with COM is limited to IIS on Windows. Since Java is the foundation of JSP, any Java/CORBA ORB can be used with JSP just as COM is used with ASP.

Another alternative is to use CORBA directly from a browser-based client application. Java applets can use CORBA directly as illustrated in Figure 9-3.

The Java applet's class files are downloaded from the Web server to the client's Web browser. The Java applet then executes within the client's Web browser and uses CORBA to access server-side CORBA objects. Using CORBA from a Java applet does not suffer from the same limitations as using DCOM

---

*For more information on JavaServer Pages, see http://java.sun.com.

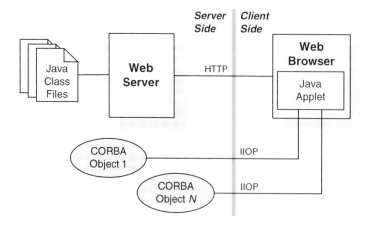

Figure 9-3. *A typical CORBA/Java applet.*

with VBScript or JScript. CORBA/Java resolves each of the following issues that were problematic in the DCOM case:

- *Browser support for Java.* Java is universally supported in almost all major browsers. Although browsers do suffer from varying levels of support for Java, there are alternatives. Sun Microsystems offers the Java Plug-in,[*] a Web browser plug-in that allows the same version of Sun's Java Runtime Environment (JRE) to be used with most of the major browsers including Internet Explorer 3.x and 4.x and Netscape 3.x and 4.x under Microsoft Windows.

- *Operating system support.* When using CORBA in a Java applet, the CORBA ORB runs entirely within the Java Virtual Machine. The CORBA ORB has no direct dependencies on the underlying operating system.

- *Security.* CORBA security is limited only by the Java security model. This security model is usually referred to as the *sandbox*. Sandbox limitations can be avoided by creating a trusted applet or by using a proxy on the Web server. (We will discuss the use of a proxy in Security Issues for Internet Clients on page 282.)

One of the more serious problems that was faced in early attempts to use CORBA in Java applets was the overhead of downloading a CORBA ORB to the

---

[*]For more information on the Java Plug-in, see http://java.sun.com.

client's browser. Beginning with version 1.2, Sun's JDK includes a fully functional CORBA ORB. By using Sun's Java Plug-in to fully support JDK 1.2, a client-based CORBA ORB is guaranteed to be present on all major Web browsers, thus reducing the overhead of using CORBA in Java applets.

Using COM with Active Server Pages

The use of COM in an Active Server Pages (ASP) application is best demonstrated by an example. Consider a situation in which an Internet application is needed to access a company's customer data. An example of such an Internet application is shown in Figure 9-4.

To use the customer application, users download the `customer.asp` page into their Web browser. After the page is loaded, a list of all customers is presented. The user can then do one of the following three things:

1. *Lookup.* The user can select a name in the customer list and look up the customer. Upon successful completion, the selected customer's information is displayed.

2. *Create.* The user can create a new customer. Upon successful completion, the newly created customer is displayed.

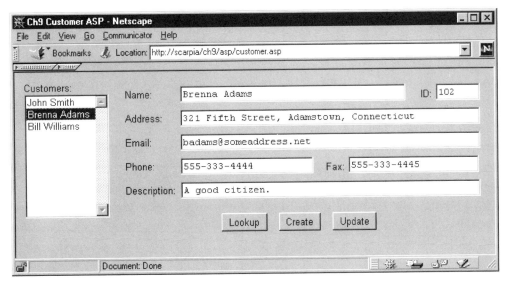

Figure 9-4. *The customer ASP application after a successful lookup.*

3. *Update.* The user can update the currently loaded customer. Upon successful completion, the updated customer is displayed.

From the client's perspective, the customer application is simply an HTML/ CGI-based application. Clicking on *Lookup, Create,* or *Update* simply performs a CGI form-post of all data contained in the form.[*] A new customer page, `customer.asp`, is returned as a response from the Web server after successful execution of the action.

On the server side, the application is implemented using COM and Active Server Pages. A COM object that implements the `ICustomer` interface is created to provide access to the customer data. The `ICustomer` interface is shown in Listing 9-1.

The `ICustomer` interface consists of the following methods:

- `GetAll()`—Used to retrieve the ids and names of the company's customers. The ids and names are returned in a `VARIANT`-wrapped `SAFEARRAY`. This method is needed to populate the list of all customers in the application.

- `Create()`—Used to create a new customer. The customer is created using information stored in the variable `info`. The variable `info` is a `VARIANT`-wrapped `SAFEARRAY` and contains the customer's name, address, phone number, and so forth. The `id` of the newly created customer is returned to the user.

- `Lookup()`—Used to look up an existing customer that corresponds to the specified `id`. If the customer exists, the `info` for the customer is returned.

- `Update()`—Used to update the customer corresponding to the specified `id`.

Before continuing with the example, it is important to note that the design of the `ICustomer` interface was influenced by the following criteria:

- *Remoting criterion.* For remoting purposes, the number of round-trips between client and server is minimized since all data about the customer is always transferred in a single operation (as opposed to getting or setting data one attribute at a time).

---

[*]CGI (Common Gateway Interface) is the standard method for implementing forms in HTML pages and is universally supported in all Web browsers.

Listing 9-1. *COM ICustomer Interface*

```
[
    object,
    uuid(3A12A51D-60B9-11D2-B2E1-00207812E629),
    dual,
    pointer_default(unique)
]
interface ICustomer : IDispatch
{
    [id(1)] HRESULT GetAll([out] VARIANT* idArray,
                           [out] VARIANT* nameArray);

    [id(2)] HRESULT Create([in] VARIANT info,
                           [out, retval] long* id);

    [id(3)] HRESULT Lookup([in] long id,
                           [out,retval] VARIANT* info);

    [id(4)] HRESULT Update([in] long id,
                           [in] VARIANT info);
};
[
    uuid(3A12A510-60B9-11D2-B2E1-00207812E629)
]
library CUSTOMERLib
{
    importlib("stdole32.tlb");
    importlib("stdole2.tlb");


    [
        uuid(3A12A51E-60B9-11D2-B2E1-00207812E629)
    ]
    coclass Customer
    {
        [default] interface ICustomer;
    };
};
```

- *Client criterion.* Since the COM object will be used from Active Server Pages, it must support an automation-compatible interface. For this reason, a VARIANT-wrapped SAFEARRAY is used rather than a COM struct to represent the customer information.

- *MTS criterion.* Recall (from COM Object Management Under Microsoft's MTS on page 194) that an identifier must be passed in each method in order to restore the state of the object after activation. Since we wish to host the `Ch9.Customer` object under MTS as a stateless object, we pass the `id` of the customer when invoking `Lookup()` and `Update()`.

Although the `ICustomer` interface defined in Listing 9-1 meets all of the preceding criteria, it is actually a very poor interface. The use of `VARIANT`-wrapped `SAFEARRAY`s to convey customer information is error-prone at best. In addition, customer instances do not maintain any identity. Client applications are forced to manage both the customer `id` and the customer information array when accessing the COM customer instance. (In Client Needs Versus Remoting Requirements on page 280, we will revisit these issues and discuss other approaches for meeting client needs as well as the aforementioned criteria.)

The COM customer instance is used by the ASP application to access all customer data. The implementation of the customer ASP application is illustrated in Figure 9-5.

Recall that `.asp` files typically consist of a mix of HTML and VBScript (or JScript) and that the scripting code can access COM objects as required. The customer ASP application consists of the following `.asp` files:

* `customer.asp`—Used to present the user interface (CGI form) as shown in Figure 9-4.

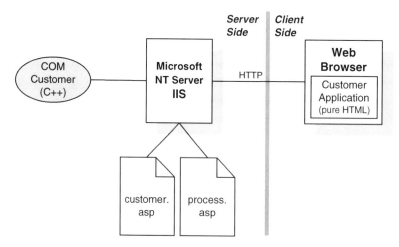

Figure 9-5. *Server-side implementation of the customer ASP application.*

- `process.asp`—Invoked whenever the user clicks on *Lookup, Create,* or *Update.* If processing succeeds, the user is redirected back to the `customer.asp` file.

Listing 9-2 demonstrates how the COM customer object is used in `customer.asp` to build the customer list when the page is accessed from IIS. The excerpt of `customer.asp` shown in Listing 9-2 illustrates the following key features:

- *ASP pages consist of a mixture of HTML and VBScript.* In `customer.asp`, the VBScript is delimited by `<% %>` as shown in lines 4–28 and lines 36–41.

- *Functions and subprocedures can be declared within the VBScript.* The `getAll()` subprocedure (lines 5–23) creates an instance of the `Ch9.Customer` object and calls `GetAll()` on the customer object to retrieve the ids and names of all customers.

- *Variables can be declared at the page level for later use in the page.* On line 25, the `customerIDs` and `customerNames` variables are declared. These variables are initialized by a call to the `getAll()` subprocedure on line 26 and are later used on lines 38 and 39.

By default, all VBScript code is processed on the server side before the page is downloaded to the client's browser. For this example, the generated code that ends up getting downloaded to the client's browser would appear as shown in Listing 9-3.

Note that, in Listing 9-3, the BODY of `customer.asp` consists primarily of a FORM whose action is defined as `process.asp`. Because *Lookup, Create,* and *Update* are defined as submit buttons in the form, clicking on those buttons will do a form-post to `process.asp`. The `process.asp` file contains VBScript subprocedures that interact with the COM customer object. If processing of `process.asp` by the Web server succeeds, the user is immediately redirected back to `customer.asp` with updated data. The main point to note is that since HTML/CGI is being used, each interaction with the server requires an HTTP request to the server followed by a reply (page) that must be downloaded to the client's browser.

Accessing the COM customer object from `process.asp` is done in much the same way as was done in `customer.asp` (see Listing 9-2). The rest of the customer ASP application is an exercise in how to use Active Server Pages and has nothing to do with how ASP accesses COM objects.

Listing 9-2. *Excerpt from customer.asp*

```
1  <HTML>
2  <BODY BGCOLOR="#d3d3d3">
3
4  <%
5      Sub getAll(ids, names)
6          On Error Resume Next
7
8          'Get a customer wrapper instance.
9          Dim cust
10         Set cust = Server.CreateObject("Ch9.Customer")
11         If Err.number <> 0 Then
12             'Handle error
13             Exit Sub
14         End If
15
16         'Get all ids and names from the customer.
17         Call cust.GetAll(ids, names)
18
19         If Err.number <> 0 Then
20             'Handle error
21             Exit Sub
22         End If
23     End Sub
24
25     Dim customerIDs, customerNames
26     Call getAll(customerIDs, customerNames)
27     ...
28 %>
29 <FORM action=process.asp method=post>
30 <!-- **************** Customer List **************** -->
31 <font size=2 face=sans-serif>
32   Customers:<BR>
33 </font>
34
35 <SELECT size=10 name=customerID>
36 <%
37     For i = 0 To UBound(customerIDS)
38         Response.Write("<OPTION value=" & customerIDS(i))
39         Response.Write(">" & customerNames(i) & vbcrlf)
40     Next
41 %>
42 </SELECT>
43 </FORM>
44 </BODY>
45 </HTML>
```

Listing 9-3. *Client Browser's View of customer.asp*

```
<HTML>
<BODY BGCOLOR="#d3d3d3">
<FORM action=process.asp method=post>

<font size=2 face=sans-serif>
  Customers:<BR>
</font>

<SELECT size=10 id=select1 name=customerID>
<OPTION value=101>John Smith
<OPTION value=102>Brenna Adams
<OPTION value=103>Bill Williams
</SELECT>

</FORM>
</BODY>
</HTML>
```

Using CORBA in a Java Applet

CORBA can be used from a Java applet to access server-side resources. In fact, a Java applet using a Java/CORBA ORB is considered a first-class entity in the CORBA ORB universe. Consider once again the case where an Internet application is needed to access a company's customer data. An example of a CORBA/Java applet that implements such an Internet application is shown in Figure 9-6.

Using a CORBA/Java applet to access customer data offers an approach that is radically different from the use of Active Server Pages. In contrast to the Active Server Pages approach, which relies on constant interaction with the Web server, a CORBA/Java applet is a fully functional client-side application that can access server-side resources without using the Web server.

To use the customer application, users download the `CustomerApplet.html` page into their Web browser. The `CustomerApplet.html` page contains an `<OBJECT>` tag that specifies the applet code (Java `.class` files) to be downloaded from the Web server.[*] After the page is loaded, the applet is started, and

---

[*]Because our applet uses Sun's Java Plug-in rather than the Java Virtual Machine supported by the browser, we rely on an object tag rather than on an applet tag.

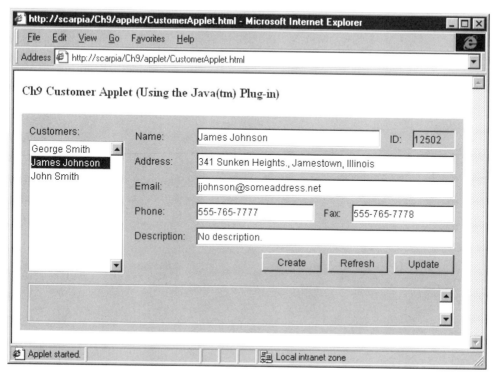

Figure 9-6. *The customer CORBA/Java applet.*

a list of customers is presented to the user. The user can then do one of the following four things:

1. *Lookup.* The user can select a name in the customer list. Upon selection, the applet will perform a lookup of the selected customer and display the selected customer's information.

2. *Create.* The user can create a new customer.

3. *Refresh.* The user can refresh the data for the currently selected customer.

4. *Update.* The user can update the currently selected customer.

On the server side, a CORBA object is implemented that supports the `Customer` and `CustomerManager` interfaces shown in Listing 9-4.

The `CustomerManager` interface defines the factory interface for creating `Customer` instances. (We discussed the need for factory objects in CORBA

Listing 9-4. *CORBA Customer and CustomerManager Interfaces*

```
// Ch9.idl
module Ch9
{
    typedef sequence<long>   LongSeq;
    typedef sequence<string> StringSeq;

    exception CustomerExc
    {
        string reason;
    };

    struct CustomerInfo
    {
        long   id;
        string name;
        string address;
        string phone;
        string fax;
        string email;
        string desc;
    };

    interface Customer
    {
        void getAll(out LongSeq ids,
                    out StringSeq names) raises(CustomerExc);

        long create(in CustomerInfo info) raises(CustomerExc);

        CustomerInfo lookup(in long id) raises(CustomerExc);

        CustomerInfo getInfo() raises(CustomerExc);

        void setInfo(in CustomerInfo info) raises(CustomerExc);
    };

    interface CustomerManager
    {
        Customer createCustomer();
    };
};
```

Factories on page 82.) The `Customer` interface presented in Listing 9-4 defines the core functionality needed to implement the customer applet. The `Customer` interface consists of the following methods:

- `getAll()`—Used to retrieve the ids and names of the company's customers. This method is needed to populate the list of all customers when the applet is loaded.

- `create()`—Used to create a new customer. Note that the CORBA implementation takes as a parameter a fully defined `CustomerInfo` struct representing the customer info (as opposed to a `VARIANT` in the customer ASP application). If successful, the CORBA object instance is associated with the newly created customer.

- `lookup()`—Used to look up the customer associated with the specified `id`. If successful, the CORBA object instance is associated with the customer, and the customer information is returned as a `CustomerInfo` struct.

- `getInfo()`—Used to retrieve the customer information associated with the current CORBA customer instance.

- `setInfo()`—Used to update the customer information associated with the current CORBA customer instance.

The customer CORBA/Java applet directly accesses the customer CORBA object without accessing the Web server. The Web server is no longer needed by the applet after the applet has been downloaded and initialized. The implementation of the customer CORBA/Java applet is illustrated in Figure 9-7.

A typical scenario for using the customer CORBA/Java applet is as follows:

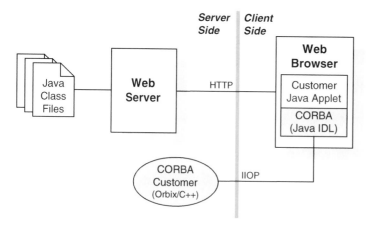

Figure 9-7. *Implementation of the customer CORBA/Java applet.*

1. The user requests the `CustomerApplet.html` page from the Web server.

2. The Web server downloads the `CustomerApplet.html` page to the client Web browser. The Java `.class` files that are required to execute the applet are also downloaded.

3. The applet is initialized and uses the client-side Java IDL CORBA ORB to access the Orbix/C++ customer object on the server.

4. The applet retrieves the names and ids of the company's customers.

5. The user selects, creates, refreshes, and updates customers. These actions require further interaction with the Orbix/C++ CORBA customer server via the Java IDL CORBA ORB.

To create the CORBA-related files needed by the client applet, we first need to run the `idltojava` compiler provided with the Java IDL ORB product on the `Ch9.idl` file:

```
// idltojava ships as an extension to the Java IDL CORBA product
idltojava Ch9.idl
```

Because the interface definitions for `Customer` and `CustomerManager` are defined within a CORBA IDL module named `Ch9`, a Java package named `Ch9` is generated containing all of the `Ch9` CORBA files needed to access the `Customer` and `CustomerManager` CORBA objects.

Before the Java IDL CORBA ORB can be used in the applet, it must be initialized as shown here:

```
public class CustomerApplet extends Applet {
    public void init() {
        try {
            // Initialize the ORB.
            org.omg.CORBA.ORB orb = ORB.init(this, null);
            ...
```

The ORB reference created by calling `ORB.init()` can then be used to obtain the handle on the `CustomerManager` instance:

```
// Get the CustomerManager instance.
org.omg.CORBA.Object obj;
obj = orb.string_to_object(ior);
Ch9.CustomerManager mgr = Ch9.CustomerManagerHelper.narrow(obj);
```

For the example discussed in this section, we pass the IOR (introduced on page 36) of the `CustomerManager` CORBA object to the customer applet as an applet parameter in the `CustomerApplet.html` file. A more robust method for obtaining references to persistent CORBA objects like the `CustomerManager` instance would be to use a CORBA naming service.

Once we have obtained a reference to the `CustomerManager` factory object, we can create a `Customer` object as shown here:

```
// Create the customer.
Ch9.Customer cust = mgr.createCustomer();
```

To complete initial loading of the customer applet, we obtain the ids and names of all customers. These ids and names can then be used to populate the customer list in the applet:

```
// Get ids and names of all customers.
LongSeqHolder ids = new LongSeqHolder();
StringSeqHolder names = new StringSeqHolder();
cust.getAll(ids, names);
```

Looking up an existing customer, creating a new customer, refreshing the current customer, and updating the current customer are all accomplished by directly calling the customer object in the same manner as the call to `getAll()`. The Java applet running in the client-side Web browser has full access to the CORBA customer object that is running on the server machine.

The Push Technology Alternative

Using the Internet as a distribution mechanism for end-user applications has both advantages and disadvantages. The greatest advantage is that casual users (e.g., Web surfers) can use an Active Server Pages (ASP) application or Java applet without having to go through a complex and tedious installation on their client machines. The Web browser manages all installation and initialization issues on the client machine.

The convenience of using a browser-hosted Internet application comes at a significant cost. An ASP application requires extensive interaction between the user's Web browser and the Web server. Each interaction in an ASP application requires one or more HTTP requests from the client machine to the Web server. This can place a heavy load on the Web server and can result in poor overall performance when many users try to use the application simultaneously. While CORBA/Java applets can remove some of the burden on the Web server, initializing a Java applet in a Web browser is often a very expensive task. The use of a Java applet almost always requires the download of a significant number of class files before the applet can begin execution. This download time can be especially frustrating when downloading a Java applet over a slow network connection such as a phone modem.

The main problem with browser-based client applications is that users are forced to download the same files from the Web server over and over again. This is often referred to as a *pull* approach since the user (with the help of the Web browser) pulls applications on demand. In the case of a Java applet, all of the applet's class files need to be downloaded every time the Web browser is restarted (Web browsers do not usually cache Java class files on the client machine across invocations). When CORBA is used in a Java applet, the problem is exacerbated because the CORBA ORB's class files need to be downloaded as well. While the use of a client-side CORBA ORB such as Java IDL can eliminate the overhead of downloading CORBA files, the problem still exists for the rest of the Java class files associated with an applet.

The *push* approach offers an alternative to the pull approach used by Web browsers. When using the push approach, the push application is pushed to the client side. All use of the push application then occurs on the client side without further involvement by the push server. This makes subsequent invocations of the client application much more efficient. The push approach is illustrated in Figure 9-8.

In addition to first-time downloading of the push application to the client tier, most push products also allow for efficient updates of the push application after the initial download. The term *push* is therefore a bit of a misnomer. The push is actually configured to periodically check for updates to the push application and pull (as opposed to push) those updates at regular intervals. This is in contrast to the Web browser approach, where the user makes a specific request to download (pull) the application on demand.

One of the leading vendors in the push arena is Marimba, Inc.[*] Marimba offers a product called *Castanet* that can be used to efficiently distribute and update a wide range of application types via the Internet. In the Castanet product, Marimba refers to a push server as a *Transmitter* and a push receiver as a *Tuner.*

---

*For more information on Marimba and Castanet, see http://www.marimba.com.

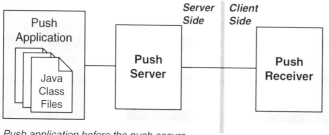

Push application before the push occurs.

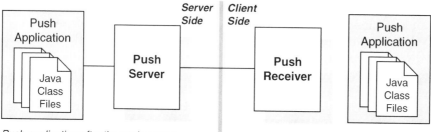

Push application after the push occurs.

Figure 9-8. *Using the push approach for a Java application.*

Push technology such as Marimba's Castanet allows COM and CORBA applications of all types to be distributed as Internet applications. In addition to Java applications, Castanet can be used to also install and manage updates to Windows desktop applications such as Visual Basic, Visual C++, and Visual J++ applications. The key point to remember is that the Internet is a distribution mechanism and that there are powerful alternatives to the convenient but often inefficient Web browser approach.

Summary

The emergence of the Internet client application as a viable alternative to the traditional desktop application has had a profound effect on overall enterprise strategy. The Internet offers an irresistible software distribution mechanism that allows vendors to reach a larger number of clients in a much shorter time period. This represents a win-win approach since both vendors and clients benefit.

Microsoft's Active Server Pages (ASP) technology and CORBA/Java applets represent two distinct approaches for using distributed objects to implement Internet client applications. The Active Server Pages approach can be used to create highly portable applications since the ASP pages that get downloaded to the client can be tailored to use standard HTML. ASP applications do, however, impose a high level of overhead on the Web server since the Web server performs all real processing. In contrast, Java applets are fully operational applications that run in the context of the user's Web browser. This places the processing load on the client machine.

The Internet is actually a distribution mechanism rather than a specific type of client application. Although Internet applications are generally considered to be applications that execute in the context of a Web browser, push technology, such as Marimba's Castanet, offers a powerful alternative to the Web browser distribution model. Perhaps a better classification of Internet applications is that they operate on a wider range of platforms. Both ASP applications and Java applets can be used on a multitude of platforms, including Windows, Macintosh, and UNIX. The importance of the Internet as a distribution mechanism becomes most noticeable when attempting to support a diverse range of operating system platforms.

Up to this point, we have introduced fairly basic approaches for creating desktop clients and Internet clients. In the next chapter, we will discuss fundamental design issues that arise when we are creating COM and CORBA client applications. We will also examine the issues that arise when we attempt to create client applications that access both COM and CORBA servers.

Chapter 10

Client Design Considerations

Topics Covered in This Chapter

- Remoting Requirements and Design Issues
- Client Needs Versus Remoting Requirements
- Security Issues for Internet Clients
- Migrating from the Desktop to the Internet

In an ideal world, the use of COM and CORBA would have little effect on the design and implementation of client applications. COM and CORBA would simply provide object-oriented access to distributed resources. The catch to all of this is that the resources being accessed are distributed and that temporal issues must be considered when accessing anything nonlocal. Communication across a network is several orders of magnitude more expensive (and error-prone) than accessing local memory. This communication expense must be taken into account when accessing distributed objects.

The most basic requirement for accessing distributed resources is to minimize the number of requests made between clients and servers. It is usually best to retrieve all data required from a server with the fewest number of actual client requests. Another important requirement is to ensure secure access to valuable server resources. These requirements often convolute the interface of a distributed object and make a distributed object awkward to use in a broad range of client environments.

In this chapter, we'll examine and address some of the remoting, security, and usability issues related to the use of COM and CORBA in client applications. We'll conclude this chapter by examining how COM and CORBA objects can be used concurrently from desktop as well as Internet client applications.

Remoting Requirements and Design Issues

The use of distributed objects necessitates an awareness of two basic remoting requirements:

1. Minimize network traffic.

2. Minimize the number of stateful connections between clients and servers.

The requirement to minimize network traffic applies to the use of all types of distributed resources, including distributed objects implemented with COM and CORBA. The most effective method for minimizing network traffic with COM and CORBA is to minimize the invocations against an interface by sending and receiving a greater amount of data on each transmission between client and server. For example, consider the following COM interface:

```
interface ICustomer : IDispatch
{
    [id(1), propget] HRESULT name    ([out, retval] BSTR*);
    [id(2), propget] HRESULT address([out, retval] BSTR*);
    [id(3), propget] HRESULT phone   ([out, retval] BSTR*);
};
```

If the preceding interface is used, a client that wishes to retrieve all of the information associated with a particular customer is forced to make three requests to the ICustomer server. A better approach (from a remoting perspective) is to provide a single method that retrieves all customer information in a single call. An approach that uses a single method and exhibits a coarser granularity is shown here:

```
typedef struct CustomerInfo
{
    BSTR name;
    BSTR address;
    BSTR phone;
} CustomerInfo_t;

interface ICustomer : IUnknown
{
    HRESULT Lookup([out,retval] CustomerInfo_t* info);
};
```

The biggest problem with this approach is that we can no longer use the ICustomer interface from COM automation environments such as VBScript.

In the case of a more complicated interface, such as one that utilizes a nested structure, we would not be able to use the interface from environments such as Visual J++. The only client environment that can be guaranteed to work with a custom interface is Visual C++. Note that we could instead use a VARIANT-wrapped SAFEARRAY as a return argument, but this would result in a weakly defined interface. In general, creating interfaces that manipulate only VARIANTs is poor design and is likely to result in unforeseen errors due to the lack of adequate compile-time type checking.

The use of a struct to minimize network traffic is a common practice when creating CORBA interfaces. Such an approach is demonstrated by the following CORBA IDL definition:

```
struct CustomerInfo
{
    string name;
    string address;
    string phone;
};

interface Customer
{
    CustomerInfo getInfo();
};
```

Although the use of a struct with both COM and CORBA makes sense from a remoting perspective, it is hardly the ideal interface from a client perspective. Clients generally desire an interface that supports finer granularity. Such interfaces often exhibit high overhead from a remoting perspective. (We will examine this issue more closely in the next section.)

The other remoting requirement is to minimize the number of stateful connections between clients and servers. In The Need for Stateless Objects on page 191, we discussed how a distributed object system can allow for stateless and inexpensive connections. If a product such as Microsoft Transaction Server or BEA Systems' M3 is used, the number of stateful connections can be minimized by properly designing the server-side objects.

CORBA is often described as a superior remoting architecture when compared to COM. This is actually not the case in terms of fundamentals. Both COM and CORBA support remoting equally well in most situations. The main difference is that COM was primarily used as an in-process component model during its early stages. Because of its in-process use, many COM components were designed to work well as in-process DLLs rather than as remote distributed objects. Interfaces designed for in-process usage are often poor interfaces for remote servers because remoting issues such as call latency are not considered. In contrast, CORBA has always been treated as a remoting architecture. The designers of good CORBA interfaces always place a high priority on the ability of those interfaces to function in remote settings.

Client Needs Versus Remoting Requirements

Remoting requirements cannot be ignored when designing distributed objects. Interfaces that facilitate remoting, however, often fall short of client application needs. As discussed in the last section, the interface that supported individual retrieval of a customer's name, address, and phone number was abandoned in favor of an interface that supported retrieval of all customer information at once. From a client perspective (as opposed to a remoting perspective), the first approach that retrieves one attribute at a time is much simpler to use. It is far simpler to retrieve attributes one at a time from a single object than to retrieve a `struct` and maintain that data separately within the client application.

In the case of COM, there is also a serious limitation regarding the use of a custom COM interface (e.g., one that uses a `struct`) in environments other than Visual C++. A custom interface cannot be used from COM automation environments such as VBScript. Two approaches for dealing with the COM incompatibility issue for automation environments are

1. *Multiple interface approach.* Create a single COM object that supports an automation (`IDispatch`) interface in addition to a customer interface.

2. *Wrapper approach.* Create a separate in-process dual interface COM object that wraps the functionality of the distributed object. The wrapper can then be used by any COM client.

With the first approach, the creation of a COM object that supports both custom and automation interfaces suffers from several major deficiencies. As we stated earlier, an automation interface cannot meet both remoting and client requirements. If an automation interface attempts to meet remoting requirements, it will most likely rely on `VARIANT`s as arguments and lack adequate compile-time type checking. If an automation interface provides access methods for each data member, it will be too inefficient to use in a heavily loaded distributed system.

The wrapper approach is superior to the multiple interface approach. The main cost of using a wrapper is that two COM objects (the distributed object and the wrapper) need to be designed, implemented, and maintained instead of one. The actual performance overhead of adding an in-process wrapper, which then calls a remote distributed object, is negligible.

In terms of creating wrappers, COM holds a distinct and significant advantage over CORBA. COM's support for creating in-process components allows wrappers to be created that work across multiple development environments. A COM in-process wrapper can be implemented in Visual C++ and then used from a diverse set of clients implemented in Visual C++, Visual J++, Visual Basic, and VBScript. Note that the wrapper can be implemented in something other than Visual C++ if the wrapper implementation environment can adequately access the interface supported by the distributed object. Figure 10-1 illustrates the COM wrapper approach.

While COM offers the ability to implement a wrapper as a COM component, it is certainly possible to create a wrapper using more conventional techniques. For example, a wrapper can be implemented as a Visual Basic class if it is needed only by Visual Basic clients (assuming that the Visual Basic environment supports the interface of the distributed object). The main advantage of using the COM approach is that the wrapper has to be written only once for all client environment types. CORBA does not offer this capability since its support for in-process components does not usually work across multiple programming language environments.

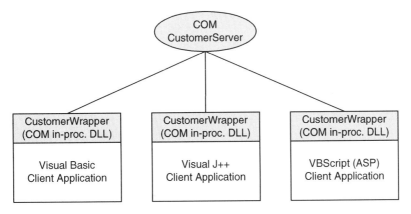

Figure 10-1. *Using a COM wrapper in multiple client environments.*

The main purpose of a distributed object wrapper is to provide an interface to a distributed object that is better suited for the client. The implementation of a client-side wrapper has the potential to offer the following advantages over accessing the distributed object directly:

- *Reliability.* Because a wrapper is local to a client's process, an instance of a wrapper can be instantiated by a client without worrying about remoting issues. Issues related to establishing a reliable connection to a remote distributed object can be handled by the wrapper. This frees clients from having to worry about remoting issues when using a wrapped distributed object.

- *Usability.* A wrapper's interface is oriented toward client needs rather than toward remoting requirements. The client orientation of a wrapper should result in a more usable interface for clients. In the case of COM, a wrapper is required if the client environment is incompatible with the distributed object's interface.

- *Caching.* An instance of a wrapper can maintain a cache of data associated with a remote distributed object. This cache can be used by clients to reduce the number of requests that need to be made to a remote server.

- *Recovery.* A multitude of errors can occur when using a distributed resource. For example, a connection can be broken due to a hardware failure. A wrapper can be designed to automatically recover when failures occur, thereby relieving clients from having to implement redundant recovery mechanisms.

Balancing remoting requirements against client needs is often a difficult task. In most cases, it is generally best to focus on remoting requirements when designing a distributed object. Client needs can best be met by providing a wrapper around the distributed object. Given the ability of wrappers to offer advantages such as reliability, usability, caching, and recovery, it is almost always prudent to provide a wrapper rather than to attempt to meet client needs in a distributed object interface.

Security Issues for Internet Clients

Maintaining security is paramount when providing Internet access to server-side assets. It is also important to assure end users that Internet applications are safe to use on client machines. To spare application designers from having to spend an inordinate amount of resources on guaranteeing security, Internet client approaches such as Active Server Pages (ASP) and Java applets provide default mechanisms for meeting both client and server security requirements. In this section, we will describe the default security mechanisms that are provided when using Active Server Pages and browser-based Java applets.

Security Issues When Using Active Server Pages

Client-side security is rarely an issue when using Active Server Pages. In most ASP applications, the pages that get downloaded to the client browser use only HTML and JavaScript. Web browsers provide built-in security that prevents HTML and JavaScript from accessing client machine resources. The only risk occurs when browser extensions such as browser plug-ins (including ActiveX controls) are used. In such cases, users are generally warned when the installation of plug-ins can compromise security.

The Active Server Pages approach offers a high level of security on the server since all server-side resources are accessed directly by IIS. The client's browser does not directly access server side resources. Database connections, connections to COM objects, and so on, are all confined to the ASP application running under IIS. In addition, IIS provides an extra level of security by impersonating a special user when accessing COM servers from ASP pages. By default, the user that is impersonated is named IUSR_ServerName. For example, all COM interactions from the Ch10 ASP application running under IIS on a server named SCARPIA would impersonate the user named IUSR_SCARPIA. Figure 10-2 demonstrates how the user name can be set from the Internet Service Manager for a specific ASP application.

The default user that gets assigned by IIS for ASP applications is special in that it can access only a limited subset of server resources. One of the most important restrictions is that IUSR_ServerName is defined as a local account rather than as a domain account. It therefore cannot access COM servers on remote machines. While this may seem overly restrictive, it ensures that COM servers on remote machines are secured against inadvertent access by Internet clients.

There are several approaches for working around the restriction regarding remote access to COM servers. The most obvious solution is to assign a domain user to the ASP application. This is unwise since it opens up a security hole for accessing server-side resources. Instead, Microsoft recommends the use of an intermediate local component (i.e., a proxy) that can then be

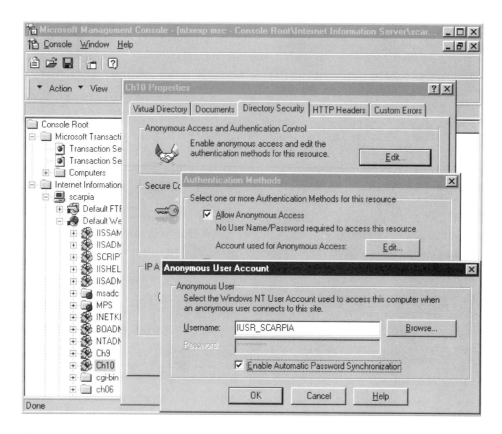

Figure 10-2. *Setting the default user name for an ASP application.*

used to access the remote COM server.* The intermediate component can be installed under MTS to run with an identity that has access to the remote server. Such an approach is illustrated in Figure 10-3.

In Figure 10-3, the IIS ASP application running on SCARPIA does not use the remote COM customer server directly; instead, IIS uses the local COM server, CustomerProxy. IIS is forced to use a local proxy because IIS impersonates the local account, IUSR_SCARPIA, whenever it interacts with COM objects.

The COM CustomerProxy server that is illustrated in Figure 10-3 is hosted under MTS and runs as the domain identity PSW\jason. The PSW\jason account is allowed to launch and execute the remote COM customer server.

---

*This approach is described in knowledge base article Q159311 and can be found at
http://support.microsoft.com/support/kb/articles/q159/3/11.asp.

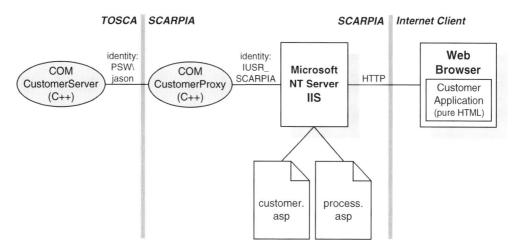

Figure 10-3. *Accessing a remote COM server from an ASP application.*

`CustomerProxy` can therefore communicate with the COM customer server running on TOSCA. By using the `CustomerProxy` server, the ASP application running under IIS is able to communicate with the remote COM customer server.

The performance overhead of using a proxy as illustrated in Figure 10-3 is negligible. The cost of accessing the local proxy should be insignificant compared to the cost of accessing the remote customer server. In almost all situations, the added security benefits of using a proxy outweigh any performance overhead.

Security Issues When Using Java Applets

The security issues related to using Java applets are radically different from the ones related to Active Server Pages. Java applets are fully functional applications that run on the client machine. Because the Java code of an applet executes on the client machine, it is necessary to ensure that the applet does not adversely affect client resources.

Since its introduction, Java has provided for varying degrees of security by allowing a security manager to be specified that controls the Java Virtual Machine's interactions with external systems. Web browsers control the security manager for any applets that execute within the Web browser's JVM. The default security model used by Web browsers for Java applets is typically referred to as the *sandbox.*

The sandbox security model is simple and quite restrictive. Under the default security model, a Java applet is allowed to communicate only with the server from which it was downloaded (i.e., the code base for the applet). A Java applet is not allowed to directly access the client's local file system, local memory, or any external hosts besides the Web server. Any attempts to do so are stopped by the security manager. Limiting the applet in such a manner prevents malicious applets from accessing resources on the client machine and also prevents access to other machines within the client's view. Keep in mind that the client's view consists of all machines within the client's Intranet (i.e., all machines behind the client's firewall). Enforcement of the sandbox by the Web browser is critical when using applets from unknown and/or unreliable sources.

The sandbox security model prevents applets from communicating with CORBA objects running on servers other than the Web server. Two approaches for circumventing sandbox restrictions when attempting to access remote CORBA servers are

1. *Signed applet approach.* An applet can be signed and can express the need to contact machines other than the Web server. If the user chooses to trust the applet, the applet can break out of the sandbox.

2. *Proxy approach.* A proxy can be created for the CORBA object on the remote server. The applet communicates with the proxy, which, in turn, communicates with the remote CORBA server. This approach conforms to the rules of the sandbox security model.

The use of signed applets is most appropriate when distributing trusted applets to a well-defined set of clients. This would typically be the case when deploying an applet within an Intranet (or a well-defined Extranet). The main problem with signed applets has been the lack of a standard approach for deploying those applets across the primary Web browsers. The use of signed applets also requires trust by the client—something that should not be taken lightly by Internet clients in general.

The other alternative for accessing remote CORBA servers is to use a proxy. The proxy approach is illustrated in Figure 10-4.

In Figure 10-4, the Java applet does not use the remote CORBA customer server directly. The applet instead uses the CORBA `CustomerProxy` server on `SCARPIA`. `SCARPIA` hosts the Web server from which the applet was down-

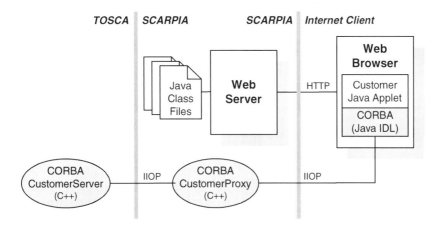

Figure 10-4. *Accessing a remote CORBA server from a Java applet.*

loaded. The applet is forced to use the proxy because the sandbox security constraints allow the applet to interact only with the machine from which the applet was downloaded. The CORBA CustomerProxy server communicates with the remote customer server running on TOSCA. By using the CustomerProxy server, the applet is able to communicate with the remote CORBA customer server. Implementing a proxy is a fairly trivial task since it is simply a pass-through to the remote server. An alternative is to use a vendor-specific CORBA product that dynamically creates proxies. Both Inprise and Iona offer this capability with their CORBA/Java products.

Another security issue related to the use of CORBA/Java applets is IIOP transmission through a firewall. Firewalls prevent Internet access to Intranet resources. In most situations, firewall products are configured to allow HTTP requests to flow freely across the firewall. This allows clients within an Intranet to communicate via HTTP with external resources. A CORBA ORB, however, relies on IIOP rather than on HTTP for communicating between clients and servers. Most firewalls do not allow the transmission of IIOP packets. The OMG is working on a CORBA/Firewall Security specification that will be included with CORBA 3.0. This specification defines how firewall products will manage IIOP traffic across a firewall.

Several of the CORBA vendors offer proprietary solutions that allow IIOP traffic to be wrapped in the HTTP protocol, thereby allowing for communication. Such an approach is referred to as *HTTP tunneling.* HTTP tunneling is somewhat inefficient and is at best a temporary solution until firewall products add support for the transmission of IIOP.

Relying on vendor extensions to support automatic proxies and HTTP tunneling is problematic in that the specific vendor's CORBA ORB must be used by the client. Using a vendor-specific CORBA ORB negates the advantages of using the universal Java IDL ORB, which is freely available when using a browser that supports JDK 1.2 (or by using the Java Plug-in from Sun). The main advantage of the Java IDL ORB is that it is preinstalled on client machines. The vendor-specific ORB requires download and installation by the client.

Building a custom solution to the proxy and firewall problems so that the Java IDL ORB can be used requires significant effort. As stated earlier, the proxy issue can be circumvented by manually creating a proxy object. Resolving the firewall issue, however, requires significant effort when dealing with existing firewall products that allow transmission of HTTP only.

Migrating from the Desktop to the Internet

One constant in the software universe is that software requirements will change. Nowhere is this more evident than in the current trend to rapidly migrate traditional desktop applications to the Internet. When considering the Internet, one cannot help but notice that a lot of changes have occurred in a very short period of time. The pace of change has left many wondering what tomorrow's standards will be and what steps should be taken today to maintain competitive advantage. Will Microsoft Windows continue to dominate as a client platform or will the allure of the Internet result in an alternate platform that better meets end-user needs? Will COM, CORBA, or some other technology dominate the distributed object arena?

COM, CORBA, Windows, Java, and so on, are all likely to remain important for the foreseeable future. There will almost certainly be cases where each technology is best suited for a particular purpose. In the face of rapid change, the only recourse for software strategists is to ensure that their architectures are flexible enough to adapt to change.

In this section, we will examine a simple set of servers and clients that demonstrate how COM and CORBA can be used together in a multitude of situations. The examples are intended to show how the same COM and CORBA servers can be used from a traditional Visual Basic desktop client, an Active Server Pages application, and a CORBA/Java applet. The main goal of the examples is to demonstrate that various combinations of clients and servers that use COM and CORBA can coexist. A design that supports such coexistence is resilient in the face of change and can leverage the inherent strengths of each technology wherever it is deemed most appropriate.

Implementing the COM and CORBA Customer Servers

In Chapter 9, we explored an ASP application and a CORBA/Java applet that utilized COM and CORBA customer servers. In this section, we'll revisit the customer servers and redesign them so that they can be used in a heterogeneous environment that supports both COM and CORBA. We'll also improve on the original designs of those servers based on the design issues that were identified earlier in this chapter. The server implementations include the following improvements:

- *Improvement of COM customer interface.* The `ICustomer` interface uses a `struct` rather than a `VARIANT` to convey customer information.

- *Creation of COM customer wrapper.* Using a `struct` in the `ICustomer` interface results in a custom interface that cannot be used from automation clients. The `CustomerWrapper` COM object simplifies usage of `ICustomer` and allows access to `ICustomer` from automation clients.

- *Creation of proxy objects.* For security reasons, a proxy is needed by IIS to access the remote COM customer server. A proxy is also needed by the CORBA/Java applet so that it can access the remote CORBA customer server.

The same COM customer server and CORBA customer server will be used by all three of the example clients in Implementing the COM and CORBA Customer Clients on page 303.

The COM Customer Server and Proxy

The first step in creating the COM customer server is to define the `ICustomer` interface. The `ICustomer` interface is presented in Listing 10-1 and has the following characteristics:

- *CustomerInfo struct.* A `struct` is used to convey all customer information when calling methods on the `ICustomer` interface.

- *Init( ) method.* The `ICustomer` interface supports an `Init()` method that accepts connection information to be used when a COM object instance that implements `ICustomer` is initialized.

Listing 10-1. COM ICustomer Interface

```
// customer.idl

import "oaidl.idl";
import "ocidl.idl";

    typedef struct CustomerInfo
    {
        long id;
        BSTR name;
        BSTR address;
        BSTR phone;
        BSTR fax;
        BSTR email;
        BSTR desc;
    } CustomerInfo_t;

    [
        uuid(B25E6290-5C93-11d2-B2E0-00207812E629),
        helpstring("Ch10 ICustomer Interface"),
        pointer_default(unique)
    ]
    interface ICustomer : IUnknown
    {
        HRESULT Init([in] BSTR connectionInfo,
                    [out,retval] VARIANT* ctx);

        HRESULT GetAll([in] VARIANT ctx,
                    [out] VARIANT* idArray,
                    [out] VARIANT* nameArray);

        HRESULT Create([in,out] VARIANT* ctx,
                    [in] CustomerInfo_t* info,
                    [out,retval] long* id);

        HRESULT Lookup([in,out] VARIANT* ctx,
                    [in] long id,
                    [out,retval] CustomerInfo_t* info);

        HRESULT GetInfo([in] VARIANT ctx,
                    [out,retval] CustomerInfo_t* info);

        HRESULT SetInfo([in] VARIANT ctx,
                    [in] CustomerInfo_t* info);
    };
```

- *Variant context.* A `VARIANT` is used to represent the context that gets passed as a parameter when an `ICustomer` method is invoked.

One thing that is conspicuously absent from the `customer.idl` description shown in Listing 10-1 is a `library` section. The reason is that we are not defining a specific COM class but are instead defining an interface to be implemented by multiple COM servers. The `ICustomer` interface is implemented by the `CustomerServer` and `CustomerProxy` COM servers. As we shall see, support for a single interface (`ICustomer`) allows the `CustomerServer` and `CustomerProxy` COM objects to be used interchangeably by clients.

The IDL definitions for `CustomerServer` and `CustomerProxy` are shown in Listing 10-2. Both `CustomerServer.idl` and `CustomerProxy.idl` import the `ICustomer` interface defined in `customer.idl`. The `CustomerServer` and `CustomerProxy` COM classes both declare `ICustomer` as their default interface (as shown in Listing 10-2).

The `connectionInfo` that gets passed to the `Init()` method of `ICustomer` is used in different ways by the `CustomerServer` and `CustomerProxy` COM servers. The `connectionInfo` is actually not used at all by `CustomerServer`; however, in the case of `CustomerProxy`, `connectionInfo` specifies the host name of the `CustomerServer` with which the `CustomerProxy` instance communicates. The `CustomerProxy` implementation of `Init()` creates an instance of `CustomerServer` on the specified host. The `CustomerProxy` instance then uses the `CustomerServer` instance created in `Init()` when acting as a proxy for a client. The different uses of `connectionInfo` with `CustomerServer` and `CustomerProxy` are illustrated in Figure 10-5.

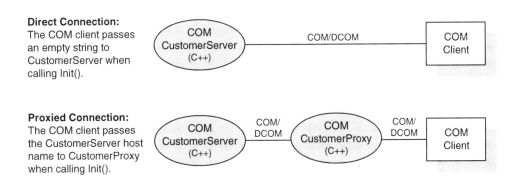

Figure 10-5. *The COM customer server and proxy.*

Listing 10-2. *COM IDL Description of CustomerServer and CustomerProxy*

```
// CustomerServer.idl
import "oaidl.idl";
import "ocidl.idl";
import "customer.idl";   // defines Ch10 ICustomer interface
[
    uuid(C7D01100-5BCB-11D2-B2DF-00207812E629), version(1.0),
    helpstring("Ch10 CustomerServer Type Library")
]
library CUSTOMERSERVERLib
{
    importlib("stdole32.tlb");
    importlib("stdole2.tlb");
    [
        uuid(C7D0110E-5BCB-11D2-B2DF-00207812E629),
        helpstring("Ch10 CustomerServer Class")
    ]
    coclass CustomerServer
    {
        [default] interface ICustomer;
    };
};
```

```
// CustomerProxy.idl
import "oaidl.idl";
import "ocidl.idl";
import "customer.idl";   // defines Ch10 ICustomer interface
[
    uuid(9B12A880-5C67-11D2-B2E0-00207812E629), version(1.0),
    helpstring("Ch10 CustomerProxy Type Library")
]
library CUSTOMERPROXYLib
{
    importlib("stdole32.tlb");
    importlib("stdole2.tlb");
    [
        uuid(9B12A88E-5C67-11D2-B2E0-00207812E629),
        helpstring("Ch10 CustomerProxy Class")
    ]
    coclass CustomerProxy
    {
        [default] interface ICustomer;
    };
};
```

The other interesting characteristic present in the `ICustomer` interface is the context variable that gets passed as a parameter to each `ICustomer` method. Recall (from COM Object Management Under Microsoft's MTS on page 194) that context data must be passed to each method in order to restore the state of the object after activation. Since we wish to host the `CustomerServer` and `CustomerProxy` objects under MTS as stateless objects, we maintain context data on the client side that gets passed to the server on each method invocation.

`ICustomer` relies on a `VARIANT` rather than on a specific data type (such as an integer) to hold context data. The use of a `VARIANT` allows various server types that implement the `ICustomer` interface to store different types of context data. In the example presented in this chapter, the customer id is always maintained in the context data. Different servers that implement the `ICustomer` interface may need to store other types of context data in addition to the customer id. For example, the `CustomerProxy` object may need to store the host name of the remote `CustomerServer` object as part of the context.[*]

In situations where the context can have different meanings when using different servers, the context should always be treated as an opaque type by clients. Clients should not use or manipulate the data stored internally in the context. The context is manipulated only by the `ICustomer` methods as described here:

- `Init()`—Creates the initial context to be used by the client.

- `GetAll()`—Uses the context created by `Init()`.

- `Create()`—Uses the context created by `Init()` and updates the context to reflect the newly created customer. The id of the newly created customer is stored in the context.

- `Lookup()`—Uses the context created by `Init()` and updates the context to reflect the customer retrieved by the lookup. The id of the retrieved customer is stored in the context.

- `GetInfo()`—Uses the context generated as a result of a `Create()` or `Lookup()`.

- `SetInfo()`—Uses the context generated as a result of a `Create()` or `Lookup()`.

---

[*]Although the actual implementation of `CustomerProxy` used in this chapter does not store anything in the context besides the customer id, the use of a `VARIANT` does make it possible.

The ICustomer interface is a COM custom interface and therefore necessitates the creation of a proxy–stub DLL (see Table 8-3 on page 237 for more information). The proxy–stub DLL must be installed on both the client and server machines where ICustomer is used. Keep in mind that proxy–stub DLLs are used to marshal interfaces and are therefore associated with interfaces rather than with specific server implementations. Since CustomerServer and CustomerProxy both implement ICustomer, only one proxy–stub DLL needs to be installed for both servers.

The COM Customer Wrapper

The ICustomer interface focuses on remoting requirements rather than on client needs. Because of its orientation toward remoting, ICustomer suffers from the following deficiencies when we attempt to use it from client applications:

- *Automation deficiency.* The ICustomer interface is a custom interface that cannot be used by COM automation clients. This prevents usage of ICustomer in environments such as Active Server Pages that support automation only.

- *Coarse-grained data access.* Clients that use ICustomer must manage a struct of data when setting and retrieving customer data. Such an approach is appropriate from a remoting standpoint but is awkward to use from client applications.

- *Context management.* Clients are forced to manage context data in addition to an ICustomer interface pointer when working with customers. Clients should need only a single object handle to manage a customer instance.

The best approach for correcting these deficiencies is to write a simple in-process COM component that wraps access to ICustomer with an interface that is more conducive for client use. The CustomerWrapper component defined in Listing 10-3 provides a wrapper for ICustomer that resolves all of the preceding deficiencies.

The CustomerWrapper component defined in Listing 10-3 is implemented using Visual Basic. This is done strictly as a matter of convenience. Note that using Visual Basic is possible only because all constructs used by the ICustomer interface map to Visual Basic. When the interface being wrapped is too complex for languages such as Visual Basic, the wrapper must be written in C++.

Listing 10-3. *COM IDL Description of CustomerWrapper*

```
[
  uuid(D5460249-5D84-11D2-B2E0-00207812E629)
]
library Ch10
{
    importlib("Stdole2.tlb");
    interface _CustomerWrapper;


    [
      dual,
      uuid(D5460259-5D84-11D2-B2E0-00207812E629)
    ]
    interface _CustomerWrapper : IDispatch
    {
        [id(1)] HRESULT Init([in] BSTR progID,
                             [in] BSTR serverName,
                             [in] BSTR connectionInfo);
        [id(2)] HRESULT GetAll([in, out] VARIANT* ids,
                               [in, out] VARIANT* names);
        [id(3)] HRESULT CreateNewInstance();
        [id(4)] HRESULT LookupExistingInstance([in] long id);
        [id(5)] HRESULT RefreshInstance();
        [id(6)] HRESULT UpdateInstance();

        [id(7), propget] HRESULT id([out, retval] long* );
        [id(7), propput] HRESULT id([in] long );

        [id(8), propget] HRESULT name([out, retval] BSTR*);
        [id(8), propput] HRESULT name([in] BSTR );

        [id(9), propget] HRESULT address([out, retval] BSTR*);
        [id(9), propput] HRESULT address([in] BSTR );

        ... properties for phone, fax, email, and desc
    };


    [
      uuid(D546024B-5D84-11D2-B2E0-00207812E629),
      version(1.0)
    ]
    coclass CustomerWrapper
    {
        [default] interface _CustomerWrapper;
    };
};
```

The `CustomerWrapper` component implements the `_CustomerWrapper` inter-face and corrects the `ICustomer` client deficiencies as follows:

- *Automation capability.* The `CustomerWrapper` component supports a dual interface that can be used from all COM client environments.

- *Fine-grained data access.* The `_CustomerWrapper` interface supports fine-grained access to all customer data. The `CustomerWrapper` caches customer data so that access to individual elements such as name, address, and so on, can be done in a performant manner.

- *Context management.* The `CustomerWrapper` component manages the context data internally. Clients do not have to manage context data. The wrapper automatically passes the context data instance as required when utilizing the wrapped `ICustomer` interface pointer.

`CustomerWrapper` wraps the `ICustomer` interface rather than a specific imple-mentation of `ICustomer`. `CustomerWrapper` can therefore be used to wrap any COM component that implements the `ICustomer` interface. For our example, `CustomerWrapper` is used to wrap `CustomerServer` and `CustomerProxy`.[*] This is made possible by defining an `Init()` method for `CustomerWrapper` that works with multiple `ICustomer` COM servers. The arguments used by the `CustomerWrapper` `Init()` method are

- `progID`—Identifies the `ICustomer` server to be instantiated by the wrapper (e.g., `Ch10.CustomerServer`, `Ch10.CustomerProxy`, etc.).

- `serverName`—Identifies the machine where the `ICustomer` server to be wrapped is located.

- `connectionInfo`—Is passed to the `ICustomer` server when its `Init()` method is called by the wrapper.

The implementation of the `CustomerWrapper` `Init()` method is shown in Listing 10-4.

In Listing 10-4, the `Init()` method uses the Visual Basic `CreateObject()` method to create the appropriate `ICustomer` server (corresponding to `progID`) on the designated host machine (corresponding to `serverName`). If the `ICustomer` instance is successfully created, the `ICustomer` interface pointer's `Init()` method is invoked with the connection information. Note that the `CustomerWrapper` instance maintains handles on the `ICustomer` inter-face pointer returned by `CreateObject()` as well as the context instance returned by the call to `ICustomer::Init()`. These handles are required by

---

[*]`CustomerWrapper` will also be used to wrap the `CustomerBridge` component later in this chapter.

Listing 10-4. *Excerpt from CustomerWrapper Implementation*

```
'Excerpt from CustomerWrapper.cls

Private mCustomer As ICustomer
Private mCtx As Variant
Private mCustomerInfo As CustomerInfo

Public Sub Init(ByVal progId As String, _
                ByVal serverName As String, _
                ByVal connectionInfo As String)
On Error GoTo ErrorHandler
    Set mCustomer = CreateObject(progId, serverName)
    mCtx = mCustomer.Init(connectionInfo)
Exit Sub
ErrorHandler:
    'handle error
End Sub

Public Sub LookupExistingInstance(ByVal id As Long)
On Error GoTo ErrorHandler
    mCustomerInfo = mCustomer.Lookup(mCtx, id)
Exit Sub
ErrorHandler:
    'handle error
End Sub

Public Property Get name() As String
    name = mCustomerInfo.name
End Property
```

the other methods of the wrapper when they are invoked. This is demonstrated by the `LookupExistingInstance()` method, which uses the `mCtx` variable, when calling `Lookup()` on the `mCustomer` interface pointer.

The CORBA Customer Server and Proxy

The first step in creating the CORBA customer server is to define the `Customer` interface. The CORBA `Customer` and `CustomerManager` interfaces are presented in Listing 10-5. The `Customer` and `CustomerManager` interfaces are identical to the ones presented in Chapter 9 (Listing 9-4 on page 269) with the following exceptions:

- *Module name.* The module is named `Ch10` rather than `Ch9`.

Listing 10-5. *CORBA Customer and CustomerManager Interfaces*

```
// Ch10.idl    CORBA IDL description of Customer interface.

module Ch10
{
    typedef sequence<long>   LongSeq;
    typedef sequence<string> StringSeq;

    exception CustomerExc
    {
        string reason;
    };

    struct CustomerInfo
    {
        long   id;
        string name;
        string address;
        string phone;
        string fax;
        string email;
        string desc;
    };

    interface Customer
    {
        void init(in string connectionInfo) raises(CustomerExc);

        void getAll(out LongSeq ids,
                    out StringSeq names) raises(CustomerExc);

        long create(in CustomerInfo info) raises(CustomerExc);

        CustomerInfo lookup(in long id) raises(CustomerExc);

        CustomerInfo getInfo() raises(CustomerExc);

        void setInfo(in CustomerInfo info) raises(CustomerExc);
    };

    interface CustomerManager
    {
        Customer createCustomer();
    };
};
```

- *Init( ) method.* The `Customer` interface supports an `init()` method that accepts connection information to be used when a CORBA `Customer` instance is initialized.

The `Customer` and `CustomerManager` interfaces presented in Listing 10-5 are used when implementing both the `CustomerServer` and `CustomerProxy` CORBA servers. The `connectionInfo` that gets passed to the `init()` method of the `Customer` interface is used in different ways by the `CustomerServer` and `CustomerProxy` CORBA servers. The `connectionInfo` is actually not used at all by `CustomerServer`; however, in the case of `CustomerProxy`, `connectionInfo` specifies the IOR (interoperable object reference) of the `CustomerServer` with which the `CustomerProxy` instance communicates. The `CustomerProxy` implementation of `init()` creates an instance of `CustomerServer` using the specified IOR. The `CustomerProxy` instance then uses the `CustomerServer` instance created in `init()` when acting as a proxy for a client. The different uses of `connectionInfo` with the `CustomerServer` and `CustomerProxy` CORBA servers are illustrated in Figure 10-6.

One cannot help but notice that major changes were made to the COM customer server presented in Chapter 9 when creating the COM customer server for this chapter. In contrast, the CORBA server changed very little. This is mostly due to the original COM server's inability to meet both remoting and client requirements, whereas the original CORBA customer server focused only on remoting requirements. The problems with the COM customer server of Chapter 9 were resolved in this chapter by modifying the `ICustomer` interface to better meet remoting requirements and by creating a COM `CustomerWrapper` component to meet client needs.

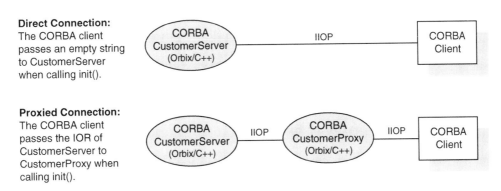

Direct Connection:
The CORBA client passes an empty string to CustomerServer when calling init().

Proxied Connection:
The CORBA client passes the IOR of CustomerServer to CustomerProxy when calling init().

Figure 10-6. *The CORBA customer server and proxy.*

Although we are not creating a CORBA customer wrapper, there is little doubt that such a wrapper can be very useful. The CORBA `Customer` interface is not very client-friendly in that it forces clients to manipulate customer data by using a `struct`. A wrapper can be used to eliminate the use of the `struct` by clients. In addition, a wrapper can handle complex tasks such as automatic recovery when connections between clients and servers fail. The major problem with creating such a wrapper is that such an approach requires a separate wrapper to be written for each programming language since CORBA lacks support for cross-language in-process components.

The ability of COM to provide cross-language in-process components is one of its greatest strengths. It is also true, however, that COM's advantage in the area of cross-language in-process components is limited to the Windows platform, where Microsoft has the greatest degree of control over the runtime environment. Although COM is beginning to appear on non-Windows platforms, COM is not adequately supported on those platforms in any language other than C++.

Implementing the COM/CORBA Customer Bridge

A fundamental goal of this chapter is to demonstrate that COM and CORBA can be used together in the same runtime environment. Up to this point in the book, we have described a multitude of COM and CORBA clients and servers; however, we have not described how COM clients work with CORBA servers or how CORBA clients work with COM servers. In this section, we will describe components that bridge COM clients with the CORBA customer server and CORBA clients with the COM customer server.

The most straightforward approach for bridging COM and CORBA is to write specialized components that use both COM and CORBA internally to map one model to the other. With such an approach, a development platform must be chosen that adequately supports both models. C++ is an obvious choice since it is fully supported by both COM and CORBA. For CORBA support, we rely on Iona's Orbix to meet the CORBA requirements of the bridging components.

The COM-to-CORBA Customer Bridge

The first half of the bridging solution necessitates the implementation of a COM `CustomerBridge` component that allows COM clients to use the CORBA `CustomerServer` component. The COM `CustomerBridge` component is

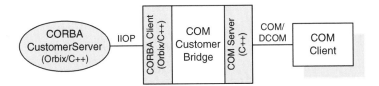

Figure 10-7. *The COM customer bridge.*

both a CORBA client and a COM server. A conceptual view of the COM `CustomerBridge` component is shown in Figure 10-7.

The COM `CustomerBridge` component uses Iona's Orbix to communicate with the CORBA `CustomerServer` component. In this regard, the COM `CustomerBridge` component is a typical CORBA client. Although Orbix was chosen for both the COM `CustomerBridge` and CORBA `CustomerServer` components, a mix of IIOP-compliant CORBA products could have been used instead. The only criterion is that both components communicate with each other using IIOP.

In addition to being a CORBA client, the COM `CustomerBridge` component is also a COM server. As was the case with the COM `CustomerServer` and COM `CustomerProxy` components, the COM `CustomerBridge` component implements the `ICustomer` interface defined in Listing 10-1. The IDL definition of the COM `CustomerBridge` component is shown in Listing 10-6.

Support for the `ICustomer` interface by the COM `CustomerBridge` component allows it to be used interchangeably with the COM `CustomerServer` and COM `CustomerProxy` components. COM clients that use the COM `CustomerWrapper` component simply need to use the appropriate `progID` and connection information when initializing the component. All other invocations of the `ICustomer` methods are done in the same way for each server type. The end result is that COM clients use the CORBA `CustomerServer` component through the COM `CustomerBridge` component in the same way that they would use the COM `CustomerServer` component. (This will be demonstrated in The Visual Basic Customer Client on page 304.)

The CORBA-to-COM Customer Bridge

The other half of the bridging solution necessitates the implementation of a CORBA `CustomerBridge` component that allows CORBA clients to use the COM `CustomerServer` component. The CORBA `CustomerBridge` component

Listing 10-6. IDL Description of COM CustomerBridge

```
// CustomerBridge.idl
import "oaidl.idl";
import "ocidl.idl";
import "customer.idl";    // defines Ch10 ICustomer interface
[
    uuid(C17A3EE0-5CC4-11D2-B2E0-00207812E629), version(1.0),
    helpstring("Ch10 CustomerBridge Type Library")
]
library CUSTOMERBRIDGELib
{
    importlib("stdole32.tlb");
    importlib("stdole2.tlb");
    [
        uuid(C17A3EEE-5CC4-11D2-B2E0-00207812E629),
        helpstring("Ch10 CustomerBridge Class")
    ]
    coclass CustomerBridge
    {
        [default] interface ICustomer;
    };
};
```

is both a COM client and a CORBA server. A conceptual view of the CORBA `CustomerBridge` component is shown in Figure 10-8.

The CORBA `CustomerBridge` uses COM to communicate with the COM `CustomerServer` component. In this regard, the CORBA `CustomerBridge` component is a typical COM client.

In addition to being a COM client, the CORBA `CustomerBridge` component uses Iona's Orbix to implement a CORBA server. As was the case with the CORBA `CustomerServer` and CORBA `CustomerProxy` components, the CORBA `CustomerBridge` component implements the `Customer` and `CustomerManager` interfaces defined in Listing 10-5.

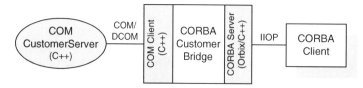

Figure 10-8. The CORBA customer bridge.

Support for the `Customer` interface by the CORBA `CustomerBridge` component allows it to be used interchangeably with the CORBA `CustomerServer` and CORBA `CustomerProxy` components. The end result is that CORBA clients use the COM `CustomerServer` component through the CORBA `CustomerBridge` component in the same way that they would use the CORBA `CustomerServer` or CORBA `CustomerProxy` components. (This is demonstrated in The CORBA/Java Customer Client on page 310.)

Implementing the COM and CORBA Customer Clients

The customer servers, proxies, and bridges that we have created up to this point will be used by the desktop and Internet clients. To illustrate the power and flexibility of the components implemented so far, three client applications will be implemented that use those components to access customer data that is managed by both the COM and CORBA customer servers. The three client approaches that will be used are

1. Visual Basic desktop client

2. Active Server Pages (ASP) application

3. CORBA/Java applet

Table 10-1. *Mapping of Client Applications to Target Users*

Client Type	Target Users	Rationale
Visual Basic desktop client	Intranet power users	Users working within an Intranet expect the utmost in performance and presentation. Visual Basic is able to take maximal advantage of the Windows platform in terms of both performance and presentation.
Active Server Pages (ASP) application	Internet casual users	Active Server Pages applications usually generate Web pages that use highly portable HTML and CGI. An Active Server Pages application is most appropriate for casual users rather than for power users due to the limitations of the HTML/CGI approach.
CORBA/Java applet	Intranet/ Extranet power users	A CORBA/Java applet is a first-class application that runs on the client machine. The downside is that complex Java applets incur significant performance penalties in both download speed and execution time. Some of these performance limitations can be overcome by faster hardware and faster network connections as are generally used by Intranet/Extranet power users.

The three client applications that are presented in this section reflect three distinct user groups that might need to be targeted by an enterprise application being deployed on the Internet. A mapping of the three client approaches to their specific user groups is described in Table 10-1.

Regardless of the user type being targeted in a specific situation, the three client approaches presented in this section demonstrate the use of COM and CORBA from a diverse set of COM and CORBA client environments.

The Visual Basic Customer Client

The Visual Basic customer client application is shown in Figure 10-9. The most interesting aspect of the Visual Basic client is that it supports connections to both the COM customer server and the CORBA customer server. Note that CORBA is not directly supported in the Visual Basic development environment. The client application therefore relies on the COM `CustomerBridge`

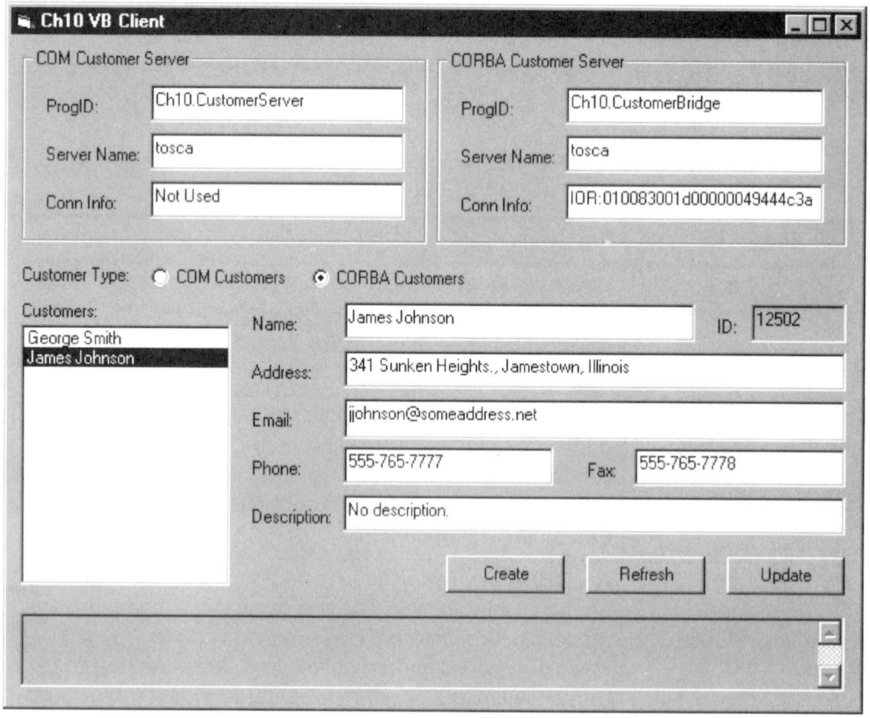

Figure 10-9. The Visual Basic customer client.

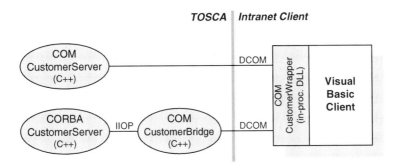

Figure 10-10. *Using COM and CORBA from the Visual Basic client.*

component when communicating with the CORBA `CustomerServer` component. The components that are used by the Visual Basic client application are identified in Figure 10-10.

As shown in Figure 10-10, the Visual Basic client actually relies on the COM `CustomerWrapper` component when using the other customer components. Recall that the COM `CustomerServer` component and the COM `CustomerBridge` component both implement the `ICustomer` interface. Also recall that the COM `CustomerWrapper` component is used to wrap the `ICustomer` interface. The Visual Basic client therefore needs to maintain only a single instance of the COM `CustomerWrapper` component when working with both the COM and CORBA customer servers. The Visual Basic client creates the single instance of the COM `CustomerWrapper` component when the Visual Basic application is started by using the following `Form_Load()` method:

```
Dim g_customer As CustomerWrapper

Private Sub Form_Load()
    Set g_customer = CreateObject("Ch10.CustomerWrapper")
End Sub
```

Whenever the user selects the *COM Customers* or *CORBA Customers* option button in the Visual Basic application, `g_customer` is reinitialized using the appropriate COM and CORBA server information. For example, the following code is executed when the user selects the *COM Customers* option button in the application:

```
Private Sub optCom_Click()
    'Initialize the COM wrapper.
    Call g_customer.Init(txtComProgID.Text, _
                         txtComServerName.Text, _
                         txtComConnInfo.Text)

    'Populate the customer list.
    Dim i
    Dim names As Variant

    Call g_customer.GetAll(g_currIds, names)

    For i = 0 To UBound(names)
        Call lstCustomers.AddItem(names(i))
    Next i
End Sub
```

In the implementation of `optCom_Click()`, the COM `CustomerWrapper` instance is initialized based on the *COM Customer Server* settings in the application. After the `CustomerWrapper` instance is initialized, it is used to populate the customer list.

The same strategy is used when the user selects the *CORBA Customers* option button. The following code is invoked when such an event occurs:

```
Private Sub optCorba_Click()
    'Initialize the COM wrapper.
    Call g_customer.Init(txtCorbaProgID.Text, _
                         txtCorbaServerName.Text, _
                         txtCorbaConnInfo.Text)

    'Populate the customer list.
    Dim i
    Dim ids As Variant, names As Variant
    Call g_customer.GetAll(ids, names)

    For i = 0 To UBound(names)
        Call lstCustomers.AddItem(names(i))
    Next i
End Sub
```

After the COM `CustomerWrapper` instance is initialized, the client application does not need to know whether the customer instance is implemented using COM or CORBA. The wrapper simply invokes the COM `CustomerServer` component or COM `CustomerBridge` component that corresponds with the last call to the wrapper's `Init()` method.

One other point worth mentioning is the location of the COM `CustomerBridge` component. In Figure 10-10, the COM `CustomerBridge` component is installed on the same machine as the CORBA `CustomerServer` component. Note that the bridge component could have also been installed on the same machine as the Visual Basic client application.

Determining where to install the bridge component is highly dependent on the situation. If the bridge component is installed near the CORBA server (as was done in Figure 10-10), the CORBA ORB does not need to be installed on the client machine. Note that, in Figure 10-10, all communication between the client machine and the server machine uses COM (and not IIOP). The other option is to install the bridge component on the client machine. Installing the bridge component on the client machine does have its advantages. If the server machine does not support COM and supports only CORBA (as might be the case with a UNIX server), the bridge component must be installed on the client. IIOP can then be used to communicate between the client machine and server machine.

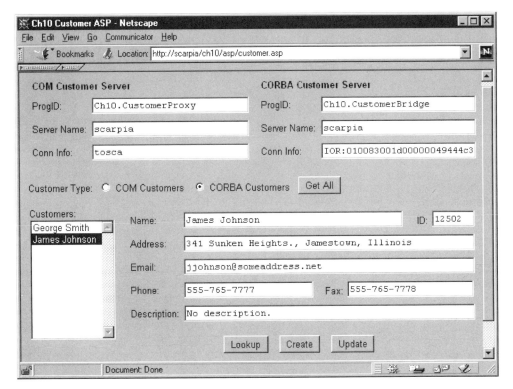

Figure 10-11. *The Active Server Pages customer client.*

The Active Server Pages Customer Client

The Active Server Pages (ASP) customer client application is shown in Figure 10-11. The ASP application presented in this chapter extends the ASP application presented in Using COM with Active Server Pages on page 261. The extensions allow the use of both the COM customer server and the CORBA customer server. Note that CORBA is not directly supported in the ASP VBScript environment. The ASP client application therefore relies on the COM CustomerBridge component when communicating with the CORBA CustomerServer component. The components that are used by the ASP client application are identified in Figure 10-12.

As shown in Figure 10-12, IIS actually relies on the COM CustomerWrapper component when using the other customer components. For security reasons, IIS uses the COM CustomerProxy component to communicate with the remote COM CustomerServer component.

Recall that the COM CustomerProxy component and the COM CustomerBridge component both implement the ICustomer interface. Also recall that the COM CustomerWrapper component is used to wrap the ICustomer interface. The ASP application therefore needs to use only the COM CustomerWrapper component when working with both the COM and CORBA customer servers.

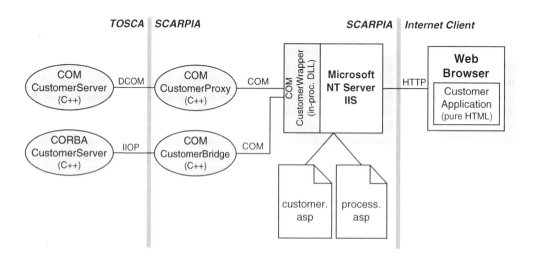

Figure 10-12. Using COM and CORBA from the ASP client.

To keep things simple, the ASP customer application creates an instance of the COM `CustomerWrapper` component every time a request is made by the client. The wrapper instance is released after processing of the page has completed. The following excerpt from the `process.asp` file demonstrates how the wrapper instance is created and initialized in the ASP customer application:

```
<%
    Function getCustomerWrapper(outCust)
        On Error Resume Next
        getCustomerWrapper = False

        'Create the wrapper instance
        Set outCust = Server.CreateObject("Ch10.CustomerWrapper")
        If Err.number <> 0 Then
            'handle error
        End If

        'Initialize the wrapper to use COM or CORBA
        If Request.Form("customerType") = "com" Then
            Call outCust.Init(Request.Form("comProgID"), _
                            Request.Form("comServerName"), _
                            Request.Form("comConnInfo"))
        Else
            Call outCust.Init(Request.Form("corbaProgID"), _
                            Request.Form("corbaServerName"), _
                            Request.Form("corbaConnInfo"))
        End If

        If Err.number <> 0 Then
            'handle error
        End If

        getCustomerWrapper = True
    End Function
%>
```

The `getCustomerWrapper()` function first creates an instance of the wrapper. It then examines the CGI variables that were sent as part of the request from the user's Web browser. The ASP `Request.Form()` function is used to examine the CGI variables. If the user selects the *COM Customers* option button in the Web browser, the wrapper is initialized to use the appropriate COM customer component; otherwise, the COM `CustomerBridge` component is used to communicate with the CORBA `CustomerServer` component.

After the COM `CustomerWrapper` instance is initialized, the rest of the processing that occurs does not need to know whether the customer instance is implemented using COM or CORBA. The wrapper simply invokes the COM

`CustomerProxy` component or COM `CustomerBridge` component that corresponds with the last call to the wrapper instance's `Init()` method.

The CORBA/Java Customer Client

The CORBA/Java customer client applet is shown in Figure 10-13. The applet presented in this chapter extends the applet presented in Using CORBA in a Java Applet on page 267. The extensions allow the use of both the COM customer server and the CORBA customer server. Note that COM support is not guaranteed in the client applet's environment (as would be the case when using any browser besides Internet Explorer). The CORBA/Java applet therefore relies on the CORBA `CustomerBridge` component when communicating

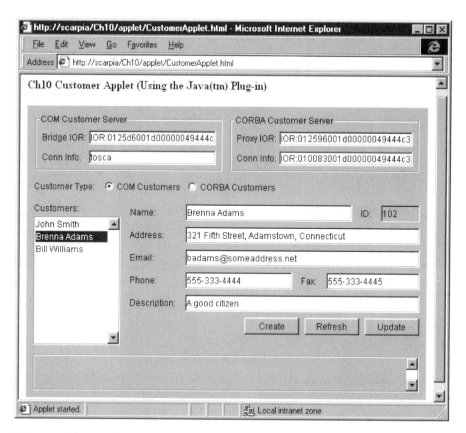

Figure 10-13. *The CORBA/Java customer client.*

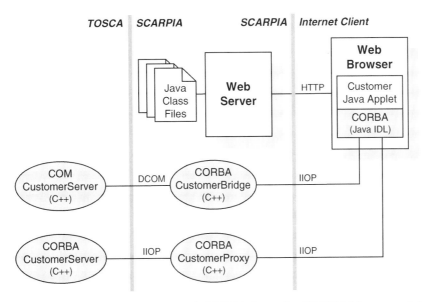

Figure 10-14. *Using COM and CORBA from the CORBA/Java applet.*

with the COM `CustomerServer` component. The components that are used by the CORBA/Java applet are identified in Figure 10-14.

As shown in Figure 10-14, the CORBA/Java applet does not use a wrapper component as did the Visual Basic and ASP client applications. The applet instead uses the customer components directly. For security reasons, the CORBA/Java applet uses the CORBA `CustomerProxy` component to communicate with the remote CORBA `CustomerServer` component.

Recall that the CORBA `CustomerBridge` component and the CORBA `CustomerProxy` component both implement the `Customer` interface. The applet uses a single `Customer` object reference to manipulate both COM customers and CORBA customers. The `Customer` object reference is declared as an instance variable of the applet's main panel as shown here:

```
import Ch10.*;

class CustomerPanel extends JPanel
{
    Ch10.Customer m_customer = null;
    . . .
```

Whenever the user selects the *COM Customers* or *CORBA Customers* option button in the applet, `m_customer` is reinitialized using the appropriate COM and CORBA server information. For example, the following code is executed when the user selects the *COM Customers* option button in the applet:

```
void loadComCustomers()
{
    try
    {
        // Get the Customer Manager instance.
        org.omg.CORBA.Object obj;
        obj = m_orb.string_to_object(txtComBridgeIOR.getText());
        CustomerManager cm = CustomerManagerHelper.narrow(obj);

        // Create the customer.
        m_customer = cm.createCustomer();

        // Initialize the customer.
        m_customer.init(txtComServerName.getText());

        // Get names and ids of all customers.
        StringSeqHolder names = new StringSeqHolder();
        m_customer.getAll(m_ids, names);

        // Initialize the list.
        lstCustomers.setListData(names.value);
    }
    catch (Throwable t)
    {
        // handle error
    }
}
```

In the implementation of `loadComCustomers()`, the `Customer` object reference is initialized based on the *COM Customer Server* settings in the applet. After `m_customer` is initialized, it is used to populate the customer list in the applet.

The same strategy is used when the user selects the *CORBA Customers* option button. The following code is invoked when such an event occurs:

```
void loadCorbaCustomers()
{
    try
    {
        // Get the Customer Manager instance.
        org.omg.CORBA.Object obj;
```

```
            obj = m_orb.string_to_object(txtCorbaProxyIOR.getText());
            CustomerManager cm = CustomerManagerHelper.narrow(obj);

            // Create the customer.
            m_customer = cm.createCustomer();

            // Initialize the customer.
            m_customer.init(txtCorbaConnInfo.getText());

            // Get names and ids of all customers.
            StringSeqHolder names = new StringSeqHolder();
            m_customer.getAll(m_ids, names);

            // Initialize the list.
            lstCustomers.setListData(names.value);
        }

        catch (Throwable t)
        {
            // handle error
        }
    }
```

After `m_customer` is initialized, the rest of the applet uses `m_customer` as a generic `Customer` object reference and does not need to know whether the customer instance is implemented using COM or CORBA.

Migration Summary

In this section, we have demonstrated the use of both COM and CORBA servers from a diverse range of COM and CORBA client environments. The diverse client environments reflect the migration of desktop applications to the Internet—a common situation in today's marketplace. Support for COM and CORBA client environments was accomplished by creating server components, proxy components, and bridge components. Server components are generally used to implement the core functionality and business logic of some real-world entity (such as a customer). Proxy components are required to provide a level of indirection that helps to ensure the security of other remote components in the network; proxy components are often needed when supporting Internet clients. Bridge components allow the use of CORBA servers by COM clients and vice versa.

When using the approach demonstrated in this section, the amount of effort that is required to support both COM and CORBA by creating servers, proxies, and bridges can be somewhat daunting. The example that we used was actually a brute-force approach for solving a simple problem. This was done intentionally to expose the nuances of using COM and CORBA in three very different client environments. A goal of the example was to demonstrate as many combinations of COM and CORBA as possible.

Some of the effort that is required to create proxy components and bridge components can be eliminated by using commercial tools. Several CORBA vendors offer products that support dynamic proxy creation when security exceptions occur. This would eliminate the need for creating CORBA proxy servers. In addition, most of the CORBA vendors now provide dynamic bidirectional bridging products that facilitate interworking between COM and CORBA.

The actual cost of implementing and maintaining proxy and bridge components ultimately depends on one's ability to stabilize component interfaces early in the development cycle. If the interfaces can be frozen, the proxy and bridge components will be inexpensive to maintain since they are merely an indirection to other server components. If the interfaces change frequently, the cost of maintaining the proxy and bridge components can become prohibitive.

Client-Side Summary

Our goal when we started Part III was to explore the primary client environments that utilize COM and CORBA. We have identified two distinct client platforms: the desktop client platform that is dominated by Microsoft Windows and the Internet platform that is usually associated with Web browser applications. The desktop platform continues to be important since it provides the greatest combination of stability, power, and performance. The Internet platform is becoming increasingly popular because of its incredible appeal as a software distribution mechanism.

In Chapter 8, we delved into the desktop client arena. Because of the pervasive presence of Microsoft Windows, we almost immediately segued into an exploration of COM client approaches. We explored the various types of COM interfaces (i.e., custom, automation, and dual interfaces). We then examined several of the key development environments for creating Windows desktop applications that use COM.

The impact of the Internet on client application development was explored in Chapter 9. Whereas COM totally dominates the Windows desktop, both COM and CORBA have a strong foothold on the Internet platform. We explored the use of COM in Active Server Pages and the use of CORBA in Java applets. We also discussed the use of push technology as an alternative to the Web browser approach.

In this chapter, we examined a number of design issues that come into play when creating COM and CORBA client applications. These issues center around the need to focus on remoting requirements rather than on client needs when designing interfaces for distributed objects. In most cases, client needs are better met by creating client-oriented wrappers for the distributed objects being used. We also examined security issues related to the use of COM in Active Server Pages and the use of CORBA in Java applets. This chapter (and Part III) culminated with a thorough examination of how COM and CORBA servers can be used in a diverse range of COM and CORBA client environments.

We concluded this chapter with a programming example that demonstrates the most straightforward approach for bridging COM and CORBA—the creation of custom bridging components. In Part IV, we will explore various approaches that support the use of both COM and CORBA in enterprise applications. In addition to custom bridging approaches, we will discuss commercial bridging products and the emergence of enterprise application servers.

Part IV

Bridging COM and CORBA

Introduction

COM and CORBA each offer distinct advantages when we are creating a distributed object solution. On the Windows platform, COM dominates on both the server and client side; Microsoft provides a powerful set of services for creating a COM-based distributed system. On both Windows and non-Windows platforms, multiple vendors offer CORBA ORBs and services that can be used to create a CORBA-based infrastructure.

To leverage the advantages of both COM and CORBA, bridging approaches must be used that allow COM and CORBA to be integrated within a distributed solution. For small systems, custom bridging components can be manually created that allow clients and servers of different object systems to communicate. For larger systems, a commercial bridging product should be used to minimize the design, implementation, and maintenance costs that would be incurred when manually creating custom components. An alternative to using a commercial bridging product is to use an enterprise application server product that supports both COM and CORBA.

Part IV focuses on integration approaches for COM and CORBA when we are creating distributed solutions that rely on both technologies.

- Chapter 11 examines the use of custom bridging components to bridge between COM and CORBA. When custom bridging components are created, a development environment that supports both COM and CORBA must be used. This chapter addresses the use of C++ and Java-based environments to create custom bridging components.

- Chapter 12 examines the use of commercial bridging products to bridge between COM and CORBA. A full COM/CORBA interworking specification is contained in the OMG's CORBA 2.2 specification. This chapter examines that interworking specification as well as a number of commercial bridging products that claim some level of conformance with the specification.

- Chapter 13 discusses the recent emergence of enterprise application servers. Enterprise application servers provide a distributed object framework for creating sophisticated distributed applications. This chapter focuses on enterprise application servers that are based on COM, CORBA, and Enterprise JavaBeans.

After completing Part IV, you will better understand how to integrate COM and CORBA when you are creating distributed object solutions. Understanding the various integration approaches will allow you to leverage the various strengths of both COM and CORBA by using each technology where it is most appropriate.

Chapter 11

Custom Bridging Approaches

Topics Covered in This Chapter

- Overview of Bridging Example
- Using C++ to Bridge COM and CORBA
- Using Microsoft's JVM as a Bridge
- Other COM/CORBA Bridging Approaches

One approach for bridging COM and CORBA is to manually create components that bridge the two distributed object domains. The primary advantage of such an approach is that there is no dependency on third-party commercial bridging products. The disadvantage is the potential costs associated with design, implementation, and maintenance of custom bridging components. The trade-off between these advantages and disadvantages is dependent on the number of bridging components that must be created.

The requirement to bridge COM and CORBA most often occurs when we attempt to use COM clients with CORBA servers. COM has traditionally been associated with Windows desktop client applications, while CORBA has been used on server-side non-Windows platforms. For this reason, we will focus primarily on bridging COM clients with CORBA servers in this chapter.

When custom bridging components are created, software development environments that support both COM and CORBA must be utilized. In this chapter, we will examine three such environments. Visual C++ on the Windows platform provides excellent support for COM and is also supported by all of the major CORBA vendors. Microsoft's Java Virtual Machine (JVM) supports COM and can be used with CORBA/Java ORBs to create custom bridging components. A pure Java implementation of COM along with CORBA/Java ORBs also allows bridging components to be used with non-Microsoft JVMs.

Overview of Bridging Example

COM's legacy is tied to the rise of Microsoft Windows as the dominant desktop client platform. In contrast, CORBA has evolved primarily as a server-side distributed object infrastructure on non-Windows platforms. As Windows becomes more established as a server platform, client applications including CORBA-based clients will need to interact with COM servers. At the present time, however, CORBA clients rarely use COM servers. Given the current typical usage of COM and CORBA, the bridging example presented in this chapter focuses on the use of a COM client with a CORBA server.

A custom bridging component is typically implemented using a software development environment that supports both COM and CORBA. The bridging example in this chapter demonstrates a custom bridging component that allows a Visual Basic client to use an Orbix/C++ CORBA server. Figure 11-1 illustrates how the bridging example is implemented.

As shown in Figure 11-1, the custom bridging component acts as a CORBA client and as a COM server. This allows the Visual Basic client to use the Orbix CORBA server via the bridging component. The bridging component can use any CORBA ORB product that adequately supports IIOP. The bridging example demonstrated in this chapter uses an Orbix CORBA server. The Orbix CORBA server supports IIOP, thereby allowing access by IIOP-based clients. The CORBA IDL for the Orbix server is shown in Listing 11-1.

The CORBA server supports two interfaces. The `CorbaServerFactory` interface defines a simple factory method that is used to create `CorbaServer` instances. The `CorbaServer` interface provides methods to test the ability of clients to communicate with the Orbix server. For example, the `GetServerType()` method returns a string indicating how the CORBA server is implemented.

Figure 11-1. *Implementation of the bridging example.*

Listing 11-1. *CORBA IDL for Orbix Server*

```
// Ch11.idl

module Ch11
{
    interface CorbaServer
    {
        string GetServerType();
        string GetTestString();
        void   SetTestString(in string str);
    };

    interface CorbaServerFactory
    {
        CorbaServer createCorbaServer();
    };
};
```

A Visual Basic COM client is used to demonstrate access to the Orbix server. The Visual Basic COM client application is shown in Figure 11-2.

The most interesting aspect illustrated in Figure 11-2 is that when the user presses the *Initialize* button, three parameters are required by the client application to communicate with the CORBA server. These parameters are *ProgID*,

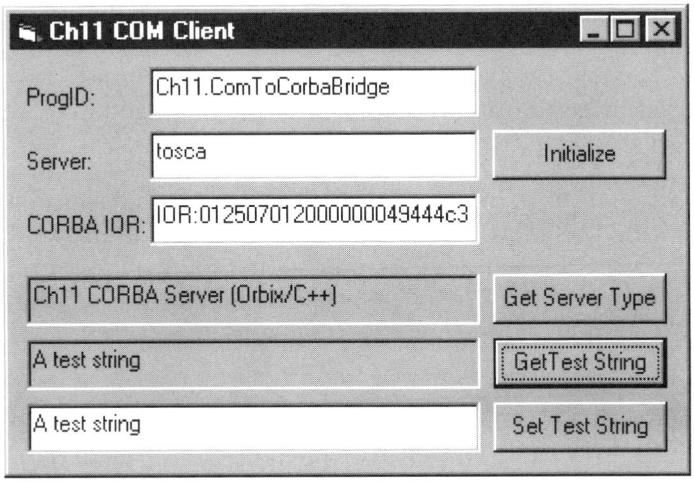

Figure 11-2. *The Visual Basic COM client.*

Server, and *CORBA IOR*. The *ProgID* and *Server* parameters are used to locate the COM server that implements the custom bridging component. The *CORBA IOR* is used by the bridging component during initialization to locate the `CorbaServerFactory` object. After initialization is complete, the Visual Basic client can use the bridging component to interact with the Orbix server. Specific technologies that can be used to implement the custom bridging component will be discussed throughout the remainder of this chapter.

Using C++ to Bridge COM and CORBA

The C++ programming language offers the most mature environment for hosting a COM/CORBA bridging component. The use of COM with C++ is supported in the Visual C++ development environment as well as in a wide variety of non-Windows platforms, including all of the major UNIX variants. COM's internal architecture is obviously rooted in C++ and is therefore fully accessible from C++ development environments. On the CORBA front, all of the major CORBA products have provided C++ support for a substantial period of time. For example, Iona's Orbix has supported C++ since 1993.

The advantages of using C++ to create a COM/CORBA custom bridging component are largely a result of the maturity that COM and CORBA have attained with regard to C++. Because of its maturity, C++ often provides the most performant and robust environment for creating COM- or CORBA-based server components.

The main disadvantage of using C++ to create custom bridging components is that C++ is difficult to use (especially in comparison to Java). One significant challenge when using C++ is correctly managing the lifetime of COM and CORBA objects. In C++, reference counting must be carefully managed to avoid resource leaks and/or dangling references.

An example of how C++ can be used to bridge COM and CORBA was described in Chapter 10 in Implementing the COM/CORBA Customer Bridge on page 300. In that section, Iona's Orbix is used with Visual C++ to create a custom bridging component that allows a Visual Basic client to interact with an Orbix/C++ server. In addition, a second bridging component was described that allows a CORBA/Java client to interact with a COM server.

In many ways, Java is superior to C++ for creating COM/CORBA bridging components. With regard to both COM and CORBA, Java alleviates many of the issues related to reference counting. As Java matures, it also appears that many of the issues related to performance and robustness will also be resolved. Java is already beginning to supplant C++ as the primary language of choice when we are creating COM and CORBA server objects. The rest of this chapter will focus on Java-based approaches for creating custom bridging components.

Using Microsoft's JVM as a Bridge

The most straightforward approach for creating a Java-based COM/CORBA bridging component is to use Microsoft's Java Virtual Machine. Microsoft's JVM has built-in support for COM and can also be used with most of the major CORBA/Java ORB products. With this approach, it is important to check with the CORBA vendor to ensure adequate support for the version of the Microsoft JVM being used.

Using a CORBA/Java ORB with Microsoft's JVM

Version 1.2 of Sun's Java Development Kit ships with Java IDL, a lightweight implementation of a CORBA 2.0 compliant ORB. In this chapter, we'll use a version of Java IDL that is compatible with the Microsoft JVM.[*] All of the CORBA-related class files are stored in a Java `.jar` file called `javaidl.jar`. To use Java IDL with Microsoft's JVM, the registry must be updated as follows:

```
REGEDIT4

[HKEY_LOCAL_MACHINE\SOFTWARE\Microsoft\Java VM]
"Classpath"="C:\\WINNT\\java\\classes\\classes.zip;
           C:\\WINNT\\java\\classes;.;
           c:\\winnt\\java\\javaidl.jar"
```

The preceding registry entry makes all of the Java IDL classes available whenever the Microsoft JVM is used. This includes use of the Microsoft JVM from inside the Visual J++ development environment. If a CORBA/Java ORB other than Java IDL is used, the appropriate `.zip` or `.jar` files associated with the CORBA/Java ORB should be added to the `Classpath` registry entry. Once a CORBA/Java ORB is usable from the Microsoft JVM, the Microsoft JVM can be used to create COM/CORBA custom bridging components.

---

[*]At the time of this writing, the version of Java IDL and the corresponding `idltojava` compiler that are used in this chapter are pre-release versions that work with JDK 1.1. This is necessary since, at the time of this writing, Microsoft had not yet upgraded its JVM to support the Java IDL classes that are included in JDK 1.2.

Figure 11-3. *Implementing the bridging component using the Microsoft JVM.*

A COM-to-CORBA Bridge

Figure 11-3 illustrates how Microsoft's JVM is used to implement the custom bridging component.

The bridging component shown in Figure 11-3 acts as both a CORBA client and as a COM server. To access the CORBA server, the `idltojava` compiler that comes with Java IDL is used to generate Java-based CORBA stubs for the `Ch11.idl` file shown in Listing 11-1. These CORBA stubs are used by the bridging component to access the Orbix server.

The bridging component implements a COM server corresponding to the following COM IDL:

```
// ComToCorbaBridge.idl
import "oaidl.idl";
import "ocidl.idl";

    [
        object,
        uuid(6222C240-9B5A-11d2-B301-00207812E629),
        dual,
        pointer_default(unique)
    ]
    interface IComToCorbaBridge : IDispatch
    {
        [id(1)] HRESULT Init([in] BSTR corbaFactoryIOR);
        [id(2)] HRESULT GetServerType([out, retval] BSTR* str);
        [id(3)] HRESULT GetTestString([out,retval] BSTR* str);
        [id(4)] HRESULT SetTestString([in] BSTR str);
    };

[
    uuid(6222C241-9B5A-11d2-B301-00207812E629),
    version(1.0),
]
```

```
library Ch11
{
    importlib("stdole32.tlb");
    importlib("stdole2.tlb");

    [
        uuid(6222C242-9B5A-11d2-B301-00207812E629),
    ]
    coclass ComToCorbaBridge
    {
        [default] interface IComToCorbaBridge;
    };
};
```

The Visual J++ development environment is used to create the bridging component. The bridging component is a COM DLL that implements the COM IDL just shown. An excerpt from the implementation class of the bridging component is shown here:

```
// Excerpt from ComToCorbaBridge.java
//     This class implements the Ch11.ComToCorbaBridge COM object.

package comtocorbabridge;


import com.ms.com.*;
import com.ms.com.IUnknown;
import com.ms.com.Variant;
import Ch11.*;                 // CORBA-generated stubs
import org.omg.CORBA.ORB;   // Java IDL CORBA class


/** @com.register(clsid=6222C242-9B5A-11D2-B301-00207812E629,
    typelib=6222C241-9B5A-11D2-B301-00207812E629, version="1.0",
    description="Ch11 ComToCorbaBridge Class")
*/
public class ComToCorbaBridge
                implements IUnknown,com.ms.com.NoAutoScripting,
                    comtocorbabridge.IComToCorbaBridgeDefault
{
    CorbaServer m_srv;  // generated CORBA stub class


    public void Init(String corbaFactoryIOR)
    {
```

```
        try
        {
            // Initialize the ORB.
            ORB orb = ORB.init(new String[0], null);

            // Get the factory instance.
            org.omg.CORBA.Object obj;
            obj = orb.string_to_object(corbaFactoryIOR);

            CorbaServerFactory factory =
                CorbaServerFactoryHelper.narrow(obj);

            // Create a CorbaServer object.
            m_srv = factory.createCorbaServer();
        }
        catch (Throwable t)
        {
            throw new com.ms.com.ComFailException("" + t);
        }
    }


    public String GetServerType()
    {
        try
        {
            return m_srv.GetServerType();
        }
        catch (Throwable t)
        {
            throw new com.ms.com.ComFailException("" + t);
        }
    }


    ...
}
```

The implementation of the bridging component maintains a handle on a
`CorbaServer` instance for each instance of the bridging component. The
`CorbaServer` instance is created when the user calls the COM object's `Init()`
method with the IOR corresponding to the Orbix `CorbaServerFactory`
instance. As is demonstrated in the `GetServerType()` method, the COM
object (i.e., bridging component) simply redirects client requests to the CORBA
object instance that it manages.

A Visual Basic Client

The Visual Basic client that is used to test the Microsoft JVM-based bridging component was shown earlier in Figure 11-2. Recall that in order to initialize the client, three parameters are required. Assume that the parameters have the following values:

- *ProgID* = "Ch11.ComToCorbaBridge"

- *Server* = "tosca"

- *CORBA IOR* = "IOR:012507012000000049444c3..."

When the user presses the *Initialize* button in the Visual Basic client application, the following Visual Basic code is invoked:

```
Dim g_obj As IComToCorbaBridge

Private Sub cmdInit_Click()
    Set g_obj = CreateObject(txtProgID.Text, txtServer.Text)
    Call g_obj.Init(txtCorbaFactoryIOR.Text)
End Sub
```

The Visual Basic client maintains a global variable, g_obj, that holds an IComToCorbaBridge interface pointer to the currently active Ch11.ComToCorbaBridge instance. The cmdInit_Click() method first creates an instance of the COM object (using the *ProgID* and *Server* name) and initializes g_obj. The IComToCorbaBridge::Init() method is then invoked to associate g_obj with a CORBA server instance (as was described in the previous subsection).

Once g_obj has been initialized, the other Visual Basic client methods simply invoke g_obj as shown here:

```
Private Sub cmdGetServerType_Click()
    txtServerType.Text = g_obj.GetServerType()
End Sub
```

The Ch11.ComToCorbaBridge component that is associated with g_obj redirects requests to the CorbaServer instance and returns the results to the Visual Basic client. Except for the CORBA IOR that is passed as a parameter during initialization, the Visual Basic COM client is not aware that CORBA is being used.

Other COM/CORBA Bridging Approaches

Up to this point, we have used Microsoft's Visual C++ and Microsoft's Java Virtual Machine (JVM) only to provide the COM support that is required to create custom bridging components. COM support along with the appropriate CORBA ORB allows for the creation of custom bridging components. There are many other techniques that can be used to create bridges between COM and CORBA. In this section, we'll briefly discuss several third-party products that facilitate COM/CORBA integration. We'll also examine directions that Microsoft may take in the future that would allow Java and COM to be used on a wider range of platforms.

Using COM in Non-Microsoft JVMs

Microsoft's Java Virtual Machine is the only JVM that provides built-in support for COM. To use COM from non-Microsoft JVMs, a third-party software package is required. The following two vendors both provide Java software packages that allow COM to be used from non-Microsoft JVMs:

1. Linar, Ltd., at `http://www.linar.com`. Linar offers a Java-based product called *Jintegra* that allows COM server objects to be used from Java applications executing in any of the major JVMs. Jintegra also allows Java classes to be used from COM clients.

2. Neva Object Technology, Inc., at `http://www.nevaobject.com`. Neva Object Technology offers a Java-based product called *Java2COM* that allows COM server objects to be used from Java applications executing in any of the major JVMs.

Either of these products can be used with a CORBA/Java ORB to create COM/CORBA bridging components. Bridging components created in this manner would not be dependent on Microsoft's JVM but would instead rely on third-party implementations of COM for Java.

Bridging ActiveX and JavaBeans

Several products support bridging between ActiveX components and JavaBeans components. Products that bridge the ActiveX and JavaBeans component models can also be used to bridge COM and CORBA. The following two products are complementary in that one can be used to bridge COM clients with

CORBA servers while the other can be used to bridge CORBA clients with COM servers:

1. Sun Microsystems, at `http://java.sun.com/beans/software/bridge`. Sun provides a product called *JavaBeans Bridge for ActiveX* that allows JavaBeans to be used as ActiveX components from COM client applications. To bridge from COM to CORBA, CORBA server functionality can be wrapped in a JavaBean, and the JavaBean can then be exposed as an ActiveX control to a COM client.

2. Gensym Corporation (`http://www.gensym.com/java`). Gensym provides a product called *BeanXporter*. This product allows ActiveX components to be used as JavaBeans from Java client applications. To bridge from CORBA to COM, COM server functionality can be wrapped in an ActiveX component and the ActiveX component can then be exposed as a JavaBean to a CORBA/Java server. The CORBA/Java server can then expose a CORBA interface to CORBA clients.

Using Environments That Support COM and CORBA

Several distributed application development environments support COM and CORBA clients as is evidenced by the following vendors:

1. NobleNet, Inc., at `http://www.noblenet.com`. NobleNet offers a distributed application development environment called *Nouveau*. Distributed applications that are implemented with Nouveau can be used from both COM and CORBA clients. This allows Nouveau applications to bridge the COM and CORBA domains.

2. ObjectSpace, Inc., at `http://www.objectspace.com`. ObjectSpace offers a distributed object product called *Voyager*. Distributed objects that are implemented under Voyager can be used from CORBA clients. ObjectSpace has also announced plans to add COM support. If Voyager does eventually support both COM and CORBA, it will be possible to use Voyager to create COM/CORBA bridging components.

In addition to the products just listed, a number of enterprise application server products are emerging that also facilitate integration with both COM and CORBA. (We will discuss enterprise application servers and their support for COM and CORBA in Chapter 13.)

Future Java/COM Support from Microsoft

Microsoft's Java Virtual Machine provides a powerful mechanism for using COM with Java. The major disadvantage of using Microsoft's JVM for creating COM/CORBA bridging components is that Microsoft's JVM is available only on the Windows platform. Custom bridging components that rely on Microsoft's JVM must therefore be hosted on the Windows platform. This could be problematic in several situations. For example, it would not be possible to deploy a Microsoft JVM-based COM-to-CORBA bridging component on the same machine as a CORBA server if the CORBA server was running on a non-Windows platform.

If Microsoft implemented at least one of the following two approaches, Java and COM could be used on a wider range of platforms:

1. Provide support for the Microsoft JVM on non-Windows platforms.

2. Provide a pure Java version of COM. This would allow COM to be used from all of the major Java Virtual Machines.

At the time of this writing, it should be noted that neither of these two approaches currently supports Microsoft's strategy to establish Windows as the dominant server platform. If Microsoft decides that support for Java and COM on non-Windows platforms is important in the future, Microsoft will probably support at least one of the approaches. Support for either approach would greatly simplify the development of COM/CORBA bridging components on non-Windows platforms.

Summary

The custom bridging approach is most appropriate when we are building small systems that require only the creation of a small number of bridging components. As we demonstrated in this chapter (and in Chapter 10), the design and the implementation of bridging components require significant effort. First, a software development environment that supports both COM and CORBA (e.g., Visual C++ or Visual J++) must be used to create the bridging components. In addition, the creation of custom bridging components requires expertise with both COM and CORBA. Such an approach is obviously inappropriate when we are creating a large system.

With large systems that require a considerable amount of COM/CORBA integration, a commercial bridging product should be used rather than attempting to implement a large number of custom bridging components. In the next chapter, we will examine the use of commercial bridging products. Commercial bridging products provide high-level tools that greatly reduce the effort required to bridge COM and CORBA.

Chapter 12

Commercial Bridging Approach

Topics Covered in This Chapter

- COM/CORBA Interworking Specification
- Vendor Support for COM/CORBA Bridging
- A Commercial Bridging Example
- Bridging COM/CORBA Services

The use of custom components to bridge COM and CORBA can become cumbersome in a large enterprise system. The design and the implementation of custom bridging components require a high level of expertise with both COM and CORBA. Many issues must be considered, including differences in the COM and CORBA object models as well as differences in the life cycles of COM and CORBA object instances. The proliferation of custom bridging components also adds to the overall deployment and maintenance costs of any large COM/CORBA software system.

Several software vendors have recognized the need to provide high-level tool support for bridging the COM and CORBA domains. Most of these vendors are CORBA ORB vendors that offer COM/CORBA bridging products that are tailored toward their specific CORBA products. The OMG's CORBA 2.2 specification contains a well-defined specification for a COM/CORBA interworking architecture. All of the major commercial bridging products claim some level of conformance with the OMG's COM/CORBA interworking specification.

One vendor that is conspicuously absent from the list of vendors that offer COM/CORBA bridging products is Microsoft. Because COM dominates on the client desktop as well as Microsoft's server-side offerings, a COM/CORBA bridging product does not appear to be important to Microsoft's overall distributed object strategy. In contrast, the CORBA vendors are forced to acknowledge COM's dominance on the Windows platform and must therefore provide strong support for COM. This is generally accomplished by providing a commercially supported COM/CORBA bridging product. In this chapter, we will explore the functionality that is typically provided by a commercial COM/CORBA bridging product.

COM/CORBA Interworking Specification

Revision 2.2 of the OMG's CORBA specification contains a comprehensive specification for a COM/CORBA interworking architecture.[*] The section of the CORBA specification that deals with COM/CORBA interworking comprises more than 140 pages. The primary chapters of the CORBA 2.2 specification that are related to COM/CORBA interworking are

- Chapter 15, Interworking Architecture

- Chapter 16, Mapping: COM and CORBA

- Chapter 17, Mapping: OLE Automation and CORBA

Note that separate chapters are required for describing distinct mappings with regard to COM custom interfaces and COM automation interfaces. A full description of the interworking architecture would require a significant amount of effort and goes well beyond the scope of this book.[†] There are, however, several key areas that merit discussion.

The interworking specification identifies a number of similarities between COM and CORBA that facilitate the creation of an interworking architecture. The most important similarity is that both COM and CORBA rely on the notion of interfaces for exposing external entry points to COM and CORBA servers. The specification also notes that, in most cases, it is possible to directly map between CORBA interfaces and COM custom interfaces (i.e., nonautomation interfaces). CORBA interfaces and COM custom interfaces both allow for user-defined data types such as structs, unions, and arrays as well as for a rich set of primitive data types.

Simply providing COM custom interfaces is inappropriate in terms of the needs of COM clients. Many types of COM clients depend on COM automation interfaces rather than on COM custom interfaces (see COM Client Approaches on

---

[*]The CORBA 2.2 specification, which includes the complete COM/CORBA interworking specification, can be obtained at http://www.omg.org.

[†]For a list of references that focus on COM/CORBA bridging, see page 375.

page 218). For this reason, the COM/CORBA interworking specification must also address the mapping between CORBA and COM automation.

Recall that support for automation is highly restrictive with regard to the supported data types. Chapter 17 of the COM/CORBA interworking specification describes how user-defined types such as CORBA structs are mapped to an automation-compliant interface. In the case of CORBA structs, the interworking specification describes how a *helper* automation object is created for each CORBA-defined struct.

In addition to issues surrounding custom and automation COM interfaces, the COM/CORBA interworking specification addresses the following critical mapping issues:

- *Mapping of COM's multiple interface model to CORBA.* Recall that a COM object can support multiple distinct COM interfaces. The interworking specification describes how COM's multiple interface model is mapped to CORBA.

- *Mapping of CORBA's multiple inheritance to COM.* CORBA allows for multiple inheritance in the interface inheritance hierarchy. COM does not. The interworking specification addresses how such differences are resolved.

- *Mapping CORBA Exceptions to COM HRESULTs and COM error objects.* CORBA supports exceptions in CORBA IDL. COM relies on the use of a 32-bit integer (i.e., HRESULT) to convey error information. COM also allows other error information such as a textual description of an error to be passed in a COM error object. The interworking specification describes the mapping between CORBA exceptions and COM HRESULTs. The interworking specification also describes the use of COM error objects.

The interworking specification introduces the concepts of views and targets. In the context of the specification, a *view* is associated with a client (i.e., COM client or CORBA client) while the *target* is associated with a server (i.e., COM server or CORBA server). Because the interworking specification addresses both COM custom interfaces as well as COM automation interfaces, mappings between the following views and targets are addressed:

- COM custom interface view of CORBA target.

- CORBA view of COM custom interface target.

- COM automation interface view of CORBA target.

- CORBA view of COM automation interface target.

The bridging mechanism used to map COM and CORBA can be either generic or interface-specific. A *generic* mapping is accomplished by performing the mapping dynamically at runtime. An *interface-specific* mapping is accomplished by creating the mapping at compile time and compiling the mapping implementation into the client application. Flexibility as well as a number of various performance implications must be considered when choosing between a generic mapping approach and an interface-specific mapping approach. While the generic mapping approach offers greater flexibility, the interface-specific mapping approach generally offers better levels of performance.

Controlling the lifetime of server objects requires careful programming when bridging COM and CORBA. Recall that COM relies on a distributed reference-counting mechanism to destroy unreferenced server instances. In contrast, CORBA decouples client reference counting from server reference counting and requires additional effort to destroy server objects that are no longer in use. The COM and CORBA views that get generated by a bridging product are actually COM and CORBA server objects whose lifetimes must also be managed.

In the case where a COM client wishes to use a CORBA server instance, an intermediate COM view of the CORBA server instance is automatically created by the bridging product. If the COM client wants to destroy the CORBA server instance, it must call `remove()` or some other implementation-specific method on the COM view. The view then calls the appropriate method on the CORBA server instance to destroy it; otherwise, the CORBA server instance continues to survive. Note that the COM view instance still remains after making such a call. When there are no longer any clients using the COM view instance, COM's distributed reference-counting mechanism automatically destroys the view instance.

In the case where a CORBA client wishes to use a COM server instance, an intermediate CORBA view of the COM server instance is automatically created by the bridging product. To delete the CORBA view of the COM server instance, the CORBA client must explicitly call `LifeCycleObject::remove()` on the CORBA view instance. Note that the interworking specification mandates that all generated CORBA views support the `LifeCycleObject` interface. Because of distributed reference counting, the COM server instance will automatically be destroyed when there are no longer any views referencing it.

The interworking specification also addresses how servers get bound to views. For example, COM clients must be able to bind specific CORBA servers to their respective COM views. The interworking specification describes specific mechanisms that allow the binding of CORBA servers to COM views as well as COM servers to CORBA views.

The OMG's COM/CORBA interworking specification establishes a foundation for commercial COM/CORBA bridging products. The interworking specification is geared primarily for implementors of bridging products rather than for end users. The most important point to note is that the specification allows for consistency (e.g., consistency of naming and typing conventions) across different vendors' bridging products. Such consistency insulates client applications against the possibility of product changes. For example, proper support for the specification would allow a new CORBA ORB and bridging product to be used in an existing enterprise application without forcing all client applications to be rewritten. This is clearly advantageous when maintaining large software systems.

Vendor Support for COM/CORBA Bridging

Several software vendors offer commercial bridging products that comply with the OMG's COM/CORBA interworking specification (or at least part of it). Most of the vendors that offer commercial bridging products are CORBA ORB vendors. The bridging products that are offered by specific CORBA ORB vendors are generally tailored to work with their particular CORBA ORB products. One notable exception to this rule is Visual Edge Software.

Visual Edge does not directly market a specific CORBA ORB but instead focuses on a wide range of middleware utilities for CORBA, COM, and Java. Visual Edge's patented bridging technology, ObjectBridge, works with all of the primary CORBA ORB products and also includes support for generic IIOP. Generic IIOP support allows ObjectBridge to be used with virtually any IIOP-compliant CORBA ORB. In addition to offering its own bridging product, Visual Edge has also licensed its bridging solution to several CORBA ORB vendors.

Vendors that have licensed Visual Edge's ObjectBridge technology include CORBA heavyweights such as BEA, Visigenic (which was later acquired by Inprise), and Expersoft. Except for minor adaptations for each particular CORBA ORB, the look and feel should therefore be the same when using the commercial bridging solutions offered by Visual Edge, BEA, Inprise, and Expersoft. (We will briefly look at how Visual Edge's product is used later in this chapter.)

While many CORBA vendors rely on Visual Edge's bridging technology to meet their COM/CORBA bridging needs, several major vendors have created their own bridging products. The most notable vendors in this category are Iona and PeerLogic. Iona offers OrbixCOMet, a full-featured bridging product. PeerLogic offers the DAIS COM2CORBA bridge, a bridging product that focuses on mapping between CORBA and COM automation.[*]

Although Microsoft does not directly offer a commercial COM/CORBA bridging product, it has shown some interest in the bridging arena by licensing COM to both Iona and Visual Edge Software. This should help Iona and Visual Edge to continue improving their support for COM within their respective bridging products.

A Commercial Bridging Example

The best way to understand the capabilities of a commercial bridging product is to use such a product in an example. The overall goal when using a commercial bridging product is to minimize the need to understand two distinct distributed object architectures. For example, a COM developer should be able to use the bridge to create a COM view of a CORBA object without having to understand CORBA. Similarly, a CORBA developer should be able to work with COM objects in a CORBA framework. In this section, we will examine a commercial COM/CORBA bridging product and demonstrate the use of an Orbix/C++ CORBA server from a Visual Basic COM client. We will also discuss how the bridging product can be used to access COM servers from CORBA clients.

Selecting a Commercial Bridging Product

There are several commercial bridging products that can be used to bridge Iona's Orbix with COM. One such product is Visual Edge's ObjectBridge COM/CORBA Enterprise Client.[†] We will hereafter refer to Visual Edge's bridging product simply as *ObjectBridge*. Our choice of bridging products is fairly arbitrary since we could have used other bridging products such as Iona's Orbix-COMet. We selected Visual Edge's product because it is fairly vendor-neutral and supports all of the primary CORBA products, including Iona Orbix.

---

[*]In August of 1998, PeerLogic obtained an exclusive source code license for ICL's DAIS product line, including the DAIS COM2CORBA product.

[†]For more information on Visual Edge's ObjectBridge COM/CORBA Enterprise Client, see http://www.visualedge.com.

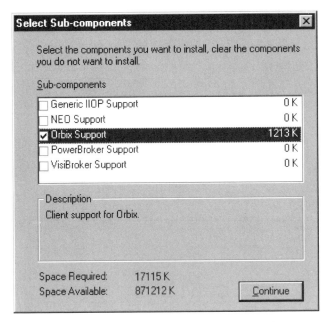

Figure 12-1. *Supporting Orbix in ObjectBridge.*

Despite its neutrality with regard to vendors, ObjectBridge does require some Orbix-specific information when the product is installed for use with Orbix. The first step is to indicate that Orbix is to be used. This is accomplished during installation as shown in Figure 12-1.

The next step is to indicate the locations of the Orbix naming service and interface repository as shown in Figure 12-2.

ObjectBridge relies on a CORBA naming service and interface repository during both development and deployment. CORBA servers must therefore be registered with the naming service. During development, the CORBA naming service and interface repository are used by ObjectBridge to determine available CORBA services and create COM/CORBA interface mappings. After deployment, ObjectBridge uses the naming service to locate existing CORBA services.

The CORBA Server

A CORBA server is needed to demonstrate the use of ObjectBridge. The IDL for the CORBA server is shown in Listing 12-1. The CORBA server is imple-

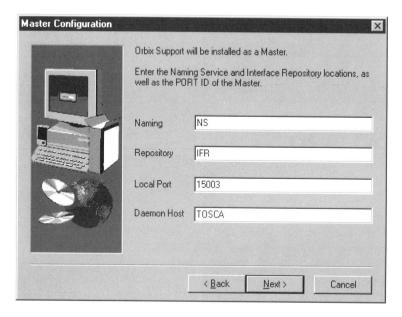

Figure 12-2. *Supporting Orbix naming service and interface repository.*

mented using Orbix/C++. To use the CORBA server with ObjectBridge, the CORBA server must be registered with the Orbix naming service and Orbix interface repository.

From a COM/CORBA mapping perspective, the CORBA IDL that is specified in Listing 12-1 has the following interesting characteristics:

- *CORBA sequences.* The CORBA IDL defines a sequence of `long`s, `LongSeq`, as well as a sequence of `string`s, `StringSeq`. These sequence types are used by the `Customer::getAll()` method to convey the ids and names of all `Customer` instances that are available in the CORBA customer server.

- *CORBA exception.* The CORBA IDL defines the `CustomerExc` exception. This exception can be thrown by any of the methods defined in the `Customer` interface.

- *CORBA struct.* The CORBA IDL defines the `CustomerInfo` struct. This struct is used as a parameter to all `Customer` methods that manipulate information related to a `Customer` instance.

- *Multiple interfaces.* The CORBA IDL defines the `Ch12` module that contains two distinct interfaces, `Customer` and `CustomerManager`. The

Listing 12-1. *IDL for CORBA Customer Server*

```
// Ch12.idl
module Ch12
{
    typedef sequence<long>   LongSeq;
    typedef sequence<string> StringSeq;

    exception CustomerExc  { string reason; };

    struct CustomerInfo
    {
        long   id;
        string name;
        string address;
        string phone;
        string fax;
        string email;
        string desc;
    };

    interface Customer
    {
        void getAll(out LongSeq ids,
                    out StringSeq names) raises(CustomerExc);
        long create(in CustomerInfo info) raises(CustomerExc);
        CustomerInfo lookup(in long id) raises(CustomerExc);
        CustomerInfo getInfo() raises(CustomerExc);
        void setInfo(in CustomerInfo info) raises(CustomerExc);
    };

    interface CustomerManager
    {
        Customer createCustomer();
    };
};
```

`CustomerManager` interface defines a CORBA factory that is used to create instances of `Customer`.

In the next section, we will examine how ObjectBridge maps the CORBA IDL to COM interfaces. Then, in Using the CORBA Server from a Visual Basic Client on page 346, we will examine how the ObjectBridge COM mapping is used from a Visual Basic COM client.

Creating a COM View for the CORBA Server

With ObjectBridge, it is relatively simple to create a COM view for a CORBA server. ObjectBridge provides an Administrator application for performing such tasks. The ObjectBridge Administrator application is shown in Figure 12-3. In Figure 12-3, an ObjectBridge service named `Ch12` provides a COM automation view for the `Ch12CustomerManager` CORBA interfaces defined in Listing 12-1.

The steps required to create a service like the one shown in Figure 12-3 are very simple and require little expertise with COM or CORBA.

The first step is to create an ObjectBridge service. For our example, we have chosen to name the service `Ch12`. To create the service, we invoke the *New Service...* menu item from the Administrator's *File* menu. This pops up a dialog that allows us to create a new service with a specified name. Note that ObjectBridge can support multiple ObjectBridge services. (We will describe the creation of a second service in Using COM Servers from CORBA Clients on page 352.)

The second step is to indicate what types of clients will use the ObjectBridge service. Since we will be using the service from a Visual Basic application, we

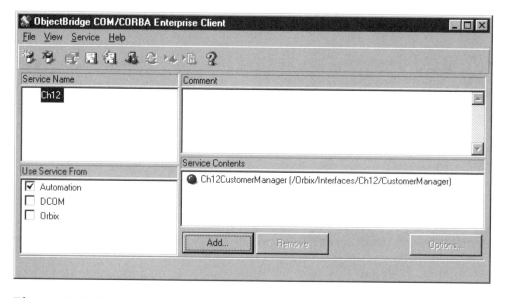

Figure 12-3. *Creating a service in the ObjectBridge Administrator.*

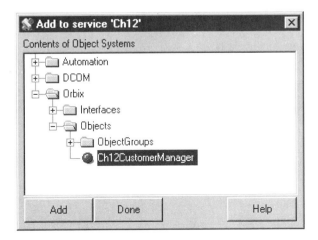

Figure 12-4. *Adding the CORBA server to the Ch12 ObjectBridge service.*

select the *Automation* check box. As we will show later in this section, COM dual interfaces will be created for the CORBA objects that are being mapped to COM automation.

The third step is to indicate the CORBA objects that will be supported by the Ch12 ObjectBridge service. The *Add...* button in the Administrator is used to pop up a dialog that allows the user to select the distributed objects to be supported. The dialog for adding the Ch12CustomerManager Orbix server is shown in Figure 12-4.

After completing the third step, we need to install the changes made to this point. To install the newly created service, we simply invoke the *Install Changes* menu item from the Administrator's *Service* menu. After we install the changes, the CORBA object can be used from COM clients.

At this point, it is advantageous (although not necessary) to generate bindings that clients can use to facilitate the use of the Ch12 ObjectBridge service. To generate bindings, we invoke the *Generate Bindings* menu item from the Administrator's *Service* menu. This pops up the *Generate Bindings* dialog shown in Figure 12-5.

A large number of choices are available with regard to the types of bindings that can be generated.[*] As illustrated in Figure 12-5, we have chosen to gener-

---

[*]Note that the DCOM-related bindings are available only if DCOM has been selected as a client type in the ObjectBridge Administrator (see Figure 12-3).

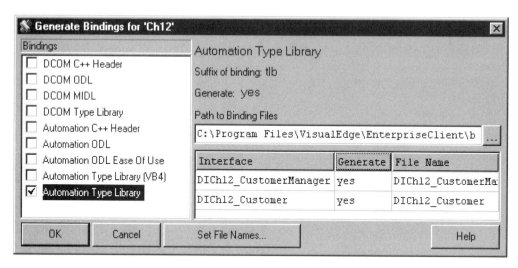

Figure 12-5. Generating COM bindings for the CORBA server.

ate COM automation type libraries since we will be using the `Ch12` Object-Bridge service from a Visual Basic application. The automation bindings that get generated for CORBA interfaces are dual interfaces. For example, the COM automation bindings that get created for the CORBA `Customer` interface defined in Listing 12-1 are as follows:

```
// excerpt from DICh12_Customer.odl
    [
        odl, dual, oleautomation, version(1.0),
        uuid(bf239b9f-0d63-10d9-1de3-54d188a33421)
    ]

    interface DICh12_Customer : IDispatch
    {
        [ id(7), helpstring("Method raises: DICh12_CustomerExc") ]
        HRESULT create(
            [in] DICh12_CustomerInfo* info,
            [in,out,optional] VARIANT* exceptionInfo,
            [out,retval] int* returnValue);

        [ id(8), helpstring("Method raises: DICh12_CustomerExc") ]
        HRESULT getAll(
            [out] VARIANT* ids,
            [out] VARIANT* names,
            [in,out,optional] VARIANT* exceptionInfo);
```

```
    [ id(9), helpstring("Method raises: DICh12_CustomerExc") ]
    HRESULT getInfo(
        [in,out,optional] VARIANT* exceptionInfo,
        [out,retval] DICh12_CustomerInfo** returnValue);

    [ id(10), helpstring("Method raises: DICh12_CustomerExc") ]
    HRESULT lookup(
        [in] int id,
        [in,out,optional] VARIANT* exceptionInfo,
        [out,retval] DICh12_CustomerInfo** returnValue);

    [ id(11), helpstring("Method raises: DICh12_CustomerExc") ]
    HRESULT setInfo(
        [in] DICh12_CustomerInfo* info,
        [in,out,optional] VARIANT* exceptionInfo);

};
```

ObjectBridge maps the CORBA sequences (i.e., `LongSeq` and `StringSeq`) defined in Listing 12-1 to COM VARIANTs. As we shall see in the next section, the VARIANTs that get associated with the CORBA sequences are actually VARIANT-wrapped SAFEARRAYs and are easily used from Visual Basic.

Recall (from Dual Interfaces on page 229) that dual interfaces cannot support user-defined types. For this reason, CORBA structs and exceptions must be mapped to COM interfaces. For example, the COM automation bindings that get created for the CORBA `CustomerInfo` struct defined in Listing 12-1 are as follows:

```
// excerpt from DICh12_Customer.odl
    [
        odl, dual, oleautomation, version(0.0),
        uuid(c1136e20-7442-4fd7-1de8-5c1c49db809e)
    ]

    interface DICh12_CustomerInfo : DICORBAStruct
    {
        [id(128),propget] HRESULT id([out,retval] int* rtrn);
        [id(128),propput] HRESULT id([in] int valueToPut);

        [id(129),propget] HRESULT name([out,retval] BSTR* rtrn);
        [id(129),propput] HRESULT name([in] BSTR valueToPut);

        [id(130),propget] HRESULT address([out,retval] BSTR* rtrn);
        [id(130),propput] HRESULT address([in] BSTR valueToPut);
        ...
    };
```

The mapping of CORBA structs and exceptions to COM interfaces can have serious performance implications. Each access of a CORBA struct member forces a COM method call to the COM view. If the COM view is implemented as a local server or remote server, the cost of accessing a struct will probably be prohibitive; however, since the COM view is generally run as an in-process COM object, the performance overhead of accessing the struct through the interface methods is usually inconsequential.

In addition to COM automation support, ObjectBridge also supports the mapping of CORBA objects to COM custom interfaces. This is accomplished by supporting *DCOM* clients in the ObjectBridge Administrator and by generating the DCOM-related bindings. With this approach, CORBA structs and exceptions are mapped to COM structs. The downside is that the COM view that gets generated is not automation-compliant and might therefore be unusable from environments other than C++.

Using the CORBA Server from a Visual Basic Client

The Visual Basic COM client application is shown in Figure 12-6. The Visual Basic client application relies on the COM view of the CORBA server that was generated in the previous section. Recall that we generated type library bindings for the COM view. These type library bindings are used by Visual Basic

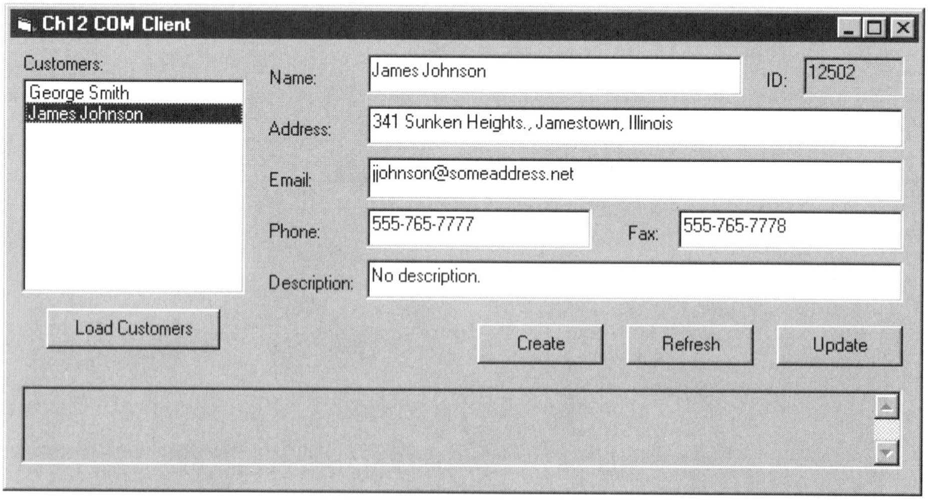

Figure 12-6. *The Visual Basic COM client.*

when creating the Visual Basic client application. The actual type library references that are used in the Visual Basic project are shown in Figure 12-7.

As shown in Figure 12-7, the Visual Basic project relies on the following three type libraries.

1. *DICh12_Customer Library.* This type library provides the COM interface corresponding to the CORBA `Customer` interface defined in Listing 12-1. It also provides COM interfaces corresponding to the CORBA `CustomerInfo` struct as well as the CORBA `CustomerExc` exception object.

2. *DICh12_CustomerManager Library.* This type library provides the COM interface corresponding to the CORBA `CustomerManager` interface defined in Listing 12-1.

3. *ObjectBridge OLE/COM Support (3.0).* This type library provides a number of COM interfaces for interacting with the ObjectBridge system. The only interface that is used in our example is the `DICORBAFactoryEx` interface.

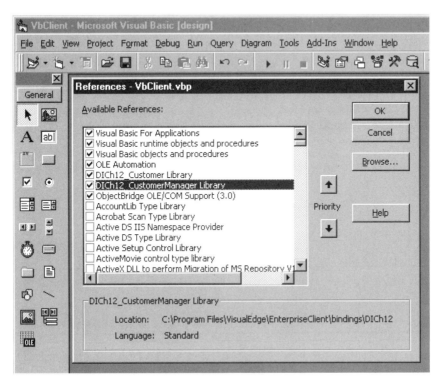

Figure 12-7. *Referencing bridge-related COM objects in the Visual Basic project.*

This interface provides a method for creating instances of the COM `CustomerInfo` object corresponding to the CORBA `CustomerInfo` struct.

The Visual Basic code that is used to create a `Customer` instance is shown here:

```
Dim g_customer As DICh12_Customer

Private Sub CreateComCustomer()
    Dim mgr As DICh12_CustomerManager

    'Obtain a handle on the Ch12CustomerManager CORBA server.
    Set mgr = CreateObject("Ch12.Ch12CustomerManager")

    'Obtain a handle on a Customer instance.
    Set g_customer = mgr.createCustomer()
End Sub
```

In this example, `g_customer` is defined as a global `Customer` reference. To create the `Customer` instance, a `CustomerManager` handle must first be obtained. ObjectBridge defines a `ProgID` in the Windows system registry that corresponds to the appropriate CORBA server. This `ProgID` is used in the call to `CreateObject()`. The `ProgID` is based on the ObjectBridge service name (i.e., `Ch12`) and CORBA server name (i.e., `Ch12CustomerManager`). Once a handle on the `CustomerManager` server has been obtained, the `createCustomer()` method is invoked to create a `Customer` instance.

Recall that the CORBA method `Customer::getAll()` returns CORBA sequences as shown here:

```
// excerpt from Ch12.idl
module Ch12
{
    typedef sequence<long>   LongSeq;
    typedef sequence<string> StringSeq;
    ...

    interface Customer
    {
        void getAll(out LongSeq ids,
                    out StringSeq names) raises(CustomerExc);

        ...
    };
};
```

The Visual Basic client handles these sequences as follows:

```
Dim currIds, names As Variant
Call g_customer.getAll(currIds, names)

For i = 0 To UBound(names)
    Call lstCustomers.AddItem(names(i))
Next i
```

Note that the `names` variable is treated as an ordinary Visual Basic array. The CORBA sequences `LongSeq` and `StringSeq` map to `VARIANT`-wrapped `SAFEARRAY`s that are easily used from COM dual interface clients.

There are several issues that must be considered when working with CORBA structs. Recall from the last section that the CORBA `CustomerInfo` struct is mapped to a COM interface when mapping CORBA to COM automation. Two distinct cases must be handled when using a struct. The simplest case occurs when a call to the COM view returns a COM object corresponding to the struct as shown here:

```
Private Sub lstCustomers_Click()
On Error GoTo ErrorHandler
    'Get id for selected item in list.
    Dim id As Long
    id = CLng(g_currIds(lstCustomers.ListIndex))
    txtID.Text = "" & id

    'Look up customer.
    Dim info As DICh12_CustomerInfo
    Set info = g_customer.lookup(id)

    'Display customer name and address.
    txtName.Text = info.Name
    txtAddress.Text = info.address
Exit Sub

ErrorHandler:
    txtStatus.Text = Err.Source & ": " & Err.Description
End Sub
```

In this example, `info` is returned by the call to `g_customer.lookup()`. The `info` object is then used to retrieve the customer information.

The other case with regard to struct usage occurs when the client must create an instance of the COM struct object to pass as a parameter to a COM method. The following example creates a COM struct object and passes it as a parameter to a COM method:

```
Private Sub cmdUpdate_Click()
On Error GoTo ErrorHandler

    'The factory is used to create empty instances of a struct.
    Dim factory As DICORBAFactoryEx
    Set factory = CreateObject("EnterpriseClient.Factory")

    'Create an info object to hold the customer's data.
    Dim info As DICh12_CustomerInfo
    Set info = factory.CreateType(g_customer, "CustomerInfo")

    'Set the customer attributes.
    info.Name = txtName.Text
    info.address = txtAddress.Text
    info.phone = txtPhone.Text
    info.fax = txtFax.Text
    info.email = txtEmail.Text
    info.Desc = txtDesc.Text

    'Update customer.
    Call g_customer.setInfo(info)
Exit Sub

ErrorHandler:
    txtStatus.Text = Err.Source & ": " & Err.Description
End Sub
```

In this example, a COM object instance is created that supports the `DICORBAFactoryEx` interface.[*] The factory instance is then used to create an `info` object. The `info` object is then used to hold all pertinent customer information and is passed as a parameter to `g_customer.setInfo()`.

The last example that we need to examine is the handling of CORBA exceptions in the Visual Basic client. Recall that the `Customer::create()` method can raise an exception. The CORBA IDL describing the `Customer::create()` method is as follows:

```
// excerpt from Ch12.idl
module Ch12
{
    exception CustomerExc  { string reason; };
    ...
```

---

[*]The `DICORBAFactoryEx` interface is defined in the *ObjectBridge OLE/COM Support* type library.

```
interface Customer
{
    long create(in CustomerInfo info) raises(CustomerExc);
    ...
};
};
```

The Visual Basic client handles CORBA exceptions as follows:

```
'Create the customer.
Dim excep As Object
Call g_customer.Create(info, excep)

'Check for CORBA exception.
Select Case (excep.EX_majorCode)
    Case 1: 'system exception
        txtStatus.Text = "CORBA System Exception Occurred!"
    Case 2: 'user exception
        txtStatus.Text = "CORBA User Exception: " & excep.reason
End Select
```

If a method is capable of throwing a CORBA exception, the COM view of that method allows an exception object to be passed as a parameter to the method. The exception object can then be queried to determine the following exception status:

- *No exception.* If the exception's EX_majorCode is equal to 0, the exception object should be ignored.

- *System exception.* If the exception's EX_majorCode is equal to 1, a CORBA system exception occurred.

- *User exception.* If the exception's EX_majorCode is equal to 2, a user-defined exception occurred. Various fields of the user-defined exception can then be accessed to determine the reason for the exception.

The most important point to note in this section is that the creation of the Visual Basic client application required practically no understanding of CORBA. ObjectBridge was used to rapidly create a robust COM view of the CORBA customer server.

Using COM Servers from CORBA Clients

As was the case when creating a COM view for a CORBA server, it is just as simple to create a CORBA view for a COM server when using a commercial bridging product like ObjectBridge. Consider the case where a CORBA client application needs to manipulate an Excel spreadsheet. In Figure 12-8, an ObjectBridge service named `excel` provides a CORBA view for the `Excel Application` server.

After creating the `excel` service, ObjectBridge now supports two distinct services. The `Ch12` service provides a COM view of the CORBA `Customer` server. The `excel` service provides a CORBA view of the `Excel Application` server (i.e., a COM automation server).

The *Add to service* dialog is used to add the `Excel` automation server to the ObjectBridge `excel` service. The `Excel Application` object is selected as shown in Figure 12-9.

The last step is to generate CORBA IDL that describes the CORBA view of the COM automation server. This is done using the *Generate Bindings* dialog as shown in Figure 12-10.

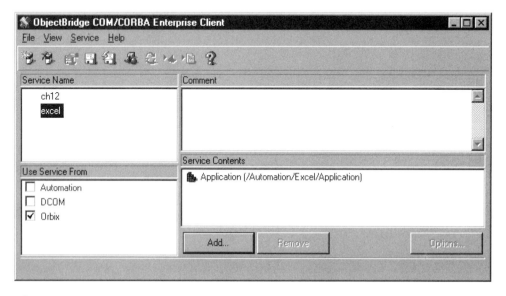

Figure 12-8. *Creating an Excel service in the ObjectBridge Administrator.*

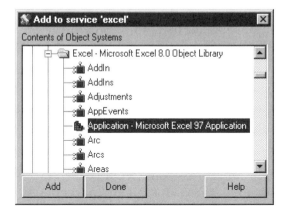

Figure 12-9. *Adding an Excel automation server to the Excel ObjectBridge service.*

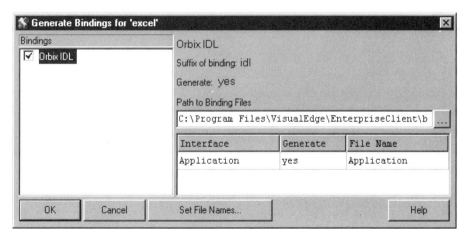

Figure 12-10. *Generating CORBA IDL bindings for the Excel automation server.*

The generated CORBA IDL can then be used to create CORBA client stubs that allow a CORBA client application to access the CORBA view of the `Excel` automation server. The most important point to note is that very little COM knowledge is needed to create the CORBA view of the COM automation server.

Bridging COM/CORBA Services

In this chapter, we have examined how commercial bridging products can be used to access CORBA servers from COM clients and vice versa. While the ability of a commercial bridging product to provide base-level interoperability between COM and CORBA is important, one cannot help but wonder how interoperability can be achieved between COM and CORBA services such as those supporting transactions and security. Of all the services, transaction support is probably the most critical.

The most obvious strategy to avoid interoperability problems between various implementations of a service is simply to avoid interoperability altogether. While this may sound overly restrictive, adequate support does not yet exist to support interworking across different implementations of sophisticated services such as those supporting transactions and security. For example, there are currently no commercial products that allow transactions to span the Microsoft Transaction Service (MTS) and a CORBA-compliant Object Transaction Service (OTS). To avoid the need to interoperate across different implementations of a service, the enterprise must be partitioned appropriately. (We discussed the need for such partitioning in Partitioning the Enterprise on page 107.)

With regard to bridging MTS to other commercial transaction services, one of the most interesting initiatives in this area has occurred with Microsoft and Iona. Iona has announced that it plans to integrate Microsoft Transaction Server (MTS) and Iona's OrbixOTM. Due to the pervasive nature of Microsoft products, it seems likely that many other vendors will also seek to integrate with Microsoft's distributed object services as Microsoft's distributed object products become more established in the marketplace.

Summary

A commercial bridging product is generally required when working in a large environment that makes heavy use of both COM and CORBA. Attempting to use custom components in a large environment inevitably results in increased maintenance costs. A dependency on custom components also necessitates personnel who are competent with both COM and CORBA in order to maintain the custom bridging components.

The primary commercial bridging products that are currently available all comply to some degree with the OMG's COM/CORBA interworking specification. In this chapter, we explored how one of those products, Visual Edge's ObjectBridge, can be used to bridge COM and CORBA. A commercial bridging product such as the one offered by Visual Edge is important for many reasons. The most important of these reasons is that it allows a developer who has expertise in only one distributed object system to seamlessly use distributed objects that are implemented in another distributed object system. For example, with the help of ObjectBridge, a COM developer would need little understanding of CORBA in order to access a CORBA server from a COM client.

The recent emergence of enterprise application servers will further necessitate COM/CORBA integration. Enterprise application servers will probably need to support both COM and CORBA clients and servers. In the next chapter, we will attempt to define what constitutes an enterprise application server with an emphasis on implications related to support for COM and CORBA. We will define criteria for evaluating enterprise application servers and compare different approaches that rely on COM, CORBA, and Enterprise JavaBeans.

Chapter 13

Enterprise Application Servers

Topics Covered in This Chapter

- Emergence of Enterprise Application Servers
- Enterprise Application Server Criteria
- Enterprise Application Server Approaches

Building a large distributed system with COM and/or CORBA is hard. In fact, designing and implementing any large multi-tier system always require a considerable amount of effort. The added effort is mostly due to the large number of infrastructure issues that apply to any large distributed system. Software vendors are evolving improved software development and runtime environments that facilitate the creation and deployment of distributed object systems. These environments are often referred to as *enterprise application servers*.

One of the primary goals of an enterprise application server is to free developers from having to concern themselves with infrastructure issues (e.g., legacy support, transactions, security, etc.) so that they can instead focus on actual business problems. Enterprise application servers must support a range of legacy systems as well as client environments. This includes support for clients and servers that are implemented with both COM and CORBA. In this regard, an enterprise application server can be used as a bridge between COM and CORBA although it is actually intended to solve a wider range of problems.

In this chapter, we'll attempt to define what constitutes an enterprise application server. This is important due to the disparity that exists among the application server products that are offered by various vendors. We'll explore a number of approaches that enterprise application servers can use, including COM, CORBA, and Enterprise JavaBeans.

Emergence of Enterprise Application Servers

In creating the middle tier in a 3-tier system, the fundamental goal is to move business logic out of the client (as well as the database in the case of stored procedures) to middle-tier servers on which the business logic can best be managed. In almost all cases, issues related to transactions, security, performance, fault tolerance, and so on, often override the fundamental task of implementing business logic in the middle tier. This places an incredible burden on developers in that they must possess expertise in areas that are totally unrelated to the business logic that they are implementing. Application server environments are intended to relieve programmers from having to deal with infrastructure issues so that they can instead focus on business logic implementation.

Early Web Application Servers

The rapid growth of the Internet has resulted in the proliferation of 3-tier Web-based applications. Web-based applications typically consist of a thin client tier (HTML/CGI), a middle tier (which generates HTML), and a database tier. Early Web-based applications were implemented in an ad hoc manner using a variety of scripting and compiler-based development tools. Such tools were inadequate when creating Web-based applications of complexity beyond a certain threshold. It quickly became evident that a development environment tailored for Web-based applications was needed. Such environments are often referred to as *Web application servers*. The typical use of a Web application server is illustrated in Figure 13-1.

When compared to an ad hoc approach, the use of a Web application server offers one or more of the following advantages:

- *Programming utilities.* The Web application server environment provides a number of utilities that facilitate the creation of client Web pages.

- *Platform portability.* The Web application server shields implementors from platform differences. Such platform differences may include both the operating system platform (NT, Solaris, etc.) as well as the Web server platform (Microsoft IIS, Netscape Enterprise Server, Apache, etc.).

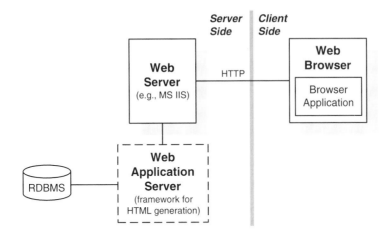

Figure 13-1. *A typical Web application server.*

- *Load balancing.* The Web application server distributes requests across multiple servers in order to support a large number of Internet clients.

- *Database support.* The Web application server environment facilitates use of relational database management systems.

- *Web-site management.* The Web application server environment provides tools that assist in management of Web-site content.

As stated earlier, the introduction of Web application servers was a direct response to the high demand for Web-based applications. This was due to the growing demand of users on the Internet. Web application servers provide a framework for the development of multi-tiered Web-based applications. It seems logical that such a framework could be extended to support distributed object applications in addition to conventional Web-based applications.

The Need for Enterprise Application Servers

Throughout this book, we have focused on the use of COM and CORBA in the widest possible range of situations. COM and CORBA both have much to offer in terms of client and server technology. In addition, the COM and CORBA domains can be bridged, thereby allowing the use of both COM and CORBA in

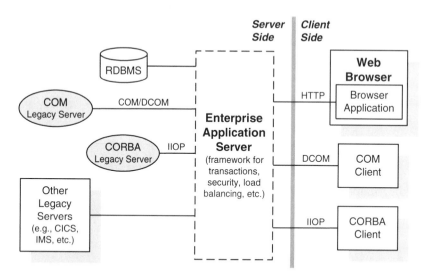

Figure 13-2. *A typical enterprise application server.*

a specific enterprise solution. Despite these advances, it is still difficult to build a substantial distributed system using COM and/or CORBA.

The early Web application server environments provided a precursor to advanced application servers that are better able to support COM and CORBA. These advanced application servers support a much wider range of clients and legacy systems than their Web application server predecessors. Because these advanced application servers are aimed at meeting enterprise needs as opposed to just Web application needs, they are often referred to as *enterprise application servers*. The typical use of an enterprise application server is illustrated in Figure 13-2.

Software vendors are very much aware of the need for enterprise application servers. In fact, every major vendor in the COM/CORBA arena is currently working on or has already released an enterprise application server product. The widespread availability of these enterprise application servers will greatly assist developers and will fuel the use of COM and CORBA in the enterprise.

Enterprise Application Server Criteria

Enterprise application servers first appeared on the market near the end of 1998. Because of their recent emergence, it is difficult to differentiate between the products of various vendors. The criteria presented in Table 13-1 are not intended to be comprehensive but are instead intended to differentiate among products by accentuating the strengths and weaknesses of the various enterprise application server approaches.

Table 13-1. *Enterprise Application Server Criteria*

Criterion	Test	Comments
Client support	Does the application server support the targeted client environments?	Possible client types include Internet (HTTP), COM, and CORBA clients. In Java environments, Java RMI is also important.
Legacy system support	Does the application server support strategic legacy systems?	Possible legacy systems include COM and CORBA servers as well as mainframe systems such as CICS and IMS.
Database access	Does the application server support the targeted database systems?	New enterprise applications almost always rely on one or more RDBMSs.
Distributed transactions	Does the application server support distributed transactions?	Distributed transactions are essential in order to maintain integrity in a distributed application.
Security	Does the application server support security and privacy?	Conventional security issues such as authentication and authorization are important. Issues related to privacy and integrity are also important.
Naming services	Does the application server support naming and location of services?	Naming services provide for registration and location of provided services.
Event services	Does the application server support event propagation to clients?	Clients need to be updated when various events occur in the system. This requires some type of event service support.
Development environment	Is the application server supported in the appropriate development environments?	Highly visual development environments are needed to make developers more productive because of the complexity of distributed applications.
Portability	Will it be possible to deploy the enterprise application on all targeted platforms?	It is often necessary to deploy an enterprise application on more than one platform.
Scalability	Does the application server support large numbers of clients?	To achieve scalability, an application server needs to provide automatic load balancing as well as resource pooling.

The weight of each criterion will obviously depend on the overall goals of the distributed application to be implemented. In addition, each enterprise application server vendor is likely to offer unique features, thus resulting in additional criteria that may be important for a specific situation.

The criteria in Table 13-1 present a significant challenge for the enterprise application server vendors. The good news is that several vendors are already creating environments that meet many of these criteria. As enterprise application server products mature, it should become much simpler to create systems that utilize COM and CORBA.

Enterprise Application Server Approaches

A staggering number of vendors are currently vying for the dominant position in the enterprise application server arena. Competition is intense, and the application server market will probably change dramatically in the near term. Despite the turbulence in the market, it is still important to recognize the various enterprise application server approaches. Distributed object frameworks such as COM, CORBA, and Java RMI (in the case of Enterprise JavaBeans) can be used to provide the infrastructure for an enterprise application server. In this section, the criteria presented in Table 13-1 will be used to identify the strengths and weaknesses of each distributed object approach.

COM Approach

Microsoft's overwhelming support for COM on the Windows platform makes the COM approach somewhat different from that of an enterprise application server. Under Windows, Microsoft controls the platform and is therefore much more than an application server vendor. An overview of how Windows/COM meets the enterprise application server criteria is presented in Table 13-2.

The weaknesses identified in Table 13-2 are fairly insignificant. One noticeable weakness is the fact that CORBA clients are not supported. Reconciling this weakness is actually more of a problem for CORBA vendors than for Microsoft. CORBA vendors recognize the importance of COM on the Windows platform and are therefore forced to provide bidirectional bridging products that allow integration between COM and CORBA. Most of the other weaknesses that are identified in Table 13-2 will be addressed in upcoming versions of COM and Windows NT.

Table 13-2. *Windows/COM Handling of Enterprise Application Server Criteria*

Criterion	Handling of Criterion
Client support	Microsoft supports Internet (HTTP) clients through its Active Server Pages technology. COM clients are fully supported. CORBA clients are not supported.
Legacy system support	Microsoft supports a significant number of traditional legacy systems such as CICS, IMS, and AS/400 flat files (see Legacy Support When Using COM on page 128 for more information). Legacy CORBA servers are not supported.
Database access	Microsoft provides several COM-based APIs, including Microsoft ADO, for accessing RDBMSs. ODBC is typically used as the underlying API.
Distributed transactions	Microsoft Transaction Server (MTS) and Distributed Transaction Coordinator (DTC) are used to support distributed transactions (see COM, MTS, and the Distributed Transaction Coordinator on page 148 for more information).
Security	COM provides low-level built-in security. Microsoft Transaction Server provides role-based security (see MTS Security on page 170 for more information).
Naming services	COM generally relies on the Windows system registry on each machine. Microsoft will provide improved naming capabilities in the Active Directory Services that will be supported in the next version of Windows.
Event services	COM currently relies on an automation-oriented approach known as *connection points*. The next version of COM will improve on connection points and support a rich publish/subscribe mechanism.
Development environment	Microsoft provides tremendous support for COM-based development in its Visual Studio product offering. Development tools include Visual C++, Visual Basic, and Visual J++.
Portability	COM and related services such as MTS are supported only on the Windows platform.
Scalability	MTS works with the ODBC Driver Manager to pool database connections. Automatic load balancing will be supported in the next version of COM.

While Microsoft continues to aggressively improve its COM-based tools and environment, it does not appear that Microsoft will place much effort in improving on COM's greatest weakness—the lack of support for COM and

COM-related tools on non-Windows platforms. For the foreseeable future, the use of COM beyond basic support for C++ will be nonexistent on all platforms other than Windows.

Committing to COM for enterprise application development inevitably results in a commitment to Windows as the primary middle-tier server platform. The strengths that are described in Table 13-2 demonstrate why Microsoft's offering is so attractive. Microsoft appears to be betting that its highly integrated enterprise application platform will entice customers to exclusively use the Windows server platform as opposed to using other more traditional platforms.

CORBA Approach

CORBA provides a mature distributed object infrastructure for an enterprise application server. This maturity is demonstrated by the long period of time that CORBA products have been available on a multitude of major server platforms. Maturity is also demonstrated by the rich set of services that are now being offered by all of the primary CORBA vendors. An overview of how CORBA meets the enterprise application server criteria is presented in Table 13-3.

Inprise is one of several software vendors that is using CORBA as the infrastructure for its enterprise application server. Inprise possesses an excellent combination of resources to meet the high demands of a full-fledged enterprise application server. In addition to its highly respected development tools, Inprise also possesses a robust set of CORBA products that were obtained through the acquisition of Visigenic in early 1998. Other vendors that possess many of the ingredients needed to create a CORBA-based enterprise application server include Iona, BEA, and IBM.

Limited development environment support is the most significant weakness of the CORBA approach. This is in contrast to the COM/Windows approach. On Windows, Microsoft has been able to build a rich development environment by focusing a considerable amount of resources on a single platform. The CORBA vendors do not have this luxury and must instead focus their resources on issues such as language and platform portability as well as a number of sophisticated services (transaction, security, etc.).

The introduction of Java as a dominant CORBA development platform has given CORBA vendors a new opportunity to meet their development environment requirements. By using a pure Java approach to achieve cross-platform support, CORBA servers can be developed on one platform and deployed on

Table 13-3. *CORBA Handling of Enterprise Application Server Criteria*

Criterion	Handling of Criterion
Client support	Direct support for Internet clients (HTTP) is vendor-specific. CORBA clients are fully supported. COM clients are supported through a COM/CORBA bridging product.
Legacy system support	Several CORBA vendors provide support for major legacy systems. CORBA is also well suited to wrap legacy systems because of its multiplatform support (see Legacy Support When Using CORBA on page 133 for more information).
Database access	Third-party tools and products are typically used for accessing RDBMSs.
Distributed transactions	All of the primary CORBA vendors currently support a CORBA-compliant Object Transaction Service (see CORBA and the Object Transaction Service on page 156 for more information).
Security	All of the primary CORBA vendors currently support SSL as well as a CORBA-compliant Security Service (see The CORBA Security Service on page 175 for more information).
Naming services	All of the primary CORBA vendors currently support a CORBA-compliant Naming Service.
Event services	All of the primary CORBA vendors currently support a CORBA-compliant Event Service.
Development environment	Development environment support varies greatly across CORBA vendors. Inprise offers direct support for VisiBroker in its development environments.
Portability	Each of the primary CORBA vendors supports most of the major server platforms. Cross-vendor interoperability is also possible in most cases.
Scalability	Provisions for scalability vary greatly across vendors. CORBA vendors provide proprietary mechanisms for load balancing and resource pooling. Support for the POA in upcoming releases of CORBA products will provide a standardized infrastructure for creating scalable CORBA servers.

another. This allows complex CORBA servers to be developed on the Windows platform using the most advanced Java development tools (most of which only run on Windows). These Java-based CORBA servers can then be deployed on other traditional server platforms that support compliant Java Virtual Machines.

Enterprise JavaBeans Approach

The Enterprise JavaBeans specification* describes an alternative to the COM and CORBA approaches for supporting an enterprise application server. An Enterprise JavaBean (EJB) typically relies on Java RMI to support remote method invocations between EJB clients and servers. In Java RMI on page 20, we pointed out that RMI is not appropriate for general-purpose use because it can be used only with the Java programming language. The Enterprise Java-Beans specification addresses this problem by listing CORBA compatibility as a primary goal. The EJB specification also specifies that arguments, return types, and exceptions must be valid types in the OMG's Java-to-IDL mapping specification. It currently appears that many of the EJB application server vendors will attempt to support CORBA clients in addition to RMI-based Java clients.

Compatibility between Enterprise JavaBeans and CORBA is achieved at the wire level. The Internet Inter-ORB Protocol (IIOP) has been extended by the OMG to fully support Java RMI. This allows for but does not guarantee interoperability between Java RMI servers and CORBA clients. There are at least two issues that affect RMI/CORBA interoperability:

1. The arguments, return types, and exceptions used by an RMI server must be valid types in the OMG's Java-to-IDL mapping specification. Note that several EJB vendors have not yet committed to IIOP and do not enforce this restriction when using their EJB servers.

2. EJB vendors will need to do extensive testing to prove that their servers are interoperable with CORBA ORBs and other EJB servers. This is a maturity issue related to the ongoing efforts of EJB vendors to comply with EJB and CORBA specifications.

The Enterprise JavaBeans specification also describes mappings between the CORBA naming, transaction, and security services and their Java counter-parts. Enterprise JavaBeans and CORBA complement each other and rely on each other's inherent strengths to solve a larger set of problems. Enterprise JavaBeans provides a powerful component framework for creating distributed objects in Java, while CORBA provides cross-language (e.g., Java/C++) support where required.

Version 1.0 of the Enterprise JavaBeans specification was released in March of 1998. By the end of 1998, a number of vendors, including BEA/WebLogic, Per-

---

*The Enterprise JavaBeans specification is available at `http://java.sun.com`.

sistence Software, GemStone Systems, and Novera, claimed to provide EJB server products that fully supported the 1.0 specification. This is quite remarkable when compared to the amount of time that it took to support COM and CORBA in a similar manner. Despite the relative youth of EJB application servers, several EJB servers have managed to meet a substantial number of

Table 13-4. EJB Handling of Enterprise Application Server Criteria

Criterion	Handling of Criterion
Client support	Direct support for Internet clients (HTTP) is vendor-specific. Java RMI clients are supported. COM clients are poorly supported. CORBA clients are supported (or soon will be supported) by many EJB vendors.
Legacy system support	Support for legacy systems is vendor-specific. EJB is well suited to wrap legacy systems because Java is supported on all major platforms.
Database access	The JDBC Database Access API can be used with all major RDBMSs. JDBC can also be bridged to RDBMSs using ODBC drivers.
Distributed transactions	The EJB specification describes the use of the Java Transaction Service (JTS) with EJB for handling distributed transactions. All of the primary EJB vendors support a JTS.
Security	The EJB specification describes the use of standard Java security (as defined in the JDK's java.security package) with EJB. In addition, the EJB specification describes a role-based security model.
Naming services	The EJB specification describes the use of the Java Naming and Directory Interface (JNDI). All of the primary EJB vendors support the use of JNDI.
Event services	Support for event services is vendor-specific.
Development environment	EJB development environment support is currently limited; however, extensive support for EJB is planned in Inprise's JBuilder and Symantec's Visual Cafe environments.
Portability	EJB is highly portable across all major platforms. Cross-vendor interoperability is currently limited but is expected to improve significantly as EJB matures.
Scalability	EJB servers can use JDBC 2.0 solutions that support the pooling of database connections. The EJB specification describes pooling of Enterprise JavaBean instances. EJB vendors provide proprietary mechanisms for load balancing.

the enterprise application server criteria. An overview of how EJB meets the enterprise application server criteria is presented in Table 13-4.

All of the weaknesses identified in Table 13-4 can be attributed to the immaturity of Enterprise JavaBeans in the marketplace. These weaknesses include

- *Limited support for COM clients.* Several vendors have provided limited support for COM clients; however, such support is insufficient for a large enterprise endeavor. This is an area where vendors can leverage the OMG's COM/CORBA interworking architecture. Vendors should be able to adapt COM/CORBA bridging products to support interactions between COM and EJB in a comprehensive manner.

- *Limited support for event services.* Version 1.0 of the EJB specification does not mention how asynchronous events should be handled. This issue needs to be addressed in future specifications of EJB.

- *Limited interoperability across vendors.* Version 1.0 of the EJB specification purposely left certain areas of the specification open with regard to how EJB servers should be implemented, thereby creating interoperability problems. This issue needs to be addressed in future specifications of EJB.

The Enterprise JavaBeans specification introduces a powerful architecture for component-based server-side development. The weaknesses just described will almost certainly be addressed as EJB matures. If these weaknesses can be eliminated, EJB application servers will provide a powerful and platform-independent alternative to Microsoft's highly integrated Windows/COM approach.

Summary

In this chapter, we have examined the COM, CORBA, and Enterprise Java-Beans approaches for supporting enterprise application servers. When engaging in new enterprise application development, it is extremely important to choose the right enterprise application server product. Enterprise application servers provide an end-to-end solution for building sophisticated distributed object applications. As we have stated on numerous occasions, the building of such applications can be very difficult. Enterprise application servers are intended to handle infrastructure issues, thereby allowing developers to focus on business problems rather than on infrastructure problems. Successful reduction of infrastructure complexity makes distributed application development much easier.

Although we have examined three distinct approaches, competition exists between only two distinct camps. Microsoft's COM approach competes with a combined CORBA/EJB approach. The COM approach is inherently dependent on the Windows platform, while the CORBA/EJB approach is inherently cross-platform.

Microsoft offers an incredibly powerful and well-integrated environment for creating a distributed object application. In the race to create the most attractive enterprise application environment, Microsoft has a tremendous head start. Microsoft has managed to cover (or will cover in upcoming releases) all of the significant requirements for enterprise application development and deployment. The most significant problem with Microsoft's approach is that such an approach ends up requiring Windows as the server platform. Most large enterprises are unwilling to make such a large commitment to a single platform.

The other approach is to use CORBA, EJB, or both. The combination of CORBA and EJB can be used to create a flexible multiplatform enterprise application. This is in contrast to Microsoft, which focuses solely on Windows. CORBA and EJB do not compete with each other. Instead, CORBA and EJB complement each other's strengths. This is evidenced by the rapid movement of the OMG and primary CORBA vendors to embrace and support EJB. The most significant new functionality being added to the CORBA 3.0 specification is the addition of a CORBA component model. The CORBA component model is intended to interoperate with EJB. In addition to the OMG's efforts, the EJB specification lists CORBA compatibility as a primary goal.

The convergence of CORBA and EJB poses a significant threat to Microsoft's quest to make Windows the dominant server platform. If the CORBA/EJB application server vendors are able to create a robust development environment that can compete with the COM-based environment offered by Microsoft, the only differentiator that remains will be that of platform. In terms of platform support, the CORBA/EJB approach clearly offers greater flexibility.

Given Microsoft's head start and considerable resources, the CORBA/EJB application server vendors will have a difficult time keeping up with the powerful COM-based environment that Microsoft is creating for the Windows platform. For the foreseeable future, the choice of a particular enterprise application approach will hinge greatly on the willingness of enterprises to commit to Windows as the primary server platform. Enterprises that do not want to rely so heavily on Windows will undoubtedly turn to enterprise application servers that are based on CORBA and/or EJB.

Chapter 14

Conclusion

We have traveled a great distance to reach this point. Mapping out the terrain surrounding both COM and CORBA is an ambitious endeavor. In this chapter, we'll attempt to tie everything together by summarizing the main topics that we've covered throughout the book. If you missed any of the key points mentioned in the summary herein, we recommend that you reread the appropriate section.

A Summary of What We've Covered

Embracing COM and CORBA (Part I)

In Chapters 1 and 2, we discussed the rise in stature of distributed object systems and presented a rationale as to why COM and CORBA have become the dominant distributed object architectures.

In Chapter 3, we examined the technical fundamentals of using COM and CORBA, such as object creation, object invocation, and so forth. This examination relied on several basic programming examples that demonstrated the similarities and differences of COM and CORBA. (For a summary of similarities and differences, see Table 3-4.) After the examination, it was fairly obvious that at the basic level, COM and CORBA are very similar.

In terms of fundamentals, the most significant difference between COM and CORBA is support (or lack of support) for distributed garbage collection. COM provides built-in mechanisms to support distributed garbage collection, while CORBA does not specify such a mechanism. It should be noted that distributed garbage collection is a complex and potentially expensive operation and that both the COM and CORBA camps have excellent reasons for choosing their respective approaches with regard to cleanup of distributed objects.

Because of performance and fault tolerance issues, cases can be made for and against implicit support for distributed garbage collection.

The primary goal of Part I was to demonstrate that at the basic level, COM and CORBA are very similar. In fact, based on technical fundamentals alone (with the exception of distributed garbage collection), there is nothing significant that differentiates one from the other. Instead, choosing where COM and CORBA are most appropriate depends on many other factors, including operating system platform, distributed object services (e.g., transaction service, security service, etc.), and development tool support.

COM and CORBA on the Server (Part II)

In Chapter 4, we examined the use of COM and CORBA on the server side of the enterprise. We first discussed the need to partition the enterprise. In general, COM and CORBA should not be mixed within a specific server-side enterprise partition since integration issues can become problematic. We then identified an assessment strategy that can be used to determine whether COM or CORBA should be used for a specific enterprise partition. (For an example that demonstrates this strategy, see Table 4-2.)

In Chapter 5, we examined a wide range of platform-related issues that must be considered when selecting COM and CORBA as a server-side infrastructure. Platform issues center around operating system support, support for legacy systems (such as MVS, AS/400, etc.), and development tool support. While Microsoft provides solid legacy system support as well as exceptional development tools, it does so at the expense of operating system platform support. CORBA clearly dominates the distributed object arena on non-Windows platforms.

In Chapter 6, we examined essential services that are required when creating robust server-side distributed objects. We focused on support for transactions, security, messaging, and management of COM and CORBA server objects. Note that other services such as those supporting naming/directory and events are also important; however, they are handled in very different ways with regard to COM and CORBA.

In Chapter 7, we looked at several intangibles that often influence the choice of COM and CORBA in a particular situation. These intangibles include a number of nontechnical issues such as vendor perception, vendor lock-in, and availability of development staff. All too often, such intangibles exert a dispro-portionate amount of influence on decisions related to COM and CORBA.

The primary goal of Part II was to demonstrate that COM and CORBA each offer distinct advantages on the server side and that a decision to use one or the other in a specific area of the enterprise should be carefully evaluated. The assessment strategy presented in Chapter 4 provides a basis for performing such an evaluation.

COM and CORBA on the Client (Part III)

In Chapter 8, we focused on the use of COM from desktop client applications. Microsoft Windows is the dominant desktop operating system, and Microsoft's COM is therefore the dominant distributed object architecture for Windows cli-ent applications. We examined the use of custom, automation, and dual COM interfaces from COM client applications. We also looked at several program-ming examples using the primary COM development environments: Visual Basic, Visual C++, and Visual J++.

In Chapter 9, we examined the use of COM and CORBA with Internet client applications. COM and CORBA each possess distinct strengths when used to implement Internet applications. We examined the use of COM with Active Server Pages as well as CORBA in CORBA/Java applets. We also discussed the use of push technology as an alternative to browser-based client solutions.

In Chapter 10, we discussed design considerations that must be taken into account when creating COM and CORBA client applications. Performance issues related to remote method invocation must be considered when design-ing the interfaces of distributed objects. As a result, interfaces end up being rather unfriendly from a client perspective. In Chapter 10, we also discussed how remoting requirements can be met while still providing client-friendly interfaces. We also examined a programming example that used both desktop (COM) and Internet (COM and CORBA) clients with COM and CORBA servers.

The primary goal of Part III was to demonstrate that COM and CORBA each offer distinct advantages on the client side. To leverage the advantages of both COM and CORBA in the overall solution, the selection of COM and CORBA on the client side should be done independently of the technology being used on the server side. For example, the need to support Windows desktop clients using COM should not prohibit the use of CORBA as the distributed infra-structure on the server side.

Bridging COM and CORBA (Part IV)

In Chapter 11, we discussed a multitude of custom bridging approaches that can be used to bridge the COM and CORBA domains. We focused on the use of Microsoft's Visual C++ and Microsoft's Java Virtual Machine to create custom bridging components. We also described several third-party products that can be used to facilitate the bridging of COM and CORBA. We noted that custom bridging approaches should be used only when a small amount of COM/CORBA integration is required.

In Chapter 12, we discussed the OMG's COM/CORBA interworking specification. We also identified several vendors who implement commercial COM/CORBA bridging products that comply to some degree with the OMG's specification. Commercial bridging products provide high-level tools that simplify bridging between COM and CORBA. We provided an example that used a commercial bridging product (Visual Edge Software's ObjectBridge) to bridge a Visual Basic COM client with an Iona Orbix CORBA server.

In Chapter 13, we discussed the emergence of enterprise application servers. Enterprise application servers, as defined in Chapter 13, are software development and runtime environments that facilitate the creation and deployment of distributed object systems. COM, CORBA, and Enterprise JavaBeans (EJB) are all distributed object infrastructures that can be used to implement an enterprise application server. As enterprise application servers mature, they will almost certainly need to support interaction with both COM and CORBA. In Chapter 13, we identified criteria for enterprise application servers and then used those criteria to assess the appropriateness of COM, CORBA, and EJB for implementing an enterprise application server.

The primary goal of Part IV was to show that COM and CORBA can be used together. Custom bridging approaches should be used only when a small amount of COM/CORBA integration is required. In larger systems where greater integration is required, a commercial bridging product or enterprise application server product should be used.

Farewell

Weaving COM and/or CORBA into a complex distributed system requires considerable knowledge and effort. This book should provide you with valuable knowledge and direction. Regardless of whether you choose COM, CORBA, EJB, or all of the above, we wish you well and hope that we were able to help.

Appendix A

References

On COM

- David Chappell. *Understanding ActiveX and OLE* (Microsoft Press, 1996).

- Dale Rogerson. *Inside COM* (Microsoft Press, 1997).

- Don Box. *Essential COM* (Addison-Wesley, 1998).

On CORBA

- Jon Siegel et al. *CORBA Fundamentals and Programming* (John Wiley & Sons, 1996).

- Michi Henning, Stephen Vinoski. *Advanced CORBA Programming with C++* (Addison-Wesley, 1999).

- Robert Orfali, Dan Harkey, Jeri Edwards. *Instant CORBA* (John Wiley & Sons, 1997).

- *The Common Object Request Broker: Architecture and Specification* (OMG, 1998). Available from the OMG at `http://www.omg.org`.

On COM/CORBA Bridging

- Michael Rosen, David Curtis. *Integrating CORBA and COM Applications* (John Wiley & Sons, 1998).

- Ronan Geraghty et al. *COM-CORBA Interoperability* (Prentice Hall, 1999).

Appendix B

Examples Available for Download

This appendix describes the organization of the source code that constitutes the examples used throughout the book. The source code described in this appendix can be downloaded from `http://www.pobox.com/~pritchard/com_corba.html`.

The source code is organized by chapter. The relevant examples and corresponding directories are as described next.

Chapter 3 Examples

Directory: `book/ch03`

Purpose: Contains source code for the examples presented in Chapter 3. These examples are intended to demonstrate the fundamentals of using COM and CORBA.

Clients

Directory: `book/ch03/clients`

Purpose: Contains source code for the COM and CORBA client applications presented in Chapter 3.

COM C++ Client

Directory: `book/ch03/clients/com_cpp_client`

Purpose: Demonstrates use of a COM server from a Visual C++/MFC client application.

COM Visual Basic Client

Directory: `book/ch03/clients/com_vb_client`

Purpose: Demonstrates use of a COM server from a Visual Basic client application.

CORBA C++ Client

Directory: `book/ch03/clients/corba_cpp_client`

Purpose: Demonstrates use of a CORBA server from a C++ client application. The client application uses Iona Orbix and IIOP to communicate with the CORBA server.

CORBA Java Client

Directory: `book/ch03/clients/corba_java_client`

Purpose: Demonstrates use of a CORBA server from a Java client application. The client application uses Inprise's VisiBroker for Java and IIOP to communicate with the CORBA server.

Servers

Directory: `book/ch03/servers`

Purpose: Contains source code for the COM and CORBA servers presented in Chapter 3.

COM IDL

Directory: `book/ch03/servers/midl`

Purpose: Contains a COM IDL and type library description of the COM server used in Chapter 3.

CORBA IDL

Directory: `book/ch03/servers/idl`

Purpose: Contains a CORBA IDL description of the CORBA server used in Chapter 3.

COM C++ Server

Directory: `book/ch03/servers/com_cpp_server`

Purpose: Provides the COM server that is used by the COM Visual C++ and Visual Basic clients in Chapter 3. The COM server is implemented using Visual C++ and ATL.

CORBA C++ Server

Directory: `book/ch03/servers/corba_cpp_server`

Purpose: Provides the CORBA server that is used by the CORBA C++ and Java clients in Chapter 3. The CORBA server is implemented using Visual C++ and Iona Orbix.

Chapter 6 Examples

Directory: `book/ch06`

Purpose: Contains source code for the examples presented in Chapter 6. These examples are intended to demonstrate essential services supporting transactions, security, and messaging.

MTS Example

Directory: `book/ch06/mts_example`

Purpose: Contains source code for COM MTS servers and a COM client that demonstrates the use of MTS to manage distributed transactions.

MTS Account Server

Directory: `book/ch06/mts_example/account`

Purpose: Provides a COM MTS server that implements an *Account* object that participates in an MTS distributed transaction. This server is implemented using Visual C++ and ATL.

MTS Teller Server

Directory: `book/ch06/mts_example/teller`

Purpose: Provides a COM MTS server that implements a *Teller* object that uses MTS to guarantee transfers between two accounts. This server is implemented using Visual C++ and ATL.

MTS Client

Directory: `book/ch06/mts_example/client`

Purpose: Demonstrates use of the MTS *Teller* server from a Visual Basic client application.

COM Security

Directory: `book/ch06/com_security`

Purpose: Contains source code for COM servers and clients that demonstrates the use of COM and MTS to manage security.

COM Secure Agent Server

Directory: `book/ch06/com_security/com_agent`

Purpose: Provides a COM server that demonstrates basic COM security constructs. This server is implemented using Visual C++ and ATL.

COM Secure Client

Directory: `book/ch06/com_security/com_client`

Purpose: Demonstrates use of basic COM security constructs from a Visual C++ client application.

MTS Secure Account Server

Directory: `book/ch06/com_security/mts_secure_account`

Purpose: Provides a COM MTS server that demonstrates the use of MTS security. This server is implemented using Visual Basic.

MTS Secure Client

Directory: `book/ch06/com_security/mts_secure_client`

Purpose: Demonstrates use of MTS security from a Visual Basic client application.

MSMQ Example

Directory: `book/ch06/msmq_example`

Purpose: Contains source code for two Visual Basic applications that communicate using MSMQ.

MSMQ Market Application

Directory: `book/ch06/msmq_example/market`

Purpose: Demonstrates use of MSMQ by simulating a simple market that processes orders from traders. Traders place orders in an MSMQ queue. After processing an order, the *Market* application places a response in a separate queue. The *Market* application is implemented using Visual Basic.

MSMQ Trader Application

Directory: `book/ch06/msmq_example/trader`

Purpose: Demonstrates use of MSMQ by simulating a simple trader that places orders in an MSMQ queue. The *Trader* application then waits for responses in a separate queue. The *Trader* application is implemented using Visual Basic.

Chapter 8 Examples

Directory: `book/ch08`

Purpose: Contains source code for the examples presented in Chapter 8. These examples are intended to demonstrate various COM interface approaches.

Automation Interface Approach

Directory: `book/ch08/automation_interface_approach`

Purpose: Contains source code for a COM automation server and client applications that use the automation server.

Visual J++ Server

Directory: `book/ch08/automation_interface_approach/vjserver`

Purpose: Provides a COM server that implements an automation interface.

Visual Basic Client

Directory: `book/ch08/automation_interface_approach/vbclient`

Purpose: Demonstrates use of a COM automation server from a Visual Basic client application.

Visual C++ Client

Directory: `book/ch08/automation_interface_approach/vcclient`

Purpose: Demonstrates use of a COM automation server from a Visual C++ client application.

Visual J++ Client

Directory: `book/ch08/automation_interface_approach/vjclient`

Purpose: Demonstrates use of a COM automation server from a Visual J++ client application.

Custom Interface Approach

Directory: `book/ch08/custom_interface_approach`

Purpose: Contains source code for a COM custom interface server and client applications that use the custom interface server.

Visual C++ Server

Directory: `book/ch08/custom_interface_approach/vcserver`

Purpose: Provides a COM server that implements a custom interface.

Visual Basic Client

Directory: `book/ch08/custom_interface_approach/vbclient`

Purpose: Demonstrates use of a COM custom interface server from a Visual Basic client application.

Visual C++ Client

Directory: `book/ch08/custom_interface_approach/vcclient`

Purpose: Demonstrates use of a COM custom interface server from a Visual C++ client application.

Visual J++ Client

Directory: `book/ch08/custom_interface_approach/vjclient`

Purpose: Demonstrates use of a COM custom interface server from a Visual J++ client application.

Dual Interface Approach

Directory: `book/ch08/dual_interface_approach`

Purpose: Contains source code for COM dual interface servers and client applications that use the dual interface servers.

Visual Basic Server

Directory: `book/ch08/dual_interface_approach/vbserver`

Purpose: Provides a COM server that implements a dual interface. Demonstrates the implementation of a dual interface server using Visual Basic.

Visual C++ Server

Directory: `book/ch08/dual_interface_approach/vcserver`

Purpose: Provides a COM server that implements a dual interface. Demonstrates the implementation of a dual interface server using Visual C++.

Visual J++ Server

Directory: `book/ch08/dual_interface_approach/vjserver`

Purpose: Provides a COM server that implements a dual interface. Demonstrates the implementation of a dual interface server using Visual J++.

Visual Basic Client

Directory: `book/ch08/dual_interface_approach/vb_com_client`

Purpose: Demonstrates use of COM dual interface servers from a Visual Basic client application.

Visual Basic Automation Client

Directory: `book/ch08/dual_interface_approach/vb_automation_client`

Purpose: Demonstrates use of COM dual interface servers from a Visual Basic client application. This Visual Basic client uses automation to communicate with the dual interface servers by declaring all COM references as type `Object`.

Visual C++ Client

Directory: `book/ch08/dual_interface_approach/vcclient`

Purpose: Demonstrates use of COM dual interface servers from a Visual C++ client application.

Visual J++ Client

Directory: `book/ch08/dual_interface_approach/vjclient`

Purpose: Demonstrates use of COM dual interface servers from a Visual J++ client application.

Chapter 9 Examples

Directory: `book/ch09`

Purpose: Contains source code for the examples presented in Chapter 9. These examples are intended to demonstrate use of COM and CORBA in Internet applications.

Clients

Directory: `book/ch09/clients`

Purpose: Contains source code for the COM and CORBA client applications presented in Chapter 9.

COM Active Server Pages Client

Directory: `book/ch09/clients/com_asp_client`

Purpose: Demonstrates use of a COM server from an Active Server Pages client application.

CORBA Java Applet

Directory: `book/ch09/clients/corba_java_applet`

Purpose: Demonstrates use of a CORBA server from a Java applet.

Servers

Directory: `book/ch09/servers`

Purpose: Contains source code for the COM and CORBA servers presented in Chapter 9.

COM IDL

Directory: `book/ch09/servers/midl`

Purpose: Contains a COM IDL description of the COM server used in Chapter 9.

CORBA IDL

Directory: `book/ch09/servers/idl`

Purpose: Contains a CORBA IDL description of the CORBA server used in Chapter 9.

COM Server

Directory: `book/ch09/servers/com_server`

Purpose: Provides the COM server that is used by the Active Server Pages client application. The COM server is implemented using Visual C++ and ATL.

CORBA Server

Directory: `book/ch09/servers/corba_server`

Purpose: Provides the CORBA server that is used by the Java applet. The CORBA server is implemented using Visual C++ and Iona Orbix.

Chapter 10 Examples

Directory: `book/ch10`

Purpose: Contains source code for the examples presented in Chapter 10. These examples are intended to demonstrate use of COM and CORBA in desktop and Internet applications. This includes use of a CORBA server from COM clients as well as a COM server from a CORBA client.

Clients

Directory: `book/ch10/clients`

Purpose: Contains source code for the COM and CORBA client applications presented in Chapter 10.

COM Active Server Pages Client

Directory: `book/ch10/clients/com_asp`

Purpose: Demonstrates use of a COM server and a CORBA server from an Active Server Pages client application.

COM Visual Basic Client

Directory: `book/ch10/clients/com_vb`

Purpose: Demonstrates use of a COM server and a CORBA server from a Visual Basic client application.

CORBA Java Applet

Directory: `book/ch10/clients/corba_java_applet`

Purpose: Demonstrates use of a COM server and a CORBA server from a Java applet.

Servers

Directory: `book/ch10/servers`

Purpose: Contains source code for the COM and CORBA servers presented in Chapter 10.

COM IDL

Directory: `book/ch10/servers/midl`

Purpose: Contains a COM IDL description of the COM server used in Chapter 10.

CORBA IDL

Directory: `book/ch10/servers/idl`

Purpose: Contains a CORBA IDL description of the CORBA server used in Chapter 10.

COM Customer Interface

Directory: `book/ch10/servers/com_customer_interface`

Purpose: Defines the COM customer interface used by the COM customer server, COM customer proxy, and COM-to-CORBA bridge components. A batch file is also defined that creates a proxy–stub DLL for the COM customer interface.

COM Customer Wrapper

Directory: `book/ch10/servers/com_customer_wrapper`

Purpose: Provides a lightweight wrapper (in-process DLL) that wraps any server that implements the COM customer interface. The wrapper is implemented using Visual Basic.

COM Customer Server

Directory: `book/ch10/servers/com_customer_server`

Purpose: Provides the COM server that is used by the ASP client, Visual Basic client, and Java applet. The COM server is implemented using Visual C++ and ATL.

COM Customer Proxy

Directory: `book/ch10/servers/com_customer_proxy`

Purpose: Provides the COM server that acts as a proxy to the COM customer server. The COM server is implemented using Visual C++ and ATL.

COM-to-CORBA Bridge

Directory: `book/ch10/servers/com_to_corba_bridge`

Purpose: Provides the COM server that acts as a bridge from COM clients to the CORBA customer server. The COM server is implemented using Visual C++, ATL, and Iona Orbix.

CORBA Customer Server

Directory: `book/ch10/servers/corba_customer_server`

Purpose: Provides the CORBA server that is used by the ASP client, Visual Basic client, and Java applet. The CORBA server is implemented using Visual C++ and Iona Orbix.

CORBA Customer Proxy

Directory: `book/ch10/servers/corba_customer_proxy`

Purpose: Provides the CORBA server that acts as a proxy to the CORBA customer server. The CORBA server is implemented using Visual C++ and Iona Orbix.

CORBA-to-COM Bridge

Directory: `book/ch10/servers/corba_to_com_bridge`

Purpose: Provides the CORBA server that acts as a bridge from CORBA clients to the COM customer server. The CORBA server is implemented using Visual C++ and Iona Orbix.

Chapter 11 Examples

Directory: `book/ch11`

Purpose: Contains source code for the examples presented in Chapter 11. These examples are intended to demonstrate custom COM/CORBA bridging approaches.

COM IDL

Directory: `book/ch11/midl`

Purpose: Contains a COM IDL and type library description of the COM server used in Chapter 11.

CORBA IDL

Directory: `book/ch11/idl`

Purpose: Contains a CORBA IDL description of the CORBA server used in Chapter 11.

COM Client

Directory: `book/ch11/com_client`

Purpose: Demonstrates use of a CORBA server from a Visual Basic client application.

COM-to-CORBA Bridge

Directory: `book/ch11/com_to_corba_bridge`

Purpose: Provides the COM server that acts as a bridge from COM clients to the CORBA server. The COM server is implemented using Microsoft's JVM and Sun Microsystems' Java IDL CORBA ORB.

CORBA Server

Directory: `book/ch11/corba_server`

Purpose: Provides the CORBA server that is used by the COM client in Chapter 11. The CORBA server is implemented using Visual C++ and Iona Orbix.

Chapter 12 Examples

Directory: `book/ch12`

Purpose: Contains source code for the examples presented in Chapter 12. These examples are intended to demonstrate use of a commercial COM/CORBA bridging product.

Bindings Generated by Commercial Bridging Product

Directory: `book/ch12/bindings`

Purpose: Contains COM bindings for a CORBA server and CORBA bindings for a COM server that were automatically generated by Visual Edge Software's ObjectBridge COM/CORBA Enterprise Client.

COM Client

Directory: `book/ch12/com_client`

Purpose: Demonstrates use of a CORBA server from a Visual Basic client application. The client relies on Visual Edge Software's ObjectBridge COM/CORBA Enterprise Client product.

CORBA Server

Directory: `book/ch12/corba_server`

Purpose: Provides the CORBA server that is used by the Visual Basic COM client application. The CORBA server is implemented using Visual C++ and Iona Orbix.

Appendix C

Selected Example Code

MyCheckingAccount Classes (from Ch. 3)

COM/C++ MyCheckingAccount Class

```cpp
// ****************************************************************
// MyCheckingAccount.h
// ****************************************************************

#ifndef MyCheckingAccount_h
#define MyCheckingAccount_h

#include "Ch3ComCppServer.h"

class MyCheckingAccount
{
public:
    MyCheckingAccount();
    virtual ~MyCheckingAccount();

    // Reset
    void Reset();

    // Initialization
    BOOL Init(const CString& name,
              const CString& server,
              CString& errmsg);

    BOOL InitUsingFactory(const CString& name,
                          const CString& server,
                          CString& errmsg);

    // Properties
    double  GetBalance();
    CString GetName();
    CString GetServerName() const;

    // Methods
    BOOL Deposit(double amount);
    BOOL Withdraw(double amount);
    BOOL WithdrawCheck(int checkNumber, double amount);

    // Predicates
    BOOL IsEnabled() const    { return m_isEnabled; }
```

```
    // Test QueryInterface()
    BOOL ResetInterfaces();
    BOOL SetInterfaces(IUnknown* pIUnknown);

private:
    IAccount*          m_pIAccount;
    IAccountInit*      m_pIAccountInit;
    ICheckingAccount* m_pICheckingAccount;

    BOOL    m_isEnabled;
    CString m_serverName;

    CString GetErrMsg(HRESULT hr);
};

#endif // MyCheckingAccount_h




// ***************************************************************
// MyCheckingAccount.cpp
// ***************************************************************

#include "stdafx.h"
#include "MyCheckingAccount.h"

#include "Ch3ComCppServer_i.c"

MyCheckingAccount::MyCheckingAccount()
{
    m_isEnabled = FALSE;
    m_pIAccount           = NULL;
    m_pIAccountInit       = NULL;
    m_pICheckingAccount = NULL;
}

MyCheckingAccount::~MyCheckingAccount()
{
    Reset();
}

void MyCheckingAccount::Reset()
{
    m_isEnabled = FALSE;
    m_serverName = "";

    if (m_pIAccount) m_pIAccount->Release();
    m_pIAccount = NULL;

    if (m_pIAccountInit) m_pIAccountInit->Release();
    m_pIAccountInit = NULL;

    if (m_pICheckingAccount) m_pICheckingAccount->Release();
    m_pICheckingAccount = NULL;
}
```

```
BOOL MyCheckingAccount::Init(const CString& name,
                             const CString& serverName,
                             CString& errmsg)
{
    Reset();

    // Create server info.
    COSERVERINFO  serverInfo;
    COSERVERINFO* pServerInfo;
    if ( serverName.IsEmpty() )
    {
        // Use local server.
        pServerInfo = NULL;
    }
    else
    {
        serverInfo.dwReserved1 = 0;
        serverInfo.dwReserved2 = 0;
        serverInfo.pwszName    = serverName.AllocSysString();
        serverInfo.pAuthInfo   = NULL;
        pServerInfo = &serverInfo;
    }

    // Create MULTI_QI array to get all pertinent interfaces.
    MULTI_QI mqi[] =
    {
        {&IID_IAccount,        NULL, 0},
        {&IID_IAccountInit,    NULL, 0},
        {&IID_ICheckingAccount, NULL, 0},
    };

    // Create a server object instance.
    HRESULT hr;
    hr = CoCreateInstanceEx
            (CLSID_Ch3CheckingAccount, NULL,
             CLSCTX_LOCAL_SERVER | CLSCTX_REMOTE_SERVER,
             pServerInfo, 3, mqi);

    ::SysFreeString(serverInfo.pwszName);

    if ( !SUCCEEDED(hr) )
    {
        errmsg = "CoCreateInstanceEx() failed (1)\n   ";
        errmsg += GetErrMsg(hr);
        return FALSE;
    }

    // Assign the interface pointers and server name.
    m_pIAccount         = (IAccount*)mqi[0].pItf;
    m_pIAccountInit     = (IAccountInit*)mqi[1].pItf;
    m_pICheckingAccount = (ICheckingAccount*)mqi[2].pItf;
    m_serverName = serverName;

    // Initialize the name.
    BSTR bstrName = name.AllocSysString();
    hr = m_pIAccountInit->Init(bstrName);
    ::SysFreeString(bstrName);
```

```
    if ( !SUCCEEDED(hr) )
    {
        if (hr == E_INVALID_NAME)
            errmsg = "Invalid name!";
        else
            errmsg = "Failed to initialize account!";
        Reset();
        return FALSE;
    }
    m_isEnabled = TRUE;

    return TRUE;
}

BOOL MyCheckingAccount::InitUsingFactory(const CString& name,
                                         const CString& serverName,
                                         CString& errmsg)
{
    Reset();

    // Create server info.
    COSERVERINFO  serverInfo;
    COSERVERINFO* pServerInfo;
    if ( serverName.IsEmpty() )
    {
        // Use local server.
        pServerInfo = NULL;
    }
    else
    {
        serverInfo.dwReserved1 = 0;
        serverInfo.dwReserved2 = 0;
        serverInfo.pwszName    = serverName.AllocSysString();
        serverInfo.pAuthInfo   = NULL;
        pServerInfo = &serverInfo;
    }

    // Get the factory ...
    IClassFactory* pIClassFactory;
    HRESULT hr;
    hr = CoGetClassObject
            (CLSID_Ch3CheckingAccount,
             CLSCTX_LOCAL_SERVER | CLSCTX_REMOTE_SERVER,
             pServerInfo,
             IID_IClassFactory,
             (void**)&pIClassFactory);

    ::SysFreeString(serverInfo.pwszName);

    if ( !SUCCEEDED(hr) )
    {
        errmsg = "CoGetClassObject() failed\n    ";
        errmsg += GetErrMsg(hr);
        return FALSE;
    }

    // Create the instance ...
    IUnknown* pIUnknown;
```

```
    hr = pIClassFactory->CreateInstance(NULL,
                                        IID_IUnknown,
                                        (void**)&pIUnknown);
    pIClassFactory->Release();

    if ( !SUCCEEDED(hr) )
    {
        errmsg = "CreateInstance() failed\n    ";
        errmsg += GetErrMsg(hr);
        return FALSE;
    }

    // Set the interfaces.
    if ( !SetInterfaces(pIUnknown) )
    {
        errmsg = "InitUsingFactory: SetInterfaces() failed";
        return FALSE;
    }

    // Initialize the name.
    BSTR bstrName = name.AllocSysString();
    hr = m_pIAccountInit->Init(bstrName);
    ::SysFreeString(bstrName);

    if ( !SUCCEEDED(hr) )
    {
        if (hr == E_INVALID_NAME)
            errmsg = "Invalid name!";
        else
            errmsg = "Failed to initialize account!";
        Reset();
        return FALSE;
    }
    m_isEnabled = TRUE;

    return TRUE;
}

double MyCheckingAccount::GetBalance()
{
    if (m_pIAccount == NULL)
        return 0.0;
    double val;
    HRESULT hr = m_pIAccount->get_Balance(&val);

    if ( !SUCCEEDED(hr) )
        val = -999.0;
    return val;
}

CString MyCheckingAccount::GetName()
{
    CString name;
    if (m_pIAccount == NULL)
        return name;
    BSTR bstrName;
    HRESULT hr = m_pIAccount->get_Name(&bstrName);
```

```
    if ( !SUCCEEDED(hr) )
        name = "Error!";
    else
        name = bstrName;
    ::SysFreeString(bstrName);
    return name;
}

CString MyCheckingAccount::GetServerName() const
{
    return m_serverName;
}

BOOL MyCheckingAccount::Deposit(double amount)
{
    if (m_pIAccount == NULL)
        return FALSE;
    HRESULT hr = m_pIAccount->Deposit(amount);
    if ( !SUCCEEDED(hr) )
        TRACE("MyCheckingAccount::Deposit() failed");
    return SUCCEEDED(hr);
}

BOOL MyCheckingAccount::Withdraw(double amount)
{
    if (m_pIAccount == NULL)
        return FALSE;
    HRESULT hr = m_pIAccount->Withdraw(amount);
    if ( !SUCCEEDED(hr) )
        TRACE("MyCheckingAccount::Withdraw() failed");
    return SUCCEEDED(hr);
}

BOOL MyCheckingAccount::WithdrawCheck(int checkNumber,
                                      double amount)
{
    if (m_pICheckingAccount == NULL)
        return FALSE;
    HRESULT hr;
    hr = m_pICheckingAccount->WithdrawUsingCheck(checkNumber,
                                                 amount);
    if ( !SUCCEEDED(hr) )
        TRACE("MyCheckingAccount::WithdrawUsingCheck() failed");
    return SUCCEEDED(hr);
}

BOOL MyCheckingAccount::ResetInterfaces()
{
    TRACE("Resetting interfaces...\n");
    if (m_pIAccount != NULL)
        m_pIAccount->AddRef();
    return SetInterfaces(m_pIAccount);
}

BOOL MyCheckingAccount::SetInterfaces(IUnknown* pIUnknown)
{
    if (pIUnknown == NULL)
        return FALSE;
```

```
    // Reset all interface pointers.
    Reset();
    HRESULT hr;
    void*   pInterface = NULL;

    // Query the IUnknown interface to get the
    // ICheckingAccount interface.
    hr = pIUnknown->QueryInterface(IID_ICheckingAccount,
                                   &pInterface);
    if ( !SUCCEEDED(hr) )
    {
        TRACE("MyCheckingAccount::SetInterfaces() failed(1)\n");
        Reset();
        return FALSE;
    }
    m_pICheckingAccount = (ICheckingAccount*)pInterface;

    // Query the ICheckingAccount interface to get the
    // IAccount interface.
    hr = m_pICheckingAccount->QueryInterface(IID_IAccount,
                                             &pInterface);
    if ( !SUCCEEDED(hr) )
    {
        TRACE("MyCheckingAccount::SetInterfaces() failed(2)\n");
        Reset();
        return FALSE;
    }
    m_pIAccount = (IAccount*)pInterface;

    // Query the IAccount interface to get the
    // IAccountInit interface.
    hr = m_pIAccount->QueryInterface(IID_IAccountInit,
                                     &pInterface);
    if ( !SUCCEEDED(hr) )
    {
        TRACE("MyCheckingAccount::SetInterfaces() failed(3)\n");
        Reset();
        return FALSE;
    }
    m_pIAccountInit = (IAccountInit*)pInterface;

    m_isEnabled = TRUE;
    return TRUE;
}
```

COM/Visual Basic MyCheckingAccount Class

```
'MyCheckingAccount.cls

Option Explicit

Private Const CLSIDAccount As String = _
    "{B5F3E300-B376-11D1-BB1E-00207812E629}"
```

```
Private mIAccount As IAccount
Private mIAccountInit As IAccountInit
Private mICheckingAccount As ICheckingAccount
Private mIsEnabled As Boolean

Public Property Get AccountName() As String
    On Error GoTo ErrorHandler
    AccountName = mIAccount.name
Exit Property
ErrorHandler:
    Debug.Print "MyCheckingAccount::AccountName propget failed"
End Property


Public Property Get Balance() As Double
    On Error GoTo ErrorHandler
    Balance = mIAccount.Balance
Exit Property
ErrorHandler:
    Debug.Print "MyCheckingAccount::Balance propget failed"
End Property


Public Property Get isEnabled() As Boolean
    isEnabled = mIsEnabled
End Property


Public Function Deposit(amount As Double) As Boolean
    On Error GoTo ErrorHandler
    Call mIAccount.Deposit(amount)
    Deposit = True
Exit Function
ErrorHandler:
    Debug.Print "MyCheckingAccount::Deposit() failed"
    Deposit = False
End Function


Public Function Init(name As String, _
                     server As String) As Boolean
On Error GoTo ErrorHandler
    Dim account As IUnknown
    Dim bridge As New DCOMBridge

    'Make sure that the name is set to something.
    If Len(name) = 0 Then
        name = ""
    End If

    'Reset all interface pointers before initializing.
    Call Reset

    'Create an instance of the checking account.
    If Len(server) > 0 Then
        'Use the bridge to create a remote instance.
        Set account = _
            bridge.CreateRemoteInstance(CLSIDAccount, _
```

```
                                              server, _
                                              False)
    Else
        'Create an instance locally.
        Set account = New Ch3CheckingAccount
    End If

    'Initialize the interface pointers.
    Set mIAccount = account
    Set mIAccountInit = account
    Set mICheckingAccount = mIAccount

    'Initialize the account object.
    Call mIAccountInit.Init(name)
    mIsEnabled = True
    Init = True
Exit Function
ErrorHandler:
    Call Reset
    Debug.Print "MyCheckingAccount::Init() failed"
    Debug.Print "Err.Description : " + Err.Description
    Debug.Print "Err.Number      : " + "0x" + Hex(Err.Number)
    Init = False
End Function


Public Sub Reset()
    mIsEnabled = False
    Set mIAccount = Nothing
    Set mIAccountInit = Nothing
    Set mICheckingAccount = Nothing
End Sub


Public Function Withdraw(amount As Double) As Boolean
    On Error GoTo ErrorHandler
    Call mIAccount.Withdraw(amount)
    Withdraw = True
Exit Function
ErrorHandler:
    Debug.Print "MyCheckingAccount::Withdraw() failed"
    Withdraw = False
End Function


Public Function WithdrawCheck(checkNumber As Integer, _
                              amount As Double) _
                              As Boolean
    On Error GoTo ErrorHandler
    Call mICheckingAccount.WithdrawUsingCheck(checkNumber, _
                                              amount)
    WithdrawCheck = True
Exit Function
ErrorHandler:
    Debug.Print "MyCheckingAccount::WithdrawCheck() failed"
    WithdrawCheck = False
End Function
```

CORBA/C++ MyCheckingAccount Class

```
// ************************************************************
// MyCheckingAccount.h
// ************************************************************


#ifndef MyCheckingAccount_h
#define MyCheckingAccount_h

#include "Ch3.hh"


class MyCheckingAccount
{
public:
    MyCheckingAccount();
    virtual ~MyCheckingAccount();

    // Reset
    void Reset();

    // Initialization
    BOOL Init(const char* name, const char* factoryIOR);

    // Properties
    double      GetBalance();
    const char* GetFactoryIOR() const;
    const char* GetName();

    // Methods
    BOOL Deposit(double amount);
    BOOL Withdraw(double amount);
    BOOL WithdrawCheck(int checkNumber, double amount);

    // Predicates
    BOOL IsEnabled() const  { return m_isEnabled; }

private:
    Ch3::CheckingAccount_var m_account;

    CORBA::ORB m_orb;

    char m_factoryIOR[1024];
    char m_name[256];
    BOOL m_isEnabled;

    Ch3::CheckingAccountFactory_ptr LocateFactory(const char* ior);
};


#endif // MyCheckingAccount_h
```

```cpp
// ****************************************************************
// MyCheckingAccount.cpp
// ****************************************************************

#include "MyCheckingAccount.h"
#include <iostream.h>


MyCheckingAccount::MyCheckingAccount()
{
    m_orb = CORBA::Orbix;
    m_factoryIOR[0] = '\0';
    m_name[0] = '\0';
    m_isEnabled = FALSE;
}


MyCheckingAccount::~MyCheckingAccount()
{
    Reset();
}


void MyCheckingAccount::Reset()
{
    m_isEnabled = FALSE;
    m_factoryIOR[0] = '\0';
    m_name[0] = 0;

    if ( !CORBA::is_nil(m_account) )
    {
        m_account->destroy();
        m_account = Ch3::CheckingAccount::_nil();
    }
}


BOOL MyCheckingAccount::Init(const char* name,
                            const char* factoryIOR)
{
    BOOL ok = FALSE;

    try
    {
        Reset();

        // Locate checking account factory.
        Ch3::CheckingAccountFactory_var factory;
        factory = LocateFactory(factoryIOR);

        if (CORBA::is_nil(factory))
            return FALSE;

        // Create a checking account instance.
        m_account = factory->create();

        // Initialize the account for the name.
        m_account->init(name);
```

```
        // Demonstrate implicit widening ...
        //    m_account is declared as type CheckingAccount_var
        Ch3::CheckingAccount_ptr pCheckingAccount = m_account;
        Ch3::Account_ptr         pAccount         = m_account;
        Ch3::AccountInit_ptr     pAccountInit     = m_account;

        Ch3::Account_var vAccount =
            Ch3::CheckingAccount::_duplicate(m_account);
        cout << "implicit widening check (pAccount) ==> "
             << pAccount->balance()
             << endl << flush;
        cout << "implicit widening check (vAccount) ==> "
             << vAccount->balance()
             << endl << flush;

        // Finish initialization.
        m_isEnabled = TRUE;
        ok = TRUE;
    }
    catch (Ch3::InvalidNameException& exc)
    {
        Reset();
        cerr << "MyCheckingAccount::Init: "
             << "InvalidNameException! - "
             << exc.reason << endl;
        ok = FALSE;
    }
    catch (CORBA::SystemException& se)
    {
        Reset();
        cerr << "MyCheckingAccount::Init: "
             << "CORBA::SystemException!"
             << endl;
        ok = FALSE;
    }
    return ok;
}

double MyCheckingAccount::GetBalance()
{
    if ( !IsEnabled() )
        return -9.99;
    double bal = -9.99;
    try
    {
        bal = m_account->balance();
    }
    catch (CORBA::SystemException& se)
    {
        cerr << "MyCheckingAccount::GetBalance: "
             << "CORBA::SystemException!"
             << endl;
    }
    return bal;
}
```

```cpp
const char* MyCheckingAccount::GetName()
{
    if ( !IsEnabled() )
        return "";
    try
    {
        m_name[0] = '\0';
        CORBA::String_var name = m_account->name();
        strcpy(m_name, name);
    }
    catch (CORBA::SystemException& se)
    {
        cerr << "MyCheckingAccount::GetName: "
             << "CORBA::SystemException!"
             << endl;
    }
    return m_name;
}

const char* MyCheckingAccount::GetFactoryIOR() const
{
    return m_factoryIOR;
}

BOOL MyCheckingAccount::Deposit(double amount)
{
    if ( !IsEnabled() )
        return FALSE;
    BOOL ok = FALSE;
    try
    {
        m_account->deposit(amount);
        ok = TRUE;
    }
    catch (CORBA::SystemException& se)
    {
        cerr << "MyCheckingAccount::Deposit: "
             << "CORBA::SystemException!"
             << endl;
        ok = FALSE;
    }

    return ok;
}

BOOL MyCheckingAccount::Withdraw(double amount)
{
    if ( !IsEnabled() )
        return FALSE;
    BOOL ok = FALSE;
    try
    {
        m_account->withdraw(amount);
        ok = TRUE;
    }
    catch (CORBA::SystemException& se)
    {
        cerr << "MyCheckingAccount::Withdraw: "
```

```
                    << "CORBA::SystemException!"
                    << endl;
            ok = FALSE;
        }
        return ok;
}

BOOL MyCheckingAccount::WithdrawCheck(int checkNumber,
                                     double amount)
{
    if ( !IsEnabled() )
        return FALSE;
    BOOL ok = FALSE;
    try
    {
        m_account->withdrawUsingCheck(checkNumber, amount);
        ok = TRUE;
    }
    catch (CORBA::SystemException& se)
    {
        cerr << "MyCheckingAccount::WithdrawCheck: "
             << "CORBA::SystemException!"
             << endl;
        ok = FALSE;
    }

    return ok;
}

Ch3::CheckingAccountFactory_ptr
MyCheckingAccount::LocateFactory(const char* ior)
{
    Ch3::CheckingAccountFactory_var factory;
    try
    {
        // Obtain an object reference corresponding to
        // the IOR.
        CORBA::Object_var obj;
        cout << ior << endl;
        obj = m_orb.string_to_object((char*)ior);

        if (CORBA::is_nil(obj))
        {
            cerr << "LocateFactory: null object" << endl;
            return Ch3::CheckingAccountFactory::_nil();
        }

        // Narrow to a factory object.
        factory = Ch3::CheckingAccountFactory::_narrow(obj);

        if (CORBA::is_nil(factory))
        {
            cerr << "LocateFactory: null factory" << endl;
            return Ch3::CheckingAccountFactory::_nil();
        }
    }
    catch (CORBA::SystemException& se)
    {
```

```
            cerr << "LocateFactory: CORBA::SystemException!"
                << endl;
            return Ch3::CheckingAccountFactory::_nil();
    }

    // Return the factory.
    // return factory;  // this compiles but is incorrect
    return Ch3::CheckingAccountFactory::_duplicate(factory);
}
```

CORBA/Java MyCheckingAccount Class

```
// MyCheckingAccount.java

import Ch3.CheckingAccount;
import Ch3.CheckingAccountFactory;
import Ch3.CheckingAccountFactoryHelper;
import Ch3.InvalidNameException;
import org.omg.CORBA.ORB;

class MyCheckingAccount
{
    CheckingAccount m_account;
    String          m_factoryIOR = "";
    String          m_name = "";
    ORB             m_orb;

    boolean m_isEnabled = false;

    public MyCheckingAccount(ORB orb)
    {
        m_orb = orb;
    }

    public void reset()
    {
        m_isEnabled = false;
        m_factoryIOR = "";
        m_name = "";

        if (m_account != null)
        {
            m_account.destroy();
            m_account = null;
        }
    }

    public void init(String name, String factoryIOR)
    {
        reset();

        try
        {
            // Locate the factory ...
            org.omg.CORBA.Object obj =
```

```
                m_orb.string_to_object(factoryIOR);

            CheckingAccountFactory factory =
                CheckingAccountFactoryHelper.narrow(obj);

            // Create an account ...
            m_account = factory.create();

            // Initialize the account ...
            m_account.init(name);
            m_isEnabled = true;
        }
        catch (InvalidNameException e)
        {
            e.printStackTrace();
            reset();
        }
        catch (org.omg.CORBA.SystemException e)
        {
            e.printStackTrace();
            reset();
        }
    }

    public double getBalance()
    {
        double result = -9.99;

        try
        {
            result = m_account.balance();
        }
        catch (org.omg.CORBA.SystemException e)
        {
            e.printStackTrace();
        }

        return result;
    }

    public String getFactoryIOR()
    {
        return m_factoryIOR;
    }

    public String getName()
    {
        String name = "";

        try
        {
            name = m_account.name();
        }
        catch (org.omg.CORBA.SystemException e)
        {
            e.printStackTrace();
        }
```

```java
            return name;
    }

    public void deposit(double amount) throws MyAccountExc
    {
        try
        {
            m_account.deposit(amount);
        }
        catch (org.omg.CORBA.SystemException e)
        {
            e.printStackTrace();
            throw new MyAccountExc("deposit() failed");
        }
    }

    public void withdraw(double amount) throws MyAccountExc
    {
        try
        {
            m_account.withdraw(amount);
        }
        catch (org.omg.CORBA.SystemException e)
        {
            e.printStackTrace();
            throw new MyAccountExc("withdraw() failed");
        }
    }

    public void withdrawCheck(int checkNumber,
                              double amount) throws MyAccountExc
    {
        try
        {
            m_account.withdrawUsingCheck(checkNumber, amount);
        }
        catch (org.omg.CORBA.SystemException e)
        {
            e.printStackTrace();
            throw new MyAccountExc("withdrawCheck() failed");
        }
    }

    public boolean isEnabled()
    {
        return m_isEnabled;
    }
}

class MyAccountExc extends Exception
{
    MyAccountExc(String reason)
    {
        super(reason);
    }
}
```

MTS Components (from Ch. 6)

Ch6Teller MTS Component

```
// ***************************************************************
// Teller.h
// ***************************************************************

#ifndef __TELLER_H_
#define __TELLER_H_

#include "resource.h"        // main symbols
#include <mtx.h>

#import "Ch6Account.dll" no_namespace

class ATL_NO_VTABLE CTeller :
    public CComObjectRootEx<CComSingleThreadModel>,
    public CComCoClass<CTeller, &CLSID_Teller>,
    public IObjectControl,
    public IDispatchImpl<ITeller,
                         &IID_ITeller,
                         &LIBID_CH6TELLERLib>
{
public:
    CTeller() {}

DECLARE_REGISTRY_RESOURCEID(IDR_TELLER)
DECLARE_NOT_AGGREGATABLE(CTeller)

BEGIN_COM_MAP(CTeller)
    COM_INTERFACE_ENTRY(ITeller)
    COM_INTERFACE_ENTRY(IObjectControl)
    COM_INTERFACE_ENTRY(IDispatch)
END_COM_MAP()

// IObjectControl
public:
    STDMETHOD(Activate)();
    STDMETHOD_(BOOL, CanBePooled)();
    STDMETHOD_(void, Deactivate)();

    CComPtr<IObjectContext> m_spObjectContext;

// ITeller
public:
    STDMETHOD(GetBalance)(/*[in]*/ BSTR accountName,
                          /*[out,retval]*/ double* amount);

    STDMETHOD(Transfer)(/*[in]*/ BSTR fromAccount,
                        /*[in]*/ BSTR toAccount,
                        /*[in]*/ double amount);

protected:
    IAccountPtr m_pIAccount_A;
```

```
    IAccountPtr m_pIAccount_B;

    void InitializeAccounts();
};

#endif //__TELLER_H_


// ****************************************************************
// Teller.cpp
// ****************************************************************

#include "stdafx.h"
#include "Ch6Teller.h"
#include "Teller.h"

HRESULT CTeller::Activate()
{
    HRESULT hr = GetObjectContext(&m_spObjectContext);
    if (FAILED(hr))
        return hr;

    InitializeAccounts();

    return S_OK;
}

void CTeller::InitializeAccounts()
{
    HRESULT hr;

    // Get a handle on the MTS context object.
    CComPtr<IObjectContext> spObjectContext;
    ::GetObjectContext(&spObjectContext);

    // Create an Account object instance in the transaction
    // context of this Teller object. This object will be
    // associated with Account A.
    IAccount* pIAccount;
    hr = spObjectContext->CreateInstance(__uuidof(Account),
                                         __uuidof(IAccount),
                                         (LPVOID*)&pIAccount);
    if (FAILED(hr)) return;

    m_pIAccount_A.Attach(pIAccount);  // Account A's object

    // Create another Account object instance in the transaction
    // context of this Teller object. This object will be
    // associated with Account B.
    hr=spObjectContext->CreateInstance(__uuidof(Account),
                                       __uuidof(IAccount),
                                       (LPVOID*)&pIAccount);
    if (FAILED(hr)) return;

    m_pIAccount_B.Attach(pIAccount);  // Account B's object
}

BOOL CTeller::CanBePooled()
```

```
{
    return TRUE;
}

void CTeller::Deactivate()
{
    m_pIAccount_A.Release();
    m_pIAccount_B.Release();
    m_spObjectContext.Release();
}

STDMETHODIMP CTeller::GetBalance(BSTR accountName,
                                 double* amount)
{
    try
    {
        *amount = m_pIAccount_A->GetBalance(accountName);
    }
    catch (...)
    {
        m_spObjectContext->SetAbort();
        return E_FAIL;
    }

    m_spObjectContext->SetComplete();
    return S_OK;
}

STDMETHODIMP CTeller::Transfer(BSTR fromAccount,
                               BSTR toAccount,
                               double amount)
{
    // Get a handle on the MTS context object.
    CComPtr<IObjectContext> spObjectContext;
    ::GetObjectContext(&spObjectContext);

    try
    {
        // Transfer the money.
        m_pIAccount_A->Withdraw(fromAccount, amount);
        m_pIAccount_B->Deposit(toAccount, amount);
    }
    catch (...)
    {
        // If either Withdraw() or Deposit() throws an
        // exception, abort the transaction.
        spObjectContext->SetAbort();
        return E_FAIL;
    }

    // The call to SetComplete() will begin the two-phase
    // commit of the Transfer() operation.
    spObjectContext->SetComplete();
    return S_OK;
}
```

Ch6Account MTS Component

```
// ***************************************************************
// Account.h
// ***************************************************************

#ifndef __ACCOUNT_H_
#define __ACCOUNT_H_

#include "resource.h"        // main symbols
#include <mtx.h>
#include <comdef.h>

class ATL_NO_VTABLE CAccount :
    public CComObjectRootEx<CComSingleThreadModel>,
    public CComCoClass<CAccount, &CLSID_Account>,
    public IObjectControl,
    public IDispatchImpl<IAccount, &IID_IAccount,
                         &LIBID_CH6ACCOUNTLib>
{
public:
    CAccount() {}

DECLARE_REGISTRY_RESOURCEID(IDR_ACCOUNT)
DECLARE_NOT_AGGREGATABLE(CAccount)

BEGIN_COM_MAP(CAccount)
    COM_INTERFACE_ENTRY(IAccount)
    COM_INTERFACE_ENTRY(IObjectControl)
    COM_INTERFACE_ENTRY(IDispatch)
END_COM_MAP()

// IObjectControl
public:
    STDMETHOD(Activate)();
    STDMETHOD_(BOOL, CanBePooled)();
    STDMETHOD_(void, Deactivate)();

    CComPtr<IObjectContext> m_spObjectContext;

// IAccount
public:
    STDMETHOD(Withdraw)(/*[in]*/ BSTR accountName,
                        /*[in]*/ double amount);

    STDMETHOD(Deposit)(/*[in]*/ BSTR accountName,
                       /*[in]*/ double amount);

    STDMETHOD(GetBalance)(/*[in]*/ BSTR accountName,
                          /*[out,retval]*/ double* balance);

protected:
    BOOL AdjustBalanceInDatabase(const _bstr_t& db,
                                 const _bstr_t& accountName,
                                 double amount);

    double DbGetBalance(const _bstr_t& db,
```

```
                              const _bstr_t& accountName);
};

#endif //__ACCOUNT_H_



// ****************************************************************
// Account.cpp
// ****************************************************************

#include "stdafx.h"
#include "Ch6Account.h"
#include "Account.h"

#import  <msado15.dll> no_namespace
#include <stdio.h>

const double INVALID_AMOUNT = -999.99;

HRESULT CAccount::Activate()
{
    HRESULT hr = ::GetObjectContext(&m_spObjectContext);
    if (SUCCEEDED(hr))
        return S_OK;
    return hr;
}

BOOL CAccount::CanBePooled()
{
    return TRUE;
}

void CAccount::Deactivate()
{
    m_spObjectContext.Release();
}

STDMETHODIMP CAccount::GetBalance(BSTR accountName,
                                  double* balance)
{
    // Determine the database that the account is
    // associated with.
    const char* db = (_bstr_t("A") == _bstr_t(accountName)) ?
                     "RDBMS_A" :
                     "RDBMS_B";

    // Get the balance out of the database.
    *balance = DbGetBalance(db, accountName);

    m_spObjectContext->SetComplete();
    return S_OK;
}

STDMETHODIMP CAccount::Deposit(BSTR accountName, double amount)
{
    // Get a handle on the MTS context object.
    CComPtr<IObjectContext> spObjectContext;
```

```
    ::GetObjectContext(&spObjectContext);

    // Determine the database that the account is
    // associated with.
    const char* db = (_bstr_t("A") == _bstr_t(accountName)) ?
                     "RDBMS_A" :
                     "RDBMS_B";

    // Adjust the balance in the database.
    if ( !AdjustBalanceInDatabase(db, accountName, amount) )
    {
        // Abort the transaction.
        spObjectContext->SetAbort();
        return E_FAIL;
    }

    // Let MTS know that this part of the transaction
    // is complete.
    spObjectContext->SetComplete();
    return S_OK;
}

STDMETHODIMP CAccount::Withdraw(BSTR acctName, double amount)
{
    // Get a handle on the MTS context object.
    CComPtr<IObjectContext> spObjectContext;
    ::GetObjectContext(&spObjectContext);

    // Determine the database that the account is
    // associated with.
    const char* db = (_bstr_t("A") == _bstr_t(acctName)) ?
                     "RDBMS_A" :
                     "RDBMS_B";

    // Adjust the balance in the database.
    if ( !AdjustBalanceInDatabase(db, acctName, amount * -1.0) )
    {
        // Abort the transaction.
        spObjectContext->SetAbort();
        return E_FAIL;
    }

    // Let MTS know that this part of the transaction
    // is complete.
    spObjectContext->SetComplete();
    return S_OK;
}

BOOL CAccount::AdjustBalanceInDatabase(const _bstr_t& db,
                                       const _bstr_t& acctName,
                                       double amount)
{
    _ConnectionPtr pConnection = NULL;

    try
    {
        // Connect to the database ...
        pConnection = new _ConnectionPtr(__uuidof(Connection));
```

```
        pConnection->Open(db,
                          _bstr_t("sa"),
                          _bstr_t(""),
                          -1);

        char buff[128];
        sprintf(buff, "%f ", amount);

        // Build the update statement ...
        _bstr_t query("UPDATE Account ");
        query += "SET balance = balance + ";
        query += buff;
        query += "WHERE name = '";
        query += acctName;
        query += "'";

        // Execute the query ...
        pConnection->Execute(query, NULL, adCmdText);

        pConnection->Close();
        return TRUE;
    }
    catch (...)
    {
        // Make sure that the connection gets closed.
        try { pConnection->Close(); } catch (...) {}
        return FALSE;
    }
}

double CAccount::DbGetBalance(const _bstr_t& db,
                             const _bstr_t& accountName)
{
    // Force a failure if amount < 0 ...
    _ConnectionPtr pConnection = NULL;

    try
    {
        // Connect to the database ...
        pConnection = new _ConnectionPtr(__uuidof(Connection));

        pConnection->Open(db,
                          _bstr_t("sa"),
                          _bstr_t(""),
                          -1);

        // Build the query to get the balance ...
        _bstr_t query("SELECT balance FROM Account ");
        query += "WHERE name = '";
        query += accountName;
        query += "'";

        // Execute the query ...
        _RecordsetPtr pResults =
            pConnection->Execute(query, NULL, adCmdText);

        if (pResults->GetBOF())
```

```
        {
            pConnection->Close();
            return INVALID_AMOUNT;
        }

        // Return the resulting balance ...
        long col = 0;
        _variant_t val =
            pResults->GetFields()->GetItem(col)->GetValue();

        pConnection->Close();
        return (double)val;
    }
    catch (...)
    {
        // Make sure that the connection gets closed.
        try { pConnection->Close(); } catch (...) {}
        return INVALID_AMOUNT;
    }
}
```

MSMQ Applications (from Ch. 6)

Trader MSMQ Application

```
'Trader application

Option Explicit

Const ORDER_Q_HOST = "scarpia"
Const ORDER_Q_LABEL = "stock_market_orders"
Const ORDER_Q_GUID = "{FDDCFE21-F8FC-11d1-B266-00207812E629}"

Const NOTIFY_Q_HOST = "scarpia"
Const NOTIFY_Q_LABEL = "trader_notifications"
Const NOTIFY_Q_GUID = "{FDDCFE22-F8FC-11d1-B266-00207812E629}"

Dim gOrderQ As MSMQQueue
Dim gNotifyQ As MSMQQueue
Dim WithEvents gNotifyQEvents As MSMQEvent

Private Sub Form_Load()
    'Open the order queue to place orders.
    Call OpenQ(ORDER_Q_HOST, ORDER_Q_LABEL, _
               ORDER_Q_GUID, MQ_SEND_ACCESS, gOrderQ)

    'Open the notify queue to be notified when orders
    'are fulfilled.
    Call OpenQ(NOTIFY_Q_HOST, NOTIFY_Q_LABEL, _
               NOTIFY_Q_GUID, MQ_RECEIVE_ACCESS, gNotifyQ)

    'Receive event notification when new messages are added
    'to the order queue.
```

```
    Set gNotifyQEvents = New MSMQEvent
    gNotifyQ.EnableNotification gNotifyQEvents
End Sub

Private Sub cmdPlaceOrder_Click()
    Dim msg As New MSMQMessage
    Dim order As String

    'Determine priority of the message.
    If optSell.Value = True Then
        msg.Priority = 7    'Sell orders have highest priority
    Else
        msg.Priority = 3    'Buy orders have lower priority
    End If

    'We don't want orders to be recoverable
    msg.Delivery = MQMSG_DELIVERY_EXPRESS

    'We want orders to time out if they haven't been fetched
    'from the queue within 10 minutes (600 seconds).
    msg.MaxTimeToReceive = 600

    'Track the order placement in the status area.
    order = GetOrderString
    txtStatus.Text = txtStatus.Text + "Order: " + _
                     order + vbCrLf

    'Set the message body and label and send the message.
    msg.Body = GetOrderString
    msg.Label = "Order"
    msg.Send gOrderQ          'And send the message
End Sub

Private Sub gNotifyQEvents_Arrived(ByVal q As Object, _
                                   ByVal cursor As Long)

    Dim msgIn As MSMQMessage
    Dim strTextIn As String

    'Get an MSMQQueue interface pointer for the notifyQ
    Dim notifyQ As MSMQQueue
    Set notifyQ = q

    'Get the message out of the queue
    '(time out after 100 milliseconds)
    Set msgIn = notifyQ.Receive(ReceiveTimeout:=100)
    If Not msgIn Is Nothing Then
        strTextIn = msgIn.Body          'Read the message body
        txtStatus.Text = txtStatus.Text + _
                         strTextIn + vbCrLf
    End If

    'Reenable event firing
    notifyQ.EnableNotification gNotifyQEvents
End Sub


Private Sub OpenQ(ByVal qHost As String, _
```

```
                ByVal qLabel As String, _
                ByVal qGuid As String, _
                ByVal qMode As Long, _
                ByRef q As MSMQQueue)

    Dim query As New MSMQQuery
    Dim qinfos As MSMQQueueInfos
    Dim qinfo As MSMQQueueInfo

    'Locate the queue.
    Set qinfos = query.LookupQueue(Label:=qLabel, _
                                   ServiceTypeGuid:=qGuid)
    Set qinfo = qinfos.Next

    'Create the queue if the query did not find one.
    If qinfo Is Nothing Then
        Set qinfo = New MSMQQueueInfo
        qinfo.PathName = qHost + "\" + qLabel
        qinfo.Label = qLabel
        qinfo.ServiceTypeGuid = qGuid
        qinfo.Create
    End If

    'Open the queue (qMode can be set to peek, send, or receive)
    Set q = qinfo.Open(qMode, 0)
End Sub


Private Function GetOrderString() As String
    Dim order As String

    If optSell.Value = True Then
        order = "Sell "
    Else
        order = "Buy "
    End If
    order = order + txtNumShares.Text + " shares of "
    order = order + txtSymbolName.Text + " @ "
    order = order + txtPrice.Text

    GetOrderString = order
End Function

Private Sub cmdClearStatus_Click()
    txtStatus.Text = ""
End Sub
```

Stock Market MSMQ Application

```
'Stock Market Application

Option Explicit

Const ORDER_Q_HOST = "scarpia"
Const ORDER_Q_LABEL = "stock_market_orders"
Const ORDER_Q_GUID = "{FDDCFE21-F8FC-11d1-B266-00207812E629}"
```

```
Const NOTIFY_Q_HOST = "scarpia"
Const NOTIFY_Q_LABEL = "trader_notifications"
Const NOTIFY_Q_GUID = "{FDDCFE22-F8FC-11d1-B266-00207812E629}"

Dim WithEvents gOrderQEvents As MSMQEvent
Dim gOrderQ As MSMQQueue
Dim gNotifyQ As MSMQQueue

Private Sub Form_Load()
    'Open the order queue to receive orders.
    Call OpenQ(ORDER_Q_HOST, ORDER_Q_LABEL, _
               ORDER_Q_GUID, MQ_RECEIVE_ACCESS, gOrderQ)

    'Open the notify queue to notify the trader when orders
    'are fulfilled.
    Call OpenQ(NOTIFY_Q_HOST, NOTIFY_Q_LABEL, _
               NOTIFY_Q_GUID, MQ_SEND_ACCESS, gNotifyQ)

    'Receive event notification when new messages are added
    'to the order queue.
    Set gOrderQEvents = New MSMQEvent
    gOrderQ.EnableNotification gOrderQEvents
End Sub

Private Sub cmdFulfillOrder_Click()
    Dim msg As New MSMQMessage
    Dim order As String
    Dim indx As Integer

    'Determine the selected order to be fulfilled.
    indx = lstOrders.ListIndex
    If indx < 0 Then
        Exit Sub
    End If

    'Get order and remove it from the list.
    order = lstOrders.List(indx)
    Call lstOrders.RemoveItem(indx)

    'Set the priority (3 is the normal MSMQ default)
    msg.Priority = 3

    'We want notifications to be recoverable.
    msg.Delivery = MQMSG_DELIVERY_RECOVERABLE

    'We want notifications to live forever until retrieved
    'by the trader (INFINITE is the normal MSMQ default)

    'Set the body and label and send the message.
    msg.Body = "Fulfilled: " + order
    msg.Label = "Fulfilled"
    msg.Send gNotifyQ
End Sub

Private Sub gOrderQEvents_Arrived(ByVal q As Object, _
                                  ByVal cursor As Long)
    Dim msgIn As MSMQMessage
    Dim strTextIn As String
```

```
    'Get an MSMQQueue interface pointer for the orderQ
    Dim orderQ As MSMQQueue
    Set orderQ = q

    'Get the message out of the queue
    '(time out after 100 milliseconds)
    Set msgIn = orderQ.Receive(ReceiveTimeout:=100)
    If Not msgIn Is Nothing Then
        strTextIn = msgIn.Body        'Read the message body
        lstOrders.AddItem (strTextIn) 'Add the order to the list
    End If

    'Reenable event firing
    orderQ.EnableNotification gOrderQEvents
End Sub

Private Sub OpenQ(ByVal qHost As String, _
                  ByVal qLabel As String, _
                  ByVal qGuid As String, _
                  ByVal qMode As Long, _
                  ByRef q As MSMQQueue)

    Dim query As New MSMQQuery
    Dim qinfos As MSMQQueueInfos
    Dim qinfo As MSMQQueueInfo

    'Locate the queue.
    Set qinfos = query.LookupQueue(Label:=qLabel, _
                                   ServiceTypeGuid:=qGuid)
    Set qinfo = qinfos.Next

    'Create the queue if the query did not find one.
    If qinfo Is Nothing Then
        Set qinfo = New MSMQQueueInfo
        qinfo.PathName = qHost + "\" + qLabel
        qinfo.Label = qLabel
        qinfo.ServiceTypeGuid = qGuid
        qinfo.Create
    End If

    'Open the queue (qMode can be set to peek, send, or receive)
    Set q = qinfo.Open(qMode, 0)
End Sub
```

Index

Effective COM

50 Ways to Improve Your COM and MTS-based Applications
Don Box, Keith Brown, Tim Ewald, and Chris Sells
Addison-Wesley Object Technology Series

Effective COM offers fifty concrete guidelines for COM derived from the
communal wisdom formed over years of COM-based development. This book
is targeted at developers who are living and breathing COM, humbled by its
complexity and challenged by the breadth of distributed object computing.
These four COM experts provide insight on complex subjects such as the
differences between pure C++ development and COM-based C++ development, COM interface design, concurrency and apartments, and security.

0-201-37968-6 • Paperback • 240 pages • ©1999

Essential COM

Don Box
Addison-Wesley Object Technology Series

This groundbreaking book helps developers go beyond simplistic applications
of COM to become truly effective COM programmers. This book offers a
thorough explanation of COM's basic vocabulary, provides a complete
Distributed COM application to illustrate programming techniques, and
includes the author's test library of COM utility code. By showing you the
why of COM, and not just the *how*, Don Box enables you to apply the model
creatively and effectively to everyday programming problems.

0-201-63446-5 • Paperback • 464 pages • ©1998

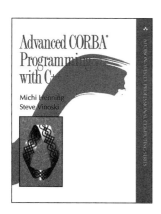

Advanced CORBA® Programming with C++

Michi Henning and Steve Vinoski
Addison-Wesley Professional Computing Series

Here is the CORBA book that every C++ software engineer has been waiting
for. This book provides designers and developers with the tools required to
understand CORBA technology at the architectural, design, and source code
levels. The authors offer hands-on explanations for building efficient applications, as well as lucid examples that provide practical advice on avoiding
costly mistakes.

0-201-37927-9 • Paperback • 1120 pages • ©1999

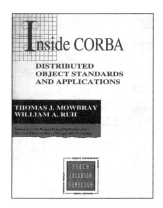

Inside CORBA

Distributed Object Standards and Applications
Thomas J. Mowbray and William A. Ruh
Addison-Wesley Object Technology Series

Inside CORBA is a comprehensive, up-to-date, and authoritative guide to distributed object architecture, software development, and CORBA standards. It includes the latest coverage of the new CORBA IDL Language Mapping for the Java programming language and comprehensive coverage of the CORBA 2 standard and CORBA services. The authors outline essential lessons learned from experienced CORBA managers and architects to ensure successful adoption and migration to CORBA technology.

0-201-89540-4 • Paperback • 400 pages • ©1997

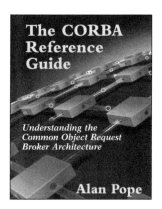

The CORBA Reference Guide

Understanding the Common Object Request Broker Architecture
Alan Pope

This book offers a clear explanation of CORBA and a complete reference to the standard. *The CORBA Reference Guide* provides a general background in distributed systems and explains the base architecture as well as the services and facilities that extend this architecture. Of particular note, the book details the most sophisticated security framework that has been developed for any architecture to date and covers interoperability with other ORBs.

0-201-63386-8 • Paperback • 432 pages • ©1998

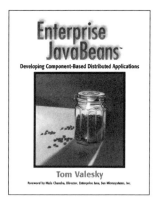

Enterprise JavaBeans™

Developing Component-Based Distributed Applications
Tom Valesky

Enterprise JavaBeans™ will put you on the fast track and get you results. Begin with an overview of Enterprise JavaBeans—its architecture, its components, and its compelling advantages. Next, start coding and walk through each stage of Enterprise JavaBeans development, mastering stateful and stateless session beans, as well as bean-managed and container-managed entity beans. Discover how to write client programs that use server-side Enterprise JavaBeans, as well as how to package and deploy distributed applications.

0-201-60446-9 • Paperback • 352 pages • ©1999

Addison-Wesley Computer and Engineering Publishing Group

How to Interact with Us

1. Visit our Web site

http://www.awl.com/cseng

When you think you've read enough, there's always more content for you at Addison-Wesley's web site. Our web site contains a directory of complete product information including:

- Chapters
- Exclusive author interviews
- Links to authors' pages
- Tables of contents
- Source code

You can also discover what tradeshows and conferences Addison-Wesley will be attending, read what others are saying about our titles, and find out where and when you can meet our authors and have them sign your book.

2. Subscribe to Our Email Mailing Lists

Subscribe to our electronic mailing lists and be the first to know when new books are publishing. Here's how it works: Sign up for our electronic mailing at **http://www.awl.com/cseng/mailinglists.html**. Just select the subject areas that interest you and you will receive notification via email when we publish a book in that area.

3. Contact Us via Email

cepubprof@awl.com
Ask general questions about our books.
Sign up for our electronic mailing lists.
Submit corrections for our web site.

bexpress@awl.com
Request an Addison-Wesley catalog.
Get answers to questions regarding your order or our products.

innovations@awl.com
Request a current Innovations Newsletter.

webmaster@awl.com
Send comments about our web site.

mary.obrien@awl.com
Submit a book proposal.
Send errata for an Addison-Wesley book.

cepubpublicity@awl.com
Request a review copy for a member of the media interested in reviewing new Addison-Wesley titles.

We encourage you to patronize the many fine retailers who stock Addison-Wesley titles. Visit our online directory to find stores near you or visit our online store: **http://store.awl.com/** or call 800-824-7799.

Addison Wesley Longman
Computer and Engineering Publishing Group
One Jacob Way, Reading, Massachusetts 01867 USA
TEL 781-944-3700 • FAX 781-942-3076